SELECTED SOLUTIONS MANUAL

Karen C. Timberlake
LOS ANGELES VALLEY COLLEGE

WITH CONTRIBUTIONS FROM

Mark Quirie
ALGONQUIN COLLEGE

GENERAL, ORGANIC, AND BIOLOGICAL

CHEMISTRY

STRUCTURES OF LIFE

Fourth Edition

Karen C. Timberlake

PEARSON

Boston Columbus Indianapolis New York San Francisco Upper Saddle River
Amsterdam Cape Town Dubai London Madrid Milan Munich Paris Montréal Toronto
Delhi Mexico City São Paulo Sydney Hong Kong Seoul Singapore Taipei Tokyo

Editor in Chief: Adam Jaworski
Executive Editor: Jeanne Zalesky
Senior Marketing Manager: Jonathan Cottrell
Associate Editor: Jessica Neumann
Assistant Editor: Coleen McDonald
Managing Editor, Chemistry and Geosciences: Gina M. Cheselka
Production Project Manager and Manufacturing Buyer: Dorothy Cox
Production Management and Composition: PreMediaGlobal
Cover Design: Seventeenth Street Studios
Cover Photo Credit: Fernando Alonso Herrero/iStockphoto

www.pearsonhighered.com

1 2 3 4 5 6 7 8 9—BRR—16 15 14 13 12

ISBN 10: 0-321-76703-9; ISBN 13: 978-0-321-76703-5

Contents

Chapter 1
Chemistry and Measurements

1.1 Many chemicals are listed on a vitamin bottle, such as vitamin A, vitamin B_3, vitamin B_{12}, vitamin C, and folic acid.

1.3 No. All of the ingredients listed are chemicals.

1.5 Among the things you might do to help yourself succeed in chemistry are: attend class regularly, review the *Learning Goals*, keep a problem notebook, read the text actively, read the chapter before lecture, form a study group, and take advantage of your instructor's office hours.

1.7 Ways you can enhance your learning of chemistry:
  a. Form a study group.
  c. Visit the professor during office hours.
  e. Become an active learner.
  f. Work the Learning Exercises in the *Study Guide*.

1.9 **a.** A liter (L) is a unit of volume.
  b. A centimeter (cm) is a unit of length.
  c. A kilometer (km) is a unit of length.
  d. A second (s) is a unit of time.

1.11 **a.** The unit is a meter, which is a unit of length.
  b. The unit is a gram, which is a unit of mass.
  c. The unit is a liter, which is a unit of volume.
  d. The unit is a second, which is a unit of time.
  e. The unit is a degree Celsius, which is a unit of temperature.

1.13 **a.** Move the decimal point four places to the left to give 5.5×10^4 m.
  b. Move the decimal point two places to the left to give 4.8×10^2 g.
  c. Move the decimal point six places to the right to give 5×10^{-6} cm.
  d. Move the decimal point four places to the right to give 1.4×10^{-4} s.
  e. Move the decimal point three places to the right to give 7.85×10^{-3} L.
  f. Move the decimal point five places to the left to give 6.7×10^5 kg.

1.15 **a.** The value 7.2×10^3 cm, which is also 72×10^2 cm, is larger than 8.2×10^2 cm.
  b. The value 3.2×10^{-2} kg, which is also 320×10^{-4} kg, is larger than 4.5×10^{-4} kg.
  c. The value 1×10^4 L, which is also 10 000 L, is larger than 1×10^{-4} L or 0.0001 L.
  d. The value 6.8×10^{-2} m, which is also 0.068 m, is larger than 0.000 52 m.

1.17 **a.** The standard number is 1.2 times the power 10^4, or 10 000, which gives 12 000 s.
  b. The standard number is 8.25 times the power 10^{-2}, or 0.01, which gives 0.0825 kg.
  c. The standard number is 4 times the power 10^6, or 1 000 000, which gives 4 000 000 g.
  d. The standard number is 5 times the power 10^{-3}, or 0.001, which gives 0.005 m.

1.19   Measured numbers are obtained using some type of measuring device. Exact numbers are numbers obtained by counting items or using a definition that compares two units in the same measuring system.

    a.   The value 67.5 kg is a measured number; measurement of mass requires a measuring device.

    b.   The value 2 tablets is obtained by counting, making it an exact number.

    c.   The values in the metric definition 1 m = 1000 mm are exact numbers.

    d.   The value 1720 km is a measured number; measurement of distance requires a measuring device.

1.21   Measured numbers are obtained using some type of measuring device. Exact numbers are numbers obtained by counting items or using a definition that compares two units in the same measuring system.

    a.   3 hamburgers is a counted/exact number; the value 6 oz of meat is obtained using a measuring device, so it is a measured number.

    b.   Neither are measured numbers; both 1 table and 4 chairs are counted/exact numbers.

    c.   Both 0.75 lb of grapes and 350 g of butter are obtained using a measuring device, so they are both measured numbers.

    d.   Neither are measured numbers; the values in a definition are exact numbers.

1.23   **a.**   The zeros at the beginning of a decimal number are not significant; only the zero in the last decimal place following the 8 is significant.

    b.   The zero between nonzero digits is significant.

    c.   Both zeros in a number with a decimal point are significant.

    d.   The zero in the coefficient of a number written in scientific notation is significant.

    e.   None; zeros used as placeholders in a large number without a decimal point are not significant.

1.25   **a.**   All five numbers are significant figures (5 SFs).

    b.   Only the two nonzero numbers are significant (2 SFs); the preceding zeros are placeholders.

    c.   Only the two nonzero numbers are significant (2 SFs); the zeros that follow are placeholders.

    d.   All three numbers in the coefficient of a number written in scientific notation are significant (3 SFs).

    e.   All four numbers to the right of the decimal point, including the last zero, in a decimal number are significant (4 SFs).

    f.   All three numbers including the zeros at the end of a decimal number are significant (3 SFs).

1.27   **a.**   11.00 m (4 SFs) contains more significant figures than does 11.0 m (3 SFs).

    b.   405.0 K (4 SFs) contains more significant figures than does 405 K (3 SFs).

    c.   0.0120 s (3 SFs) contains more significant figures than does 12 000 s (2 SFs).

    d.   250.0 L (4 SFs) contains more significant figures than does 2.5×10^{-2} L (2 SFs).

1.29   **a.**   1.85 kg; the last digit is dropped since it is 4 or less.

    b.   184 L; since the fourth digit is 4 or less, the last four digits are dropped.

    c.   0.004 74 cm; since the fourth significant digit (the first digit to be dropped) is 5 or greater, the last retained digit is increased by 1 when the last four digits are dropped.

    d.   8810 m; since the fourth digit (the first digit to be dropped) is 5 or greater, the last retained digit is increased by 1 when the last digit is dropped (a nonsignificant zero is added at the end as a placeholder).

    e. 1.83×10^{5} s; since the fourth digit is 4 or less, the last digit is dropped. The $\times 10^{5}$ is retained so that the magnitude of the answer is not changed.

1.31   **a.** $45.7 \times 0.034 = 1.6$; two significant figures are allowed since 0.034 has 2 SFs.

    b. $0.002\ 78 \times 5 = 0.01$; one significant figure is allowed since 5 has 1 SF.

c. $\dfrac{34.56}{1.25} = 27.6$; three significant figures are allowed since 1.25 has 3 SFs.

d. $\dfrac{(0.2465)(25)}{1.78} = 3.5$; two significant figures are allowed since 25 has 2 SFs.

1.33 **a.** 45.48 cm + 8.057 cm = 53.54 cm; two decimal places are allowed since 45.48 cm has two decimal places.

b. 23.45 g + 104.1 g + 0.025 g = 127.6 g; one decimal place is allowed since 104.1 g has one decimal place.

c. 145.675 mL − 24.2 mL = 121.5 mL; one decimal place is allowed since 24.2 mL has one decimal place.

d. 1.08 L − 0.585 L = 0.50 L; two decimal places are allowed since 1.08 L has two decimal places.

1.35 The km/h markings indicate how many kilometers (how much distance) will be traversed in 1 hour's time if the speed is held constant. The mph (mi/h) markings indicate the same distance traversed but measured in miles during the 1 hour of travel.

1.37 **a.** mg
b. dL
c. km
d. pg
e. μL
f. ns

1.39 **a.** 0.01 (or 1×10^{-2})
b. 1000 (or 1×10^{3})
c. 0.001 (or 1×10^{-3})
d. 1 000 000 000 000 (or 1×10^{12})
e. 1 000 000 (or 1×10^{6})
f. 0.000 000 000 001 (or 1×10^{-12})

1.41 **a.** 1 m = 100 cm
b. 1 m = 1×10^{9} nm
c. 1 mm = 0.001 m
d. 1 L = 1000 mL

1.43 **a.** kilogram, since 10^{3} g is greater than 10^{-3} g
b. milliliter, since 10^{-3} L is greater than 10^{-6} L
c. km, since 10^{3} m is greater than 10^{0} m
d. kL, since 10^{3} L is greater than 10^{-1} L
e. nanometer, since 10^{-9} m is greater than 10^{-12} m

1.45 **a.** 1 m = 100 cm; $\dfrac{100\ cm}{1\ m}$ and $\dfrac{1\ m}{100\ cm}$

b. 1 g = 1000 mg; $\dfrac{1000\ mg}{1\ g}$ and $\dfrac{1\ g}{1000\ mg}$

c. $1\,L = 1000\,mL$; $\dfrac{1000\,mL}{1\,L}$ and $\dfrac{1\,L}{1000\,mL}$

d. $1\,dL = 100\,mL$; $\dfrac{100\,mL}{1\,dL}$ and $\dfrac{1\,dL}{100\,mL}$

1.47 **a.** $1\text{ yard} = 3\text{ ft}$; $\dfrac{3\,ft}{1\text{ yard}}$ and $\dfrac{1\text{ yard}}{3\,ft}$; the numbers 1 and 3 are both exact.

b. $1\,kg = 2.20\,lb$; $\dfrac{2.20\,lb}{1\,kg}$ and $\dfrac{1\,kg}{2.20\,lb}$; the number 1 is exact; the number 2.20 has 3 SFs.

c. $1\,min = 60\,sec$; $\dfrac{60\,s}{1\,min}$ and $\dfrac{1\,min}{60\,s}$; the numbers 1 and 60 are both exact.

d. 1 gal of gasoline = 27 mi; $\dfrac{27\,mi}{1\text{ gal gasoline}}$ and $\dfrac{1\text{ gal gasoline}}{27\,mi}$; the number 1 is exact; the number 27 has 2 SFs.

e. 100 g of sterling silver = 93 g of silver; $\dfrac{93\text{ g silver}}{100\text{ g sterling silver}}$ and $\dfrac{100\text{ g sterling silver}}{93\text{ g silver}}$; the number 100 is exact; the number 93 has 2 SFs.

1.49 **a.** $1\,s = 3.5\,m$; $\dfrac{3.5\,m}{1\,s}$ and $\dfrac{1\,s}{3.5\,m}$; the number 1 is exact; the number 3.5 has 2 SFs.

b. 1 day = 3500 mg of potassium; $\dfrac{3500\text{ mg potassium}}{1\text{ day}}$ and $\dfrac{1\text{ day}}{3500\text{ mg potassium}}$; the number 1 is exact; the number 3500 has 2 SFs.

c. 1 gal of gasoline = 46.0 km; $\dfrac{46.0\,km}{1\text{ gal gasoline}}$ and $\dfrac{1\text{ gal gasoline}}{46.0\,km}$; the number 1 is exact; the number 46.0 has 3 SFs.

d. 1 tablet = 50. mg of Atenolol; $\dfrac{50.\text{ mg Atenolol}}{1\text{ tablet}}$ and $\dfrac{1\text{ tablet}}{50.\text{ mg Atenolol}}$; the number 1 is exact; the number 50. has 2 SFs.

e. 1 kg of plums = 29 μg of pesticide; $\dfrac{29\,\mu\text{g pesticide}}{1\text{ kg plums}}$ and $\dfrac{1\text{ kg plums}}{29\,\mu\text{g pesticide}}$; the number 1 is exact; the number 29 has 2 SFs.

f. 1 tablet = 81 mg of aspirin; $\dfrac{81\text{ mg aspirin}}{1\text{ tablet}}$ and $\dfrac{1\text{ tablet}}{81\text{ mg aspirin}}$; the number 1 is exact; the number 81 has 2 SFs.

1.51 **a.** **Given** 175 cm   **Need** meters

Plan cm → m $\dfrac{1\,m}{100\,cm}$

Set Up $175\text{ cm} \times \dfrac{1\,m}{100\text{ cm}} = 1.75\,m$ (3 SFs)

b. Given 5500 mL   **Need** liters

Plan mL → L $\dfrac{1\,L}{1000\,mL}$

Set Up 5500 mL $\times \dfrac{1\,L}{1000\,mL} = 5.5\,L$ (2 SFs)

c. Given 0.0055 kg   **Need** grams

Plan kg → g $\dfrac{1000\,g}{1\,kg}$

Set Up 0.0055 kg $\times \dfrac{1000\,g}{1\,kg} = 5.5\,g$ (2 SFs)

1.53   **a. Given** 0.750 qt   **Need** milliliters

Plan qt → mL $\dfrac{946\,mL}{1\,qt}$

Set Up 0.750 qt $\times \dfrac{946\,mL}{1\,qt} = 710.\,mL$ (3 SFs)

b. Given 11.8 stones   **Need** kilograms

Plan stones → lb → kg $\dfrac{14.0\,lb}{1\,stone}\quad\dfrac{1\,kg}{2.20\,lb}$

Set Up 11.8 stones $\times \dfrac{14.0\,lb}{1\,stone} \times \dfrac{1\,kg}{2.20\,lb} = 75.1\,kg$ (3 SFs)

c. Given 19.5 in.   **Need** millimeters

Plan in. → cm → mm $\dfrac{2.54\,cm}{1\,in.}\quad\dfrac{10\,mm}{1\,cm}$

Set Up 19.5 in. $\times \dfrac{2.54\,cm}{1\,in.} \times \dfrac{10\,mm}{1\,cm} = 495\,mm$ (3 SFs)

d. Given 0.50 μm   **Need** inches

Plan μm → m → in. $\dfrac{1\,m}{1\times10^{6}\,\mu m}\quad\dfrac{39.4\,in.}{1\,m}$

Set Up 0.50 μm $\times \dfrac{1\,m}{1\times10^{6}\,\mu m} \times \dfrac{39.4\,in.}{1\,m} = 2.0\times10^{-5}\,in.$ (2 SFs)

1.55   **a. Given** 78.0 ft (length)   **Need** meters

Plan ft → in. → cm → m $\dfrac{12\,in.}{1\,ft}\quad\dfrac{2.54\,cm}{1\,in.}\quad\dfrac{1\,m}{100\,cm}$

Set Up 78.0 ft $\times \dfrac{12\,in.}{1\,ft} \times \dfrac{2.54\,cm}{1\,in.} \times \dfrac{1\,m}{100\,cm} = 23.8\,m$ (length) (3 SFs)

b. **Given** 27.0 ft (width), 23.8 m (length)   **Need** area in square meters (m^2)

Plan ft → in. → cm → m, then length (m), width (m) → m^2

$$\frac{12 \text{ in.}}{1 \text{ ft}} \quad \frac{2.54 \text{ cm}}{1 \text{ in.}} \quad \frac{1 \text{ m}}{100 \text{ cm}} \qquad Area = length \times width$$

Set Up $27.0 \text{ ft} \times \dfrac{12 \text{ in.}}{1 \text{ ft}} \times \dfrac{2.54 \text{ cm}}{1 \text{ in.}} \times \dfrac{1 \text{ m}}{100 \text{ cm}} = 8.23 \text{ m (width) (3 SFs)}$

∴ Area = 23.8 m × 8.23 m = 196 m^2 (3 SFs)

c. **Given** 23.8 m (length), 185 km/h (speed)   **Need** seconds

Plan m → km → h → min → s $\dfrac{1 \text{ km}}{1000 \text{ m}} \quad \dfrac{1 \text{ h}}{185 \text{ km}} \quad \dfrac{60 \text{ min}}{1 \text{ h}} \quad \dfrac{60 \text{ s}}{1 \text{ min}}$

Set Up $23.8 \text{ m} \times \dfrac{1 \text{ km}}{1000 \text{ m}} \times \dfrac{1 \text{ h}}{185 \text{ km}} \times \dfrac{60 \text{ min}}{1 \text{ h}} \times \dfrac{60 \text{ s}}{1 \text{ min}} = 0.463 \text{ s (3 SFs)}$

1.57 **a.** **Given** 250 L of water   **Need** gallons of water

Plan L → qt → gal $\dfrac{1.06 \text{ qt}}{1 \text{ L}} \quad \dfrac{1 \text{ gal}}{4 \text{ qt}}$

Set Up $250 \text{ L} \times \dfrac{1.06 \text{ qt}}{1 \text{ L}} \times \dfrac{1 \text{ gal}}{4 \text{ qt}} = 66 \text{ gal (2 SFs)}$

b. **Given** 0.024 g of sulfa drug, 8-mg tablets   **Need** number of tablets

Plan g of sulfa drug → mg of sulfa drug → number of tablets $\dfrac{1000 \text{ mg}}{1 \text{ g}} \quad \dfrac{1 \text{ tablet}}{8 \text{ mg sulfa drug}}$

Set Up $0.024 \text{ g sulfa drug} \times \dfrac{1000 \text{ mg}}{1 \text{ g}} \times \dfrac{1 \text{ tablet}}{8 \text{ mg sulfa drug}} = 3 \text{ tablets (1 SF)}$

c. **Given** 34-lb child, 115 mg of ampicillin/kg of body mass   **Need** milligrams of ampicillin

Plan lb of body mass → kg of body mass → mg of ampicillin $\dfrac{1 \text{ kg}}{2.20 \text{ lb}} \quad \dfrac{115 \text{ mg ampicillin}}{1 \text{ kg body mass}}$

Set Up $34 \text{ lb body mass} \times \dfrac{1 \text{ kg body mass}}{2.20 \text{ lb body mass}} \times \dfrac{115 \text{ mg ampicillin}}{1 \text{ kg body mass}}$

= 1800 mg of ampicillin (2 SFs)

1.59 Each of the following requires a percent factor from the problem information:
a. **Given** 325 g of crust, 46.7% oxygen   **Need** grams of oxygen

Plan g of crust → g of oxygen

(percent equality: 100 g of crust = 46.7 g of oxygen) $\dfrac{46.7 \text{ g oxygen}}{100 \text{ g crust}}$

Set Up $325 \text{ g crust} \times \dfrac{46.7 \text{ g oxygen}}{100 \text{ g crust}} = 152 \text{ g of oxygen (3 SFs)}$

b. **Given** 1.25 g of crust, 2.1% magnesium   **Need** grams of magnesium

Plan g of crust → g of magnesium

(percent equality: 100 g of crust = 2.1 g of magnesium) $\dfrac{2.1\ \text{g magnesium}}{100\ \text{g crust}}$

Set Up $1.25\ \text{g crust} \times \dfrac{2.1\ \text{g magnesium}}{100\ \text{g crust}} = 0.026$ g of magnesium (2 SFs)

c. **Given** 10.0 oz of fertilizer, 15% nitrogen   **Need** grams of nitrogen

Plan oz of fertilizer → lb of fertilizer → g of fertilizer → g of nitrogen

(percent equality: 100 g of fertilizer = 15 g of nitrogen) $\dfrac{1\ \text{lb}}{16\ \text{oz}}\quad \dfrac{454\ \text{g}}{1\ \text{lb}}\quad \dfrac{15\ \text{g nitrogen}}{100\ \text{g fertilizer}}$

Set Up $10.0\ \text{oz fertilizer} \times \dfrac{1\ \text{lb}}{16\ \text{oz}} \times \dfrac{454\ \text{g}}{1\ \text{lb}} \times \dfrac{15\ \text{g nitrogen}}{100\ \text{g fertilizer}} = 43$ g of nitrogen (2 SFs)

d. **Given** 5.0 kg of pecans, 22.0% pecans   **Need** pounds of chocolate bars

Plan kg of pecans → kg of bars → lb of bars

(percent equality: 100 kg of bars = 22.0 kg of pecans) $\dfrac{100\ \text{kg choc. bars}}{22.0\ \text{kg pecans}}\quad \dfrac{2.20\ \text{lb}}{1\ \text{kg}}$

Set Up $5.0\ \text{kg pecans} \times \dfrac{100\ \text{kg choc. bars}}{22.0\ \text{kg pecans}} \times \dfrac{2.20\ \text{lb}}{1\ \text{kg}} = 50.$ lb of chocolate bars (2 SFs)

1.61 Because the density of aluminum is $2.70\ \text{g/cm}^3$, silver is $10.5\ \text{g/cm}^3$, and lead is $11.3\ \text{g/cm}^3$, we can identify the unknown metal by calculating its density as follows:

$$\text{Density} = \frac{\text{mass of metal}}{\text{volume of metal}} = \frac{217\ \text{g}}{19.2\ \text{cm}^3} = 11.3\ \text{g/cm}^3\ (3\ \text{SFs})$$

∴ the metal is lead.

1.63 Density is the mass of a substance divided by its volume. $\text{Density} = \dfrac{\text{mass (grams)}}{\text{volume (mL)}}$. The densities of solids and liquids are usually stated in g/mL or g/cm^3, so in some problems the units will need to be converted.

a. $\text{Density} = \dfrac{\text{mass (grams)}}{\text{volume (mL)}} = \dfrac{24.0\ \text{g}}{20.0\ \text{mL}} = 1.20$ g/mL (3 SFs)

b. **Given** 0.250 lb of butter, 130. mL   **Need** density (g/mL)

Plan lb → g, then calculate density $\dfrac{454\ \text{g}}{1\ \text{lb}}$

Set Up $0.250\ \text{lb} \times \dfrac{454\ \text{g}}{1\ \text{lb}} = 114$ g (3 SFs), ∴ $\text{Density} = \dfrac{\text{mass}}{\text{volume}} = \dfrac{114\ \text{g}}{130.\ \text{mL}} = 0.877$ g/mL (3 SFs)

c. **Given** 20.0 mL initial volume, 34.5 mL final volume, 45.0 g   **Need** density (g/mL)

Plan calculate volume by difference; then calculate density

Set Up volume of gem: 34.5 mL total − 20.0 mL water = 14.5 mL

$$\therefore \text{Density} = \frac{\text{mass}}{\text{volume}} = \frac{45.0\ \text{g}}{14.5\ \text{mL}} = 3.10\ \text{g/mL (3 SFs)}$$

d. **Given** 0.100 pt, 115.25 g initial, 182.48 g final   **Need** density (g/mL)

Plan pt → qt → L → mL, then calculate mass by difference

$$\frac{1\ \text{qt}}{2\ \text{pt}}\ \frac{1\ \text{L}}{1.06\ \text{qt}}\ \frac{1000\ \text{mL}}{1\ \text{L}}, \text{ then calculate the density}$$

Set Up $0.100\ \text{pt} \times \dfrac{1\ \text{qt}}{2\ \text{pt}} \times \dfrac{1\ \text{L}}{1.06\ \text{qt}} \times \dfrac{1000\ \text{mL}}{1\ \text{L}} = 47.2\ \text{mL (3 SFs)}$

mass of liquid = 182.48 g − 115.25 g = 67.23 g

$$\therefore \text{Density} = \frac{\text{mass}}{\text{volume}} = \frac{67.23\ \text{g}}{47.2\ \text{mL}} = 1.42\ \text{g/mL (3 SFs)}$$

1.65 In these problems, the density is used as a conversion factor.
   a. **Given** 1.50 kg of ethanol, 0.79 g/mL (density)   **Need** liters of ethanol

Plan kg → g → mL → L $\dfrac{1000\ \text{g}}{1\ \text{kg}}\ \dfrac{1\ \text{mL}}{0.79\ \text{g}}\ \dfrac{1\ \text{L}}{1000\ \text{mL}}$

Set Up $1.50\ \text{kg} \times \dfrac{1000\ \text{g}}{1\ \text{kg}} \times \dfrac{1\ \text{mL}}{0.79\ \text{g}} \times \dfrac{1\ \text{L}}{1000\ \text{mL}} = 1.9\ \text{L of ethanol (2 SFs)}$

b. **Given** 6.5 mL of mercury, 13.6 g/mL (density)   **Need** grams of mercury

Plan mL → g $\dfrac{13.6\ \text{g}}{1\ \text{mL}}$

Set Up $6.5\ \text{mL} \times \dfrac{13.6\ \text{g}}{1\ \text{mL}} = 88\ \text{g of mercury (2 SFs)}$

c. **Given** 225 mL of bronze, 7.8 g/mL (density)   **Need** ounces of bronze

Plan mL → g → lb → oz $\dfrac{7.8\ \text{g}}{1\ \text{mL}}\ \dfrac{1\ \text{lb}}{454\ \text{g}}\ \dfrac{16\ \text{oz}}{1\ \text{lb}}$

Set Up $225\ \text{mL} \times \dfrac{7.8\ \text{g}}{1\ \text{mL}} \times \dfrac{1\ \text{lb}}{454\ \text{g}} \times \dfrac{16\ \text{oz}}{1\ \text{lb}} = 62\ \text{oz of bronze (2 SFs)}$

d. **Given** 12.0 gal of gasoline, 0.74 g/mL (density)   **Need** kilograms of gasoline

Plan gal → qt → mL → g → kg $\dfrac{4\ \text{qt}}{1\ \text{gal}}\ \dfrac{946\ \text{mL}}{1\ \text{qt}}\ \dfrac{0.74\ \text{g}}{1\ \text{mL}}\ \dfrac{1\ \text{kg}}{1000\ \text{g}}$

Set Up $12.0\ \text{gal} \times \dfrac{4\ \text{qt}}{1\ \text{gal}} \times \dfrac{946\ \text{mL}}{1\ \text{qt}} \times \dfrac{0.74\ \text{g}}{1\ \text{mL}} \times \dfrac{1\ \text{kg}}{1000\ \text{g}} = 34\ \text{kg of gasoline (2 SFs)}$

1.67 Specific gravity is the ratio of the density of the sample to the density of water.

a. Specific gravity $= \dfrac{\text{density of sample}}{\text{density of H}_2\text{O}} = \dfrac{1.030 \text{ g/mL}}{1.00 \text{ g/mL}} = 1.03$ (3 SFs)

b. Calculate the density and then the specific gravity:

Density $= \dfrac{\text{mass}}{\text{volume}} = \dfrac{45.0 \text{ g}}{40.0 \text{ mL}} = 1.13$ g/mL

Specific gravity $= \dfrac{\text{density of sample}}{\text{density of H}_2\text{O}} = \dfrac{1.13 \text{ g/mL}}{1.00 \text{ g/mL}} = 1.13$ (3 SFs)

c. Rearrange the formula for specific gravity by multiplying both sides of the equation by the density of H_2O:

(Specific gravity) $\times$ (density of H_2O) = density of sample

0.85 (oil sp gr) $\times$ 1.00 g/mL (H_2O density) = 0.85 g/mL (oil density) (2 SFs)

1.69 A successful study plan would include:
b. Working the *Sample Problems* as you go through a chapter.
c. Going to your professor's office hours.

1.71 You should record the mass of the object as 32.075 g. Because the balance will measure mass to the nearest 0.001 g, the mass values should be reported to 0.001 g.

1.73 **a.** 2.0500 m (5 SFs) contains more significant figures than does 0.0205 m (3 SFs).
b. 600.0 K (4 SFs) contains more significant figures than does 60 K (1 SF).
c. 0.000 705 s (3 SFs) contains more significant figures than does 75 000 s (2 SFs).
d. 2.550×10^{-2} L (4 SFs) contains more significant figures than does 2550 L (3 SFs).

1.75 **a.** The number of legs is a counted number; it is exact.
b. The height is measured with a ruler or tape measure; it is a measured number.
c. The number of chairs is a counted number; it is exact.
d. The area is measured with a ruler or tape measure; it is a measured number.

1.77 **a.** length = 6.96 cm; width = 4.75 cm (Each answer may vary in the estimated digit.)
b. length = 69.6 mm; width = 47.5 mm
c. There are three significant figures in the length measurement.
d. There are three significant figures in the width measurement.
e. Area = length $\times$ width = 6.96 cm $\times$ 4.75 cm = 33.1 cm^2
f. Since there are three significant figures in the width and length measurements, there are three significant figures in the calculated area.

1.79 **Given** 18.5 mL initial volume, 23.1 mL final volume, 8.24 g mass **Need** density (g/mL)

Plan calculate volume by difference; then calculate density

Set Up The volume of the object is 23.1 mL − 18.5 mL = 4.6 mL.

$\therefore$ Density $= \dfrac{\text{mass}}{\text{volume}} = \dfrac{8.24 \text{ g}}{4.6 \text{ mL}} = 1.8$ g/mL (2 SFs)

1.81 **a.** To round off 0.000 012 58 L to three significant figures, drop the final digit (8) and increase the last retained digit by 1 to give 0.000 012 6 L or 1.26×10^{-5} L.

b. To round off 3.528×10^2 kg to three significant figures, drop the final digit (8) and increase the last retained digit by 1 to give 3.53×10^2 kg.

c. To round off 125 111 m to three significant figures, drop the final three digits (111) and add three zeros as placeholders to give 125 000 m or 1.25×10^5 m.

d. To express 58.703 g to three significant figures, drop the final two digits (03) to give 58.7 g.

1.83 The total mass is the sum of the individual components. 137.25 g + 84 g + 43.7 g = 265 g
No places to the right of the decimal point are allowed since the mass of the fudge sauce (84 g) has no digits to the right of the decimal point.

1.85 This problem requires several conversion factors. When you write out the unit plan, be sure you know a conversion factor you can use for each step. A possible unit plan follows:

Given 7500 ft, 55.0 m/min   **Need** minutes

Plan ft $\rightarrow$ in. $\rightarrow$ cm $\rightarrow$ m $\rightarrow$ min $\dfrac{12 \text{ in.}}{1 \text{ ft}}$ $\dfrac{2.54 \text{ cm}}{1 \text{ in.}}$ $\dfrac{1 \text{ m}}{100 \text{ cm}}$ $\dfrac{1 \text{ min}}{55.0 \text{ m}}$

Set Up $7500 \text{ ft} \times \dfrac{12 \text{ in.}}{1 \text{ ft}} \times \dfrac{2.54 \text{ cm}}{1 \text{ in.}} \times \dfrac{1 \text{ m}}{100 \text{ cm}} \times \dfrac{1 \text{ min}}{55.0 \text{ m}} = 42 \text{ min}$ (2 SFs)

1.87 **a.** **Given** 8.0 oz   **Need** number of crackers

Plan oz $\rightarrow$ number of crackers $\dfrac{6 \text{ crackers}}{0.50 \text{ oz}}$

Set Up $8.0 \text{ oz} \times \dfrac{6 \text{ crackers}}{0.50 \text{ oz}} = 96 \text{ crackers}$ (2 SFs)

b. **Given** 10 crackers, 4 g of fat/serving   **Need** ounces of fat

Plan number of crackers $\rightarrow$ servings $\rightarrow$ g of fat $\rightarrow$ lb of fat $\rightarrow$ oz of fat

$\dfrac{1 \text{ serving}}{6 \text{ crackers}}$ $\dfrac{4 \text{ g fat}}{1 \text{ serving}}$ $\dfrac{1 \text{ lb}}{454 \text{ g}}$ $\dfrac{16 \text{ oz}}{1 \text{ lb}}$

Set Up $10 \text{ crackers} \times \dfrac{1 \text{ serving}}{6 \text{ crackers}} \times \dfrac{4 \text{ g fat}}{1 \text{ serving}} \times \dfrac{1 \text{ lb}}{454 \text{ g}} \times \dfrac{16 \text{ oz}}{1 \text{ lb}} = 0.2 \text{ oz of fat}$ (1 SF)

c. **Given** 50 boxes, 140 mg of sodium/serving   **Need** grams of sodium

Plan boxes $\rightarrow$ oz $\rightarrow$ servings $\rightarrow$ mg of sodium $\rightarrow$ g of sodium

$\dfrac{8.0 \text{ oz}}{1 \text{ box}}$ $\dfrac{1 \text{ serving}}{0.50 \text{ oz}}$ $\dfrac{140 \text{ mg sodium}}{1 \text{ serving}}$ $\dfrac{1 \text{ g}}{1000 \text{ mg}}$

Set Up $50 \text{ boxes} \times \dfrac{8.0 \text{ oz}}{1 \text{ box}} \times \dfrac{1 \text{ serving}}{0.50 \text{ oz}} \times \dfrac{140 \text{ mg sodium}}{1 \text{ serving}} \times \dfrac{1 \text{ g sodium}}{1000 \text{ mg sodium}}$

$= 110 \text{ g of sodium}$ (2 SFs)

1.89   **Given** 0.45 lb of avocado, 48 pesos/kg, 13.0 pesos/dollar   **Need** cost in cents

Plan lb → kg → pesos → dollars → cents $\dfrac{1\ kg}{2.20\ lb}$ $\dfrac{48\ pesos}{1\ kg}$ $\dfrac{1\ dollar}{13.0\ pesos}$ $\dfrac{100\ cents}{1\ dollar}$

Set Up $0.45\ \cancel{lb} \times \dfrac{1\ \cancel{kg}}{2.20\ \cancel{lb}} \times \dfrac{48\ \cancel{pesos}}{1\ \cancel{kg}} \times \dfrac{1\ \cancel{dollar}}{13.0\ \cancel{pesos}} \times \dfrac{100\ cents}{1\ \cancel{dollar}} = 76\ cents\ (2\ SFs)$

1.91   **a.**   **Given** 65 kg of body mass, 3.0% fat   **Need** pounds of fat

Plan kg of body mass → kg of fat → lb of fat

(percent equality: 100 kg of body mass = 3.0 kg of fat) $\dfrac{3.0\ kg\ fat}{100\ kg\ body\ mass}$ $\dfrac{2.20\ lb\ fat}{1\ kg\ fat}$

Set Up $65\ \cancel{kg\ body\ mass} \times \dfrac{3.0\ \cancel{kg\ fat}}{100\ \cancel{kg\ body\ mass}} \times \dfrac{2.20\ lb\ fat}{1\ \cancel{kg\ fat}} = 4.3\ lb\ of\ fat\ (2\ SFs)$

b.   **Given** 3.0 L of fat, 0.94 g/mL (density)   **Need** pounds of fat

Plan L → mL → g → lb $\dfrac{1000\ mL}{1\ L}$ $\dfrac{0.94\ g}{1\ mL}$ $\dfrac{1\ lb}{454\ g}$

Set Up $3.0\ \cancel{L} \times \dfrac{1000\ \cancel{mL}}{1\ \cancel{L}} \times \dfrac{0.94\ \cancel{g}}{1\ \cancel{mL}} \times \dfrac{1\ lb}{454\ \cancel{g}} = 6.2\ lb\ of\ fat\ (2\ SFs)$

1.93   **Given** 215 mL initial volume, 285 mL final volume, 11.3 g/mL (density of lead)

Need grams of lead

Plan calculate the volume by difference and use the density to convert   mL → g $\dfrac{11.3\ g}{1\ mL}$

Set Up The difference between the initial volume of the water and its volume with the lead object will give us the volume of the lead object: 285 mL total − 215 mL water = 70. mL of lead, then

$70.\ \cancel{mL\ lead} \times \dfrac{11.3\ g\ lead}{1\ \cancel{mL\ lead}} = 790\ g\ of\ lead\ (2\ SFs)$

1.95   **Given** 27.0 cm^3 of sterling silver, 10.3 g/cm^3 (density), 92.5% silver   **Need** ounces of pure silver

Plan cm^3 of sterling → g of sterling → g of silver → lb of silver → oz of silver

(percent equality: 100 g of sterling = 92.5 g of silver)

$\dfrac{10.3\ g\ sterling}{1\ cm^3\ sterling}$ $\dfrac{92.5\ g\ silver}{100\ g\ sterling}$ $\dfrac{1\ lb}{454\ g}$ $\dfrac{16\ oz}{1\ lb}$

Set Up $27.0\ \cancel{cm^3\ sterling} \times \dfrac{10.3\ \cancel{g\ sterling}}{1\ \cancel{cm^3\ sterling}} \times \dfrac{92.5\ \cancel{g\ silver}}{100\ \cancel{g\ sterling}} \times \dfrac{1\ \cancel{lb}}{454\ \cancel{g}} \times \dfrac{16\ oz}{1\ \cancel{lb}}$

$= 9.07\ oz\ of\ pure\ silver\ (3\ SFs)$

1.97 **Given** 325 tubes of sunscreen, 4.0 oz/tube, 2.50% benzyl salicylate   **Need** kilograms of benzyl salicylate

Plan tubes → oz of sunscreen → lb of sunscreen → kg of sunscreen → kg of benzyl salicylate

(percent equality: 100 kg of sunscreen = 2.50 kg of benzyl salicylate)

$$\frac{4.0 \text{ oz sunscreen}}{1 \text{ tube}} \quad \frac{1 \text{ lb}}{16 \text{ oz}} \quad \frac{1 \text{ kg}}{2.20 \text{ lb}} \quad \frac{2.50 \text{ kg benzyl salicylate}}{100 \text{ kg sunscreen}}$$

Set Up $325 \text{ tubes} \times \dfrac{4.0 \text{ oz sunscreen}}{1 \text{ tube}} \times \dfrac{1 \text{ lb}}{16 \text{ oz}} \times \dfrac{1 \text{ kg}}{2.20 \text{ lb}} \times \dfrac{2.50 \text{ kg benzyl salicylate}}{100 \text{ kg sunscreen}}$

= 0.92 kg of benzyl salicylate (2 SFs)

1.99 **Given** 3.0 h, 55 mi/h (speed), 11 km/L (mileage)   **Need** gallons of gasoline

Plan h → mi → km → L → qt → gal $\dfrac{55 \text{ mi}}{1 \text{ h}} \quad \dfrac{1 \text{ km}}{0.621 \text{ mi}} \quad \dfrac{1 \text{ L}}{11 \text{ km}} \quad \dfrac{1.06 \text{ qt}}{1 \text{ L}} \quad \dfrac{1 \text{ gal}}{4 \text{ qt}}$

Set Up $3.0 \text{ h} \times \dfrac{55 \text{ mi}}{1 \text{ h}} \times \dfrac{1 \text{ km}}{0.621 \text{ mi}} \times \dfrac{1 \text{ L}}{11 \text{ km}} \times \dfrac{1.06 \text{ qt}}{1 \text{ L}} \times \dfrac{1 \text{ gal}}{4 \text{ qt}}$

= 6.4 gal of gasoline (2 SFs)

1.101 **a.** **Given** 180 lb of body mass   **Need** cups of coffee

Plan lb of body mass → kg of body mass → mg of caffeine → fl oz of coffee → cups of coffee

$$\frac{1 \text{ kg body mass}}{2.20 \text{ lb body mass}} \quad \frac{192 \text{ mg caffeine}}{1 \text{ kg body mass}} \quad \frac{6 \text{ fl oz coffee}}{100. \text{ mg caffeine}} \quad \frac{1 \text{ cup coffee}}{12 \text{ fl oz coffee}}$$

Set Up $180 \text{ lb body mass} \times \dfrac{1 \text{ kg body mass}}{2.20 \text{ lb body mass}} \times \dfrac{192 \text{ mg caffeine}}{1 \text{ kg body mass}}$

$= 1.571 \times 10^4 \text{ mg of caffeine (2 SFs allowed)}$

$1.571 \times 10^4 \text{ mg caffeine} \times \dfrac{6 \text{ fl oz coffee}}{100. \text{ mg caffeine}} \times \dfrac{1 \text{ cup coffee}}{12 \text{ fl oz coffee}}$

= 79 cups of coffee (2 SFs)

b. **Given** milligrams of caffeine from part **a**   **Need** cans of cola

Plan mg of caffeine → cans of cola $\dfrac{1 \text{ can cola}}{50. \text{ mg caffeine}}$

Set Up $1.571 \times 10^4 \text{ mg caffeine} \times \dfrac{1 \text{ can cola}}{50. \text{ mg caffeine}} = 310 \text{ cans of cola (2 SFs)}$

c. **Given** milligrams of caffeine from part **a**   **Need** number of No-Doz tablets

Plan mg of caffeine → No-Doz tablets $\dfrac{1 \text{ No-Doz tablet}}{100. \text{ mg caffeine}}$

Set Up 1.571×10^4 ~~mg caffeine~~ $\times \dfrac{1 \text{ No-Doz tablet}}{100. \text{ mg caffeine}} = 160$ No-Doz tablets (2 SFs)

1.103 **Given** 1.50 g of silicon, 3.00 in. diameter, 2.33 g/cm^3 (density)   **Need** thickness (mm)

Plan Use the density to convert $g \to cm^3$ $\dfrac{1 \text{ cm}^3 \text{ silicon}}{2.33 \text{ g silicon}}$

and $d\,(\text{in.}) \to r\,(\text{in.}) \to r\,(\text{cm})$ $r = \dfrac{d}{2}\ \dfrac{2.54 \text{ cm}}{1 \text{ in.}}$

then rearrange the volume equation for thickness (cm) $\to$ thickness (mm)

$V = \pi r^2 h \to h = \dfrac{V}{\pi r^2}$ $\dfrac{10 \text{ mm}}{1 \text{ cm}}$

Set Up Volume of wafer: $1.50 \text{ g} \times \dfrac{1 \text{ cm}^3}{2.33 \text{ g}} = 0.644 \text{ cm}^3$

Radius of wafer: $\dfrac{3.00 \text{ in.}}{2} \times \dfrac{2.54 \text{ cm}}{1 \text{ in.}} = 3.81 \text{ cm}$

$\therefore h = \dfrac{V}{\pi r^2} = \dfrac{0.644 \text{ cm}^3}{\pi (3.81 \text{ cm})^2} = 0.0141 \text{ cm} \times \dfrac{10 \text{ mm}}{1 \text{ cm}} = 0.141 \text{ mm}$ (3 SFs)

1.105 **Given** 66.7 yd length, 12 in. wide, 0.000 30 in. thick, 2.70 g/cm^3 (density)   **Need** grams of aluminum

Plan Length: yd $\to$ ft $\to$ in. $\to$ cm $\dfrac{3 \text{ ft}}{1 \text{ yd}}\ \dfrac{12 \text{ in.}}{1 \text{ ft}}\ \dfrac{2.54 \text{ cm}}{1 \text{ in.}}$

and Width and Thickness: in. $\to$ cm $\dfrac{2.54 \text{ cm}}{1 \text{ in.}}$

then calculate Volume: cm^3 $\to$ g $\dfrac{2.70 \text{ g}}{1 \text{ cm}^3}$

$V = l \times w \times h$

Set Up Length: $66.7 \text{ yd} \times \dfrac{3 \text{ ft}}{1 \text{ yd}} \times \dfrac{12 \text{ in.}}{1 \text{ ft}} \times \dfrac{2.54 \text{ cm}}{1 \text{ in.}} = 6100 \text{ cm}$

Width: $12 \text{ in.} \times \dfrac{2.54 \text{ cm}}{1 \text{ in.}} = 30. \text{ cm}$

Depth: $0.000 \ 30 \text{ in.} \times \dfrac{2.54 \text{ cm}}{1 \text{ in.}} = 0.000 \ 76 \text{ cm}$

Volume $= 6100 \text{ cm} \times 30. \text{ cm} \times 0.000 \ 76 \text{ cm} = 140 \text{ cm}^3$

then $140 \text{ cm}^3 \times \dfrac{2.70 \text{ g}}{1 \text{ cm}^3} = 3.8 \times 10^2$ g of aluminum (2 SFs)

1.107   **Given**   1.85 g/L   **Need**   mg/dL

        Plan   g/L $\rightarrow$ mg/L $\rightarrow$ mg/dL $\dfrac{1000 \text{ mg}}{1 \text{ g}}$ $\dfrac{1 \text{ L}}{10 \text{ dL}}$

        Set Up   This problem involves two unit conversions. Convert g to mg in the numerator, and convert L to dL in the denominator.

$$\frac{1.85 \text{ g}}{1 \text{ L}} \times \frac{1000 \text{ mg}}{1 \text{ g}} \times \frac{1 \text{ L}}{10 \text{ dL}} = 185 \text{ mg/dL (3 SFs)}$$

2.1   **a.** Potential energy is stored in the water at the top of the waterfall.
　　　b. Kinetic energy is displayed as the kicked ball moves.
　　　c. Potential energy is stored in the chemical bonds in the coal.
　　　d. Potential energy is stored in the skier at the top of the hill.

2.3   **a.** Potential energy increases as a roller coaster climbs up a ramp in a roller-coaster ride.
　　　b. Potential energy decreases as a skier begins to ski downhill.
　　　c. Potential energy decreases as water drops from the top of a waterfall.

2.5   **a.**   **Given** 3.0 h, 270 kJ/h　　**Need** joules

　　　　　Plan h $\rightarrow$ kJ $\rightarrow$ J　　　$\dfrac{1000 \text{ J}}{1 \text{ kJ}}$

　　　　　Set Up $3.0 \text{ h} \times \dfrac{270 \text{ kJ}}{1.0 \text{ h}} \times \dfrac{1000 \text{ J}}{1 \text{ kJ}} = 8.1 \times 10^5 \text{ J (2 SFs)}$

　　　b.   **Given** 3.0 h, 270 kJ/h　　**Need** kilocalories

　　　　　Plan h $\rightarrow$ kJ $\rightarrow$ J $\rightarrow$ cal $\rightarrow$ kcal　　　$\dfrac{1000 \text{ J}}{1 \text{ kJ}}$　$\dfrac{1 \text{ cal}}{4.184 \text{ J}}$　$\dfrac{1 \text{ kcal}}{1000 \text{ cal}}$

　　　　　Set Up $3.0 \text{ h} \times \dfrac{270 \text{ kJ}}{1.0 \text{ h}} \times \dfrac{1000 \text{ J}}{1 \text{ kJ}} \times \dfrac{1 \text{ cal}}{4.184 \text{ J}} \times \dfrac{1 \text{ kcal}}{1000 \text{ cal}} = 190 \text{ kcal (2 SFs)}$

2.7   The Fahrenheit temperature scale is still used in the United States. A normal human body temperature is 98.6 °F on this scale. To convert her 99.8 °F temperature to the equivalent reading on the Celsius scale, the following calculation must be performed:

$$T_C = \frac{(T_F - 32)}{1.8} = \frac{(99.8 - 32)}{1.8} = \frac{67.8}{1.8} = 37.7 \text{ °C (3 SFs) (1.8 and 32 are exact numbers)}$$

Because a normal body temperature is 37.0 on the Celsius scale, her temperature of 37.7 °C would indicate a mild fever.

2.9   To convert Celsius to Fahrenheit: $T_F = 1.8(T_C) + 32$

　　　To convert Fahrenheit to Celsius: $T_C = \dfrac{(T_F - 32)}{1.8}$ (1.8 and 32 are exact numbers)

　　　To convert Celsius to Kelvin: $T_K = T_C + 273$
　　　To convert Kelvin to Celsius: $T_C = T_K - 273$

　　　a. $T_F = 1.8(T_C) + 32 = 1.8(37.0) + 32 = 66.6 + 32 = 98.6 \text{ °F}$

　　　b. $T_C = \dfrac{(T_F - 32)}{1.8} = \dfrac{(65.3 - 32)}{1.8} = \dfrac{33.3}{1.8} = 18.5 \text{ °C}$

　　　c. $T_K = T_C + 273 = -27 + 273 = 246 \text{ K}$

　　　d. $T_C = T_K - 273 = 224 - 273 = -49 \text{ °C}$

e. $T_C = \dfrac{(T_F - 32)}{1.8} = \dfrac{(114 - 32)}{1.8} = \dfrac{82}{1.8} = 46\ °C$

2.11 **a.** $T_C = \dfrac{(T_F - 32)}{1.8} = \dfrac{(106 - 32)}{1.8} = \dfrac{74}{1.8} = 41\ °C$

  b. $T_C = \dfrac{(T_F - 32)}{1.8} = \dfrac{(103 - 32)}{1.8} = \dfrac{71}{1.8} = 39\ °C$

  No, there is no need to phone the doctor. The child's temperature is less than 40.0 °C.

2.13 *Elements* are the simplest type of pure substance, containing only one type of atom. *Compounds* contain two or more elements chemically combined in a definite proportion. In a *mixture*, two or more substances are physically mixed but not chemically combined.
  a. Baking soda contains four elements chemically combined in a definite proportion ($NaHCO_3$), which makes it a compound.
  b. A blueberry muffin is composed of several substances physically mixed together, but not chemically combined, which makes it a mixture.
  c. Ice is composed of two elements chemically combined in a definite proportion (H_2O), which makes it a compound.
  d. Zinc contains only one type of atom (Zn atoms), which makes it an element.
  e. Trimix is a physical but not chemical combination of oxygen, nitrogen, and helium gases, which makes it a mixture.

2.15 A *homogeneous mixture* has a uniform composition throughout the mixture; a *heterogeneous mixture* does not have a uniform composition.
  a. Vegetable soup is a heterogeneous mixture since it contains visible chunks of vegetables.
  b. Seawater is a homogeneous mixture since it has a uniform composition.
  c. Tea is a homogeneous mixture since it has a uniform composition.
  d. Tea with ice and lemon slices is a heterogeneous mixture since it has chunks of ice and lemon.
  e. Fruit salad is a heterogeneous mixture since it has chunks of fruit.

2.17 **a.** A gas has no definite volume or shape.
  b. In a gas, the particles do not interact with each other.
  c. In a solid, the particles are held in a rigid structure.

2.19 A *physical property* is a characteristic of the substance such as color, shape, odor, luster, size, melting point, and density. A *chemical property* is a characteristic that indicates the ability of a substance to change into a new substance.
  a. Color and physical state are physical properties.
  b. The ability to react with oxygen is a chemical property.
  c. The freezing point of a substance is a physical property.
  d. Milk souring describes chemical reactions and is thus a chemical property.

2.21 When matter undergoes a *physical change*, its state or appearance changes, but its composition remains the same. When a *chemical change* occurs, the original substance is converted into a new substance, which has different physical and chemical properties.
  a. Water vapor condensing is a physical change since the physical form of the water changes, but the composition of the substance does not.
  b. Cesium metal reacting is a chemical change since new substances form.
  c. Gold melting is a physical change since the physical state changes, but not the composition of the substance.
  d. Cutting a puzzle results in a physical change since the size and shape change, but not the composition of the substance.
  e. Grating cheese results in a physical change since the size and shape change, but not the composition of the substance.

2.23   **a.** The high reactivity of fluorine is a *chemical* property since it allows for the formation of new substances.
   b. The physical state of fluorine is a physical property.
   c. The color of fluorine is a physical property.
   d. The reactivity of fluorine with hydrogen is a chemical property since it allows for the formation of new substances.
   e. The melting point of fluorine is a physical property.

2.25   **a.** The change from a solid to liquid state is melting.
   b. Coffee is freeze-dried using the process of sublimation.
   c. Liquid water turning to ice is freezing.
   d. Ice crystals form on a package of frozen corn due to deposition.

2.27   **a.** Water vapor in clouds changing to rain is an example of condensation.
   b. Wet clothes drying on a clothesline involves evaporation.
   c. Steam forming as lava flows into the ocean involves boiling.
   d. Water droplets forming on a bathroom mirror after a hot shower involves condensation.

2.29

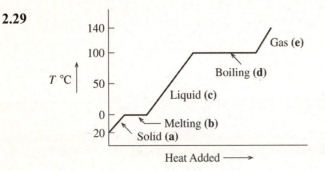

2.31   Copper, which has the lowest specific heat of the samples, would reach the highest temperature.

2.33   **a.** **Given** heat = 312 J; mass = 13.5 g; ΔT = 83.6 °C − 24.2 °C = 59.4 °C

   Need specific heat (J/g °C)

   Plan $SH = \dfrac{\text{heat}}{\text{mass} \times \Delta T}$

   Set Up specific heat (SH) = $\dfrac{312 \text{ J}}{13.5 \text{ g} \times 59.4 \text{ °C}}$ = $\dfrac{0.389 \text{ J}}{\text{g °C}}$ (3 SFs)

   b. **Given** heat = 345 J; mass = 48.2 g; ΔT = 57.9 °C − 35.0 °C = 22.9 °C

   Need specific heat (J/g °C)

   Plan $SH = \dfrac{\text{heat}}{\text{mass} \times \Delta T}$

   Set Up specific heat (SH) = $\dfrac{345 \text{ J}}{48.2 \text{ g} \times 22.9 \text{ °C}}$ = $\dfrac{0.313 \text{ J}}{\text{g °C}}$ (3 SFs)

2.35   **a.** **Given** SH_{water} = 1.00 cal/g °C; mass = 25 g; ΔT = 25 °C − 15 °C = 10. °C

   Need heat in calories

   Plan heat = mass $\times \Delta T \times SH$

   Set Up heat = 25 g $\times$ 10. °C $\times \dfrac{1.00 \text{ cal}}{\text{g °C}}$ = 250 cal (2 SFs)

b. Given $SH_{water} = 4.184$ J/g °C; mass $= 15$ g; $\Delta T = 75$ °C $- 22$ °C $= 53$ °C

Need heat in joules

Plan heat $=$ mass $\times \Delta T \times SH$

Set Up heat $= 15 \not{g} \times 53 \not{°C} \times \dfrac{4.184 \text{ J}}{\not{g} \; \not{°C}} = 3300$ J (2 SFs)

c. Given $SH_{water} = 1.00$ cal/g °C; mass $= 150$ g; $\Delta T = 77$ °C $- 15$ °C $= 62$ °C

Need heat in kilocalories

Plan heat $=$ mass $\times \Delta T \times SH$, then cal $\rightarrow$ kcal $\quad \dfrac{1 \text{ kcal}}{1000 \text{ cal}}$

Set Up heat $= 150 \not{g} \times 62 \not{°C} \times \dfrac{1.00 \not{cal}}{\not{g} \; \not{°C}} \times \dfrac{1 \text{ kcal}}{1000 \not{cal}} = 9.3$ kcal (2 SFs)

2.37 a. Given $SH_{water} = 4.184$ J/g °C $= 1.00$ cal/g °C; mass $= 25.0$ g; $\Delta T = 25.7$ °C $- 12.5$ °C $= 13.2$ °C

Need heat in joules and calories

Plan heat $=$ mass $\times \Delta T \times SH$

Set Up heat $= 25.0 \not{g} \times 13.2 \not{°C} \times \dfrac{4.184 \text{ J}}{\not{g} \; \not{°C}} = 1380$ J (3 SFs)

heat $= 25.0 \not{g} \times 13.2 \not{°C} \times \dfrac{1.00 \text{ cal}}{\not{g} \; \not{°C}} = 330.$ cal (3 SFs)

b. Given $SH_{copper} = 0.385$ J/g °C $= 0.0920$ cal/g °C; mass $= 38.0$ g;
$\Delta T = 246$ °C $- 122$ °C $= 124$ °C

Need heat in joules and calories

Plan heat $=$ mass $\times \Delta T \times SH$

Set Up heat $= 38.0 \not{g} \times 124 \not{°C} \times \dfrac{0.385 \text{ J}}{\not{g} \; \not{°C}} = 1810$ J (3 SFs)

heat $= 38.0 \not{g} \times 124 \not{°C} \times \dfrac{0.0920 \text{ cal}}{\not{g} \; \not{°C}} = 434$ cal (3 SFs)

c. Given $SH_{ethanol} = 2.46$ J/g °C $= 0.588$ cal/g °C; mass $= 15.0$ g;
$\Delta T = -42.0$ °C $- 60.5$ °C $= -102.5$ °C

Need heat in joules and calories

Plan heat $=$ mass $\times \Delta T \times SH$

Set Up heat $= 15.0 \not{g} \times (-102.5 \not{°C}) \times \dfrac{2.46 \text{ J}}{\not{g} \; \not{°C}} = -3780$ J (3 SFs)

heat $= 15.0 \not{g} \times (-102.5 \not{°C}) \times \dfrac{0.588 \text{ cal}}{\not{g} \; \not{°C}} = -904$ cal (3 SFs)

d. Given $SH_{iron} = 0.452$ J/g °C $= 0.108$ cal/g °C; mass $= 112$ g; $\Delta T = 55$ °C $- 118$ °C $= -63$ °C

Need heat in joules and calories

Plan heat $=$ mass $\times \Delta T \times SH$

Set Up heat $= 112 \cancel{g} \times (-63 \cancel{°C}) \times \dfrac{0.452 \text{ J}}{\cancel{g} \cancel{°C}} = -3200$ J (2 SFs)

heat $= 112 \cancel{g} \times (-63 \cancel{°C}) \times \dfrac{0.108 \text{ cal}}{\cancel{g} \cancel{°C}} = -760$ cal (2 SFs)

2.39 a. Given mass $= 505$ g of water; $\Delta T = 35.7$ °C $- 25.2$ °C $= 10.5$ °C;

$SH_{water} = 4.184$ J/g °C $= 1.00$ cal/g °C

Need energy in kilojoules and kilocalories

Plan heat $=$ mass $\times \Delta T \times SH$, then J $\rightarrow$ kJ $\quad \dfrac{1 \text{ kJ}}{1000 \text{ J}} \quad$ or $\quad$ cal $\rightarrow$ kcal $\quad \dfrac{1 \text{ kcal}}{1000 \text{ cal}}$

Set Up $505 \cancel{g} \times 10.5 \cancel{°C} \times \dfrac{4.184 \cancel{J}}{\cancel{g} \cancel{°C}} \times \dfrac{1 \text{ kJ}}{1000 \cancel{J}} = 22.2$ kJ (3 SFs)

$505 \cancel{g} \times 10.5 \cancel{°C} \times \dfrac{1.00 \cancel{cal}}{\cancel{g} \cancel{°C}} \times \dfrac{1 \text{ kcal}}{1000 \cancel{cal}} = 5.30$ kcal (3 SFs)

b. Given mass $= 4980$ g of water; $\Delta T = 62.4$ °C $- 20.6$ °C $= 41.8$ °C;

$SH_{water} = 4.184$ J/g °C $= 1.00$ cal/g °C

Need energy in kilojoules and kilocalories

Plan heat $=$ mass $\times \Delta T \times SH$, then J $\rightarrow$ kJ $\quad \dfrac{1 \text{ kJ}}{1000 \text{ J}} \quad$ or $\quad$ cal $\rightarrow$ kcal $\quad \dfrac{1 \text{ kcal}}{1000 \text{ cal}}$

Set Up $4980 \cancel{g} \times 41.8 \cancel{°C} \times \dfrac{4.184 \cancel{J}}{\cancel{g} \cancel{°C}} \times \dfrac{1 \text{ kJ}}{1000 \cancel{J}} = 871$ kJ (3 SFs)

$4980 \cancel{g} \times 41.8 \cancel{°C} \times \dfrac{1.00 \cancel{cal}}{\cancel{g} \cancel{°C}} \times \dfrac{1 \text{ kcal}}{1000 \cancel{cal}} = 208$ kcal (3 SFs)

2.41 a. Given 1 cup of orange juice that contains 26 g of carbohydrate, no fat, and 2 g of protein

Need total energy in kilojoules

Food Type	Mass	Energy Value	Energy
Carbohydrate	26 $\cancel{g}$ $\times$	$\dfrac{17 \text{ kJ}}{1 \cancel{g}}$ $=$	440 kJ
Protein	2 $\cancel{g}$ $\times$	$\dfrac{17 \text{ kJ}}{1 \cancel{g}}$ $=$	30 kJ
		Total energy content $=$	470 kJ (energy results rounded off to the tens place)

b. **Given** one apple that provides 72 kcal of energy and contains no fat or protein

Need grams of carbohydrate

Plan kcal → g of carbohydrate $\dfrac{1 \text{ g carbohydrate}}{4 \text{ kcal}}$

Set Up $72 \text{ kcal} \times \dfrac{1 \text{ g carbohydrate}}{4 \text{ kcal}} = 18$ g of carbohydrate (2 SFs)

c. **Given** 1 tablespoon of vegetable oil that contains 14 g of fat, and no carbohydrate or protein

Need total energy in kilocalories

Food Type	Mass	Energy Value	Energy
Fat	14 g	× $\dfrac{9 \text{ kcal}}{1 \text{ g}}$	= 130 kcal (energy results rounded off to the tens place)

d. **Given** a diet that consists of 68 g of carbohydrate, 9.0 g of fat, and 150 g of protein

Need total energy in kilocalories

Food Type	Mass	Energy Value	Energy
Carbohydrate	68 g	× $\dfrac{4 \text{ kcal}}{1 \text{ g}}$	= 270 kcal
Fat	9.0 g	× $\dfrac{9 \text{ kcal}}{1 \text{ g}}$	= 80 kcal
Protein	150 g	× $\dfrac{4 \text{ kcal}}{1 \text{ g}}$	= 600 kcal

Total energy content = 950 kcal (energy results rounded off to the tens place)

2.43 **Given** 1 cup of clam chowder that contains 16 g of carbohydrate, 12 g of fat, and 9 g of protein

Need total energy in kilojoules and kilocalories

Food Type	Mass	Energy Value	Energy
Carbohydrate	16 g	× $\dfrac{17 \text{ kJ (or 4 kcal)}}{1 \text{ g}}$	= 270 kJ (or 60 kcal)
Fat	12 g	× $\dfrac{38 \text{ kJ (or 9 kcal)}}{1 \text{ g}}$	= 460 kJ (or 110 kcal)
Protein	9 g	× $\dfrac{17 \text{ kJ (or 4 kcal)}}{1 \text{ g}}$	= 150 kJ (or 40 kcal)

Total energy content = 880 kJ (or 210 kcal) (energy results rounded off to the tens place)

2.45   To convert Celsius to Fahrenheit: $T_F = 1.8(T_C) + 32$

To convert Fahrenheit to Celsius: $T_C = \dfrac{(T_F - 32)}{1.8}$ (1.8 and 32 are exact numbers)

To convert Celsius to Kelvin: $T_K = T_C + 273$

To convert Kelvin to Celsius: $T_C = T_K - 273$

a.   convert 10 °F to °C:

$$T_C = \frac{(T_F - 32)}{1.8} = \frac{(10 - 32)}{1.8} = \frac{-22}{1.8} = -12 \text{ °C}$$

∴ 10 °C is warmer than 10 °F (−12 °C)

b.   convert 15 °F to °C:

$$T_C = \frac{(T_F - 32)}{1.8} = \frac{(15 - 32)}{1.8} = \frac{-17}{1.8} = -9.4 \text{ °C}$$

∴ 30 °C is warmer than 15 °F (−9.4 °C)

c.   convert 32 °F to °C:

$$T_C = \frac{(T_F - 32)}{1.8} = \frac{(32 - 32)}{1.8} = \frac{0}{1.8} = 0 \text{ °C}$$

∴ 32 °F (0 °C) is warmer than − 10 °C

d.   convert 200 K to °C:

$$T_C = T_K - 273 = 200 - 273 = -73 \text{ °C}$$

∴ 200 °C is warmer than 200 K (−73 °C)

2.47 $T_C = \dfrac{(T_F - 32)}{1.8} = \dfrac{(155 - 32)}{1.8} = \dfrac{123}{1.8} = 68.3 \text{ °C}$ (1.8 and 32 are exact numbers)

$T_K = T_C + 273 = 68.3 + 273 = 341 \text{ K}$ (3 SFs)

2.49   **a.**   The diagram shows two different types of atoms chemically combined in a definite proportion; it represents a compound.
   b.   The diagram shows two different types of atoms physically mixed but not chemically combined; it represents a mixture.
   c.   The diagram contains only one type of atom; it represents an element.

2.51   A *homogeneous mixture* has a uniform composition; a *heterogeneous mixture* does not have a uniform composition.
   a.   Lemon-flavored water is a homogeneous mixture since it has a uniform composition (as long as there are no lemon pieces).
   b.   Stuffed mushrooms are a heterogeneous mixture since there are mushrooms and chunks of filling.
   c.   Eye drops are a homogeneous mixture since they have a uniform composition.

2.53   **a.**   Heat is removed in the process of water freezing (liquid → solid).
   b.   Heat is added in the process of copper melting (solid → liquid).
   c.   Heat is added in the process of dry ice subliming (solid → gas).

2.55 **a.** The heat from the skin is used to evaporate the water (perspiration). Therefore, the skin is cooled.

  b. On a hot day, there are more liquid water molecules in the damp towels that have sufficient energy to become water vapor. Thus, water evaporates from the towels more quickly on a hot day.

2.57 **a.** The melting point of chloroform is about −60 °C.

  b. The boiling point of chloroform is about 60 °C.

  c. The diagonal line **A** represents the solid state as temperature increases. The horizontal line **B** represents the change from solid to liquid, or melting of the substance. The diagonal line **C** represents the liquid state as temperature increases. The horizontal line **D** represents the change from liquid to gas, or boiling of the liquid. The diagonal line **E** represents the gas state as temperature increases.

  d. At −80 °C, it is solid; at −40 °C, it is liquid; at 25 °C, it is liquid; at 80 °C, it is gas.

2.59 Sand must have a lower specific heat than water. When both substances absorb the same amount of heat, the final temperature of the sand will be higher than that of water.

2.61 **a.** **Given** a meal consisting of: cheeseburger: 34 g of carbohydrate, 29 g of fat, 31 g of protein
                                    french fries: 26 g of carbohydrate, 11 g of fat, 3 g of protein
                                    chocolate shake: 60 g of carbohydrate, 9 g of fat, 11 g of protein

  Need total energy in kilocalories

  Plan total grams of each food type, then g → kcal

  Set Up total carbohydrate = 34 g + 26 g + 60 g = 120 g

    total fat = 29 g + 11 g + 9 g = 49 g

    total protein = 31 g + 3 g + 11 g = 45 g

Food Type	Mass	Energy Value		Energy
Carbohydrate	120 g	×	$\dfrac{4 \text{ kcal}}{1 \text{ g}}$ =	480 kcal
Fat	49 g	×	$\dfrac{9 \text{ kcal}}{1 \text{ g}}$ =	440 kcal
Protein	45 g	×	$\dfrac{4 \text{ kcal}}{1 \text{ g}}$ =	180 kcal

                    Total energy content   = 1100 kcal (energy results rounded off to the tens place)

  b. **Given** 1100 kcal from meal   **Need** hours of sleeping to "burn off"

    Plan kcal → h $\dfrac{1 \text{ h sleeping}}{60 \text{ kcal}}$

    Set Up $1100 \text{ kcal} \times \dfrac{1 \text{ h sleeping}}{60 \text{ kcal}} = 18 \text{ h of sleeping (2 SFs)}$

  c. **Given** 1100 kcal from meal   **Need** hours of running to "burn off"

Plan kcal → h $\dfrac{1 \text{ h running}}{750 \text{ kcal}}$

Set Up $1100 \text{ kcal} \times \dfrac{1 \text{ h running}}{750 \text{ kcal}} = 1.5 \text{ h of running (2 SFs)}$

2.63 **a.** $T_C = \dfrac{(T_F - 32)}{1.8} = \dfrac{(134 - 32)}{1.8} = \dfrac{102}{1.8} = 56.7 \ °C$

b. $T_C = \dfrac{(T_F - 32)}{1.8} = \dfrac{(-69.7 - 32)}{1.8} = \dfrac{-101.7}{1.8} = -56.5 \ °C$

2.65 $T_C = \dfrac{(T_F - 32)}{1.8} = \dfrac{(-15 - 32)}{1.8} = \dfrac{-47}{1.8} = -26 \ °C$

$T_K = T_C + 273 = -26 + 273 = 247 \text{ K}$

2.67 *Elements* are the simplest type of pure substance, containing only one type of atom. *Compounds* contain two or more elements chemically combined in a definite proportion. In a *mixture*, two or more substances are physically mixed but not chemically combined.
   a. Carbon in pencils is an element since it contains only one type of atom (C).
   b. Carbon dioxide is a compound since it contains two elements (C, O) chemically combined.
   c. Orange juice is composed of several substances physically mixed together (for example, water, sugar, and citric acid), which makes it a mixture.
   d. Neon gas in lights is an element since it contains only one type of atom (Ne).
   e. A salad dressing made of oil and vinegar is composed of several substances physically but not chemically mixed together (for example, oil, water, and acetic acid), which makes it a mixture.

2.69 **a.** A vitamin tablet is a solid.
   b. Helium in a balloon is a gas.
   c. Milk is a liquid.
   d. Air is a mixture of gases.
   e. Charcoal is a solid.

2.71 A *physical property* is a characteristic of the substance such as color, shape, odor, luster, size, melting point, and density. A *chemical property* is a characteristic that indicates the ability of a substance to change into a new substance.
   a. The luster of gold is a physical property.
   b. The melting point of gold is a physical property.
   c. The ability of gold to conduct electricity is a physical property.
   d. The ability of gold to form a new substance with sulfur is a chemical property.

2.73 When matter undergoes a *physical change*, its state or appearance changes, but its composition remains the same. When a *chemical change* occurs, the original substance is converted into a new substance, which has different physical and chemical properties.
   a. Plant growth produces new substances, so it is a chemical change.
   b. A change of state from solid to liquid is a physical change.
   c. Chopping wood into smaller pieces results in a physical change.
   d. Burning wood, which forms new substances, results in a chemical change.

2.75 **Given** mass = 725 g of water; SH_{water} = 1.00 cal/g °C; ΔT = 37 °C − 65 °C = −28 °C

Need heat in kilocalories

Plan heat = mass $\times \Delta T \times SH$, then cal $\rightarrow$ kcal $\quad \dfrac{1\,kcal}{1000\,cal}$

Set Up heat = 725 $\cancel{g}$ × (−28 $\cancel{°C}$) × $\dfrac{1.00\,\cancel{cal}}{\cancel{g}\,\cancel{°C}}$ × $\dfrac{1\,kcal}{1000\,\cancel{cal}}$ = −20. kcal (2 SFs)

∴ 20. kcal of heat are lost from the water bottle and could be transferred to sore muscles

2.77 **Given** 1 cup of whole milk that contains 12 g of carbohydrate, 8 g of fat, and 8 g of protein

Need total energy in Calories (kilocalories)

Food Type	Mass		Energy Value		Energy
Carbohydrate	12 $\cancel{g}$	×	$\dfrac{4\,kcal}{1\,\cancel{g}}$	=	50 kcal
Fat	8 $\cancel{g}$	×	$\dfrac{9\,kcal}{1\,\cancel{g}}$	=	70 kcal
Protein	8 $\cancel{g}$	×	$\dfrac{4\,kcal}{1\,\cancel{g}}$	=	30 kcal

Total energy content = 150 kcal (150 Cal) (energy results rounded off to the tens place)

2.79 **a.** **Given** 11 kcal/1.0 g of gasoline; volume of gasoline = 1.0 gal; density = 0.74 g/mL

Need energy in megajoules (MJ)

Plan gal $\rightarrow$ qt $\rightarrow$ mL $\rightarrow$ g $\rightarrow$ kcal $\rightarrow$ cal $\rightarrow$ J $\rightarrow$ MJ $\quad \dfrac{0.74\,g\,gasoline}{1\,mL\,gasoline} \quad \dfrac{11\,kcal}{1.0\,g\,gasoline}$

Set Up 1.0 $\cancel{gal\,gasoline}$ × $\dfrac{4\,\cancel{qt}}{1\,\cancel{gal}}$ × $\dfrac{946\,\cancel{mL}}{1\,\cancel{qt}}$ × $\dfrac{0.74\,\cancel{g\,gasoline}}{1\,\cancel{mL\,gasoline}}$ × $\dfrac{11\,\cancel{kcal}}{1.0\,\cancel{g\,gasoline}}$

$\times \dfrac{1000\,\cancel{cal}}{1\,\cancel{kcal}}$ × $\dfrac{4.184\,\cancel{J}}{1\,\cancel{cal}}$ × $\dfrac{1\,MJ}{1\times10^6\,\cancel{J}}$ = 130 MJ (2 SFs)

b. **Given** 300 kJ/2.0 h of television; volume of gasoline = 1.0 gal; density = 0.74 g/mL

Need hours of television

Plan gal $\rightarrow$ qt $\rightarrow$ mL $\rightarrow$ g $\rightarrow$ kcal $\rightarrow$ cal $\rightarrow$ J $\rightarrow$ kJ $\rightarrow$ h $\quad \dfrac{0.74\,g\,gasoline}{1\,mL\,gasoline} \quad \dfrac{11\,kcal}{1.0\,g\,gasoline}$

Set Up 1.0 $\cancel{gal\,gasoline}$ × $\dfrac{4\,\cancel{qt}}{1\,\cancel{gal}}$ × $\dfrac{946\,\cancel{mL}}{1\,\cancel{qt}}$ × $\dfrac{0.74\,\cancel{g\,gasoline}}{1\,\cancel{mL\,gasoline}}$ × $\dfrac{11\,\cancel{kcal}}{1.0\,\cancel{g\,gasoline}}$

$\times \dfrac{1000\,\cancel{cal}}{1\,\cancel{kcal}}$ × $\dfrac{4.184\,\cancel{J}}{1\,\cancel{cal}}$ × $\dfrac{1\,\cancel{kJ}}{1000\,\cancel{J}}$ × $\dfrac{2.0\,h}{300\,\cancel{kJ}}$ = 860 h (2 SFs)

2.81

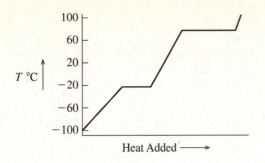

a. Carbon tetrachloride is a solid at −50 °C.
b. At −23 °C, solid carbon tetrachloride melts (solid → liquid).
c. Carbon tetrachloride is a liquid at 20 °C.
d. At 90 °C, carbon tetrachloride is a gas.
e. Both solid and liquid carbon tetrachloride will be present at the melting temperature of −23 °C.

2.83   **Given**

Copper	Water
mass = 70.0 g	mass = 50.0 g
initial temperature = 86.0 °C	initial temperature = 16.0 °C
final temperature = 24.0 °C	final temperature = 24.0 °C
SH = ? J/g °C	SH = 4.184 J/g °C

Need specific heat (SH) of copper (J/g °C)

Plan heat lost by copper = −heat gained by water

For both, heat = mass × ΔT × SH

Set Up

For water: heat gained = mass × ΔT × SH = $50.0 \, \cancel{g} \times (24.0 \, \cancel{°C} - 16.0 \, \cancel{°C}) \times \dfrac{4.184 \, J}{\cancel{g} \, \cancel{°C}} = 1670 \, J$

For copper:

∴ heat lost by copper = −1670 J

$$SH = \frac{\text{heat lost}}{\text{mass} \times \Delta T} = \frac{-1670 \, J}{70.0 \, g \times (24.0 \, °C - 86.0 \, °C)} = \frac{0.39 \, J}{g \, °C} \, (2 \, \text{SFs})$$

2.85   **a.** **Given** heat = 11 J; mass = 4.7 g; ΔT = 4.5 °C

Need specific heat (J/g °C)

Plan $SH = \dfrac{\text{heat}}{\text{mass} \times \Delta T}$

Set Up specific heat (SH) = $\dfrac{11 \, J}{4.7 \, g \times 4.5 \, °C} = \dfrac{0.52 \, J}{g \, °C} \, (2 \, \text{SFs})$

b. By comparing this calculated value to the specific heats given in Table 2.8, we would identify the unknown metal as titanium (SH = 0.523 J/g °C) rather than aluminum (SH = 0.897 J/g °C).

2.87   **Given** 0.660 g of olive oil; mass of water in calorimeter = 370. g;

SH_{water} = 4.184 J/g °C = 1.00 cal/g °C; ΔT = 38.8 °C − 22.7 °C = 16.1 °C

Need energy value of olive oil (in kJ/g and kcal/g)

Plan   heat = mass $\times \Delta T \times SH$, then J $\rightarrow$ kJ $\dfrac{1\ kJ}{1000\ J}$

Set Up   heat $= 370.\ \cancel{g} \times 16.1\ \cancel{^\circ C} \times \dfrac{4.184\ \cancel{J}}{\cancel{g}\ \cancel{^\circ C}} \times \dfrac{1\ kJ}{1000\ \cancel{J}} = 24.9$ kJ

$\therefore$ energy value $= \dfrac{\text{heat produced}}{\text{mass}} = \dfrac{24.9\ kJ}{0.660\ \text{g oil}} = 37.7$ kJ/g of olive oil (3 SFs)

heat $= 370.\ \cancel{g} \times 16.1\ \cancel{^\circ C} \times \dfrac{1\ \cancel{cal}}{\cancel{g}\ \cancel{^\circ C}} \times \dfrac{1\ kcal}{1000\ \cancel{cal}} = 5.96$ kcal

$\therefore$ energy value $= \dfrac{\text{heat produced}}{\text{mass}} = \dfrac{5.96\ kcal}{0.660\ \text{g oil}} = 9.03$ kcal/g of olive oil (3 SFs)

2.89   **Given** 1 lb of body fat; 15% (m/m) water in body fat

Need kilocalories to "burn off"

Plan Because each gram of body fat contains 15% water, a person actually loses 85 grams of fat per hundred grams of body fat. (We considered 1 lb of fat as exactly 1 lb.)

lb of body fat $\rightarrow$ g of body fat $\rightarrow$ g of fat $\rightarrow$ kcal $\dfrac{454\ \text{g body fat}}{1\ \text{lb body fat}}$ $\dfrac{85\ \text{g fat}}{100\ \text{g body fat}}$ $\dfrac{9\ kcal}{1\ \text{g fat}}$

Set Up   1 $\cancel{\text{lb body fat}} \times \dfrac{454\ \cancel{\text{g body fat}}}{1\ \cancel{\text{lb body fat}}} \times \dfrac{85\ \cancel{\text{g fat}}}{100\ \cancel{\text{g body fat}}} \times \dfrac{9\ kcal}{1\ \cancel{\text{g fat}}} = 3500$ kcal (2 SFs)

Answers to Combining Ideas from Chapters 1 and 2

CI.1 **a.** There are four significant figures in the measurement 20.17 lb.

  b. $20.17 \text{ lb} \times \dfrac{1 \text{ kg}}{2.20 \text{ lb}} = 9.17 \text{ kg (3 SFs)}$

  c. $9.17 \text{ kg} \times \dfrac{1000 \text{ g}}{1 \text{ kg}} \times \dfrac{1 \text{ cm}^3}{19.3 \text{ g}} = 475 \text{ cm}^3 \text{ (3 SFs)}$

  d. $T_F = 1.8(T_C) + 32 = 1.8(1064) + 32 = 1947 \text{ °F (4 SFs)}$

  $T_K = T_C + 273 = 1064 + 273 = 1337 \text{ K (4 SFs)}$

  e. $\Delta T = T_{final} - T_{initial} = 358 \text{ °C} - 27 \text{ °C} = 331 \text{ °C} = \text{temperature change}$

  $9.17 \text{ kg} \times \dfrac{1000 \text{ g}}{1 \text{ kg}} \times \dfrac{0.129 \text{ J}}{\text{g °C}} \times 331 \text{ °C} \times \dfrac{1 \text{ kJ}}{1000 \text{ J}} = 392 \text{ kJ (3 SFs)}$

  $9.17 \text{ kg} \times \dfrac{1000 \text{ g}}{1 \text{ kg}} \times \dfrac{0.129 \text{ J}}{\text{g °C}} \times \dfrac{1 \text{ cal}}{4.184 \text{ J}} \times 331 \text{ °C} \times \dfrac{1 \text{ kcal}}{1000 \text{ cal}} = 93.6 \text{ kcal (3 SFs)}$

  f. $9.17 \text{ kg} \times \dfrac{1000 \text{ g}}{1 \text{ kg}} \times \dfrac{\$61.08}{1 \text{ g}} = \$560\,000 \text{ or } \$5.60 \times 10^5 \text{ (3 SFs)}$

CI.3 **a.** The water has its own shape in sample B.
  b. Water sample A is represented by diagram 2, which shows the particles in a random arrangement but close together.
  c. Water sample B is represented by diagram 1, which shows the particles fixed in a definite arrangement.
  d. The state of matter indicated in diagram 1 is a *solid*; in diagram 2, it is a *liquid*; and in diagram 3, it is a *gas*.
  e. The motion of the particles is slowest in diagram 1.
  f. The arrangement of particles is farthest apart in diagram 3.
  g. The particles fill the volume of the container in diagram 3.
  h. water 45 °C → 0 °C: $\Delta T = 0 \text{ °C} - 45 \text{ °C} = -45 \text{ °C}$

  $\text{heat} = 19 \text{ g} \times (-45 \text{ °C}) \times \dfrac{4.184 \text{ J}}{\text{g °C}} \times \dfrac{1 \text{ kJ}}{1000 \text{ J}} = -3.6 \text{ kJ (2 SFs)}$

  ∴ 3.6 kJ of heat is removed

CI.5 **a.** $0.250 \text{ lb} \times \dfrac{454 \text{ g}}{1 \text{ lb}} \times \dfrac{1 \text{ cm}^3}{7.86 \text{ g}} = 14.4 \text{ cm}^3 \text{ (3 SFs)}$

  b. $30 \text{ nails} \times \dfrac{0.250 \text{ lb}}{75 \text{ nails}} \times \dfrac{454 \text{ g}}{1 \text{ lb}} \times \dfrac{1 \text{ cm}^3}{7.86 \text{ g}} \times \dfrac{1 \text{ mL}}{1 \text{ cm}^3} = 5.78 \text{ mL}$

  17.6 mL water + 5.78 mL = 23.4 mL new water level (rounded off to tenths place)

  c. $\Delta T = T_{final} - T_{initial} = 125 \text{ °C} - 16 \text{ °C} = 109 \text{ °C} = \text{temperature change}$

  $\text{heat} = \text{mass} \times \Delta T \times SH = 0.250 \text{ lb} \times \dfrac{454 \text{ g}}{1 \text{ lb}} \times 109 \text{ °C} \times \dfrac{0.452 \text{ J}}{\text{g °C}} = 5590 \text{ J or } 5.59 \times 10^3 \text{ J (3 SFs)}$

3

Atoms and Elements

3.1   **a.**   Cu is the symbol for copper.
        b.   Pt is the symbol for platinum.
        c.   Ca is the symbol for calcium.
        d.   Mn is the symbol for manganese.
        e.   Fe is the symbol for iron.
        f.   Ba is the symbol for barium.
        g.   Pb is the symbol for lead.
        h.   Sr is the symbol for strontium.

3.3   **a.**   Carbon is the element with the symbol C.
        b.   Chlorine is the element with the symbol Cl.
        c.   Iodine is the element with the symbol I.
        d.   Mercury is the element with the symbol Hg.
        e.   Silver is the element with the symbol Ag.
        f.   Argon is the element with the symbol Ar.
        g.   Boron is the element with the symbol B.
        h.   Nickel is the element with the symbol Ni.

3.5   **a.**   Sodium (Na) and chlorine (Cl) are in NaCl.
        b.   Calcium (Ca), sulfur (S), and oxygen (O) are in $CaSO_4$.
        c.   Carbon (C), hydrogen (H), chlorine (Cl), nitrogen (N), and oxygen (O) are in $C_{15}H_{22}ClNO_2$.
        d.   Calcium (Ca), carbon (C), and oxygen (O) are in $CaCO_3$.

3.7   **a.**   C, N, and O are in Period 2.
        b.   He is the element at the top of Group 8A (18).
        c.   The alkali metals are the elements in Group 1A (1).
        d.   Period 2 is the horizontal row of elements that ends with neon (Ne).

3.9   **a.**   Ca is an alkaline earth metal.
        b.   Fe is a transition element.
        c.   Xe is a noble gas.
        d.   K is an alkali metal.
        e.   Cl is a halogen.

3.11   **a.**   C is in Group 4A (14), Period 2.
        b.   He is the noble gas in Period 1.
        c.   Na is the alkali metal in Period 3.
        d.   Ca is in Group 2A (2), Period 4.
        e.   Al is in Group 3A (13), Period 3.

3.13   On the periodic table, *metals* are located to the left of the heavy zigzag line, *nonmetals* are located to the right of the line, and *metalloids* (B, Si, Ge, As, Sb, Te, Po, and At) are located along the line.
        a.   Ca is a metal.
        b.   S is a nonmetal.
        c.   Metals are shiny.
        d.   An element that is a gas at room temperature is a nonmetal.
        e.   Group 8A (18) elements are nonmetals.

    f. Br is a nonmetal.

    g. Te is a metalloid.

    h. Ag is a metal.

3.15   **a.** The electron has the smallest mass.

      b. The proton has a 1+ charge.

      c. The electron is found outside the nucleus.

      d. The neutron is electrically neutral.

3.17   **a.** True

      b. True

      c. True

      d. False; since a neutron has no charge, it is not attracted to a proton (a proton is attracted to an electron).

3.19   Thomson determined that electrons had a negative charge when he observed they were attracted to the positive electrode in a cathode ray tube.

3.21   **a.** The atomic number is the same as the number of protons in an atom.

      b. Both are needed since the number of neutrons is the (mass number) – (atomic number).

      c. The mass number is the number of particles (protons + neutrons) in the nucleus.

      d. The atomic number is the same as the number of electrons in a neutral atom.

3.23   The atomic number defines the element and is found above the symbol of the element in the periodic table.

      a. Lithium, Li, has an atomic number of 3.

      b. Fluorine, F, has an atomic number of 9.

      c. Calcium, Ca, has an atomic number of 20.

      d. Zinc, Zn, has an atomic number of 30.

      e. Neon, Ne, has an atomic number of 10.

      f. Silicon, Si, has an atomic number of 14.

      g. Iodine, I, has an atomic number of 53.

      h. Oxygen, O, has an atomic number of 8.

3.25   The atomic number gives the number of protons in the nucleus of an atom. Since atoms are neutral, the atomic number also gives the number of electrons in the neutral atom.

      a. There are 18 protons and 18 electrons in a neutral argon atom.

      b. There are 30 protons and 30 electrons in a neutral zinc atom.

      c. There are 53 protons and 53 electrons in a neutral iodine atom.

      d. There are 48 protons and 48 electrons in a neutral cadmium atom.

3.27   The atomic number is the same as the number of protons in an atom and the number of electrons in a neutral atom; the atomic number defines the element. The number of neutrons is the (mass number) – (atomic number).

Name of the Element	Symbol	Atomic Number	Mass Number	Number of Protons	Number of Neutrons	Number of Electrons
Aluminum	Al	13	27	13	$27 - 13 = 14$	13
Magnesium	Mg	12	$12 + 12 = 24$	12	12	12
Potassium	K	19	$19 + 20 = 39$	19	20	19
Sulfur	S	16	$16 + 15 = 31$	16	15	16
Iron	Fe	26	56	26	$56 - 26 = 30$	26

3.29 **a.** Since the atomic number of strontium is 38, every Sr atom has 38 protons. An atom of strontium (mass number 89) has 51 neutrons ($89 - 38 = 51\ n$). Neutral atoms have the same number of protons and electrons. Therefore, 38 protons, 51 neutrons, 38 electrons.

  b. Since the atomic number of chromium is 24, every Cr atom has 24 protons. An atom of chromium (mass number 52) has 28 neutrons ($52 - 24 = 28\ n$). Neutral atoms have the same number of protons and electrons. Therefore, 24 protons, 28 neutrons, 24 electrons.

  c. Since the atomic number of sulfur is 16, every S atom has 16 protons. An atom of sulfur (mass number 34) has 18 neutrons ($34 - 16 = 18\ n$). Neutral atoms have the same number of protons and electrons. Therefore, 16 protons, 18 neutrons, 16 electrons.

  d. Since the atomic number of bromine is 35, every Br atom has 35 protons. An atom of bromine (mass number 81) has 46 neutrons ($81 - 35 = 46\ n$). Neutral atoms have the same number of protons and electrons. Therefore, 35 protons, 46 neutrons, 35 electrons.

3.31 **a.** Since the number of protons is 15, the atomic number is 15 and the element symbol is P. The mass number is the sum of the number of protons and the number of neutrons, $15 + 16 = 31$. The atomic symbol for this isotope is $^{31}_{15}\text{P}$.

  b. Since the number of protons is 35, the atomic number is 35 and the element symbol is Br. The mass number is the sum of the number of protons and the number of neutrons, $35 + 45 = 80$. The atomic symbol for this isotope is $^{80}_{35}\text{Br}$.

  c. Since the number of electrons is 50, there must be 50 protons in a neutral atom. Since the number of protons is 50, the atomic number is 50, and the element symbol is Sn. The mass number is the sum of the number of protons and the number of neutrons, $50 + 72 = 122$. The atomic symbol for this isotope is $^{122}_{50}\text{Sn}$.

  d. Since the element is chlorine, the element symbol is Cl, the atomic number is 17, and the number of protons is 17. The mass number is the sum of the number of protons and the number of neutrons, $17 + 18 = 35$. The atomic symbol for this isotope is $^{35}_{17}\text{Cl}$.

  e. Since the element is mercury, the element symbol is Hg, the atomic number is 80, and the number of protons is 80. The mass number is the sum of the number of protons and the number of neutrons, $80 + 122 = 202$. The atomic symbol for this isotope is $^{202}_{80}\text{Hg}$.

3.33 **a.** Since the element is argon, the element symbol is Ar, the atomic number is 18, and the number of protons is 18. The atomic symbols for the isotopes with mass numbers of 36, 38, and 40 are $^{36}_{18}\text{Ar}$, $^{38}_{18}\text{Ar}$, and $^{40}_{18}\text{Ar}$, respectively.

  b. They all have the same atomic number (the same number of protons and electrons).

  c. They have different numbers of neutrons, which gives them different mass numbers.

  d. The atomic mass of argon listed on the periodic table is the weighted average atomic mass of all the naturally occurring isotopes of argon.

  e. The isotope Ar-40 ($^{40}_{18}\text{Ar}$) is the most prevalent in a sample of argon because its mass is closest to the average atomic mass of argon listed on the periodic table (39.95 amu).

3.35 $^{69}_{31}\text{Ga}$ $68.93 \times \dfrac{60.11}{100} = 41.43\ \text{amu}$

  $^{71}_{31}\text{Ga}$ $70.92 \times \dfrac{39.89}{100} = 28.29\ \text{amu}$

  _____

  Atomic mass of Ga $= 69.72\ \text{amu}$ (4 SFs)

3.37 **a.** A $1s$ orbital is spherical.

  b. A $2p$ orbital has two lobes.

  c. A $5s$ orbital is spherical.

3.39 **a.** **1 and 2**; 1*s* and 2*s* orbitals have the same shape (spherical) and can contain a maximum of two electrons.

b. **3**; 3*s* and 3*p* sublevels are in the same energy level (*n* = 3).

c. **1 and 2**; 3*p* and 4*p* sublevels contain orbitals with the same two-lobed shape and can contain the same maximum number of electrons (six).

d. **1, 2, and 3**; all of the 3*p* orbitals have two lobes, can contain a maximum of two electrons, and are in energy level *n* = 3.

3.41 **a.** There are five orbitals in the 3*d* sublevel.

b. There is one sublevel in the *n* = 1 energy level.

c. There is one orbital in the 6*s* sublevel.

d. There are nine orbitals in the *n* = 3 energy level: one 3*s* orbital, three 3*p* orbitals, and five 3*d* orbitals.

3.43 **a.** Any orbital can hold a maximum of two electrons. Thus, a 3*p* orbital has a maximum of two electrons.

b. The 3*p* sublevel contains three *p* orbitals, each of which can hold a maximum of two electrons, which gives a maximum of six electrons in the 3*p* sublevel.

c. Using $2n^2$, the calculation for the maximum number of electrons in the *n* = 4 energy level is $2(4)^2 = 2(16) = 32$ electrons.

d. The 5*d* sublevel contains five *d* orbitals, each of which can hold a maximum of two electrons, which gives a maximum of 10 electrons in the 5*d* sublevel.

3.45 Determine the number of electrons and then fill orbitals in the following order: $1s^2 2s^2 2p^6 3s^2 3p^6$

a. Boron is atomic number 5 and so it has 5 electrons. Fill orbitals as

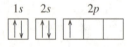

b. Aluminum is atomic number 13 and so it has 13 electrons. Fill orbitals as

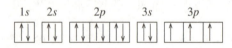

c. Phosphorus is atomic number 15 and so it has 15 electrons. Fill orbitals as

d. Argon is atomic number 18 and so it has 18 electrons. Fill orbitals as

3.47 **a.** Fe $1s^2 2s^2 2p^6 3s^2 3p^6 4s^2 3d^6$

b. Na $1s^2 2s^2 2p^6 3s^1$

c. Rb $1s^2 2s^2 2p^6 3s^2 3p^6 4s^2 3d^{10} 4p^6 5s^1$

d. As $1s^2 2s^2 2p^6 3s^2 3p^6 4s^2 3d^{10} 4p^3$

3.49 Using the periodic table, the *s* sublevel block is on the left, the *p* sublevel block is on the right, and the *d* sublevel block is in the center between the *s* and *p* blocks. The abbreviated electron configuration consists of the symbol of the preceding noble gas, followed by the electron configuration in the next period.

    a. Mg $[Ne]3s^2$

    b. Ba $[Xe]6s^2$

    c. Al $[Ne]3s^2 3p^1$

    d. Ti $[Ar]4s^2 3d^2$

3.51   **a.** S is the element with two electrons in the 3*s* and four electrons in the 3*p* sublevels.

    b. Co is the element with two electrons in the 4*s* and seven electrons in the 3*d* sublevels.

    c. Si is the element with two electrons in the 3*s* and two electrons in the 3*p* sublevels.

    d. Br is the element with two electrons in the 4*s* and five electrons in the 4*p* sublevels.

3.53   **a.** Al has three electrons in the $n = 3$ energy level, $3s^2 3p^1$.

    b. C has two 2*p* electrons, $2p^2$.

    c. Ar completes the 3*p* sublevel, $3p^6$.

    d. Zr has two electrons in the 4*d* sublevel, $4d^2$.

3.55   **a.** Zn is the tenth element in the 3*d* block; it has ten 3*d* electrons.

    b. Na is the first element in the 3*s* block; the 2*p* block in Na is complete with six electrons.

    c. As is the third element in the 4*p* block; it has three 4*p* electrons.

    d. Rb is the first element in the 5*s* block; Rb has one 5*s* electron.

3.57   **a.** Aluminum in Group 3A (13) has three valence electrons.

    b. Any element in Group 5A (15) has five valence electrons.

    c. Each halogen in Group 7A (17) has seven valence electrons.

3.59 The number of dots is equal to the number of valence electrons, as indicated by the group number.

    a. Sulfur is in Group 6A (16).

       ·S:

    b. Nitrogen is in Group 5A (15).

       ·N·

    c. Calcium is in Group 2A (2).

       Ca·

    d. Sodium is in Group 1A (1).

       Na·

    e. Gallium is in Group 3A (13).

       ·Ga·

3.61 The atomic radius of representative elements decreases going across a period from Group 1A to 8A and increases going down a group.

    a. In Period 3, Na, which is on the left, is larger than Cl.

    b. In Group 1A (1), Rb, which is farther down the group, is larger than Na.

    c. In Period 3, Na, which is on the left, is larger than Mg.

    d. In Period 5, Rb, which is on the left, is larger than I.

3.63   **a.** The atomic radius of representative elements decreases from Group 1A to 8A: Mg, Al, Si.

    b. The atomic radius of representative elements increases going down a group: I, Br, Cl.

    c. The atomic radius of representative elements decreases from Group 1A to 8A: Sr, Sb, I.

    d. The atomic radius of representative elements decreases from Group 1A to 8A: Na, Si, P.

3.65 **a.** In Br, the valence electrons are closer to the nucleus, so Br has a higher ionization energy than I.

b. In Mg, the valence electrons are closer to the nucleus, so Mg has a higher ionization energy than Sr.

c. Attraction for the valence electrons increases going from left to right across a period, giving P a higher ionization energy than Si.

d. The noble gases have the highest ionization energy in each period, which gives Xe a higher ionization energy than I.

3.67 **a.** Br, Cl, F; ionization energy decreases going down a group.

b. Na, Al, Cl; going across a period from left to right, ionization energy increases.

c. Cs, K, Na; ionization energy decreases going down a group.

d. Ca, As, Br; going across a period from left to right, ionization energy increases.

3.69 Na has a <u>larger</u> atomic size and is <u>more</u> metallic than P.

3.71 Ca, Ga, Ge, Br; since metallic character decreases from left to right across a period, Ca, in Group 2A (2), will be the most metallic, followed by Ga, then Ge, and finally Br, in Group 7A (17).

3.73 Sr has a <u>lower</u> ionization energy and is <u>more</u> metallic than Sb.

3.75 Going down Group 6A (16),

a. 1; the ionization energy <u>decreases</u>.

b. 2; the atomic size <u>increases</u>.

c. 2; the metallic character <u>increases</u>.

d. 3; the number of valence electrons <u>remains the same</u>.

3.77 In Period 2, an atom of N compared to an atom of Li has a larger (greater)

a. False; N has a smaller atomic size than Li.

b. True

c. True

d. False; N has less metallic character than Li.

e. True

3.79 Statements **b** and **c** are true. According to Dalton's atomic theory, atoms of an element are different than atoms of other elements, and atoms do not appear and disappear in a chemical reaction.

3.81 **a.** The atomic mass is the weighted average of the masses of all of the naturally occurring isotopes of the element. Isotope masses are based on the masses of all subatomic particles in the atom: protons (1), neutrons (2), and electrons (3), although almost all of that mass comes from the protons (1) and neutrons (2).

b. The number of protons (1) is the atomic number.

c. The protons (1) are positively charged.

d. The electrons (3) are negatively charged.

e. The number of neutrons (2) is the (mass number) − (atomic number).

3.83 **a.** $^{16}_{8}X$, $^{17}_{8}X$, and $^{18}_{8}X$ all have an atomic number of 8, so all have eight protons.

b. $^{16}_{8}X$, $^{17}_{8}X$, and $^{18}_{8}X$ all have an atomic number of 8, so all are isotopes of oxygen.

c. $^{16}_{8}X$ and $^{16}_{9}X$ have a mass number of 16, whereas $^{18}_{8}X$ and $^{18}_{10}X$ have a mass number of 18.

d. $^{16}_{8}X$ $(16 - 8 = 8\,n)$ and $^{18}_{10}X$ $(18 - 10 = 8\,n)$ both have eight neutrons.

3.85 **a.** $^{37}_{17}$Cl and $^{38}_{18}$Ar both have 20 neutrons ($37 - 17 = 20\,n$; $38 - 18 = 20\,n$).

b. Since both $^{36}_{14}$Si and $^{35}_{14}$Si have an atomic number of 14, they will both have 14 protons in the nucleus. Since the number of protons is 14, there must be 14 electrons in the neutral atom for both. They have different numbers of neutrons ($36 - 14 = 22\,n$; $35 - 14 = 21\,n$).

c. $^{40}_{18}$Ar and $^{39}_{17}$Cl both have 22 neutrons ($40 - 18 = 22\,n$; $39 - 17 = 22\,n$).

3.87 **a.** The diagram shows four protons and five neutrons in the nucleus of the element. Since the number of protons is four, the atomic number is 4, and the element symbol is Be. The mass number is the sum of the number of protons and the number of neutrons, $4 + 5 = 9$. The atomic symbol is $^{9}_{4}$Be.

b. The diagram shows five protons and six neutrons in the nucleus of the element. Since the number of protons is five, the atomic number is 5, and the element symbol is B. The mass number is the sum of the number of protons and the number of neutrons, $5 + 6 = 11$. The atomic symbol is $^{11}_{5}$B.

c. The diagram shows six protons and seven neutrons in the nucleus of the element. Since the number of protons is six, the atomic number is 6, and the element symbol is C. The mass number is the sum of the number of protons and the number of neutrons, $6 + 7 = 13$. The atomic symbol is $^{13}_{6}$C.

d. The diagram shows five protons and five neutrons in the nucleus of the element. Since the number of protons is five, the atomic number is 5, and the element symbol is B. The mass number is the sum of the number of protons and the number of neutrons, $5 + 5 = 10$. The atomic symbol is $^{10}_{5}$B.

e. The diagram shows six protons and six neutrons in the nucleus of the element. Since the number of protons is six, the atomic number is 6, and the element symbol is C. The mass number is the sum of the number of protons and the number of neutrons, $6 + 6 = 12$. The atomic symbol is $^{12}_{6}$C.
Both **B** ($^{11}_{5}$B) and **D** ($^{10}_{5}$B) are isotopes of boron; **C** ($^{13}_{6}$C) and **E** ($^{12}_{6}$C) are isotopes of carbon.

3.89 Atomic radius increases going down a group. Li is **D** because it would be smallest. Na is **A**, K is **C**, and Rb is **B**.

3.91 **a.** Na has the largest atomic size.
b. Cl is a halogen.
c. S has the electron configuration $1s^2 2s^2 2p^6 3s^2 3p^4$.
d. Ar, a noble gas, has the highest ionization energy.
e. Si is a metalloid.
f. Na, in Group 1A (1), has the most metallic character.
g. Mg, in Group 2A (2), has two valence electrons.

3.93 **a.** Br is in Period 4, Group 7A (17).
b. Ar is in Period 3, Group 8A (18).
c. K is in Period 4, Group 1A (1).
d. Ra is in Period 7, Group 2A (2).

3.95 On the periodic table, *metals* are located to the left of the heavy zigzag line, *nonmetals* are located to the right of the line, and *metalloids* (B, Si, Ge, As, Sb, Te, Po, and At) are located along the line.
a. Zn is a metal.
b. Co is a metal.
c. Mn is a metal.
d. I is a nonmetal.

3.97 **a.** False; A proton is a positively charged particle.
b. False; The neutron has about the same mass as a proton.
c. True
d. False; The nucleus is the tiny, dense central core of an atom.
e. True

3.99
  a. Since the atomic number of cadmium is 48, every Cd atom has 48 protons. An atom of cadmium (mass number 114) has 66 neutrons (114 − 48 = 66 n). Neutral atoms have the same number of protons and electrons. Therefore, 48 protons, 66 neutrons, 48 electrons.

  b. Since the atomic number of technetium is 43, every Tc atom has 43 protons. An atom of technetium (mass number 98) has 55 neutrons (98 − 43 = 55 n). Neutral atoms have the same number of protons and electrons. Therefore, 43 protons, 55 neutrons, 43 electrons.

  c. Since the atomic number of gold is 79, every Au atom has 79 protons. An atom of gold (mass number 199) has 120 neutrons (199 − 79 = 120 n). Neutral atoms have the same number of protons and electrons. Therefore, 79 protons, 120 neutrons, 79 electrons.

  d. Since the atomic number of radon is 86, every Rn atom has 86 protons. An atom of radon (mass number 222) has 136 neutrons (222 − 86 = 136 n). Neutral atoms have the same number of protons and electrons. Therefore, 86 protons, 136 neutrons, 86 electrons.

  e. Since the atomic number of xenon is 54, every Xe atom has 54 protons. An atom of xenon (mass number 136) has 82 neutrons (136 − 54 = 82 n). Neutral atoms have the same number of protons and electrons. Therefore, 54 protons, 82 neutrons, 54 electrons.

3.101

Name of the Element	Atomic Symbol	Number of Protons	Number of Neutrons	Number of Electrons
Sulfur	$^{34}_{16}S$	16	34 − 16 = 18	16
Nickel	$^{28+34}_{28}Ni$ or $^{62}_{28}Ni$	28	34	28
Magnesium	$^{12+14}_{12}Mg$ or $^{26}_{12}Mg$	12	14	12
Radium	$^{228}_{88}Ra$	88	228 − 88 = 140	88

3.103
  a. The 3p sublevel starts to fill after completion of the 3s sublevel.
  b. The 5s sublevel starts to fill after completion of the 4p sublevel.
  c. The 4p sublevel starts to fill after completion of the 3d sublevel.
  d. The 4s sublevel starts to fill after completion of the 3p sublevel.

3.105
  a. Iron is the sixth element in the 3d block; Fe has six 3d electrons.
  b. Barium has a completely filled 5p sublevel, which is six 5p electrons.
  c. Iodine has a completely filled 4d sublevel, which is ten 4d electrons.
  d. Radium has a filled 7s sublevel, which is two 7s electrons.

3.107
  a. Phosphorus, in Group 5A (15), is the element with electron configuration $1s^2 2s^2 2p^6 3s^2 3p^3$.
  b. Lithium is the alkali metal that is highest in Group 1A (1) and has the smallest atomic radius. (H in Group 1A (1) is a nonmetal.)
  c. Cadmium is the element with the abbreviated electron configuration $[Kr]5s^2 4d^{10}$.
  d. Nitrogen, at the top of Group 5A (15), has the highest ionization energy in that group.
  e. Sodium, the first element in Period 3, has the largest atomic radius of that period.

3.109
  a. Na is on the far left of the heavy zigzag line. Na is a metal.
  b. Na, at the beginning of Period 3, has the largest atomic radius.
  c. F, at the top of Group 7A (17) and to the far right in Period 2, has the highest ionization energy.
  d. Na has the lowest ionization energy and loses an electron most easily.
  e. Cl is found in Period 3 in Group 7A (17).

3.111
  a. Since the element is lead (Pb), the atomic number is 82, and the number of protons is 82. In a neutral atom, the number of electrons is equal to the number of protons, so there will be 82 electrons. The number of neutrons is the (mass number) − (atomic number) = 208 − 82 = 126 n. Therefore, 82 protons, 126 neutrons, 82 electrons.

    b. Since the element is lead (Pb), the atomic number is 82, and the number of protons is 82. The mass number is the sum of the number of protons and the number of neutrons, $82 + 132 = 214$. The atomic symbol for this isotope is $^{214}_{82}\text{Pb}$.

    c. Since the mass number is 214 (as in part **b**) and the number of neutrons is 131, the number of protons is the (mass number) − (number of neutrons) $= 214 − 131 = 83\ p$. Since there are 83 protons, the atomic number is 83, and the element symbol is Bi (bismuth). The atomic symbol for this isotope is $^{214}_{83}\text{Bi}$.

3.113   **a.** Atomic radius increases going down a group, which gives O the smallest atomic size in Group 6A (16).

    b. Atomic radius decreases going from left to right across a period, which gives Ar the smallest atomic size in Period 3.

    c. Ionization energy decreases going down a group, which gives C the highest ionization energy in Group 4A (14).

    d. Ionization energy increases going from left to right across a period, which gives Na the lowest ionization energy in Period 3.

    e. Metallic character increases going down a group, which gives Ra the most metallic character in Group 2A (2).

3.115 $^{28}_{14}\text{Si}$ $27.977 \times \dfrac{92.23}{100} = 25.80\ \text{amu}$

         $^{29}_{14}\text{Si}$ $28.976 \times \dfrac{4.68}{100} = 1.36\ \text{amu}$

         $^{30}_{14}\text{Si}$ $29.974 \times \dfrac{3.09}{100} = 0.926\ \text{amu}$

                  Atomic mass of Si $= 69.72\ \text{amu}$ (4 SFs)

3.117   **a.** X is a metal in Group 2A (2); Y and Z are nonmetals in the top part of Group 6A (16).

    b. X has the largest atomic radius since it is closest to the bottom left of the periodic table.

    c. Y and Z have similar properties since both have six valence electrons and are in Group 6A (16).

    d. Y has the highest ionization energy since it is closest to the top right of the periodic table.

    e. Y has the smallest atomic radius since it is closest to the top right of the periodic table.

4.1   **a.** $_2^4\text{He}$ is the symbol for an alpha particle.

b. $_{+1}^{0}e$ is the symbol for a positron.

c. $_0^0\gamma$ is the symbol for gamma radiation.

4.3   **a.**   Since the element is potassium, the element symbol is K and the atomic number is 19. The potassium isotopes with mass number 39, 40, and 41 will have the atomic symbol $_{19}^{39}\text{K}$, $_{19}^{40}\text{K}$, and $_{19}^{41}\text{K}$, respectively.

b.   Each isotope has 19 protons and 19 electrons, but they differ in the number of neutrons present. Potassium-39 has $39 - 19 = 20$ neutrons, potassium-40 has $40 - 19 = 21$ neutrons, and potassium-41 has $41 - 19 = 22$ neutrons.

4.5

Medical Use	Atomic Symbol	Mass Number	Number of Protons	Number of Neutrons
Heart imaging	$_{81}^{201}\text{Tl}$	201	81	120
Radiation therapy	$_{27}^{60}\text{Co}$	60	27	33
Abdominal scan	$_{31}^{67}\text{Ga}$	67	31	36
Hyperthyroidism	$_{53}^{131}\text{I}$	131	53	78
Leukemia treatment	$_{15}^{32}\text{P}$	32	15	17

4.7   **a.**   Since the element is copper, the element symbol is Cu and the atomic number is 29. The copper isotope with mass number 64 will have the atomic symbol $_{29}^{64}\text{Cu}$.

b.   Since the element is selenium, the element symbol is Se and the atomic number is 34. The selenium isotope with mass number 75 will have the atomic symbol $_{34}^{75}\text{Se}$.

c.   Since the element is sodium, the element symbol is Na and the atomic number is 11. The sodium isotope with mass number 24 will have the atomic symbol $_{11}^{24}\text{Na}$.

d.   Since the element is nitrogen, the element symbol is N and the atomic number is 7. The nitrogen isotope with mass number 15 will have the atomic symbol $_{7}^{15}\text{N}$.

4.9   **a.**   beta particle (β, $_{-1}^{0}e$)

b.   alpha particle (α, $_2^4\text{He}$)

c.   neutron (n, $_0^1n$)

d.   argon-38 ($_{18}^{38}\text{Ar}$)

e.   carbon-14 ($_6^{14}\text{C}$)

4.11   **a.**   1. Alpha particles do not penetrate the skin.

b.   3. Gamma radiation requires shielding protection that includes lead or thick concrete.

c.   1. Alpha particles can be very harmful if ingested.

4.13 The mass number of the radioactive atom is reduced by four when an alpha particle ($^4_2$He) is emitted. The unknown product will have an atomic number that is two less than the atomic number of the radioactive atom.

    a. $^{208}_{84}$Po $\longrightarrow$ $^{204}_{82}$Pb + $^4_2$He

    b. $^{232}_{90}$Th $\longrightarrow$ $^{228}_{88}$Ra + $^4_2$He

    c. $^{251}_{102}$No $\longrightarrow$ $^{247}_{100}$Fm + $^4_2$He

    d. $^{220}_{86}$Rn $\longrightarrow$ $^{216}_{84}$Po + $^4_2$He

4.15 The mass number of the radioactive atom is not changed when a beta particle ($^0_{-1}e$) is emitted. The unknown product will have an atomic number that is one greater than the atomic number of the radioactive atom.

    a. $^{25}_{11}$Na $\longrightarrow$ $^{25}_{12}$Mg + $^0_{-1}e$

    b. $^{20}_{8}$O $\longrightarrow$ $^{20}_{9}$F + $^0_{-1}e$

    c. $^{92}_{38}$Sr $\longrightarrow$ $^{92}_{39}$Y + $^0_{-1}e$

    d. $^{60}_{26}$Fe $\longrightarrow$ $^{60}_{27}$Co + $^0_{-1}e$

4.17 The mass number of the radioactive atom is not changed when a positron ($^0_{+1}e$) is emitted. The unknown product will have an atomic number that is one less than the atomic number of the radioactive atom.

    a. $^{26}_{14}$Si $\longrightarrow$ $^{26}_{13}$Al + $^0_{+1}e$

    b. $^{54}_{27}$Co $\longrightarrow$ $^{54}_{26}$Fe + $^0_{+1}e$

    c. $^{77}_{37}$Rb $\longrightarrow$ $^{77}_{36}$Kr + $^0_{+1}e$

    d. $^{93}_{45}$Rh $\longrightarrow$ $^{93}_{44}$Ru + $^0_{+1}e$

4.19 Balance the mass numbers and the atomic numbers in each nuclear equation.

    a. $^{28}_{13}$Al $\longrightarrow$ $^{28}_{14}$Si + $^0_{-1}e$? = $^{28}_{14}$Si   beta decay

    b. $^{180m}_{73}$Ta $\longrightarrow$ $^{180}_{73}$Ta + $^0_0\gamma$? = $^0_0\gamma$ gamma emission

    c. $^{66}_{29}$Cu $\longrightarrow$ $^{66}_{30}$Zn + $^0_{-1}e$? = $^0_{-1}e$ beta decay

    d. $^{238}_{92}$U $\longrightarrow$ $^{234}_{90}$Th + $^4_2$He   ? = $^{238}_{92}$U   alpha decay

    e. $^{188}_{80}$Hg $\longrightarrow$ $^{188}_{79}$Au + $^0_{+1}e$? = $^{188}_{79}$Au   positron emission

4.21 Balance the mass numbers and the atomic numbers in each nuclear equation.

    a. ^1_0n + $^9_4$Be $\longrightarrow$ $^{10}_4$Be   ? = $^{10}_4$Be

    b. ^1_0n + $^{131}_{52}$Te $\longrightarrow$ $^{132}_{53}$I + $^0_{-1}e$? = $^{132}_{53}$I

    c. ^1_0n + $^{27}_{13}$Al $\longrightarrow$ $^{24}_{11}$Na + $^4_2$He   ? = $^{27}_{13}$Al

    d. $^4_2$He + $^{27}_{13}$Al $\longrightarrow$ $^{30}_{15}$P + ^1_0n ? = $^{30}_{15}$P

4.23   **a.** <u>2. Absorbed dose</u> can be measured in rad.

    b. <u>3. Biological damage</u> can be measured in mrem.

    c. <u>1. Activity</u> can be measured in μCi.

    d. <u>2. Absorbed dose</u> can be measured in Gy.

4.25 $8 \; \cancel{m Gy} \times \dfrac{1 \; \cancel{Gy}}{1000 \; \cancel{mGy}} \times \dfrac{100 \; rad}{1 \; \cancel{Gy}} = 0.8 \; rad \; (1 \, SF)$

Thus, a technician exposed to a 5 rad dose of radiation received more radiation than one exposed to 8 mGy (0.8 rad) of radiation.

4.27   **a.** $70.0 \; \cancel{kg \; body \; mass} \times \dfrac{4.20 \; \mu Ci}{1 \; \cancel{kg \; body \; mass}} = 294 \; \mu Ci \; (3 \, SFs)$

       b.   from 50 rad of gamma radiation (we use a biological damage factor of 1, so 1 rad of gamma radiation = 1 rem):

$50 \; \cancel{rad} \times \dfrac{1 \; Gy}{100 \; \cancel{rad}} = 0.5 \; Gy \; (1 \, SF)$

4.29   **a.**   **2.** two half-lives:

$34 \; \cancel{days} \times \dfrac{1 \; half\text{-}life}{17 \; \cancel{days}} = 2.0 \; half\text{-}lives$

       b.   **1.** one half-life:

$20 \; \cancel{min} \times \dfrac{1 \; half\text{-}life}{20 \; \cancel{min}} = 1 \; half\text{-}life$

       c.   **3.** three half-lives:

$21 \; \cancel{h} \times \dfrac{1 \; half\text{-}life}{7 \; \cancel{h}} = 3 \; half\text{-}lives$

4.31   **a.**   After one half-life, one-half of the sample would be radioactive:

$80.0 \; mg \; of \; ^{99m}_{43}Tc \xrightarrow{1 \; half\text{-}life} 40.0 \; mg \; of \; ^{99m}_{43}Tc \; (3 \, SFs)$

       b.   After two half-lives, one-fourth of the sample would still be radioactive:

$80.0 \; mg \; of \; ^{99m}_{43}Tc \xrightarrow{1 \; half\text{-}life} 40.0 \; mg \; of \; ^{99m}_{43}Tc \xrightarrow{2 \; half\text{-}lives} 20.0 \; mg \; of \; ^{99m}_{43}Tc \; (3 \, SFs)$

       c. $18 \; \cancel{h} \times \dfrac{1 \; half\text{-}life}{6.0 \; \cancel{h}} = 3.0 \; half\text{-}lives$

$80.0 \; mg \; of \; ^{99m}_{43}Tc \xrightarrow{1 \; half\text{-}life} 40.0 \; mg \; of \; ^{99m}_{43}Tc \xrightarrow{2 \; half\text{-}lives}$

$20.0 \; mg \; of \; ^{99m}_{43}Tc \xrightarrow{3 \; half\text{-}lives} 10.0 \; mg \; of \; ^{99m}_{43}Tc \; (3 \, SFs)$

       d. $24 \; \cancel{h} \times \dfrac{1 \; half\text{-}life}{6.0 \; \cancel{h}} = 4.0 \; half\text{-}lives$

$80.0 \; mg \; of \; ^{99m}_{43}Tc \xrightarrow{1 \; half\text{-}life} 40.0 \; mg \; of \; ^{99m}_{43}Tc \xrightarrow{2 \; half\text{-}lives} 20.0 \; mg \; of \; ^{99m}_{43}Tc \xrightarrow{3 \; half\text{-}lives}$

$10.0 \; mg \; of \; ^{99m}_{43}Tc \xrightarrow{4 \; half\text{-}lives} 5.00 \; mg \; of \; ^{99m}_{43}Tc \; (3 \, SFs)$

4.33   The radiation level in a radioactive sample is cut in half with each half-life; the half-life of Sr-85 is 65 days.

For the radiation level to drop to one-fourth of its original level, $\frac{1}{4} = \frac{1}{2} \times \frac{1}{2}$ or two half-lives

$2 \; \cancel{half\text{-}lives} \times \dfrac{65 \; days}{1 \; \cancel{half\text{-}life}} = 130 \; days \; (2 \, SFs)$

For the radiation level to drop to one-eighth of its original level, $\frac{1}{8} = \frac{1}{2} \times \frac{1}{2} \times \frac{1}{2}$ or three half-lives

$3 \; \cancel{half\text{-}lives} \times \dfrac{65 \; days}{1 \; \cancel{half\text{-}life}} = 195 \; days \; (2 \, SFs)$

4.35   **a.**   Since the elements calcium and phosphorus are part of bone, any calcium or phosphorus atom, regardless of isotope, will be carried to and become part of the bony structures of the body. Once there, the radiation emitted by any radioactive isotope can be used to diagnose or treat bone diseases.

       b. $^{89}_{38}Sr \longrightarrow \, ^{89}_{39}Y + \, ^{0}_{-1}e$

         Strontium (Sr) acts much like calcium (Ca) because both are Group 2A (2) elements. The body will accumulate radioactive strontium in bones in the same way that it incorporates calcium. Once the strontium isotope is absorbed by the bone, the beta radiation will destroy cancer cells.

4.37 $4.0 \text{ mL solution} \times \dfrac{45 \, \mu Ci}{1 \text{ mL solution}} = 180 \, \mu Ci$ of selenium-75 (2 SFs)

4.39   Nuclear fission is the splitting of a large atom into smaller fragments with a simultaneous release of large amounts of energy.

4.41 $^{1}_{0}n + \, ^{235}_{92}U \longrightarrow \, ^{131}_{50}Sn + \, ^{103}_{42}Mo + 2\,^{1}_{0}n +$ energy $? = \, ^{103}_{42}Mo$

4.43   **a.**   Neutrons bombard a nucleus in the <u>fission</u> process.
       b.   The nuclear process that occurs in the Sun is <u>fusion</u>.
       c.   <u>Fission</u> is the process in which a large nucleus splits into smaller nuclei.
       d.   <u>Fusion</u> is the process in which small nuclei combine to form larger nuclei.

4.45

4.47

4.49   Half of a radioactive sample decays with each half-life:

     $6.4 \, \mu Ci$ of $^{14}_{6}C \xrightarrow{\text{1 half-life}} 3.2 \, \mu Ci$ of $^{14}_{6}C \xrightarrow{\text{2 half-lives}} 1.6 \, \mu Ci$ of $^{14}_{6}C \xrightarrow{\text{3 half-lives}}$

       $0.80 \, \mu Ci$ of $^{14}_{6}C$

     $\therefore$ the activity of carbon-14 drops to $0.80 \, \mu Ci$ in three half-lives or 3×5730 years, which makes the age of the painting 17 200 years.

4.51   **a.** $^{25}_{11}Na$ has 11 protons and $25 - 11 = 14$ neutrons.

       b. $^{61}_{28}Ni$ has 28 protons and $61 - 28 = 33$ neutrons.

       c. $^{84}_{37}Rb$ has 37 protons and $84 - 37 = 47$ neutrons.

       d. $^{110}_{47}Ag$ has 47 protons and $110 - 47 = 63$ neutrons.

4.53   **a.**   gamma emission
       b.   positron emission
       c.   alpha decay

4.55   **a.** $^{225}_{90}Th \longrightarrow \, ^{221}_{88}Ra + \, ^{4}_{2}He$

       b. $^{210}_{83}Bi \longrightarrow \, ^{206}_{81}Tl + \, ^{4}_{2}He$

    c. $^{137}_{55}\text{Cs} \longrightarrow ^{137}_{56}\text{Ba} + ^{0}_{-1}e$

    d. $^{126}_{50}\text{Sn} \longrightarrow ^{126}_{51}\text{Sb} + ^{0}_{-1}e$

    e. $^{18}_{9}\text{F} \longrightarrow ^{18}_{8}\text{O} + ^{0}_{+1}e$

4.57   **a.** $^{4}_{2}\text{He} + ^{14}_{7}\text{N} \longrightarrow ^{17}_{8}\text{O} + ^{1}_{1}\text{H}$ $? = ^{17}_{8}\text{O}$

    b. $^{4}_{2}\text{He} + ^{27}_{13}\text{Al} \longrightarrow ^{30}_{14}\text{Si} + ^{1}_{1}\text{H}$ $? = ^{1}_{1}\text{H}$

    c. $^{1}_{0}n + ^{235}_{92}\text{U} \longrightarrow ^{90}_{38}\text{Sr} + 3^{1}_{0}n + ^{143}_{54}\text{Xe}$ $? = ^{143}_{54}\text{Xe}$

    d. $^{23m}_{12}\text{Mg} \longrightarrow ^{23}_{12}\text{Mg} + ^{0}_{0}\gamma$ $? = ^{23}_{12}\text{Mg}$

4.59   **a.** $^{16}_{8}\text{O} + ^{16}_{8}\text{O} \longrightarrow ^{28}_{14}\text{Si} + ^{4}_{2}\text{He}$

    b. $^{18}_{8}\text{O} + ^{249}_{98}\text{Cf} \longrightarrow ^{263}_{106}\text{Sg} + 4^{1}_{0}n$

    c. $^{222}_{86}\text{Rn} \longrightarrow ^{218}_{84}\text{Po} + ^{4}_{2}\text{He}$

4.61   Half of a radioactive sample decays with each half-life:

$$1.2 \text{ mg of } ^{32}_{15}\text{P} \xrightarrow{\text{1 half-life}} 0.60 \text{ mg of } ^{32}_{15}\text{P} \xrightarrow{\text{2 half-lives}} 0.30 \text{ mg of } ^{32}_{15}\text{P}$$

    $\therefore$ two half-lives must have elapsed during this time (28.6 days), yielding the half-life for phosphorus-32:

$$\frac{28.6 \text{ days}}{2 \text{ half-lives}} = 14.3 \text{ days/half-life (3 SFs)}$$

4.63   **a.** $^{47}_{20}\text{Ca} \rightarrow ^{47}_{21}\text{Sc} + ^{0}_{-1}e$

    b. First, calculate the number of half-lives that have elapsed:

$$18 \text{ days} \times \frac{1 \text{ half-life}}{4.5 \text{ days}} = 4.0 \text{ half-lives}$$

    Now we can calculate the number of milligrams of calcium-47 that remain:

$$16 \text{ mg of } ^{47}_{20}\text{Ca} \xrightarrow{\text{1 half-life}} 8.0 \text{ mg of } ^{47}_{20}\text{Ca} \xrightarrow{\text{2 half-lives}} 4.0 \text{ mg of } ^{47}_{20}\text{Ca} \xrightarrow{\text{3 half-lives}}$$

$$2.0 \text{ mg of } ^{47}_{20}\text{Ca} \xrightarrow{\text{4 half-lives}} 1.0 \text{ mg of } ^{47}_{20}\text{Ca}$$

    c. Half of a radioactive sample decays with each half-life:

$$4.8 \text{ mg of } ^{47}_{20}\text{Ca} \xrightarrow{\text{1 half-life}} 2.4 \text{ mg of } ^{47}_{20}\text{Ca} \xrightarrow{\text{2 half-lives}} 1.2 \text{ mg of } ^{47}_{20}\text{Ca}$$

    $\therefore$ two half-lives have elapsed.

$$2 \text{ half-lives} \times \frac{4.5 \text{ days}}{1 \text{ half-life}} = 9.0 \text{ days (2 SFs)}$$

4.65   Half of a radioactive sample decays with each half-life:

$$320 \text{ mCi of } ^{123}_{53}\text{I} \xrightarrow{\text{1 half-life}} 160 \text{ mCi of } ^{123}_{53}\text{I} \xrightarrow{\text{2 half-lives}} 80. \text{ mCi of } ^{123}_{53}\text{I} \xrightarrow{\text{3 half-lives}}$$

$$40. \text{ mCi of } ^{123}_{53}\text{I}$$

    $\therefore$ three half-lives have elapsed.

$$3 \text{ half-lives} \times \frac{13.2 \text{ h}}{1 \text{ half-life}} = 39.6 \text{ h (3 SFs)}$$

4.67   First, calculate the number of half-lives that have elapsed:

$$24 \; \cancel{h} \times \frac{1 \text{ half-life}}{6.0 \; \cancel{h}} = 4.0 \text{ half-lives}$$

Now we can calculate the number of milligrams of technicium-99m that remain:

$$120 \text{ mg of } {}^{99m}_{43}\text{Tc} \xrightarrow{\text{1 half-life}} 60. \text{ mg of } {}^{99m}_{43}\text{Tc} \xrightarrow{\text{2 half-lives}} 30. \text{ mg of } {}^{99m}_{43}\text{Tc} \xrightarrow{\text{3 half-lives}}$$

$$15 \text{ mg of } {}^{99m}_{43}\text{Tc} \xrightarrow{\text{4 half-lives}} 7.5 \text{ mg of } {}^{99m}_{43}\text{Tc} \; (2 \text{ SFs})$$

4.69   **a.** ${}^{238}_{92}\text{U} \longrightarrow {}^{234}_{90}\text{Th} + {}^{4}_{2}\text{He}$ $? = {}^{4}_{2}\text{He}$

   b. ${}^{234}_{90}\text{Th} \longrightarrow {}^{234}_{91}\text{Pa} + {}^{0}_{-1}e$ $? = {}^{234}_{91}\text{Pa}$

   c. ${}^{226}_{88}\text{Ra} \longrightarrow {}^{222}_{86}\text{Rn} + {}^{4}_{2}\text{He}$ $? = {}^{226}_{88}\text{Ra}$

4.71   First, calculate the number of half-lives that have elapsed:

$$130 \; \cancel{\text{days}} \times \frac{1 \text{ half-life}}{32.5 \; \cancel{\text{days}}} = 4.0 \text{ half-lives}$$

Because the activity of a radioactive sample is cut in half with each half-life, the activity must have been double its present value before each half-life. For 4.0 half-lives, we need to double the value four times:

$$4.0 \; \mu\text{Ci of } {}^{141}_{58}\text{Ce} \xleftarrow{\text{1 half-life}} 8.0 \; \mu\text{Ci of } {}^{141}_{58}\text{Ce} \xleftarrow{\text{2 half-lives}} 16 \; \mu\text{Ci of } {}^{141}_{58}\text{Ce} \xleftarrow{\text{3 half-lives}}$$

$$32 \; \mu\text{Ci of } {}^{141}_{58}\text{Ce} \xleftarrow{\text{4 half-lives}} 64 \; \mu\text{Ci of } {}^{141}_{58}\text{Ce}$$

∴ the initial activity of the sample was 64 μCi. (2 SFs)

4.73   Half of a radioactive sample decays with each half-life:

$$64 \; \mu\text{Ci of } {}^{201}_{81}\text{Tl} \xrightarrow{\text{1 half-life}} 32 \; \mu\text{Ci of } {}^{201}_{81}\text{Tl} \xrightarrow{\text{2 half-lives}} 16 \; \mu\text{Ci of } {}^{201}_{81}\text{Tl} \xrightarrow{\text{3 half-lives}}$$

$$8.0 \; \mu\text{Ci of } {}^{201}_{81}\text{Tl} \xrightarrow{\text{4 half-lives}} 4.0 \; \mu\text{Ci of } {}^{201}_{81}\text{Tl}$$

∴ four half-lives must have elapsed during this time (12 days), yielding the half-life for thallium-201:

$$\frac{12 \text{ days}}{4 \text{ half-lives}} = 3.0 \text{ days/half-life} \; (2 \text{ SFs})$$

4.75 $120 \; \cancel{\text{nCi}} \times \dfrac{1 \times 10^{-9} \; \cancel{\text{Ci}}}{1 \; \cancel{\text{nCi}}} \times \dfrac{3.7 \times 10^{10} \text{ Bq}}{1 \; \cancel{\text{Ci}}} = 4400 \text{ Bq} = 4.4 \times 10^{3} \text{ Bq} \; (2 \text{ SFs})$

4.77   **a.** ${}^{180}_{80}\text{Hg} \longrightarrow {}^{176}_{78}\text{Pt} + {}^{4}_{2}\text{He}$

   b. ${}^{198}_{79}\text{Au} \longrightarrow {}^{198}_{80}\text{Hg} + {}^{0}_{-1}e$

   c. ${}^{82}_{37}\text{Rb} \longrightarrow {}^{82}_{36}\text{Kr} + {}^{0}_{+1}e$

4.79 ${}^{1}_{0}n + {}^{238}_{92}\text{U} \longrightarrow {}^{239}_{93}\text{Np} + {}^{0}_{-1}e$

Compounds and Their Bonds

5.1 Atoms with one, two, or three valence electrons will lose those electrons to acquire a noble gas electron configuration.

    a. Li loses 1 e^-.

    b. Ca loses 2 e^-.

    c. Ga loses 3 e^-.

    d. Cs loses 1 e^-.

    e. Ba loses 2 e^-.

5.3   **a.** The element with 3 protons is lithium. In a lithium ion with 2 electrons, the ionic charge would be 1+, $(3+) + (2-) = 1+$. The lithium ion is written as Li^+.

    b. The element with 9 protons is fluorine. In a fluorine ion with 10 electrons, the ionic charge would be 1−, $(9+) + (10-) = 1-$. The fluoride ion is written as F^-.

    c. The element with 12 protons is magnesium. In a magnesium ion with 10 electrons, the ionic charge would be 2+, $(12+) + (10-) = 2+$. The magnesium ion is written as Mg^{2+}.

    d. The element with 26 protons is iron. In an iron ion with 23 electrons, the ionic charge would be 3+, $(26+) + (23-) = 3+$. This iron ion is written as Fe^{3+}.

5.5   **a.** O has an atomic number of 8, which means it has 8 protons. In a neutral atom, the number of electrons equals the number of protons. An oxygen ion with a charge of 2− has gained 2 e^- to have $8 + 2 = 10$ electrons. $\therefore$ in an O^{2-} ion, there are 8 protons and 10 electrons.

    b. K has an atomic number of 19, which means it has 19 protons. In a neutral atom, the number of electrons equals the number of protons. A potassium ion with a charge of 1+ has lost 1 e^- to have $19 - 1 = 18$ electrons. $\therefore$ in a K^+ ion, there are 19 protons and 18 electrons.

    c. Br has an atomic number of 35, which means it has 35 protons. In a neutral atom, the number of electrons equals the number of protons. A bromine ion with a charge of 1− has gained 1 e^- to have $35 + 1 = 36$ electrons. $\therefore$ in a Br^- ion, there are 35 protons and 36 electrons.

    d. S has an atomic number of 16, which means it has 16 protons. In a neutral atom, the number of electrons equals the number of protons. A sulfur ion with a charge of 2− has gained 2 e^- to have $16 + 2 = 18$ electrons. $\therefore$ in a S^{2-} ion, there are 16 protons and 18 electrons.

5.7   **a.** Chlorine in Group 7A (17) gains one electron to form chloride ion, Cl^-.

    b. Potassium in Group 1A (1) loses one electron to form potassium ion, K^+.

    c. Oxygen in Group 6A (16) gains two electrons to form oxide ion, O^{2-}.

    d. Aluminum in Group 3A (13) loses three electrons to form aluminum ion, Al^{3+}.

    e. Selenium in Group 6A (16) gains two electrons to form selenide ion, Se^{2-}.

5.9   **a** (Li and Cl) and **c** (K and O) will form ionic compounds.

5.11   **a.** Na^+ and $O^{2-} \rightarrow Na_2O$

    b. Al^{3+} and $Br^- \rightarrow AlBr_3$

    c. Ba^{2+} and $N^{3-} \rightarrow Ba_3N_2$

    d. Mg^{2+} and $F^- \rightarrow MgF_2$

    e. Al^{3+} and $S^{2-} \rightarrow Al_2S_3$

5.13   **a.** Ions: K^+ and $S^{2-} \rightarrow K_2S$ Check: $2(1+) + 1(2-) = 0$

    b. Ions: Na^+ and $N^{3-} \rightarrow Na_3N$ Check: $3(1+) + 1(3-) = 0$

    c. Ions: Al^{3+} and $I^- \rightarrow AlI_3$ Check: $1(3+) + 3(1-) = 0$
    d. Ions: Ga^{3+} and $O^{2-} \rightarrow Ga_2O_3$ Check: $2(3+) + 3(2-) = 0$

5.15   **a.** aluminum oxide
       b. calcium chloride
       c. sodium oxide
       d. magnesium phosphide
       e. potassium iodide
       f. barium fluoride

5.17   Most of the transition elements form more than one positive ion. The specific ion is indicated in a name by writing a Roman numeral that is the same as the ionic charge. For example, iron forms Fe^{2+} and Fe^{3+} ions, which are named iron(II) and iron(III).

5.19   **a.** iron(II)
       b. copper(II)
       c. zinc
       d. lead(IV)
       e. chromium(III)
       f. manganese(II)

5.21   **a.** Ions: Sn^{2+} and $Cl^- \rightarrow$ tin(II) chloride
       b. Ions: Fe^{2+} and $O^{2-} \rightarrow$ iron(II) oxide
       c. Ions: Cu^+ and $S^{2-} \rightarrow$ copper(I) sulfide
       d. Ions: Cu^{2+} and $S^{2-} \rightarrow$ copper(II) sulfide
       e. Ions: Cr^{3+} and $Br^- \rightarrow$ chromium(III) bromide
       f. Ions: Zn^{2+} and $Cl^- \rightarrow$ zinc chloride

5.23   **a.** Au^{3+}
       b. Fe^{3+}
       c. Pb^{4+}
       d. Sn^{2+}

5.25   **a.** Ions: Mg^{2+} and $Cl^- \rightarrow MgCl_2$
       b. Ions: Na^+ and $S^{2-} \rightarrow Na_2S$
       c. Ions: Cu^+ and $O^{2-} \rightarrow Cu_2O$
       d. Ions: Zn^{2+} and $P^{3-} \rightarrow Zn_3P_2$
       e. Ions: Au^{3+} and $N^{3-} \rightarrow AuN$
       f. Ions: Cr^{2+} and $Cl^- \rightarrow CrCl_2$

5.27   **a.** HCO_3^-
       b. NH_4^+
       c. PO_4^{3-}
       d. HSO_4^-
       e. ClO_4^-

5.29   **a.** sulfate
       b. hypochlorite
       c. phosphate
       d. nitrate

5.31

	NO_2^-	CO_3^{2-}	HSO_4^-	PO_4^{3-}
Li^+	$LiNO_2$	Li_2CO_3	$LiHSO_4$	Li_3PO_4
Cu^{2+}	$Cu(NO_2)_2$	$CuCO_3$	$Cu(HSO_4)_2$	$Cu_3(PO_4)_2$
Ba^{2+}	$Ba(NO_2)_2$	$BaCO_3$	$Ba(HSO_4)_2$	$Ba_3(PO_4)_2$

5.33   **a.** CO_3^{2-}, sodium carbonate

b. NH_4^+, ammonium chloride

c. PO_4^{3-}, potassium phosphate

d. NO_2^-, chromium(II) nitrite

e. SO_3^{2-}, iron(II) sulfite

5.35   **a.** Ions: Ba^{2+} and $OH^- \rightarrow Ba(OH)_2$

b. Ions: Na^+ and $SO_4^{2-} \rightarrow Na_2SO_4$

c. Ions: Fe^{2+} and $NO_3^- \rightarrow Fe(NO_3)_2$

d. Ions: Zn^{2+} and $PO_4^{3-} \rightarrow Zn_3(PO_4)_2$

e. Ions: Fe^{3+} and $CO_3^{2-} \rightarrow Fe_2(CO_3)_3$

5.37   **a** (O and Cl), **c** (N and O), **d** (I and I), and **f** (C and S) will form covalent compounds.

5.39   **a.** 2 valence electrons, 1 bonding pair, no lone pairs

b. 8 valence electrons, 1 bonding pair, 3 lone pairs

c. 14 valence electrons, 1 bonding pair, 6 lone pairs

5.41   **a.** $1\ H(1\ e^-) + 1\ F(7\ e^-) = 1 + 7 = 8$ valence electrons

$$H\!:\!\ddot{\underset{\cdot\cdot}{F}}\!: \quad \text{or} \quad H\!-\!\ddot{\underset{\cdot\cdot}{F}}\!:$$

b. $1\ N(5\ e^-) + 3\ Br(7\ e^-) = 5 + 21 = 26$ valence electrons

$$:\!\ddot{\underset{\cdot\cdot}{Br}}\!:\!N\!:\!\ddot{\underset{\cdot\cdot}{Br}}\!: \quad \text{or} \quad :\!\ddot{\underset{\cdot\cdot}{Br}}\!-\!N\!-\!\ddot{\underset{\cdot\cdot}{Br}}\!:$$

c. $1\ C(4\ e^-) + 4\ H(1\ e^-) + 1\ O(6\ e^-) = 4 + 4 + 6 = 14$ valence electrons

$$H\!:\!\underset{\overset{\displaystyle H}{}}{\overset{\displaystyle H}{C}}\!:\!\ddot{\underset{\cdot\cdot}{O}}\!:\!H \quad \text{or} \quad H\!-\!\underset{\overset{|}{H}}{\overset{\overset{H}{|}}{C}}\!-\!\ddot{\underset{\cdot\cdot}{O}}\!-\!H$$

d. $2\ N(5\ e^-) + 4\ H(1\ e^-) = 10 + 4 = 14$ valence electrons

$$H\!:\!\ddot{N}\!:\!\ddot{N}\!:\!H \quad \text{or} \quad H\!-\!\underset{\overset{|}{H}}{\overset{\overset{H}{|}}{N}}\!-\!\underset{\overset{|}{H}}{\overset{\overset{H}{|}}{N}}\!-\!H$$

5.43   **a.** $1\ C(4\ e^-) + 1\ O(6\ e^-) = 4 + 6 = 10$ valence electrons

$$:\!C\!::\!O\!: \quad \text{or} \quad :\!C\!\equiv\!O\!:$$

b. $2\ C(4\ e^-) + 4\ H(1\ e^-) = 8 + 4 = 12$ valence electrons

$$
\begin{array}{cc}
\text{H}\ \ \text{H} \\
\ddot{\ }\ \ \ddot{\ } \\
\text{H:C::C:H} \quad \text{or} \quad \text{H}-\!\!\underset{\displaystyle H}{\overset{\displaystyle H}{\text{C}}}\!\!=\!\!\underset{\displaystyle H}{\overset{\displaystyle H}{\text{C}}}\!\!-\!\!\text{H}
\end{array}
$$

c. $1\ C(4\ e^-) + 2\ H(1\ e^-) + 1\ O(6\ e^-) = 4 + 2 + 6 = 12$ valence electrons

$$
\begin{array}{cc}
\text{:O:} & \text{:O:} \\
\text{:} & \| \\
\text{H:C:H} \quad \text{or} \quad \text{H}-\text{C}-\text{H}
\end{array}
$$

5.45 $1\ Cl(7\ e^-) + 1\ N(5\ e^-) + 2\ O(6\ e^-) = 7 + 5 + 12 = 24$ valence electrons

$$
\begin{array}{cc}
\text{:O:} & \text{:Ö:} \\
\| & | \\
\text{:Ċl}-\text{N}-\ddot{\text{O}}\text{:} \longleftrightarrow \text{:Ċl}-\text{N}=\ddot{\text{O}}\text{:}
\end{array}
$$

5.47 When naming covalent compounds, prefixes are used to indicate the number of each atom as shown in the subscripts of the formula. The first nonmetal is named by its elemental name; the second non-metal is named by using its elemental name with the ending changed to *ide*.
   a. 1 P and 3 Br $\rightarrow$ phosphorus tribromide
   b. 1 C and 4 Br $\rightarrow$ carbon tetrabromide
   c. 1 Si and 2 O $\rightarrow$ silicon dioxide
   d. 2 N and 3 O $\rightarrow$ dinitrogen trioxide
   e. 1 P and 5 Cl $\rightarrow$ phosphorus pentachloride

5.49   **a.** 1 C and 4 Cl $\rightarrow CCl_4$
   b. 1 C and 1 O $\rightarrow CO$
   c. 1 P and 3 Cl $\rightarrow PCl_3$
   d. 2 N and 4 O $\rightarrow N_2O_4$
   e. 1 B and 3 F $\rightarrow BF_3$
   f. 1 S and 6 F $\rightarrow SF_6$

5.51   **a.** Ions: Al^{3+} and $SO_4^{2-} \rightarrow$ aluminum sulfate
   b. Ions: Ca^{2+} and $CO_3^{2-} \rightarrow$ calcium carbonate
   c. 2N and 1 O $\rightarrow$ dinitrogen oxide
   d. Ions: Na^+ and $PO_4^{3-} \rightarrow$ sodium phosphate
   e. Ions: NH_4^+ and $SO_4^{2-} \rightarrow$ ammonium sulfate
   f. Ions: Fe^{3+} and $O^{2-} \rightarrow$ iron(III) oxide

5.53   **a.** The electronegativity values increase going from left to right across Period 2 from B to F.
   b. The electronegativity values decrease going down Group 2A (2) from Mg to Ba.
   c. The electronegativity values decrease going down Group 7A (17) from F to I.

5.55   **a.** electronegativity difference between Rb and Cl: $3.0 - 0.8 = 2.2$
   b. electronegativity difference between Cl and Cl: $3.0 - 3.0 = 0.0$
   c. electronegativity difference between N and O: $3.5 - 3.0 = 0.5$
   d. electronegativity difference between C and H: $2.5 - 2.1 = 0.4$

5.57   **a.** Electronegativity increases going up a group: K, Na, Li.
   b. Electronegativity increases going left to right across a period: Na, P, Cl.
   c. Electronegativity increases going across a period and at the top of a group: Ca, Se, O.

5.59   **a.**   Si—Br electronegativity difference: $2.8 - 1.8 = 1.0$, polar covalent
   b.   Li—F electronegativity difference: $4.0 - 1.0 = 3.0$, ionic
   c.   Br—F electronegativity difference: $4.0 - 2.8 = 1.2$, polar covalent
   d.   I—I electronegativity difference: $2.5 - 2.5 = 0.0$, nonpolar covalent
   e.   N—P electronegativity difference: $3.0 - 2.1 = 0.9$, polar covalent
   f.   C—O electronegativity difference: $3.5 - 2.5 = 1.0$, polar covalent

5.61   A dipole arrow points from the atom with the lower electronegativity value (more positive) to the atom in the bond that has the higher electronegativity value (more negative).

   a. $\overset{\delta^+\quad\delta^-}{\underset{\longrightarrow}{\text{N—F}}}$

   b. $\overset{\delta^+\quad\delta^-}{\underset{\longrightarrow}{\text{Si—Br}}}$

   c. $\overset{\delta^+\quad\delta^-}{\underset{\longrightarrow}{\text{C—O}}}$

   d. $\overset{\delta^+\quad\delta^-}{\underset{\longrightarrow}{\text{P—Br}}}$

   e. $\overset{\delta^-\quad\delta^+}{\underset{\longleftarrow}{\text{N—P}}}$

5.63   **a.**   6; Four electron groups around a central atom have a tetrahedral electron arrangement. With four bonded atoms, the shape of the molecule is tetrahedral.
   b.   5; Four electron groups around a central atom have a tetrahedral electron arrangement. With three bonded atoms (and one lone pair of electrons), the shape of the molecule is trigonal pyramidal.
   c.   3; Three electron groups around a central atom have a trigonal planar electron arrangement. With three bonded atoms, the shape of the molecule is trigonal planar.

5.65 SeO_3 $1\ Se(6\ e^-) + 3\ O(6\ e^-) = 6 + 18 = 24$ valence electrons

$$\ddot{\underset{\cdot\cdot}{O}}\text{—}\underset{\ \ \displaystyle\overset{\displaystyle:\ddot{O}:}{\|}}{Se}\text{—}\ddot{\underset{\cdot\cdot}{O}}:$$

   a.   There are <u>three</u> electron groups around the central atom.
   b.   The electron-group geometry is <u>trigonal planar</u>.
   c.   The shape of the molecule is <u>trigonal planar</u>.
   d.   The molecule is <u>nonpolar</u>.

5.67   Molecule **a** (NCl_3) and molecule **b** (PCl_3) have the same shape as PH_3 (trigonal pyramidal). Molecule **c** (BF_3) has a trigonal planar shape.

5.69   **a.**   The central O atom has four electron groups with two bonded atoms and two lone pairs of electrons, which gives OF_2 a bent shape (109°).

$$\begin{array}{c}:\ddot{F}:\\ |\\ :\ddot{F}\text{—}\ddot{O}:\end{array}$$

   b.   The central atom C has four electron groups bonded to four chlorine atoms; CCl_4 has a tetrahedral shape.

$$\begin{array}{c}:\ddot{C}l:\\ |\\ :\ddot{C}l\text{—}C\text{—}\ddot{C}l:\\ |\\ :\ddot{C}l:\end{array}$$

c. The central atom Ga has three electron groups bonded to three chlorine atoms; $GaCl_3$ has a trigonal planar shape.

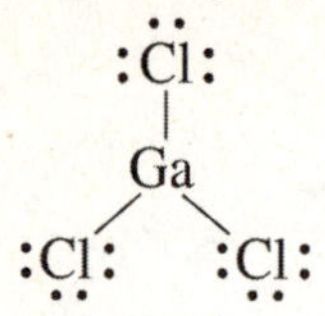

d. The central atom Se has three electron groups with two bonded atoms and one lone pair of electrons, which gives SeO_2 a bent shape (120°).

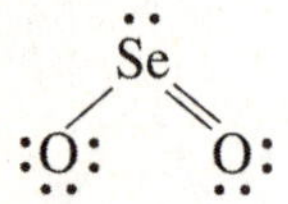

$$\overset{\displaystyle \overset{..}{Se}}{\underset{:O: \qquad O:}{}}$$

5.71 Cl_2 is a nonpolar molecule because there is a nonpolar covalent bond between Cl atoms, which have identical electronegativity values. In HCl, the bond is a polar bond because there is a large electronegativity difference, which makes HCl a polar molecule.

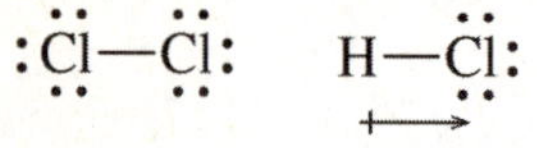

$$:\overset{..}{\underset{..}{Cl}}—\overset{..}{\underset{..}{Cl}}: \qquad H—\overset{..}{\underset{..}{Cl}}:$$
$$\text{nonpolar} \qquad \text{polar}$$

5.73 **a.** The molecule HBr contains the polar covalent H — Br bond; this single dipole makes HBr a polar molecule.

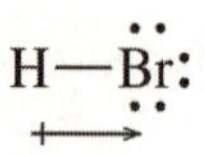

$$H—\overset{..}{\underset{..}{Br}}:$$
$$\text{polar}$$

b. The molecule NF_3 contains three polar covalent N — F bonds and a lone pair of electrons on the central N atom. This asymmetric trigonal pyramidal shape makes NF_3 a polar molecule.

polar

c. In the molecule CHF_3, there are three polar covalent C — F bonds and one nonpolar covalent C — H bond, which makes CHF_3 a polar molecule.

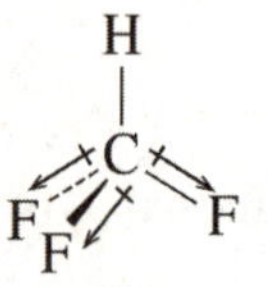

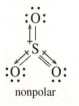
polar

d. In the molecule SO_3, there are three polar covalent S — O bonds arranged in a trigonal planar shape. This symmetric shape makes SO_3 a nonpolar molecule.

$$\overset{\displaystyle :\overset{..}{O}:}{\underset{:O: \qquad O:}{S}}$$
nonpolar

5.75 **a.** BrF is a polar molecule. An attraction between the positive end of one polar molecule and the negative end of another polar molecule is called a dipole–dipole attraction.

b. An ionic bond is an attraction between a positive and negative ion, as in KCl.

    c. CCl_4 is a nonpolar molecule. The weak attractions that occur between temporary dipoles in nonpolar molecules are called dispersion forces.

    d. Cl_2 is a nonpolar molecule. The weak attractions that occur between temporary dipoles in nonpolar molecules are called dispersion forces.

5.77 **a.** Hydrogen bonds are strong dipole–dipole attractions that occur between a partially positive hydrogen atom of one molecule and one of the strongly electronegative atoms F, O, or N in another, as is seen with CH_3OH molecules.

    b. Dispersion forces occur between temporary dipoles in nonpolar N_2 molecules.

    c. HBr is a polar molecule. Dipole–dipole attractions occur between dipoles in polar molecules.

    d. Dispersion forces occur between temporary dipoles in nonpolar CH_4 molecules.

    e. Dispersion forces occur between temporary dipoles in nonpolar CH_3CH_3 molecules.

5.79 **a.** HF would have a higher boiling point than HBr; the hydrogen bonds in HF are stronger than the dipole–dipole attractions in HBr.

    b. NaF would have a higher boiling point than HF; the ionic bonds in NaF are stronger than the hydrogen bonds in HF.

    c. $MgBr_2$ would have a higher boiling point than PBr_3; the ionic bonds in $MgBr_2$ are stronger than the dipole–dipole attractions in PBr_3.

    d. CH_3OH would have a higher boiling point than CH_4; the hydrogen bonds in CH_3OH are stronger than the dispersion forces in CH_4.

5.81 **a.** The element with 15 protons is phosphorus. In a phosphorus ion with 18 electrons, the ionic charge would be 3−, $(15+) + (18-) = 3-$. The phosphide ion is written as P^{3-}.

    b. The element with 8 protons is oxygen. Since there are also 8 electrons, this is an oxygen (O) atom.

    c. The element with 30 protons is zinc. In a zinc ion with 28 electrons, the ionic charge would be 2+, $(30+) + (28-) = 2+$. The zinc ion is written as Zn^{2+}.

    d. The element with 26 protons is iron. In an iron ion with 23 electrons, the ionic charge would be 3+, $(26+) + (23-) = 3+$. This iron ion is written as Fe^{3+}.

5.83 **a.** With 35 protons, the element is bromine (Br). Since there are 36 electrons, it is the bromide ion, Br^-.

    b. With 47 protons, the element is silver (Ag). Since there are 46 electrons, it is the silver ion, Ag^+.

    c. With 50 protons, the element is tin (Sn). Since there are 46 electrons, it is the tin ion, Sn^{4+}.

5.85 **a.** An element that forms an ion with a 2+ charge would be in Group 2A (2).

    b. The electron-dot symbol for an element in Group 2A (2) is $\dot{X}\cdot$

    c. Mg is the Group 2A (2) element in Period 3.

    d. Ions: X^{2+} and $N^{3-} \rightarrow X_3N_2$

5.87 **a.** 2; trigonal pyramidal shape, polar molecule

    b. 1; bent shape (109°), polar molecule

    c. 3; tetrahedral shape, nonpolar molecule

5.89 **a.** C—O (EN $3.5 - 2.5 = 1.0$) and N—O (EN $3.5 - 3.0 = 0.5$) are polar covalent bonds.

    b. O—O (EN $3.5 - 3.5 = 0.0$) is a nonpolar covalent bond.

    c. Ca—O (EN $3.5 - 1.0 = 2.5$) and K—O (EN $3.5 - 0.8 = 2.7$) are ionic bonds.

    d. C—O, N—O, O—O

5.91 **a.** N^{3-} has an electron configuration of $1s^2 2s^2 2p^6$.

    b. Mg^{2+} has an electron configuration of $1s^2 2s^2 2p^6$.

    c. P^{3-} has an electron configuration of $1s^2 2s^2 2p^6 3s^2 3p^6$.

    d. Al^{3+} has an electron configuration of $1s^2 2s^2 2p^6$.

    e. Li^+ has an electron configuration of $1s^2$.

5.93   **a.** Tin(IV) is Sn^{4+}.

    b. The Sn^{4+} ion has 50 protons, and $50 - 4 = 46$ electrons.

    c. Ions: Sn^{4+} and $O^{2-} \rightarrow SnO_2$

    d. Ions: Sn^{4+} and $PO_4^{3-} \rightarrow Sn_3(PO_4)_4$

5.95   **a.** The chloride ion is Cl^-.

    b. The potassium ion is K^+.

    c. The oxide ion is O^{2-}.

    d. The aluminum ion is Al^{3+}.

5.97   **a.** K^+ is the potassium ion.

    b. S^{2-} is the sulfide ion.

    c. Ca^{2+} is the calcium ion.

    d. N^{3-} is the nitride ion.

5.99   **a.** Ions: Sn^{2+} and $S^{2-} \rightarrow SnS$

    b. Ions: Pb^{4+} and $O^{2-} \rightarrow PbO_2$

    c. Ions: Ag^+ and $Cl^- \rightarrow AgCl$

    d. Ions: Ca^{2+} and $N^{3-} \rightarrow Ca_3N_2$

    e. Ions: Cu^+ and $P^{3-} \rightarrow Cu_3P$

    f. Ions: Cr^{2+} and $Br^- \rightarrow CrBr_2$

5.101 **a.** $2\ Cl(7\ e^-) + 1\ O(6\ e^-) = 14 + 6 = 20$ valence electrons

     b. $1\ C(4\ e^-) + 4\ F(7\ e^-) + 2\ Cl(7\ e^-) = 4 + 28 = 32$ valence electrons

     c. $3\ H(1\ e^-) + 1\ N(5\ e^-) + 1\ O(6\ e^-) = 3 + 5 + 6 = 14$ valence electrons

     d. $2\ H(1\ e^-) + 2\ C(4\ e^-) + 2\ Cl(7\ e^-) = 2 + 8 + 14 = 24$ valence electrons

5.103 **a.** 1 N and 3 Cl → nitrogen trichloride
    b. 2 N and 3 S → dinitrogen trisulfide
    c. 2 N and 1 O → dinitrogen oxide
    d. 2 F → fluorine (named as the element)
    e. 1 S and 2 O → sulfur dioxide
    f. 2 P and 5 O → diphosphorus pentoxide

5.105 **a.** 1 C and 1 O → CO
    b. 2 P and 5 O → P_2O_5
    c. 2 H and 1 S → H_2S
    d. 1 S and 2 Cl → SCl_2

5.107 **a.** Ionic, ions are Fe^{3+} and Cl^- → iron(III) chloride
    b. Ionic, ions are Na^+ and SO_4^{2-} → sodium sulfate
    c. Covalent, 1 N and 2 O → nitrogen dioxide
    d. Covalent, diatomic element → nitrogen
    e. Covalent, 1 P and 5 F → phosphorus pentafluoride
    f. Covalent, 1 C and 4 F → carbon tetrafluoride

5.109 **a.** Ions: Sn^{2+} and CO_3^{2-} → $SnCO_3$
    b. Ions: Li^+ and P^{3-} → Li_3P
    c. Covalent, 1 Si and 4 Cl → $SiCl_4$
    d. Ions: Mn^{3+} and O^{2-} → Mn_2O_3
    e. Covalent, diatomic element → I_2
    f. Ions: Ca^{2+} and Br^- → $CaBr_2$

5.111 **a.** C—O $(3.5-2.5=1.0)$ is more polar than C—N $(3.5-3.0=0.5)$.
    b. N—F $(4.0-3.0=1.0)$ is more polar than N—Br $(3.0-2.8=0.2)$.
    c. S—Cl $(3.0-2.5=0.5)$ is more polar than Br—Cl $(3.0-2.8=0.2)$.
    d. Br—I $(2.8-2.5=0.3)$ is more polar than Br—Cl $(3.0-2.8=0.2)$.
    e. N—F $(4.0-3.0=1.0)$ is more polar than N—O $(3.5-3.0=0.5)$.

5.113 A dipole arrow points from the atom with the lower electronegativity value (more positive) to the atom in the bond that has the higher electronegativity value (more negative).

    a. $\overset{\delta^+\ \ \delta^-}{Si—Cl} \longrightarrow$

    b. $\overset{\delta^+\ \ \delta^-}{C—N} \longrightarrow$

    c. $\overset{\delta^-\ \ \delta^+}{F—Cl} \longleftarrow$

    d. $\overset{\delta^+\ \ \delta^-}{C—F} \longrightarrow$

    e. $\overset{\delta^+\ \ \delta^-}{N—O} \longrightarrow$

5.115 **a.** Si—Cl electronegativity difference: $3.0-1.8=1.2$, polar covalent
    b. C—C electronegativity difference: $2.5-2.5=0.0$, nonpolar covalent
    c. Na—Cl electronegativity difference: $3.0-0.9=2.1$, ionic
    d. C—H electronegativity difference: $2.5-2.1=0.4$, nonpolar covalent
    e. F—F electronegativity difference: $4.0-4.0=0.0$, nonpolar covalent

5.117 **a.** $1\ N(5\ e^-)+3\ F(7\ e^-)=5+21=26$ valence electrons

$$\ddot{\underset{..}{F}}-N-\ddot{\underset{..}{F}}$$
$$|$$
$$:\ddot{\underset{..}{F}}:$$

The central atom N has four electron groups with three bonded atoms and one lone pair of electrons, which gives NF_3 a trigonal pyramidal shape.

b. $1\ Si(4\ e^-)+4\ Br(7\ e^-)=4+28=32$ valence electrons

$$:\ddot{Br}:$$
$$|$$
$$:\ddot{Br}-Si-\ddot{Br}:$$
$$|$$
$$:\ddot{Br}:$$

The central atom Si has four electron groups bonded to four bromine atoms; $SiBr_4$ has a tetrahedral shape.

c. $1\ Be(2\ e^-)+2\ Cl(7\ e^-)=2+14=16$ valence electrons

$$:\ddot{Cl}-Be-\ddot{Cl}:$$

The central atom Be has two electron groups bonded to two chlorine atoms; $BeCl_2$ has a linear shape.

d. $1\ S(6\ e^-)+2\ O(6\ e^-)=6+12=18$ valence electrons

$$\left[:\ddot{O}=\ddot{S}-\ddot{O}:\right] \longleftrightarrow \left[:\ddot{O}-\ddot{S}=\ddot{O}:\right]$$

The central atom S has three electron groups with two bonded atoms and one lone pair of electrons, which gives SO_2 a bent shape (120°).

5.119

Period	Electron-Dot Symbols	Formula of Compound	Name of Compound
3	$\cdot X\cdot$ and $\cdot \ddot{Y}\cdot$	Mg_3P_2	Magnesium phosphide
3	$\cdot X\cdot$ and $\cdot \ddot{Y}:$	Al_2S_3	Aluminum sulfide
3	$\cdot \ddot{Y}:$ and $\cdot \ddot{Y}:$	Cl_2	Chlorine
3	$\cdot \ddot{Y}\cdot$ and $\cdot \ddot{Y}:$	PCl_3	Phosphorus trichloride

5.121

Electron Configurations		Symbols of Ions			
Metal	Nonmetal	Cation	Anion	Formula of Compound	Name of Compound
$1s^2 2s^1$	$1s^2 2s^2 2p^6 3s^2 3p^4$	Li^+	S^{2-}	Li_2S	Lithium sulfide
$1s^2 2s^2 2p^6 3s^2 3p^6 4s^2$	$1s^2 2s^2 2p^6 3s^2 3p^3$	Ca^{2+}	P^{3-}	Ca_3P_2	Calcium phosphide
$1s^2 2s^2 2p^6 3s^1$	$1s^2 2s^2 2p^6 3s^2 3p^5$	Na^+	Cl^-	$NaCl$	Sodium chloride

5.123 **a.** X is in Group 1A (1); Y is in Group 6A (16).

b. ionic

c. X^+, Y^{2-}

d. X_2Y

e. Ions: X^+ and $Cl^- \rightarrow XCl$

f. Ions: Na^+ and $Y^{2-} \rightarrow Na_2Y$

g. ionic

5.125 Compounds with a metal and nonmetal are classified as ionic; compounds with two nonmetals are covalent.
   a. Ionic, ions are Li^+ and O^{2-} → lithium oxide
   b. Covalent, 2 N and 1 O → dinitrogen oxide
   c. Covalent, 1 C and 4 F → carbon tetrafluoride
   d. Covalent, 2 Cl and 1 O → dichlorine oxide

5.127 Compounds with a metal and nonmetal are classified as ionic; compounds with two nonmetals are covalent.
   a. Ionic, ions are Fe^{2+} and Cl^- → iron(II) chloride
   b. Covalent, 2 Cl and 7 O → dichlorine heptoxide
   c. Covalent, nitrogen (diatomic element)
   d. Ionic, ions are Ca^{2+} and $PO_4{}^{3-}$ → calcium phosphate
   e. Covalent, 1 P and 3 Cl → phosphorus trichloride
   f. Ionic, ions are Ca^{2+} and ClO^- → calcium hypochlorite

5.129   **a.** The molecule H_2S contains two nonpolar covalent H—S bonds (EN $2.5 - 2.1 = 0.4$) and two lone pairs of electrons on the central S atom, which gives the molecule a bent shape (109°). Since there are no dipoles from the H—S bonds, H_2S is a nonpolar molecule.

   b. The molecule NF_3 contains three polar covalent N—F bonds (EN $4.0 - 3.0 = 1.0$) and a lone pair of electrons on the central N atom, which gives the molecule a trigonal pyramidal shape. This asymmetric shape does not allow the dipoles to cancel, which makes NF_3 a polar molecule.

   c. The molecule NH_3 contains three polar covalent N—H bonds (EN $3.0 - 2.1 = 0.9$) and a lone pair of electrons on the central N atom, which gives the molecule a trigonal pyramidal shape. This asymmetric shape does not allow the dipoles to cancel, which makes NH_3 a polar molecule.

   d. The molecule CH_3Cl consists of a central atom, C, with three nonpolar covalent C—H bonds (EN $2.5 - 2.1 = 0.4$) and one polar covalent C—Cl bond (EN $3.0 - 2.5 = 0.5$). The molecule has a tetrahedral shape, but the single dipole makes CH_3Cl a polar molecule.

   e. The molecule SiF_4 consists of a central atom, Si, with four polar covalent Si—F bonds (EN $4.0 - 1.8 = 2.2$). The molecule has a tetrahedral shape, and the four dipoles cancel, which makes SiF_4 a nonpolar molecule.

5.131   **a.** Hydrogen bonding (3) involves strong dipole–dipole attractions that occur between a partially positive hydrogen atom of one polar molecule and one of the strongly electronegative atoms F, O, or N in another, as is seen with NH_3 molecules.

      b. ClF is a polar molecule (EN $4.0 - 3.0 = 1.0$). Dipole–dipole attractions (2) occur between dipoles in polar molecules.

      c. Dispersion forces (4) occur between temporary dipoles in nonpolar Br_2 molecules.

      d. Ionic bonds (1) are strong attractions between positive and negative ions, as in Cs_2O.

      e. Dispersion forces (4) occur between temporary dipoles in nonpolar C_3H_8 molecules.

      f. CH_3OH is a polar molecule and contains the polar $O—H$ bond. Hydrogen bonding (3) involves strong dipole–dipole attractions that occur between a partially positive hydrogen atom of one polar molecule and one of the strongly electronegative atoms F, O, or N in another, as is seen with CH_3OH molecules.

6

Chemical Reactions and Quantities

6.1 An equation is balanced when there are equal numbers of atoms of each element on the reactant side and on the product side.
- **a.** not balanced (2 O ≠ 3 O)
- **b.** balanced
- **c.** not balanced (6 O ≠ 5 O, 4 H ≠ 2 H)
- **d.** balanced

6.3 Place coefficients in front of formulas until you make the number of atoms of each element equal on each side of the equation.
- **a.** $N_2(g) + O_2(g) \longrightarrow 2NO(g)$
- **b.** $2HgO(s) \longrightarrow 2Hg(l) + O_2(g)$
- **c.** $4Fe(s) + 3O_2(g) \longrightarrow 2Fe_2O_3(s)$
- **d.** $2Na(s) + Cl_2(g) \longrightarrow 2NaCl(s)$
- **e.** $2Cu_2O(s) + O_2(g) \longrightarrow 4CuO(s)$

6.5
- **a.** Balance the NO_3^- ions as a group.
  $Mg(s) + 2AgNO_3(aq) \longrightarrow Mg(NO_3)_2(aq) + 2Ag(s)$
- **b.** $CuCO_3(s) \longrightarrow CuO(s) + CO_2(g)$
- **c.** $C_5H_{12}(g) + 8O_2(g) \xrightarrow{\Delta} 5CO_2(g) + 6H_2O(g)$
- **d.** Balance the NO_3^- ions as a group.
  $Pb(NO_3)_2(aq) + 2NaCl(aq) \longrightarrow PbCl_2(s) + 2NaNO_3(aq)$
- **e.** $2Al(s) + 6HCl(aq) \longrightarrow 2AlCl_3(aq) + 3H_2(g)$

6.7
- **a.** decomposition reaction
- **b.** single replacement reaction
- **c.** combustion reaction
- **d.** double replacement reaction

6.9
- **a.** single replacement reaction
- **b.** combination reaction
- **c.** decomposition reaction
- **d.** combustion reaction
- **e.** double replacement reaction
- **f.** double replacement reaction

6.11
- **a.** $Mg(s) + Cl_2(g) \longrightarrow MgCl_2(s)$
- **b.** $2HBr(g) \longrightarrow H_2(g) + Br_2(g)$
- **c.** $Mg(s) + Zn(NO_3)_2(aq) \longrightarrow Zn(s) + Mg(NO_3)_2(aq)$
- **d.** $K_2S(aq) + Pb(NO_3)_2(aq) \longrightarrow 2KNO_3(aq) + PbS(s)$
- **e.** $2C_5H_{10}(l) + 15O_2(g) \xrightarrow{\Delta} 10CO_2(g) + 10H_2O(g)$

6.13 Oxidation is the loss of electrons; reduction is the gain of electrons.
- **a.** Na^+ gains an electron to form Na^0; this is a *reduction*.
- **b.** Ni^0 loses electrons to form Ni^{2+}; this is an *oxidation*.

    c. Cr^{3+} gains electrons to form Cr^0; this is a *reduction*.

    d. $2H^+$ gain electrons to form H_2; this is a *reduction*.

6.15 An oxidized substance has lost electrons; a reduced substance has gained electrons.

    a. Zn^0 loses electrons and is oxidized. Cl_2 gains electrons and is reduced.

    b. Br^- (in NaBr) loses electrons and is oxidized. Cl_2 gains electrons and is reduced.

    c. O^{2-} (in PbO) loses electrons and is oxidized. Pb^{2+} (in PbO) gains electrons and is reduced.

    d. Sn^{2+} loses electrons and oxidized. Fe^{3+} gains electrons and is reduced.

6.17 **a.** Fe^{3+} gains an electron to form Fe^{2+}; this is a *reduction*.

    b. Fe^{2+} loses an electron to form Fe^{3+}; this is an *oxidation*.

6.19 Linoleic acid gains hydrogen atoms and is *reduced*.

6.21 **a.** $0.200 \text{ mole Ag} \times \dfrac{6.02 \times 10^{23} \text{ atoms Ag}}{1 \text{ mole Ag}} = 1.20 \times 10^{23}$ atoms of Ag (3 SFs)

    b. $0.750 \text{ mole } C_3H_8O \times \dfrac{6.02 \times 10^{23} \text{ molecules } C_3H_8O}{1 \text{ mole } C_3H_8O}$

    $= 4.52 \times 10^{23}$ molecules of C_3H_8O (3 SFs)

    c. $1.25 \text{ moles Cr} \times \dfrac{6.02 \times 10^{23} \text{ atoms Cr}}{1 \text{ mole Cr}} = 7.53 \times 10^{23}$ atoms of Cr (3 SFs)

6.23 **a.** $3.26 \times 10^{24} \text{ atoms Al} \times \dfrac{1 \text{ mole Al}}{6.02 \times 10^{23} \text{ atoms Al}} = 5.42$ moles of Al (3 SFs)

    b. $8.50 \times 10^{24} \text{ molecules } C_2H_5OH \times \dfrac{1 \text{ mole } C_2H_5OH}{6.02 \times 10^{23} \text{ molecules } C_2H_5OH}$

    $= 14.1$ moles of C_2H_5OH (3 SFs)

    c. $2.88 \times 10^{23} \text{ atoms Au} \times \dfrac{1 \text{ mole Au}}{6.02 \times 10^{23} \text{ atoms Au}} = 0.478$ mole of Au (3 SFs)

6.25 The subscripts indicate the moles of each element in one mole of that compound.

    a. $1.0 \text{ mole quinine} \times \dfrac{24 \text{ moles H}}{1 \text{ mole quinine}} = 24$ moles of H (2 SFs)

    b. $5.0 \text{ moles quinine} \times \dfrac{20 \text{ moles C}}{1 \text{ mole quinine}} = 1.0 \times 10^2$ moles of C (2 SFs)

    c. $0.020 \text{ mole quinine} \times \dfrac{2 \text{ moles N}}{1 \text{ mole quinine}} = 0.040$ mole of N (2 SFs)

6.27 **a.** $0.500 \text{ mole C} \times \dfrac{6.02 \times 10^{23} \text{ atoms C}}{1 \text{ mole C}} = 3.01 \times 10^{23}$ atoms of C (3 SFs)

b. $1.28 \text{ moles SO}_2 \times \dfrac{6.02 \times 10^{23} \text{ molecules SO}_2}{1 \text{ mole SO}_2} = 7.71 \times 10^{23}$ molecules of SO_2 (3 SFs)

c. $5.22 \times 10^{22} \text{ atoms Fe} \times \dfrac{1 \text{ mole Fe}}{6.02 \times 10^{23} \text{ atoms Fe}} = 0.0867$ mole of Fe (3 SFs)

6.29 1 mole of H_3PO_4 contains 3 moles of H atoms, 1 mole of P atoms, and 4 moles of O atoms.

a. $2.00 \text{ moles H}_3PO_4 \times \dfrac{3 \text{ moles H}}{1 \text{ mole H}_3PO_4} = 6.00$ moles of H (3 SFs)

b. $2.00 \text{ moles H}_3PO_4 \times \dfrac{4 \text{ moles O}}{1 \text{ mole H}_3PO_4} = 8.00$ moles of O (3 SFs)

c. $2.00 \text{ moles H}_3PO_4 \times \dfrac{1 \text{ mole P}}{1 \text{ mole H}_3PO_4} \times \dfrac{6.02 \times 10^{23} \text{ atoms P}}{1 \text{ mole P}} = 1.20 \times 10^{24}$ atoms of P (3 SFs)

d. $2.00 \text{ moles H}_3PO_4 \times \dfrac{4 \text{ moles O}}{1 \text{ mole H}_3PO_4} \times \dfrac{6.02 \times 10^{23} \text{ atoms O}}{1 \text{ mole O}} = 4.82 \times 10^{24}$ atoms of O (3 SFs)

6.31 **a.** $1 \text{ mole K} \times \dfrac{39.1 \text{ g K}}{1 \text{ mole K}} = 39.1$ g of K

$4 \text{ moles C} \times \dfrac{12.0 \text{ g C}}{1 \text{ mole C}} = 48.0$ g of C

$5 \text{ moles H} \times \dfrac{1.01 \text{ g H}}{1 \text{ mole H}} = 5.05$ g of H

$6 \text{ moles O} \times \dfrac{16.0 \text{ g O}}{1 \text{ mole O}} = 96.0$ g of O

1 mole of K	=	39.1 g of K
4 moles of C	=	48.0 g of C
5 moles of H	=	5.05 g of H
6 moles of O	=	96.0 g of O

$\therefore$ molar mass of $KC_4H_5O_6 = \overline{188.2 \text{ g}}$

b. $2 \text{ moles Fe} \times \dfrac{55.9 \text{ g Fe}}{1 \text{ mole Fe}} = 111.8$ g of Fe

$3 \text{ moles O} \times \dfrac{16.0 \text{ g O}}{1 \text{ mole O}} = 48.0$ g of O

2 moles of Fe	=	111.8 g of Fe
3 moles of O	=	48.0 g of O

$\therefore$ molar mass of $Fe_2O_3 = \overline{159.8 \text{ g}}$

c. $19 \text{ moles C} \times \dfrac{12.0 \text{ g C}}{1 \text{ mole C}} = 228.0 \text{ g of C}$

$20 \text{ moles H} \times \dfrac{1.01 \text{ g H}}{1 \text{ mole H}} = 20.2 \text{ g of H}$

$1 \text{ mole F} \times \dfrac{19.0 \text{ g F}}{1 \text{ mole F}} = 19.0 \text{ g of F}$

$1 \text{ mole N} \times \dfrac{14.0 \text{ g N}}{1 \text{ mole N}} = 14.0 \text{ g of N}$

$3 \text{ moles O} \times \dfrac{16.0 \text{ g O}}{1 \text{ mole O}} = 48.0 \text{ g of O}$

19 moles of C	= 228.0 g of C
20 moles of H	= 20.2 g of H
1 mole of F	= 19.0 g of F
1 mole of N	= 14.0 g of N
3 moles of O	= 48.0 g of O

$\therefore$ molar mass of $C_{19}H_{20}FNO_3$ = 329.2 g

d. $2 \text{ moles Al} \times \dfrac{27.0 \text{ g Al}}{1 \text{ mole Al}} = 54.0 \text{ g of Al}$

$3 \text{ moles S} \times \dfrac{32.1 \text{ g S}}{1 \text{ mole S}} = 96.3 \text{ g of S}$

$12 \text{ moles O} \times \dfrac{16.0 \text{ g O}}{1 \text{ mole O}} = 192.0 \text{ g of O}$

2 moles of Al	= 54.0 g of Al
3 moles of S	= 96.3 g of S
12 moles of O	= 192.0 g of O

$\therefore$ molar mass of $Al_2(SO_4)_3$ = 342.3 g

e. $1 \text{ mole Mg} \times \dfrac{24.3 \text{ g Mg}}{1 \text{ mole Mg}} = 24.3 \text{ g of Mg}$

$2 \text{ moles O} \times \dfrac{16.0 \text{ g O}}{1 \text{ mole O}} = 32.0 \text{ g of O}$

$2 \text{ moles H} \times \dfrac{1.01 \text{ g H}}{1 \text{ mole H}} = 2.02 \text{ g of H}$

1 mole of Mg	= 24.3 g of Mg
2 moles of O	= 32.0 g of O
2 moles of H	= 2.02 g of H

$\therefore$ molar mass of $Mg(OH)_2$ = 58.3 g

f. $16 \text{ moles C} \times \dfrac{12.0 \text{ g C}}{1 \text{ mole C}} = 192.0 \text{ g of C}$

$19 \text{ moles H} \times \dfrac{1.01 \text{ g H}}{1 \text{ mole H}} = 19.2 \text{ g of H}$

$3 \text{ moles N} \times \dfrac{14.0 \text{ g N}}{1 \text{ mole N}} = 42.0 \text{ g of N}$

$5 \text{ moles O} \times \dfrac{16.0 \text{ g O}}{1 \text{ mole O}} = 80.0 \text{ g of O}$

$1 \text{ mole S} \times \dfrac{32.1 \text{ g S}}{1 \text{ mole S}} = 32.1 \text{ g of S}$

16 moles of C	= 192.0 g of C
19 moles of H	= 19.2 g of H
3 moles of N	= 42.0 g of N
5 moles of O	= 80.0 g of O
1 mole of S	= 32.1 g of S

$\therefore$ molar mass of $C_{16}H_{19}N_3O_5S$ = 365.3 g

6.33 **a.** $2.00 \text{ moles Na} \times \dfrac{23.0 \text{ g Na}}{1 \text{ mole Na}} = 46.0 \text{ g of Na (3 SFs)}$

b. $2.80 \text{ moles Ca} \times \dfrac{40.1 \text{ g Ca}}{1 \text{ mole Ca}} = 112 \text{ g of Ca (3 SFs)}$

c. $0.125 \text{ mole Sn} \times \dfrac{118.7 \text{ g Sn}}{1 \text{ mole Sn}} = 14.8 \text{ g of Sn (3 SFs)}$

d. $1.76 \text{ moles Cu} \times \dfrac{63.6 \text{ g Cu}}{1 \text{ mole Cu}} = 112 \text{ g of Cu (3 SFs)}$

6.35 **a.** molar mass of NaCl = 1(23.0 g) + 1(35.5 g) = 58.5 g

$0.500 \text{ mole NaCl} \times \dfrac{58.5 \text{ g NaCl}}{1 \text{ mole NaCl}} = 29.3 \text{ g of NaCl (3 SFs)}$

b. molar mass of Na_2O = 2(23.0 g) + 1(16.0 g) = 62.0 g

$1.75 \text{ moles Na}_2\text{O} \times \dfrac{62.0 \text{ g Na}_2\text{O}}{1 \text{ mole Na}_2\text{O}} = 109 \text{ g of Na}_2\text{O (3 SFs)}$

c. molar mass of H_2O = 2(1.01 g) + 1(16.0 g) = 18.0 g

$0.225 \text{ mole H}_2\text{O} \times \dfrac{18.0 \text{ g H}_2\text{O}}{1 \text{ mole H}_2\text{O}} = 4.05 \text{ g of H}_2\text{O (3 SFs)}$

d. molar mass of CO_2 = 1(12.0 g) + 2(16.0 g) = 44.0 g

$4.42 \text{ moles CO}_2 \times \dfrac{44.0 \text{ g CO}_2}{1 \text{ mole CO}_2} = 194 \text{ g of CO}_2 \text{ (3 SFs)}$

6.37 **a.** molar mass of $MgSO_4$ = 1(24.3 g) + 1(32.1 g) + 4(16.0 g) = 120.4 g

$$5.00 \text{ moles MgSO}_4 \times \frac{120.4 \text{ g MgSO}_4}{1 \text{ mole MgSO}_4} = 602 \text{ g of MgSO}_4 \text{ (3 SFs)}$$

b. molar mass of CO_2 = 1(12.0 g) + 2(16.0 g) = 44.0 g

$$0.25 \text{ mole CO}_2 \times \frac{44.0 \text{ g CO}_2}{1 \text{ mole CO}_2} = 11 \text{ g of CO}_2 \text{ (2 SFs)}$$

6.39 **a.** $50.0 \text{ g Ag} \times \frac{1 \text{ mole Ag}}{107.9 \text{ g Ag}} = 0.463 \text{ mole of Ag (3 SFs)}$

b. $0.200 \text{ g C} \times \frac{1 \text{ mole C}}{12.0 \text{ g C}} = 0.0167 \text{ mole of C (3 SFs)}$

c. molar mass of NH_3 = 1(14.0 g) + 3(1.01 g) = 17.0 g

$$15.0 \text{ g NH}_3 \times \frac{1 \text{ mole NH}_3}{17.0 \text{ g NH}_3} = 0.882 \text{ mole of NH}_3 \text{ (3 SFs)}$$

d. molar mass of SO_2 = 1(32.1 g) + 2(16.0 g) = 64.1 g

$$75.0 \text{ g SO}_2 \times \frac{1 \text{ mole SO}_2}{64.1 \text{ g SO}_2} = 1.17 \text{ moles of SO}_2 \text{ (3 SFs)}$$

6.41 **a.** $25 \text{ g S} \times \frac{1 \text{ mole S}}{32.1 \text{ g S}} = 0.78 \text{ mole of S (2 SFs)}$

b. molar mass of SO_2 = 1(32.1 g) + 2(16.0 g) = 64.1 g

$$125 \text{ g SO}_2 \times \frac{1 \text{ mole SO}_2}{64.1 \text{ g SO}_2} \times \frac{1 \text{ mole S}}{1 \text{ mole SO}_2} = 1.95 \text{ moles of S (3 SFs)}$$

c. molar mass of Al_2S_3 = 2(27.0 g) + 3(32.1 g) = 150.3 g

$$30.1 \text{ g Al}_2\text{S}_3 \times \frac{1 \text{ mole Al}_2\text{S}_3}{150.3 \text{ g Al}_2\text{S}_3} \times \frac{3 \text{ moles S}}{1 \text{ mole Al}_2\text{S}_3} = 0.601 \text{ mole of S (3 SFs)}$$

6.43 molar mass of caffeine ($C_8H_{10}N_4O_2$)
= 8(12.0 g) + 10(1.01 g) + 4(14.0 g) + 2(16.0 g) = 194.1 g (4 SFs)

a. $0.850 \text{ mole caffeine} \times \frac{194.1 \text{ g caffeine}}{1 \text{ mole caffeine}} = 165 \text{ g of caffeine (3 SFs)}$

b. $28.0 \text{ g caffeine} \times \frac{1 \text{ mole caffeine}}{194.1 \text{ g caffeine}} = 0.144 \text{ mole of caffeine (3 SFs)}$

c. $28.0 \text{ g caffeine} \times \frac{1 \text{ mole caffeine}}{194.1 \text{ g caffeine}} \times \frac{8 \text{ moles C}}{1 \text{ mole caffeine}} = 1.15 \text{ moles of C (3 SFs)}$

d. $28.0 \text{ g caffeine} \times \frac{1 \text{ mole caffeine}}{194.1 \text{ g caffeine}} \times \frac{4 \text{ moles N}}{1 \text{ mole caffeine}} \times \frac{14.0 \text{ g N}}{1 \text{ mole N}} = 8.08 \text{ g of N (3 SFs)}$

6.45 **a.** $\dfrac{2 \text{ moles SO}_2}{1 \text{ mole O}_2}$ and $\dfrac{1 \text{ mole O}_2}{2 \text{ moles SO}_2}$; $\dfrac{2 \text{ moles SO}_2}{2 \text{ moles SO}_3}$ and $\dfrac{2 \text{ moles SO}_3}{2 \text{ moles SO}_2}$;

$\dfrac{1 \text{ mole O}_2}{2 \text{ moles SO}_3}$ and $\dfrac{2 \text{ moles SO}_3}{1 \text{ mole O}_2}$

b. $\dfrac{4 \text{ moles P}}{5 \text{ moles O}_2}$ and $\dfrac{5 \text{ moles O}_2}{4 \text{ moles P}}$; $\dfrac{4 \text{ moles P}}{2 \text{ moles P}_2\text{O}_5}$ and $\dfrac{2 \text{ moles P}_2\text{O}_5}{4 \text{ moles P}}$;

$\dfrac{5 \text{ moles O}_2}{2 \text{ moles P}_2\text{O}_5}$ and $\dfrac{2 \text{ moles P}_2\text{O}_5}{5 \text{ moles O}_2}$

6.47 **a.** $2.0 \text{ moles H}_2 \times \dfrac{1 \text{ mole O}_2}{2 \text{ moles H}_2} = 1.0 \text{ mole of O}_2$ (2 SFs)

b. $5.0 \text{ moles O}_2 \times \dfrac{2 \text{ moles H}_2}{1 \text{ mole O}_2} = 10. \text{ moles of H}_2$ (2 SFs)

c. $2.5 \text{ moles O}_2 \times \dfrac{2 \text{ moles H}_2\text{O}}{1 \text{ mole O}_2} = 5.0 \text{ moles of H}_2\text{O}$ (2 SFs)

6.49 **a.** $0.500 \text{ mole SO}_2 \times \dfrac{5 \text{ moles C}}{2 \text{ moles SO}_2} = 1.25 \text{ moles of C}$ (3 SFs)

b. $1.2 \text{ moles C} \times \dfrac{4 \text{ moles CO}}{5 \text{ moles C}} = 0.96 \text{ mole of CO}$ (2 SFs)

c. $0.50 \text{ mole CS}_2 \times \dfrac{2 \text{ moles SO}_2}{1 \text{ mole CS}_2} = 1.0 \text{ mole of SO}_2$ (2 SFs)

d. $2.5 \text{ moles C} \times \dfrac{1 \text{ mole CS}_2}{5 \text{ moles C}} = 0.50 \text{ mole of CS}_2$ (2 SFs)

6.51 **a.** $57.5 \text{ g Na} \times \dfrac{1 \text{ mole Na}}{23.0 \text{ g Na}} \times \dfrac{2 \text{ moles Na}_2\text{O}}{4 \text{ moles Na}} \times \dfrac{62.0 \text{ g Na}_2\text{O}}{1 \text{ mole Na}_2\text{O}} = 77.5 \text{ g of Na}_2\text{O}$ (3 SFs)

b. $18.0 \text{ g Na} \times \dfrac{1 \text{ mole Na}}{23.0 \text{ g Na}} \times \dfrac{1 \text{ mole O}_2}{4 \text{ moles Na}} \times \dfrac{32.0 \text{ g O}_2}{1 \text{ mole O}_2} = 6.26 \text{ g of O}_2$ (3 SFs)

c. $75.0 \text{ g Na}_2\text{O} \times \dfrac{1 \text{ mole Na}_2\text{O}}{62.0 \text{ g Na}_2\text{O}} \times \dfrac{1 \text{ mole O}_2}{2 \text{ moles Na}_2\text{O}} \times \dfrac{32.0 \text{ g O}_2}{1 \text{ mole O}_2} = 19.4 \text{ g of O}_2$ (3 SFs)

6.53 **a.** $13.6 \text{ g NH}_3 \times \dfrac{1 \text{ mole NH}_3}{17.0 \text{ g NH}_3} \times \dfrac{3 \text{ moles O}_2}{4 \text{ moles NH}_3} \times \dfrac{32.0 \text{ g O}_2}{1 \text{ mole O}_2} = 19.2 \text{ g of O}_2$ (3 SFs)

b. $6.50 \text{ g O}_2 \times \dfrac{1 \text{ mole O}_2}{32.0 \text{ g O}_2} \times \dfrac{2 \text{ moles N}_2}{3 \text{ moles O}_2} \times \dfrac{28.0 \text{ g N}_2}{1 \text{ mole N}_2} = 3.79 \text{ g of N}_2$ (3 SFs)

c. $34.0 \text{ g NH}_3 \times \dfrac{1 \text{ mole NH}_3}{17.0 \text{ g NH}_3} \times \dfrac{6 \text{ moles H}_2\text{O}}{4 \text{ moles NH}_3} \times \dfrac{18.0 \text{ g H}_2\text{O}}{1 \text{ mole H}_2\text{O}} = 54.0 \text{ g of H}_2\text{O}$ (3 SFs)

6.55   **a.** $28.0 \text{ g NO}_2 \times \dfrac{1 \text{ mole NO}_2}{46.0 \text{ g NO}_2} \times \dfrac{1 \text{ mole H}_2\text{O}}{3 \text{ moles NO}_2} \times \dfrac{18.0 \text{ g H}_2\text{O}}{1 \text{ mole H}_2\text{O}} = 3.65 \text{ g of H}_2\text{O (3 SFs)}$

   b. $15.8 \text{ g NO}_2 \times \dfrac{1 \text{ mole NO}_2}{46.0 \text{ g NO}_2} \times \dfrac{1 \text{ mole NO}}{3 \text{ moles NO}_2} \times \dfrac{30.0 \text{ g NO}}{1 \text{ mole NO}} = 3.43 \text{ g of NO (3 SFs)}$

   c. $8.25 \text{ g NO}_2 \times \dfrac{1 \text{ mole NO}_2}{46.0 \text{ g NO}_2} \times \dfrac{2 \text{ moles HNO}_3}{3 \text{ moles NO}_2} \times \dfrac{63.0 \text{ g HNO}_3}{1 \text{ mole HNO}_3} = 7.53 \text{ g of HNO}_3 \text{ (3 SFs)}$

6.57   **a.** $2\text{PbS}(s) + 3\text{O}_2(g) \xrightarrow{\Delta} 2\text{PbO}(s) + 2\text{SO}_2(g)$

   b. $29.9 \text{ g PbS} \times \dfrac{1 \text{ mole PbS}}{239.3 \text{ g PbS}} \times \dfrac{3 \text{ moles O}_2}{2 \text{ moles PbS}} \times \dfrac{32.0 \text{ g O}_2}{1 \text{ mole O}_2} = 6.00 \text{ g of O}_2 \text{ (3 SFs)}$

   c. $65.0 \text{ g PbS} \times \dfrac{1 \text{ mole PbS}}{239.3 \text{ g PbS}} \times \dfrac{2 \text{ moles SO}_2}{2 \text{ moles PbS}} \times \dfrac{64.1 \text{ g SO}_2}{1 \text{ mole SO}_2} = 17.4 \text{ g of SO}_2 \text{ (3 SFs)}$

   d. $128 \text{ g PbO} \times \dfrac{1 \text{ mole PbO}}{223.2 \text{ g PbO}} \times \dfrac{2 \text{ moles PbS}}{2 \text{ moles PbO}} \times \dfrac{239.3 \text{ g PbS}}{1 \text{ mole PbS}} = 137 \text{ g of PbS (3 SFs)}$

6.59   **a.**   theoretical yield of CS_2:

$$40.0 \text{ g C} \times \dfrac{1 \text{ mole C}}{12.0 \text{ g C}} \times \dfrac{1 \text{ mole CS}_2}{5 \text{ moles C}} \times \dfrac{76.2 \text{ g CS}_2}{1 \text{ mole CS}_2} = 50.8 \text{ g of CS}_2$$

   percent yield: $\dfrac{36.0 \text{ g CS}_2 \text{ (actual)}}{50.8 \text{ g CS}_2 \text{ (theoretical)}} \times 100\% = 70.9\% \text{ (3 SFs)}$

   b.   theoretical yield of CS_2:

$$32.0 \text{ g SO}_2 \times \dfrac{1 \text{ mole SO}_2}{64.1 \text{ g SO}_2} \times \dfrac{1 \text{ mole CS}_2}{2 \text{ moles SO}_2} \times \dfrac{76.2 \text{ g CS}_2}{1 \text{ mole CS}_2} = 19.0 \text{ g of CS}_2$$

   percent yield: $\dfrac{12.0 \text{ g CS}_2 \text{ (actual)}}{19.0 \text{ g CS}_2 \text{ (theoretical)}} \times 100\% = 63.2\% \text{ (3 SFs)}$

6.61   theoretical yield of Al_2O_3:

$$50.0 \text{ g Al} \times \dfrac{1 \text{ mole Al}}{27.0 \text{ g Al}} \times \dfrac{2 \text{ moles Al}_2\text{O}_3}{4 \text{ moles Al}} \times \dfrac{102.0 \text{ g Al}_2\text{O}_3}{1 \text{ mole Al}_2\text{O}_3} = 94.4 \text{ g of Al}_2\text{O}_3$$

Use the percent yield to convert theoretical to actual:

$$94.4 \text{ g Al}_2\text{O}_3 \times \dfrac{75.0 \text{ g Al}_2\text{O}_3}{100 \text{ g Al}_2\text{O}_3} = 70.8 \text{ g of Al}_2\text{O}_3 \text{ (actual) (3 SFs)}$$

6.63   theoretical yield of CO_2:

$$30.0 \text{ g C} \times \dfrac{1 \text{ mole C}}{12.0 \text{ g C}} \times \dfrac{2 \text{ moles CO}}{3 \text{ moles C}} \times \dfrac{28.0 \text{ g CO}}{1 \text{ mole CO}} = 46.7 \text{ g of CO}$$

   percent yield: $\dfrac{28.2 \text{ g CO (actual)}}{46.7 \text{ g CO (theoretical)}} \times 100\% = 60.4\% \text{ (3 SFs)}$

6.65 **a.** The limiting factor is the number of drivers: with only eight drivers available, only eight taxis can be used to pick up passengers.

b. The limiting factor is the number of taxis: only seven taxis are in working condition to be driven.

6.67 The limiting reactant is the one that runs out first, producing the smaller amount of product.

a. $3.0 \text{ moles N}_2 \times \dfrac{2 \text{ moles NH}_3}{1 \text{ mole N}_2} = 6.0 \text{ moles of NH}_3$

$5.0 \text{ moles H}_2 \times \dfrac{2 \text{ moles NH}_3}{3 \text{ moles H}_2} = 3.3 \text{ moles of NH}_3 \text{ (smaller number of moles)}$

The limiting reactant is 5.0 moles of H_2. (2 SFs)

b. $8.0 \text{ moles N}_2 \times \dfrac{2 \text{ moles NH}_3}{1 \text{ mole N}_2} = 16 \text{ moles of NH}_3$

$4.0 \text{ moles H}_2 \times \dfrac{2 \text{ moles NH}_3}{3 \text{ moles H}_2} = 2.7 \text{ moles of NH}_3 \text{ (smaller number of moles)}$

The limiting reactant is 4.0 moles of H_2. (2 SFs)

c. $3.0 \text{ moles N}_2 \times \dfrac{2 \text{ moles NH}_3}{1 \text{ mole N}_2} = 6.0 \text{ moles of NH}_3 \text{ (smaller number of moles)}$

$12.0 \text{ moles H}_2 \times \dfrac{2 \text{ moles NH}_3}{3 \text{ moles H}_2} = 8.00 \text{ moles of NH}_3$

The limiting reactant is 3.0 moles of N_2. (2 SFs)

6.69 **a.** $2.00 \text{ moles SO}_2 \times \dfrac{2 \text{ moles SO}_3}{2 \text{ moles SO}_2} = 2.00 \text{ moles of SO}_3 \text{ (smaller number of moles)}$

$2.00 \text{ moles O}_2 \times \dfrac{2 \text{ moles SO}_3}{1 \text{ mole O}_2} = 4.00 \text{ moles of SO}_3$

$\therefore$ SO_2 is the limiting reactant, and 2.00 moles of SO_3 can be produced. (3 SFs)

b. $2.00 \text{ moles Fe} \times \dfrac{1 \text{ mole Fe}_3\text{O}_4}{3 \text{ moles Fe}} = 0.667 \text{ mole of Fe}_3\text{O}_4$

$2.00 \text{ moles H}_2\text{O} \times \dfrac{1 \text{ mole Fe}_3\text{O}_4}{4 \text{ moles H}_2\text{O}} = 0.500 \text{ mole of Fe}_3\text{O}_4 \text{ (smaller number of moles)}$

$\therefore$ H_2O is the limiting reactant, and 0.500 mole of Fe_3O_4 can be produced. (3 SFs)

c. $2.00 \text{ moles C}_7\text{H}_{16} \times \dfrac{7 \text{ moles CO}_2}{1 \text{ mole C}_7\text{H}_{16}} = 14.0 \text{ moles of CO}_2$

$2.00 \text{ moles O}_2 \times \dfrac{7 \text{ moles CO}_2}{11 \text{ moles O}_2} = 1.27 \text{ moles of CO}_2 \text{ (smaller number of moles)}$

$\therefore$ O_2 is the limiting reactant, and 1.27 moles of CO_2 can be produced. (3 SFs)

6.71 **a.** $20.0 \text{ g Al} \times \dfrac{1 \text{ mole Al}}{27.0 \text{ g Al}} \times \dfrac{2 \text{ moles AlCl}_3}{2 \text{ moles Al}} = 0.741 \text{ mole of AlCl}_3$

$20.0 \text{ g Cl}_2 \times \dfrac{1 \text{ mole Cl}_2}{71.0 \text{ g Cl}_2} \times \dfrac{2 \text{ moles AlCl}_3}{3 \text{ moles Cl}_2} = 0.188 \text{ mole of AlCl}_3 \text{ (smaller number of moles)}$

$$0.188 \text{ mole AlCl}_3 \times \frac{133.5 \text{ g AlCl}_3}{1 \text{ mole AlCl}_3} = 25.1 \text{ g of AlCl}_3 \ (3 \text{ SFs})$$

$\therefore Cl_2$ is the limiting reactant, and 25.1 g of $AlCl_3$ can be produced.

b. $20.0 \text{ g NH}_3 \times \dfrac{1 \text{ mole NH}_3}{17.0 \text{ g NH}_3} \times \dfrac{6 \text{ moles H}_2\text{O}}{4 \text{ moles NH}_3} = 1.76 \text{ moles of H}_2\text{O}$

$20.0 \text{ g O}_2 \times \dfrac{1 \text{ mole O}_2}{32.0 \text{ g O}_2} \times \dfrac{6 \text{ moles H}_2\text{O}}{5 \text{ moles O}_2} = 0.750 \text{ mole of H}_2\text{O (smaller number of moles)}$

$0.750 \text{ mole H}_2\text{O} \times \dfrac{18.0 \text{ g H}_2\text{O}}{1 \text{ mole H}_2\text{O}} = 13.5 \text{ g of H}_2\text{O} \ (3 \text{ SFs})$

$\therefore O_2$ is the limiting reactant, and 13.5 g of H_2O can be produced.

c. $20.0 \text{ g CS}_2 \times \dfrac{1 \text{ mole CS}_2}{76.2 \text{ g CS}_2} \times \dfrac{2 \text{ moles SO}_2}{1 \text{ mole CS}_2} = 0.525 \text{ mole of SO}_2$

$20.0 \text{ g O}_2 \times \dfrac{1 \text{ mole O}_2}{32.0 \text{ g O}_2} \times \dfrac{2 \text{ moles SO}_2}{3 \text{ moles O}_2} = 0.417 \text{ mole of SO}_2 \text{(smaller number of moles)}$

$0.417 \text{ mole SO}_2 \times \dfrac{64.1 \text{ g SO}_2}{1 \text{ mole SO}_2} = 26.7 \text{ g of SO}_2 \ (3 \text{ SFs})$

$\therefore O_2$ is the limiting reactant, and 26.7 g of SO_2 can be produced.

6.73 **a.** The energy of activation is the energy required to break the bonds of the reacting molecules.
b. In exothermic reactions, the energy of the products is lower than the energy of the reactants.

c.

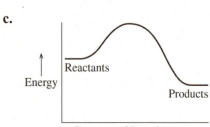

6.75 **a.** An *exothermic* reaction releases heat.
b. In an *endothermic* reaction, the energy level of the products is higher than that of the reactants.
c. The metabolism of glucose is an *exothermic* reaction, providing energy for the body.

6.77 **a.** Heat is released, which makes the reaction *exothermic* with $\Delta H = -890 \text{ kJ}$.
b. Heat is absorbed, which makes the reaction *endothermic* with $\Delta H = +65.3 \text{ kJ}$.
c. Heat is released, which makes the reaction *exothermic* with $\Delta H = -205 \text{ kcal}$.

6.79 $125 \text{ g Cl}_2 \times \dfrac{1 \text{ mole Cl}_2}{71.0 \text{ g Cl}_2} \times \dfrac{-657 \text{ kJ}}{2 \text{ moles Cl}_2} = -578 \text{ kJ} \ (3 \text{ SFs})$

$\therefore$ 578 kJ are released.

6.81 **a.** 1, 1, 2; combination reaction
b. 2, 2, 1; decomposition reaction

6.83   **a.** reactants: NO, O_2 product: NO_2
     b. $2NO(g) + O_2(g) \longrightarrow 2NO_2(g)$
     c. combination reaction

6.85   **a.** reactant: NI_3 products: N_2, I_2
     b. $2NI_3(g) \longrightarrow N_2(g) + 3I_2(g)$
     c. decomposition reaction

6.87   **a.** reactants: Cl_2, O_2 product: OCl_2
     b. $2Cl_2(g) + O_2(g) \longrightarrow 2OCl_2(g)$
     c. combination reaction

6.89   **1.**   **a.** S_2Cl_2
       b. molar mass of S_2Cl_2 = 2(32.1 g) + 2(35.5 g) = 135.2 g (4 SFs)
       c. $10.0 \text{ g } S_2Cl_2 \times \dfrac{1 \text{ mole } S_2Cl_2}{135.2 \text{ g } S_2Cl_2}$ = 0.0740 mole of S_2Cl_2 (3 SFs)

     2.   **a.** C_6H_6
       b. molar mass of C_6H_6 = 6(12.0 g) + 6(1.01 g) = 78.1 g (3 SFs)
       c. $10.0 \text{ g } C_6H_6 \times \dfrac{1 \text{ mole } C_6H_6}{78.1 \text{ g } C_6H_6}$ = 0.128 mole of C_6H_6 (3 SFs)

6.91   **a.** molar mass of dipyrithione ($C_{10}H_8N_2O_2S_2$)
     = 10(12.0 g) + 8(1.01 g) + 2(14.0 g) + 2(16.0 g) + 2(32.1 g) = 252.3 g (4 SFs)

     b. $25.0 \text{ g } C_{10}H_8N_2O_2S_2 \times \dfrac{1 \text{ mole } C_{10}H_8N_2O_2S_2}{252.3 \text{ g } C_{10}H_8N_2O_2S_2}$ = 0.0991 mole of $C_{10}H_8N_2O_2S_2$ (3 SFs)

     c. $25.0 \text{ g } C_{10}H_8N_2O_2S_2 \times \dfrac{1 \text{ mole } C_{10}H_8N_2O_2S_2}{252.3 \text{ g } C_{10}H_8N_2O_2S_2} \times \dfrac{10 \text{ moles C}}{1 \text{ mole } C_{10}H_8N_2O_2S_2}$
     = 0.991 mole of C (3 SFs)

6.93   molar mass of propane (C_3H_8) = 3(12.0 g) + 8(1.01 g) = 44.1 g (3 SFs)

     a. $1.50 \text{ moles } C_3H_8 \times \dfrac{44.1 \text{ g } C_3H_8}{1 \text{ mole } C_3H_8}$ = 66.2 g of C_3H_8 (3 SFs)

     b. $34.0 \text{ g } C_3H_8 \times \dfrac{1 \text{ mole } C_3H_8}{44.1 \text{ g } C_3H_8}$ = 0.771 mole of C_3H_8 (3 SFs)

     c. $34.0 \text{ g } C_3H_8 \times \dfrac{1 \text{ mole } C_3H_8}{44.1 \text{ g } C_3H_8} \times \dfrac{3 \text{ moles C}}{1 \text{ mole } C_3H_8} \times \dfrac{12.0 \text{ g C}}{1 \text{ mole C}}$ = 27.8 g of C (3 SFs)

     d. $0.254 \text{ g } C_3H_8 \times \dfrac{1 \text{ mole } C_3H_8}{44.1 \text{ g } C_3H_8} \times \dfrac{8 \text{ moles H}}{1 \text{ mole } C_3H_8} \times \dfrac{6.02 \times 10^{23} \text{ atoms H}}{1 \text{ mole H}}$
     = 2.77×10^{22} atoms of H (3 SFs)

6.95   **a.** $NH_3(g) + HCl(g) \longrightarrow NH_4Cl(s)$ combination reaction
     b. $Fe_3O_4(s) + 4H_2(g) \longrightarrow 3Fe(s) + 4H_2O(g)$ single replacement reaction
     c. $2Sb(s) + 3Cl_2(g) \longrightarrow 2SbCl_3(s)$ combination reaction

d. $C_5H_{12}(g) + 8O_2(g) \xrightarrow{\Delta} 5CO_2(g) + 6H_2O(g)$ combustion reaction

e. $2KBr(aq) + Cl_2(aq) \longrightarrow 2KCl(aq) + Br_2(l)$ single replacement reaction

f. $Al_2(SO_4)_3(aq) + 6NaOH(aq) \longrightarrow 3Na_2SO_4(aq) + 2Al(OH)_3(s)$ double replacement reaction

6.97 **a.** $Zn(s) + 2HCl(aq) \longrightarrow ZnCl_2(aq) + H_2(g)$

b. $BaCO_3(s) \xrightarrow{\Delta} BaO(s) + CO_2(g)$

c. $NaOH(aq) + HCl(aq) \longrightarrow NaCl(aq) + H_2O(l)$

d. $2Al(s) + 3F_2(g) \longrightarrow 2AlF_3(s)$

6.99 An oxidized substance has lost electrons; a reduced substance has gained electrons.

a. Cu^0 loses electrons and is oxidized. H^+ gains electrons and is reduced.

b. Fe^0 loses electrons and is oxidized. Ni^{2+} gains electrons and is reduced.

c. Ag^0 loses electrons and is oxidized. Cu^{2+} gains electrons and is reduced.

d. Cr^0 loses electrons and is oxidized. Ni^{2+} gains electrons and is reduced.

e. Zn^0 loses electrons and is oxidized. Cu^{2+} gains electrons and is reduced.

f. Zn^0 loses electrons and is oxidized. Pb^{2+} gains electrons and is reduced.

6.101 **a.** molar mass of lactic acid ($C_3H_6O_3$)

$= 3(12.0 \text{ g}) + 6(1.01 \text{ g}) + 3(16.0 \text{ g}) = 90.1 \text{ g (3 SFs)}$

b. $0.500 \text{ mole } C_3H_6O_3 \times \dfrac{6.02 \times 10^{23} \text{ molecules}}{1 \text{ mole } C_3H_6O_3} = 3.01 \times 10^{23} \text{ molecules of } C_3H_6O_3 \text{ (3 SFs)}$

c. $1.50 \text{ moles } C_3H_6O_3 \times \dfrac{3 \text{ moles C}}{1 \text{ mole } C_3H_6O_3} \times \dfrac{6.02 \times 10^{23} \text{ atoms C}}{1 \text{ mole C}} = 2.71 \times 10^{24} \text{ atoms of C (3 SFs)}$

d. $4.5 \times 10^{24} \text{ atoms O} \times \dfrac{1 \text{ mole O}}{6.02 \times 10^{23} \text{ atoms O}} \times \dfrac{1 \text{ mole } C_3H_6O_3}{3 \text{ moles O}} \times \dfrac{90.1 \text{ g } C_3H_6O_3}{1 \text{ mole } C_3H_6O_3}$

$= 220 \text{ g of } C_3H_6O_3 \text{ (2 SFs)}$

6.103 **a.** molar mass of zinc sulfate ($ZnSO_4$)

$= 1(65.4 \text{ g}) + 1(32.1 \text{ g}) + 4(16.0 \text{ g}) = 161.5 \text{ g (4 SFs)}$

b. molar mass of calcium iodate ($Ca(IO_3)_2$)

$= 1(40.1 \text{ g}) + 2(126.9 \text{ g}) + 6(16.0 \text{ g}) = 389.9 \text{ g (4 SFs)}$

c. molar mass of monosodium glutamate ($C_5H_8NNaO_4$)

$= 5(12.0 \text{ g}) + 8(1.01 \text{ g}) + 1(14.0 \text{ g}) + 1(23.0 \text{ g}) + 4(16.0 \text{ g}) = 169.1 \text{ g (4 SFs)}$

6.105 **a.** $0.150 \text{ mole K} \times \dfrac{39.1 \text{ g K}}{1 \text{ mole K}} = 5.87 \text{ g of K (3 SFs)}$

b. $0.150 \text{ mole } Cl_2 \times \dfrac{71.0 \text{ g } Cl_2}{1 \text{ mole } Cl_2} = 10.7 \text{ g of } Cl_2 \text{ (3 SFs)}$

c. $0.150 \text{ mole } Na_2CO_3 \times \dfrac{106.0 \text{ g } Na_2CO_3}{1 \text{ mole } Na_2CO_3} = 15.9 \text{ g of } Na_2CO_3 \text{ (3 SFs)}$

6.107 **a.** $25.0 \text{ g CO}_2 \times \dfrac{1 \text{ mole CO}_2}{44.0 \text{ g CO}_2} = 0.568$ mole of CO_2 (3 SFs)

b. $25.0 \text{ g Al(OH)}_3 \times \dfrac{1 \text{ mole Al(OH)}_3}{78.0 \text{ g Al(OH)}_3} = 0.321$ mole of $Al(OH)_3$ (3 SFs)

c. $25.0 \text{ g MgCl}_2 \times \dfrac{1 \text{ mole MgCl}_2}{95.3 \text{ g MgCl}_2} = 0.262$ mole of $MgCl_2$ (3 SFs)

6.109 **a.** $124 \text{ g C}_2\text{H}_6\text{O} \times \dfrac{1 \text{ mole C}_2\text{H}_6\text{O}}{46.1 \text{ g C}_2\text{H}_6\text{O}} \times \dfrac{1 \text{ mole C}_6\text{H}_{12}\text{O}_6}{2 \text{ moles C}_2\text{H}_6\text{O}} \times \dfrac{180.1 \text{ g C}_6\text{H}_{12}\text{O}_6}{1 \text{ mole C}_6\text{H}_{12}\text{O}_6}$

$= 242$ g of $C_6H_{12}O_6$ (3 SFs)

b. $0.240 \text{ kg C}_6\text{H}_{12}\text{O}_6 \times \dfrac{1000 \text{ g}}{1 \text{ kg}} \times \dfrac{1 \text{ mole C}_6\text{H}_{12}\text{O}_6}{180.1 \text{ g C}_6\text{H}_{12}\text{O}_6} \times \dfrac{2 \text{ moles C}_2\text{H}_6\text{O}}{1 \text{ mole C}_6\text{H}_{12}\text{O}_6} \times \dfrac{46.1 \text{ g C}_2\text{H}_6\text{O}}{1 \text{ mole C}_2\text{H}_6\text{O}}$

$= 123$ g of C_2H_6O (3 SFs)

6.111 **a.** $2NH_3(g) + 5F_2(g) \longrightarrow N_2F_4(g) + 6HF(g)$

b. $4.00 \text{ moles HF} \times \dfrac{2 \text{ moles NH}_3}{6 \text{ moles HF}} = 1.33$ moles of NH_3 (3 SFs)

$4.00 \text{ moles HF} \times \dfrac{5 \text{ moles F}_2}{6 \text{ moles HF}} = 3.33$ moles of F_2 (3 SFs)

c. $25.5 \text{ g NH}_3 \times \dfrac{1 \text{ mole NH}_3}{17.0 \text{ g NH}_3} \times \dfrac{5 \text{ moles F}_2}{2 \text{ moles NH}_3} \times \dfrac{38.0 \text{ g F}_2}{1 \text{ mole F}_2} = 143$ g of F_2 (3 SFs)

d. $3.40 \text{ g NH}_3 \times \dfrac{1 \text{ mole NH}_3}{17.0 \text{ g NH}_3} \times \dfrac{1 \text{ mole N}_2\text{F}_4}{2 \text{ moles NH}_3} \times \dfrac{104.0 \text{ g N}_2\text{F}_4}{1 \text{ mole N}_2\text{F}_4} = 10.4$ g of N_2F_4 (3 SFs)

6.113 **a.** $C_2H_6(g) + 6Cl_2(g) \longrightarrow C_2Cl_6(g) + 6HCl(g)$

b. $1.60 \text{ moles C}_2\text{Cl}_6 \times \dfrac{6 \text{ moles Cl}_2}{1 \text{ mole C}_2\text{Cl}_6} = 9.60$ moles of Cl_2 (3 SFs)

c. $50.0 \text{ g C}_2\text{H}_6 \times \dfrac{1 \text{ mole C}_2\text{H}_6}{30.1 \text{ g C}_2\text{H}_6} \times \dfrac{6 \text{ moles HCl}}{1 \text{ mole C}_2\text{H}_6} \times \dfrac{36.5 \text{ g HCl}}{1 \text{ mole HCl}} = 364$ g of HCl (3 SFs)

d. $50.0 \text{ g C}_2\text{H}_6 \times \dfrac{1 \text{ mole C}_2\text{H}_6}{30.1 \text{ g C}_2\text{H}_6} \times \dfrac{1 \text{ mole C}_2\text{Cl}_6}{1 \text{ mole C}_2\text{H}_6} \times \dfrac{237 \text{ g C}_2\text{Cl}_6}{1 \text{ mole C}_2\text{Cl}_6} = 394$ g of C_2Cl_6 (3 SFs)

6.115 $2C_2H_2(g) + 5O_2(g) \xrightarrow{\Delta} 4CO_2(g) + 2H_2O(g) + \text{energy}$
theoretical yield of CO_2:

$22.5 \text{ g C}_2\text{H}_2 \times \dfrac{1 \text{ mole C}_2\text{H}_2}{26.0 \text{ g C}_2\text{H}_2} \times \dfrac{4 \text{ moles CO}_2}{2 \text{ moles C}_2\text{H}_2} \times \dfrac{44.0 \text{ g CO}_2}{1 \text{ mole CO}_2}$

$= 76.2$ g of CO_2

percent yield: $\dfrac{62.0 \text{ g CO}_2 \text{ (actual)}}{76.2 \text{ g CO}_2 \text{ (theoretical)}} \times 100\% = 81.4\% \text{ (3 SFs)}$

6.117 **a.** $4.0 \text{ moles H}_2\text{O} \times \dfrac{1 \text{ mole C}_5\text{H}_{12}}{6 \text{ moles H}_2\text{O}} \times \dfrac{72.1 \text{ g C}_5\text{H}_{12}}{1 \text{ mole C}_5\text{H}_{12}} = 48 \text{ g of C}_5\text{H}_{12} \text{ (2 SFs)}$

b. $32.0 \text{ g O}_2 \times \dfrac{1 \text{ mole O}_2}{32.0 \text{ g O}_2} \times \dfrac{5 \text{ moles CO}_2}{8 \text{ moles O}_2} \times \dfrac{44.0 \text{ g CO}_2}{1 \text{ mole CO}_2} = 27.5 \text{ g of CO}_2 \text{ (3 SFs)}$

c. $44.5 \text{ g C}_5\text{H}_{12} \times \dfrac{1 \text{ mole C}_5\text{H}_{12}}{72.1 \text{ g C}_5\text{H}_{12}} \times \dfrac{5 \text{ moles CO}_2}{1 \text{ mole C}_5\text{H}_{12}} = 3.09 \text{ moles of CO}_2$

$108 \text{ g O}_2 \times \dfrac{1 \text{ mole O}_2}{32.0 \text{ g O}_2} \times \dfrac{5 \text{ moles CO}_2}{8 \text{ moles O}_2} = 2.11 \text{ moles of CO}_2 \text{(smaller number of moles)}$

$\therefore \text{ O}_2$ is the limiting reactant.

$2.11 \text{ moles CO}_2 \times \dfrac{44.0 \text{ g CO}_2}{1 \text{ mole CO}_2} = 92.8 \text{ g of CO}_2 \text{ (3 SFs)}$

6.119 $12.8 \text{ g Na} \times \dfrac{1 \text{ mole Na}}{23.0 \text{ g Na}} \times \dfrac{2 \text{ moles NaCl}}{2 \text{ moles Na}} = 0.557 \text{ mole of NaCl}$

$10.2 \text{ g Cl}_2 \times \dfrac{1 \text{ mole Cl}_2}{71.0 \text{ g Cl}_2} \times \dfrac{2 \text{ moles NaCl}}{1 \text{ mole Cl}_2} = 0.287 \text{ mole of NaCl (smaller number of moles)}$

$\therefore \text{ Cl}_2$ is the limiting reactant.

$0.287 \text{ mole NaCl} \times \dfrac{58.5 \text{ g NaCl}}{1 \text{ mole NaCl}} = 16.8 \text{ g of NaCl (3 SFs)}$

6.121 **a.** $3.00 \text{ g NO} \times \dfrac{1 \text{ mole NO}}{30.0 \text{ g NO}} \times \dfrac{+21.6 \text{ kcal}}{2 \text{ moles NO}} = +1.08 \text{ kcal (3 SFs)}$

$\therefore 1.08$ kcal are required.

b. $2\text{NO}(g) \longrightarrow \text{N}_2(g) + \text{O}_2(g) + 21.6 \text{ kcal}$

c. $5.00 \text{ g NO} \times \dfrac{1 \text{ mole NO}}{30.0 \text{ g NO}} \times \dfrac{-21.6 \text{ kcal}}{2 \text{ moles NO}} = -1.80 \text{ kcal (3 SFs)}$

$\therefore 1.80$ kcal are released.

6.123 **a.** $3\text{Pb(NO}_3)_2(aq) + 2\text{Na}_3\text{PO}_4(aq) \longrightarrow \text{Pb}_3(\text{PO}_4)_2(s) + 6\text{NaNO}_3(aq)$ double replacement reaction

b. $4\text{Ga}(s) + 3\text{O}_2(g) \xrightarrow{\Delta} 2\text{Ga}_2\text{O}_3(s)$ combination reaction

c. $2\text{NaNO}_3(s) \xrightarrow{\Delta} 2\text{NaNO}_2(s) + \text{O}_2(g)$ decomposition reaction

d. $\text{Bi}_2\text{O}_3(s) + 3\text{C}(s) \longrightarrow 2\text{Bi}(s) + 3\text{CO}(g)$ single replacement reaction

6.125 **a.** volume of gold bar $= l \times w \times h = 2.31 \text{ cm} \times 1.48 \text{ cm} \times 0.0758 \text{ cm} = 0.259 \text{ cm}^3$

mass of gold bar $= 0.259 \text{ cm}^3 \times \dfrac{1 \text{ mL}}{1 \text{ cm}^3} \times \dfrac{19.3 \text{ g Au}}{1 \text{ mL}} = 5.00 \text{ g of gold (3 SFs)}$

b. $5.00 \text{ g Au} \times \dfrac{1 \text{ mole Au}}{197.0 \text{ g Au}} \times \dfrac{6.02 \times 10^{23} \text{ atoms Au}}{1 \text{ mole Au}} = 1.53 \times 10^{22} \text{ atoms of Au}$ (3 SFs)

c. mass of oxygen = 5.61 g of oxide − 5.00 g of Au = 0.61 g of O

$0.61 \text{ g O} \times \dfrac{1 \text{ mole O}}{16.0 \text{ g O}} = 0.038 \text{ mole of O}$ (2 SFs)

6.127 **a.** $4Al(s) + 3O_2(g) \longrightarrow 2Al_2O_3(s)$

b. This is a combination reaction.

c. $4.50 \text{ moles Al} \times \dfrac{3 \text{ moles O}_2}{4 \text{ moles Al}} = 3.38 \text{ moles of O}_2$ (3 SFs)

d. $50.2 \text{ g Al} \times \dfrac{1 \text{ mole Al}}{27.0 \text{ g Al}} \times \dfrac{2 \text{ moles Al}_2O_3}{4 \text{ moles Al}} \times \dfrac{102.0 \text{ g Al}_2O_3}{1 \text{ mole Al}_2O_3} = 94.8 \text{ g of Al}_2O_3$ (3 SFs)

e. $13.5 \text{ g Al} \times \dfrac{1 \text{ mole Al}}{27.0 \text{ g Al}} \times \dfrac{2 \text{ moles Al}_2O_3}{4 \text{ moles Al}} = 0.250 \text{ mole of Al}_2O_3$

$8.00 \text{ g O}_2 \times \dfrac{1 \text{ mole O}_2}{32.0 \text{ g O}_2} \times \dfrac{2 \text{ moles Al}_2O_3}{3 \text{ moles O}_2} = 0.167 \text{ mole of Al}_2O_3$ (smaller number of moles)

∴ O_2 is the limiting reactant.

$0.167 \text{ mole Al}_2O_3 \times \dfrac{102.0 \text{ g Al}_2O_3}{1 \text{ mole Al}_2O_3} = 17.0 \text{ g of Al}_2O_3$ (3 SFs)

f. $45.0 \text{ g Al} \times \dfrac{1 \text{ mole Al}}{27.0 \text{ g Al}} \times \dfrac{2 \text{ moles Al}_2O_3}{4 \text{ moles Al}} = 0.833 \text{ mole of Al}_2O_3$ (smaller number of moles)

$62.0 \text{ g O}_2 \times \dfrac{1 \text{ mole O}_2}{32.0 \text{ g O}_2} \times \dfrac{2 \text{ moles Al}_2O_3}{3 \text{ moles O}_2} = 1.29 \text{ moles of Al}_2O_3$

∴ Al is the limiting reactant.

theoretical yield of Al_2O_3:

$0.833 \text{ mole Al}_2O_3 \times \dfrac{102.0 \text{ g Al}_2O_3}{1 \text{ mole Al}_2O_3} = 85.0 \text{ g of Al}_2O_3$ (3 SFs)

Use the percent yield to convert theoretical to actual:

$85.0 \text{ g Al}_2O_3 \times \dfrac{70.0 \text{ g Al}_2O_3}{100 \text{ g Al}_2O_3} = 59.5 \text{ g of Al}_2O_3$ (actual) (3 SFs)

Answers to Combining Ideas from Chapters 3 to 6

CI.7 a.

Isotope	Number of Protons	Number of Neutrons	Number of Electrons
$^{27}_{14}\text{Si}$	14	13	14
$^{28}_{14}\text{Si}$	14	14	14
$^{29}_{14}\text{Si}$	14	15	14
$^{30}_{14}\text{Si}$	14	16	14
$^{31}_{14}\text{Si}$	14	17	14

b. The electron configuration of Si is $1s^2 2s^2 2p^6 3s^2 3p^2$.

c.

$^{28}_{14}\text{Si} \qquad 27.98 \times \dfrac{92.23}{100} = 25.81 \text{ amu}$

$^{29}_{14}\text{Si} \qquad 28.98 \times \dfrac{4.67}{100} = 1.35 \text{ amu}$

$^{30}_{14}\text{Si} \qquad 29.97 \times \dfrac{3.10}{100} = 0.929 \text{ amu}$

$\overline{\qquad\qquad\text{Atomic mass of Si}\quad = 28.09 \text{ amu (4 SFs)}}$

d. $^{27}_{14}\text{Si} \longrightarrow \, ^{27}_{13}\text{Al} + \, ^{0}_{+1}e$

$^{31}_{14}\text{Si} \longrightarrow \, ^{31}_{15}\text{P} + \, ^{0}_{-1}e$

e.

$$\overset{\displaystyle :\!\ddot{\text{C}}\text{l}:}{\underset{\displaystyle :\!\ddot{\text{C}}\text{l}:}{:\ddot{\text{C}}\text{l}\!-\!\text{Si}\!-\!\ddot{\text{C}}\text{l}:}}$$

With four bonding pairs and no lone pairs, the shape of $SiCl_4$ is tetrahedral.

f. Half of a radioactive sample decays with each half-life:

$16 \ \mu\text{Ci of } ^{31}_{14}\text{Si} \xrightarrow{\text{1 half-life}} 8.0 \ \mu\text{Ci of } ^{31}_{14}\text{Si} \xrightarrow{\text{2 half-lives}} 4.0 \ \mu\text{Ci of } ^{31}_{14}\text{Si} \xrightarrow{\text{3 half-lives}}$

$2.0 \ \mu\text{Ci of } ^{31}_{14}\text{Si}$

Therefore, three half-lives have passed.

$3 \ \text{half-lives} \times \dfrac{2.6 \text{ h}}{1 \ \text{half-life}} = 7.8 \text{ h (2 SFs)}$

CI.9 a. $^{226}_{88}\text{Ra} \longrightarrow \, ^{222}_{86}\text{Rn} + \, ^{4}_{2}\text{He}$

b. $^{222}_{86}\text{Rn} \longrightarrow \, ^{218}_{84}\text{Po} + \, ^{4}_{2}\text{He}$

c. First determine how many half-lives have passed:

$15.2 \ \text{days} \times \dfrac{1 \text{ half-life}}{3.8 \ \text{days}} = 4.0 \text{ half-lives}$

The number of atoms of radon-222 that remain:

$$24\ 000 \text{ atoms of } {}^{222}_{86}\text{Rn} \xrightarrow{\text{1 half-life}} 12\ 000 \text{ atoms of } {}^{222}_{86}\text{Rn} \xrightarrow{\text{2 half-lives}} 6000 \text{ atoms of } {}^{222}_{86}\text{Rn}$$

$$\xrightarrow{\text{3 half-lives}} 3000 \text{ atoms of } {}^{222}_{86}\text{Rn} \xrightarrow{\text{4 half-lives}} 1500 \text{ atoms of } {}^{222}_{86}\text{Rn}$$

d. volume of room = 72 000 L

$$72\ 000 \text{ L air} \times \frac{2.5 \text{ pCi}}{1 \text{ L air}} \times \frac{1 \text{ Ci}}{10^{12} \text{ pCi}} \times \frac{3.7 \times 10^{10} \text{ disintegrations}/s}{1 \text{ Ci}}$$

$$\times \frac{1 \text{ alpha particle}}{1 \text{ disintegration}} \times \frac{60 \text{ s}}{1 \text{ min}} \times \frac{60 \text{ min}}{1 \text{ h}} \times \frac{24 \text{ h}}{1 \text{ day}}$$

$$= 5.8 \times 10^8 \text{ alpha particles per day (2 SFs)}$$

CI.11 **a.** Y has the higher electronegativity since it is a nonmetal in Group 7A (17).

b. In the product, X and Y form the ions X^{2+} and Y^-.

c. X has an electron configuration of $1s^2 2s^2 2p^6 3s^2$.
Y has an electron configuration of $1s^2 2s^2 2p^6 3s^2 3p^5$.

d. X^{2+} has an electron configuration of $1s^2 2s^2 2p^6$.
Y^- has an electron configuration of $1s^2 2s^2 2p^6 3s^2 3p^6$.

e. $MgCl_2$, magnesium chloride

CI.13 **a.** The molecular formula of acetone is C_3H_6O.

b. molar mass of acetone $(C_3H_6O) = 3(12.0 \text{ g}) + 6(1.01 \text{ g}) + 1(16.0 \text{ g}) = 58.1 \text{ g (3 SFs)}$

c. polar covalent bonds in C_3H_6O: C—O
nonpolar covalent bonds in C_3H_6O: C—C, C—H

d. $C_3H_6O(l) + 4O_2(g) \xrightarrow{\Delta} 3CO_2(g) + 3H_2O(g) + \text{energy}$

e. $15.0 \text{ mL } C_3H_6O \times \dfrac{0.786 \text{ g } C_3H_6O}{1 \text{ mL } C_3H_6O} \times \dfrac{1 \text{ mole } C_3H_6O}{58.1 \text{ g } C_3H_6O} \times \dfrac{4 \text{ moles } O_2}{1 \text{ mole } C_3H_6O} \times \dfrac{32.0 \text{ g } O_2}{1 \text{ mole } O_2}$

$$= 26.0 \text{ g of } O_2 \text{ (3 SFs)}$$

f. $15.0 \text{ mL } C_3H_6O \times \dfrac{0.786 \text{ g } C_3H_6O}{1 \text{ mL } C_3H_6O} \times \dfrac{-28.5 \text{ kJ}}{1 \text{ g } C_3H_6O} = -336 \text{ kJ (3 SFs)}$

∴ 336 kJ of heat were given off in the reaction.

CI.15 **a.** The formula of shikimic acid is $C_7H_{10}O_5$.

b. molar mass of shikimic acid $(C_7H_{10}O_5) = 7(12.0 \text{ g}) + 10(1.01 \text{ g}) + 5(16.0 \text{ g})$
$= 174.1 \text{ g (4 SFs)}$

c. $130 \text{ g shikimic acid} \times \dfrac{1 \text{ mole shikimic acid}}{174.1 \text{ g shikimic acid}} = 0.75 \text{ mole of shikimic acid (2 SFs)}$

d. $155 \text{ g star anise} \times \dfrac{0.13 \text{ g shikimic acid}}{2.6 \text{ g star anise}} \times \dfrac{1 \text{ capsule Tamiflu}}{0.13 \text{ g shikimic acid}}$

$$= 59 \text{ capsules of Tamiflu (2 SFs)}$$

e. molar mass of Tamiflu $(C_{16}H_{28}N_2O_4) = 16(12.0 \text{ g}) + 28(1.01 \text{ g}) + 2(14.0 \text{ g}) + 4(16.0 \text{ g})$
$= 312 \text{ g (3 SFs)}$

f. $500\ 000 \text{ people} \times \dfrac{2 \text{ capsules}}{1 \text{ day 1 person}} \times 5 \text{ days} \times \dfrac{75 \text{ mg Tamiflu}}{1 \text{ capsule}} \times \dfrac{1 \text{ g Tamiflu}}{1000 \text{ mg Tamiflu}}$

$$\times \dfrac{1 \text{ kg Tamiflu}}{1000 \text{ g Tamiflu}} = 400 \text{ kg of Tamiflu (1 SF)}$$

7.1 **a.** At higher temperatures, gas particles have greater kinetic energy, which makes them move faster.

  b. Because there are great distances between the particles of a gas, they can be pushed closer together and still remain a gas.

7.3 **a.** The temperature of a gas can be expressed in kelvins.
  b. The volume of a gas can be expressed in milliliters.
  c. The amount of a gas can be expressed in grams.
  d. Pressure can be expressed in millimeters of mercury (mmHg).

7.5 Some units used to describe the pressure of a gas are atmospheres (abbreviated atm), mmHg, torr, pounds per square inch (lb/in.^{2} or psi), pascals, kilopascals, and in. Hg.

7.7 **a.** $2.00 \text{ atm} \times \dfrac{760 \text{ torr}}{1 \text{ atm}} = 1520 \text{ torr (3 SFs)}$

  b. $2.00 \text{ atm} \times \dfrac{760 \text{ mmHg}}{1 \text{ atm}} = 1520 \text{ mmHg (3 SFs)}$

7.9 As the scuba diver ascends to the surface, external pressure decreases. If the air in the lungs, which is at a higher pressure, were not exhaled, its volume would expand and severely damage the lungs. The pressure of the gas in the lungs must adjust to changes in the external pressure.

7.11 **a.** The pressure is greater in cylinder A. According to Boyle's law, a decrease in volume pushes the gas particles closer together, which will cause an increase in the pressure.

  b.

Property	Conditions 1	Conditions 2	Know	Predict
Pressure (P)	$P_1 = 650$ mmHg	$P_2 = 1.2$ atm	P increases	
Volume (V)	$V_1 = 220$ mL	$V_2 = ?$ mL		V decreases

According to Boyle's law, $P_1 V_1 = P_2 V_2$, then

$$V_2 = V_1 \times \frac{P_1}{P_2} = 220 \text{ mL} \times \frac{650 \text{ mmHg}}{1.2 \text{ atm}} \times \frac{1 \text{ atm}}{760 \text{ mmHg}} = 160 \text{ mL (2 SFs)}$$

7.13 **a.** The pressure of the gas *increases* to two times the original pressure when the volume is halved.
  b. The pressure *decreases* to one-third the original pressure when the volume expands to three times its initial value.
  c. The pressure *increases* to ten times the original pressure when the volume decreases to one-tenth of the initial volume.

7.15 From Boyle's law, we know that pressure is inversely related to volume (for example, pressure increases when volume decreases).
  a. Volume increases; pressure must decrease.

$$P_2 = P_1 \times \frac{V_1}{V_2} = 655 \text{ mmHg} \times \frac{10.0 \text{ L}}{20.0 \text{ L}} = 328 \text{ mmHg (3 SFs)}$$

b. Volume decreases; pressure must increase.

$$P_2 = P_1 \times \frac{V_1}{V_2} = 655 \text{ mmHg} \times \frac{10.0 \text{ L}}{2.50 \text{ L}} = 2620 \text{ mmHg (3 SFs)}$$

c. The mL units must be converted to L for unit cancellation in the calculation, and because the volume decreases, pressure must increase.

$$P_2 = P_1 \times \frac{V_1}{V_2} = 655 \text{ mmHg} \times \frac{10.0 \text{ L}}{1500. \text{ mL}} \times \frac{1000 \text{ mL}}{1 \text{ L}} = 4370 \text{ mmHg (3 SFs)}$$

7.17 From Boyle's law, we know that pressure is inversely related to volume.
a. Pressure increases; volume must decrease.

$$V_2 = V_1 \times \frac{P_1}{P_2} = 50.0 \text{ L} \times \frac{760. \text{ mmHg}}{1500 \text{ mmHg}} = 25 \text{ L (2 SFs)}$$

b. The mmHg units must be converted to atm for unit cancellation in the calculation, and because the pressure increases, volume must decrease.

$$P_1 = 760. \text{ mmHg} \times \frac{1 \text{ atm}}{760 \text{ mmHg}} = 1.00 \text{ atm}$$

$$V_2 = V_1 \times \frac{P_1}{P_2} = 50.0 \text{ L} \times \frac{1.00 \text{ atm}}{4.00 \text{ atm}} = 12.5 \text{ L (3 SFs)}$$

c. The mmHg units must be converted to atm for unit cancellation in the calculation, and because the pressure decreases, volume must increase.

$$P_1 = 760. \text{ mmHg} \times \frac{1 \text{ atm}}{760 \text{ mmHg}} = 1.00 \text{ atm}$$

$$V_2 = V_1 \times \frac{P_1}{P_2} = 50.0 \text{ L} \times \frac{1.00 \text{ atm}}{0.500 \text{ atm}} = 100. \text{ L (3 SFs)}$$

7.19 Pressure decreases; volume must increase.

$$V_2 = V_1 \times \frac{P_1}{P_2} = 5.0 \text{ L} \times \frac{5.0 \text{ atm}}{1.0 \text{ atm}} = 25 \text{ L (2 SFs)}$$

7.21 **a.** *Inspiration* begins when the diaphragm flattens, causing the lungs to expand. The increased volume of the thoracic cavity reduces the pressure in the lungs such that air flows into the lungs.
b. *Expiration* occurs as the diaphragm relaxes, causing a decrease in the volume of the lungs. The pressure of the air in the lungs increases, and air flows out of the lungs.
c. *Inspiration* occurs when the pressure within the lungs is less than that of the atmosphere.

7.23 According to Charles's law, there is a direct relationship between Kelvin temperature and volume (for example, volume increases when temperature increases, if the pressure and amount of gas remain constant).
a. Diagram C shows an increased volume corresponding to an increase in temperature.
b. Diagram A shows a decreased volume corresponding to a decrease in temperature.
c. Diagram B shows no change in volume, which corresponds to no net change in temperature.

7.25 According to Charles's law, the volume of a gas is directly related to the Kelvin temperature. In all gas law computations, temperatures must be in kelvins. (Temperatures in °C are converted to K by the addition of 273.) The initial temperature for all cases here is $T_1 = 15\ °C + 273 = 288$ K.

a. Volume increases; temperature must have increased.

$$T_2 = T_1 \times \frac{V_2}{V_1} = 288\ K \times \frac{5.00\ \cancel{L}}{2.50\ \cancel{L}} = 576\ K \qquad 576\ K - 273 = 303\ °C\ (3\ SFs)$$

b. Volume decreases; temperature must have decreased.

$$T_2 = T_1 \times \frac{V_2}{V_1} = 288\ K \times \frac{1250\ \cancel{mL}}{2.50\ \cancel{L}} \times \frac{1\ \cancel{L}}{1000\ \cancel{mL}} = 144\ K$$

$144\ K - 273 = -129\ °C\ (3\ SFs)$

c. Volume increases; temperature must have increased.

$$T_2 = T_1 \times \frac{V_2}{V_1} = 288\ K \times \frac{7.50\ \cancel{L}}{2.50\ \cancel{L}} = 864\ K \qquad 864\ K - 273 = 591\ °C\ (3\ SFs)$$

d. Volume increases; temperature must have increased.

$$T_2 = T_1 \times \frac{V_2}{V_1} = 288\ K \times \frac{3550\ \cancel{mL}}{2.50\ \cancel{L}} \times \frac{1\ \cancel{L}}{1000\ \cancel{mL}} = 409\ K \qquad 409\ K - 273 = 136\ °C\ (3\ SFs)$$

7.27 According to Charles's law, the volume of a gas is directly related to the Kelvin temperature. In all gas law computations, temperatures must be in kelvins. (Temperatures in °C are converted to K by the addition of 273.) The initial temperature for all cases here is $T_1 = 75\ °C + 273 = 348$ K.

a. When temperature decreases, volume must also decrease.

$T_2 = 55\ °C + 273 = 328$ K

$$V_2 = V_1 \times \frac{T_2}{T_1} = 2500\ mL \times \frac{328\ \cancel{K}}{348\ \cancel{K}} = 2400\ mL\ (2\ SFs)$$

b. When temperature increases, volume must also increase.

$$V_2 = V_1 \times \frac{T_2}{T_1} = 2500\ mL \times \frac{680.\ \cancel{K}}{348\ \cancel{K}} = 4900\ mL\ (2\ SFs)$$

c. When temperature decreases, volume must also decrease.

$T_2 = -25\ °C + 273 = 248$ K

$$V_2 = V_1 \times \frac{T_2}{T_1} = 2500\ mL \times \frac{248\ \cancel{K}}{348\ \cancel{K}} = 1800\ mL\ (2\ SFs)$$

d. When temperature decreases, volume must also decrease.

$$V_2 = V_1 \times \frac{T_2}{T_1} = 2500\ mL \times \frac{240.\ \cancel{K}}{348\ \cancel{K}} = 1700\ mL\ (2\ SFs)$$

7.29 An increase in temperature increases the pressure inside the can. When the pressure exceeds the pressure limit of the can, it explodes.

7.31 According to Gay-Lussac's law, temperature is directly related to pressure. For example, temperature increases when the pressure increases. In all gas law computations, temperatures must be in kelvins. (Temperatures in °C are converted to K by the addition of 273.)

a. Pressure decreases; temperature must have decreased.

$$T_1 = 25\ °C + 273 = 298\ K$$

$$T_2 = T_1 \times \frac{P_2}{P_1} = 298\ K \times \frac{625\ mmHg}{745\ mmHg} = 250.\ K \qquad 250.\ K - 273 = -23\ °C\ (2\ SFs)$$

b. Pressure increases; temperature must have increased.

$$T_1 = -18\ °C + 273 = 255\ K$$

$$T_2 = T_1 \times \frac{P_2}{P_1} = 255\ K \times \frac{1250\ torr}{0.950\ atm} \times \frac{1\ atm}{760\ torr} = 441\ K \qquad 441\ K - 273 = 168\ °C\ (3\ SFs)$$

7.33 According to Gay-Lussac's law, temperature is directly related to pressure. In all gas law computations, temperatures must be in kelvins. (Temperatures in °C are converted to K by the addition of 273.)

a. When temperature decreases, pressure must also decrease.

$$T_1 = 155\ °C + 273 = 428\ K \qquad T_2 = 0\ °C + 273 = 273\ K$$

$$P_2 = P_1 \times \frac{T_2}{T_1} = 1200\ torr \times \frac{273\ K}{428\ K} = 770\ torr\ (2\ SFs)$$

b. When temperature increases, pressure must also increase.

$$T_1 = 12\ °C + 273 = 285\ K \qquad T_2 = 35\ °C + 273 = 308\ K$$

$$P_2 = P_1 \times \frac{T_2}{T_1} = 1.40\ atm \times \frac{308\ K}{285\ K} = 1.51\ atm\ (3\ SFs)$$

7.35 a. The *boiling point* is the temperature at which bubbles of vapor appear within the liquid.

b. *Vapor pressure* is the pressure exerted by a gas above the surface of its liquid.

7.37 a. On the top of a mountain, water boils below 100 °C because the atmospheric (external) pressure is less than 1 atm. The boiling point is the temperature at which the vapor pressure of a liquid becomes equal to the external (in this case, atmospheric) pressure.

b. Because the pressure inside a pressure cooker is greater than 1 atm, water boils above 100 °C. The higher temperature of the boiling water allows food to cook more quickly.

7.39 $T_1 = 25\ °C + 273 = 298\ K;$ $\qquad V_1 = 6.50\ L;$ $\qquad P_1 = 845\ mmHg$

a. $T_2 = 325\ K;$ $\qquad V_2 = 1850\ mL = 1.85\ L;$ $\qquad P_2 = ?\ atm$

$$P_2 = P_1 \times \frac{V_1}{V_2} \times \frac{T_2}{T_1} = 845\ mmHg \times \frac{6.50\ L}{1.85\ L} \times \frac{325\ K}{298\ K} \times \frac{1\ atm}{760\ mmHg} = 4.26\ atm\ (3\ SFs)$$

b. $T_2 = 12\ °C + 273 = 285\ K;$ $\qquad V_2 = 2.25\ L;$ $\qquad P_2 = ?\ atm$

$$P_2 = P_1 \times \frac{V_1}{V_2} \times \frac{T_2}{T_1} = 845\ mmHg \times \frac{6.50\ L}{2.25\ L} \times \frac{285\ K}{298\ K} \times \frac{1\ atm}{760\ mmHg} = 3.07\ atm\ (3\ SFs)$$

c. $T_2 = 47\ °C + 273 = 320.\ K;$ $\qquad V_2 = 12.8\ L;$ $\qquad P_2 = ?\ atm$

$$P_2 = P_1 \times \frac{V_1}{V_2} \times \frac{T_2}{T_1} = 845\ mmHg \times \frac{6.50\ L}{12.8\ L} \times \frac{320.\ K}{298\ K} \times \frac{1\ atm}{760\ mmHg} = 0.606\ atm\ (3\ SFs)$$

7.41 $T_1 = 212 \,°C + 273 = 485 \text{ K};$ $V_1 = 124 \text{ mL};$ $P_1 = 1.80 \text{ atm}$

$T_2 = ? \,°C;$ $V_2 = 138 \text{ mL};$ $P_2 = 0.800 \text{ atm}$

$$T_2 = T_1 \times \frac{P_2}{P_1} \times \frac{V_2}{V_1} = 485 \text{ K} \times \frac{0.800 \text{ atm}}{1.80 \text{ atm}} \times \frac{138 \text{ mL}}{124 \text{ mL}} = 240. \text{ K} \qquad 240. \text{ K} - 273 = -33 \,°C \text{ (2 SFs)}$$

7.43 The volume increases because the number of gas particles in the tire or basketball is increased.

7.45 According to Avogadro's law, the volume of a gas is directly related to the number of moles of gas.

$n_1 = 1.50$ moles of Ne; $V_1 = 8.00 \text{ L}$

a. $V_2 = V_1 \times \dfrac{n_2}{n_1} = 8.00 \text{ L} \times \dfrac{\frac{1}{2}(1.50) \text{ moles Ne}}{1.50 \text{ moles Ne}} = 4.00 \text{ L (3 SFs)}$

b. $25.0 \text{ g Ne} \times \dfrac{1 \text{ mole Ne}}{20.2 \text{ g Ne}} = 1.24$ moles of Ne added

$n_2 = 1.50$ moles Ne $+ 1.24$ moles Ne $= 2.74$ moles of Ne

$V_2 = V_1 \times \dfrac{n_2}{n_1} = 8.00 \text{ L} \times \dfrac{2.74 \text{ moles Ne}}{1.50 \text{ moles Ne}} = 14.6 \text{ L (3 SFs)}$

c. $n_2 = 1.50$ moles Ne $+ 3.50$ moles $O_2 = 5.00$ moles of gases

$V_2 = V_1 \times \dfrac{n_2}{n_1} = 8.00 \text{ L} \times \dfrac{5.00 \text{ moles}}{1.50 \text{ moles}} = 26.7 \text{ L (3 SFs)}$

7.47 At STP, 1 mole of any gas occupies a volume of 22.4 L.

a. $44.8 \text{ L } O_2 \text{ (STP)} \times \dfrac{1 \text{ mole } O_2}{22.4 \text{ L } O_2 \text{ (STP)}} = 2.00$ moles of O_2 (3 SFs)

b. $4.00 \text{ L } CO_2 \text{ (STP)} \times \dfrac{1 \text{ mole } CO_2}{22.4 \text{ L } CO_2 \text{ (STP)}} = 0.179$ mole of CO_2 (3 SFs)

c. $6.40 \text{ g } O_2 \times \dfrac{1 \text{ mole } O_2}{32.0 \text{ g } O_2} \times \dfrac{22.4 \text{ L } O_2 \text{ (STP)}}{1 \text{ mole } O_2} = 4.48 \text{ L at STP (3 SFs)}$

d. $50.0 \text{ g Ne} \times \dfrac{1 \text{ mole Ne}}{20.2 \text{ g Ne}} \times \dfrac{22.4 \text{ L Ne (STP)}}{1 \text{ mole Ne}} \times \dfrac{1000 \text{ mL}}{1 \text{ L}} = 55\,400 \text{ mL at STP (3 SFs)}$

7.49 $8.25 \text{ g Mg} \times \dfrac{1 \text{ mole Mg}}{24.3 \text{ g Mg}} \times \dfrac{1 \text{ mole } H_2}{1 \text{ mole Mg}} \times \dfrac{22.4 \text{ L } H_2 \text{ (STP)}}{1 \text{ mole } H_2} = 7.60 \text{ L of } H_2 \text{ at STP (3 SFs)}$

7.51 **Analyze the Problem:**

Property	P	V	n	R	T
Given		10.0 L	2.00 moles	$\dfrac{0.0821 \text{ L} \cdot \text{atm}}{\text{mole} \cdot \text{K}}$	27 °C 27 °C + 273 = 300. K
Need	? atm				

$$P = \frac{nRT}{V} = \frac{(2.00 \text{ moles})\left(\frac{0.0821 \text{ L} \cdot \text{atm}}{\text{mole} \cdot \text{K}}\right)(300. \text{ K})}{(10.0 \text{ L})} = 4.93 \text{ atm (3 SFs)}$$

7.53   Analyze the Problem:

Property	P	V	n	R	T
Given	845 mmHg	20.0 L		$\dfrac{62.4 \text{ L} \cdot \text{mmHg}}{\text{mole} \cdot \text{K}}$	22 °C 22 °C + 273 = 295 K
Need			? moles (? g)		

$$n = \frac{PV}{RT} = \frac{(845 \text{ mmHg})(20.0 \text{ L})}{\left(\frac{62.4 \text{ L} \cdot \text{mmHg}}{\text{mole} \cdot \text{K}}\right)(295 \text{ K})} = 0.918 \text{ mole of } O_2$$

$$0.918 \text{ mole } O_2 \times \frac{32.0 \text{ g } O_2}{1 \text{ mole } O_2} = 29.4 \text{ g of } O_2 \text{ (3 SFs)}$$

7.55 $n = 25.0 \text{ g } N_2 \times \dfrac{1 \text{ mole } N_2}{28.0 \text{ g } N_2} = 0.893 \text{ mole of } N_2$

Analyze the Problem:

Property	P	V	n	R	T
Given	630. mmHg	50.0 L	25.0 g (0.893 mole)	$\dfrac{62.4 \text{ L} \cdot \text{mmHg}}{\text{mole} \cdot \text{K}}$	
Need					? K (? °C)

$$T = \frac{PV}{nR} = \frac{(630. \text{ mmHg})(50.0 \text{ L})}{(0.893 \text{ mole})\left(\frac{62.4 \text{ L} \cdot \text{mmHg}}{\text{mole} \cdot \text{K}}\right)} = 565 \text{ K} - 273 = 292 \text{ °C (3 SFs)}$$

7.57   a. $n = 450 \text{ mL (STP)} \times \dfrac{1 \text{ L}}{1000 \text{ mL}} \times \dfrac{1 \text{ mole}}{22.4 \text{ L (STP)}} = 0.020 \text{ mole}$

$$\text{molar mass} = \frac{\text{mass}}{\text{moles}} = \frac{0.84 \text{ g}}{0.020 \text{ mole}} = 42 \text{ g/mole (2 SFs)}$$

b.   Analyze the Problem:

Property	P	V	n	R	T
Given	685 mmHg	1.00 L		$\dfrac{62.4 \text{ L} \cdot \text{mmHg}}{\text{mole} \cdot \text{K}}$	22 °C 22 °C + 273 = 295 K
Need			? moles (? molar mass)		

$$n = \frac{PV}{RT} = \frac{(685 \ \text{mmHg})(1.00 \ \text{L})}{\left(\dfrac{62.4 \ \text{L} \cdot \text{mmHg}}{\text{mole} \cdot \text{K}}\right)(295 \ \text{K})} = 0.0372 \ \text{mole}$$

$$\text{molar mass} = \frac{\text{mass}}{\text{moles}} = \frac{1.48 \ \text{g}}{0.0372 \ \text{mole}} = 39.8 \ \text{g/mole (3 SFs)}$$

c. Analyze the Problem:

Property	P	V	n	R	T
Given	0.95 atm	2.30 L		$\dfrac{0.0821 \ \text{L} \cdot \text{atm}}{\text{mole} \cdot \text{K}}$	24 °C 24 °C + 273 = 297 K
Need			? moles (? molar mass)		

$$n = \frac{PV}{RT} = \frac{(0.95 \ \text{atm})(2.30 \ \text{L})}{\left(\dfrac{0.0821 \ \text{L} \cdot \text{atm}}{\text{mole} \cdot \text{K}}\right)(297 \ \text{K})} = 0.090 \ \text{mole}$$

$$\text{molar mass} = \frac{\text{mass}}{\text{moles}} = \frac{2.96 \ \text{g}}{0.090 \ \text{mole}} = 33 \ \text{g/mole (2 SFs)}$$

7.59 **Analyze the Problem: Reactant and Reactant**

	Given	Need
Mass	55.2 g of C_4H_{10}	
Molar mass	1 mole of C_4H_{10} = 58.1 g of C_4H_{10}	
Moles		? moles of O_2
Equation	$2C_4H_{10}(g) + 13O_2(g) \xrightarrow{\Delta} 8CO_2(g) + 10H_2O(g)$	

$$55.2 \ \text{g} \ C_4H_{10} \times \frac{1 \ \text{mole} \ C_4H_{10}}{58.1 \ \text{g} \ C_4H_{10}} \times \frac{13 \ \text{moles} \ O_2}{2 \ \text{moles} \ C_4H_{10}} = 6.18 \ \text{moles of} \ O_2$$

Analyze the Problem: Using the Ideal Gas Law to Calculate Volume

Property	P	V	n	R	T
Given	0.850 atm		6.18 moles O_2	$\dfrac{0.0821 \ \text{L} \cdot \text{atm}}{\text{mole} \cdot \text{K}}$	25 °C 25 °C + 273 = 298 K
Need		? L			

$$V = \frac{nRT}{P} = \frac{(6.18 \ \text{mole})\left(\dfrac{0.0821 \ \text{L} \cdot \text{atm}}{\text{mole} \cdot \text{K}}\right)(298 \ \text{K})}{(0.850 \ \text{atm})} = 178 \ \text{L of} \ O_2 \ (3 \ \text{SFs})$$

7.61 **Analyze the Problem: Reactant and Product**

	Reactant	Product
Mass	50.0 g of KNO_3	
Molar mass	1 mole of $KNO_3 = 101.1$ g of KNO_3	
Moles		? moles of O_2
Equation	$2KNO_3(s) \xrightarrow{\Delta} 2KNO_2(s) + O_2(g)$	

$$50.0 \text{ g } KNO_3 \times \frac{1 \text{ mole } KNO_3}{101.1 \text{ g } KNO_3} \times \frac{1 \text{ mole } O_2}{2 \text{ moles } KNO_3} = 0.247 \text{ mole of } O_2$$

Analyze the Problem: Using the Ideal Gas Law to Calculate Volume

Property	*P*	*V*	*n*	*R*	*T*
Given	1.19 atm		0.247 mole O_2	$\dfrac{0.0821 \text{ L} \cdot \text{atm}}{\text{mole} \cdot \text{K}}$	35 °C 35 °C + 273 = 308 K
Need		? L			

$$V = \frac{nRT}{P} = \frac{(0.247 \text{ mole})\left(\dfrac{0.0821 \text{ L} \cdot \text{atm}}{\text{mole} \cdot \text{K}}\right)(308 \text{ K})}{(1.19 \text{ atm})} = 5.25 \text{ L of } O_2 \text{ (3 SFs)}$$

7.63 To obtain the total pressure of a gas mixture, add up all of the partial pressures using the same pressure unit.

$$P_{\text{total}} = P_{\text{Oxygen}} + P_{\text{Nitrogen}} + P_{\text{Carbon dioxide}} + P_{\text{Water vapor}}$$
$$= 98 \text{ mmHg} + 573 \text{ mmHg} + 40. \text{ mmHg} + 47 \text{ mmHg}$$
$$= 758 \text{ mmHg (3 SFs)}$$

7.65 To obtain the total pressure of a gas mixture, add up all of the partial pressures using the same pressure unit.

$$P_{\text{total}} = P_{\text{Nitrogen}} + P_{\text{Oxygen}} + P_{\text{Helium}} = 425 \text{ torr} + 115 \text{ torr} + 225 \text{ torr} = 765 \text{ torr (3 SFs)}$$

7.67 Because the total pressure of a gas mixture is the sum of the partial pressures using the same pressure unit, addition and subtraction are used to obtain the "missing" partial pressure.

$$P_{\text{Nitrogen}} = P_{\text{total}} - (P_{\text{Oxygen}} + P_{\text{Helium}}) = 925 \text{ torr} - (425 \text{ torr} + 75 \text{ torr}) = 425 \text{ torr}$$

$$425 \text{ torr} \times \frac{1 \text{ atm}}{760 \text{ torr}} = 0.559 \text{ atm (3 SFs)}$$

7.69 a. If oxygen cannot readily cross from the lungs into the bloodstream, then the partial pressure of oxygen will be lower in the blood of an emphysema patient.
   b. Breathing a higher concentration of oxygen will help to increase the supply of oxygen in the lungs and blood and raise the partial pressure of oxygen in the blood.

7.71 a. 2; the fewest number of gas particles will exert the lowest pressure.
   b. 1; the greatest number of gas particles will exert the highest pressure.

7.73   **a.** A; volume decreases when temperature decreases (at constant P and n).
     b. C; volume increases when pressure decreases (at constant n and T).
     c. A; volume decreases when the number of moles of gas decreases (at constant T and P).
     d. B; doubling the Kelvin temperature would double the volume, but when half of the gas escapes, the volume would decrease by half. These two opposing effects cancel each other, and there is no overall change in the volume (at constant P).
     e. C; increasing the moles of gas causes an increase in the volume to keep T and P constant.

7.75   **a.** The volume of the chest and lungs will decrease when compressed during the Heimlich maneuver.
     b. A decrease in volume causes the pressure to increase. A piece of food would be dislodged with a sufficiently high pressure.

7.77 $T_1 = -8\ °C + 273 = 265\ \text{K};$ $P_1 = 658\ \text{mmHg};$ $V_1 = 31\ 000\ \text{L}$

$T_2 = 0\ °C + 273 = 273\ \text{K};$ $P_2 = 760\ \text{mmHg};$ $V_2 = ?\ \text{L}$

$$V_2 = V_1 \times \frac{P_1}{P_2} \times \frac{T_2}{T_1} = 31\ 000\ \text{L} \times \frac{658\ \text{mmHg}}{760\ \text{mmHg}} \times \frac{273\ \text{K}}{265\ \text{K}} = 28\ 000\ \text{L at STP}$$

$$28\ 000\ \text{L H}_2\ \text{(STP)} \times \frac{1\ \text{mole H}_2}{22.4\ \text{L H}_2\ \text{(STP)}} \times \frac{2.02\ \text{g H}_2}{1\ \text{mole H}_2} \times \frac{1\ \text{kg H}_2}{1000\ \text{g H}_2} = 2.5\ \text{kg of H}_2\ \text{(2 SFs)}$$

7.79 $T_1 = 25\ °C + 273 = 298\ \text{K};$ $T_2 = 75\ °C + 273 = 348\ \text{K}$

$P_1 = 10.\ \text{atm};$ $P_2 = ?\ \text{atm}$

$$P_2 = P_1 \times \frac{T_2}{T_1} = 10.\ \text{atm} \times \frac{348\ \text{K}}{298\ \text{K}} = 12\ \text{atm (2 SFs)}$$

7.81 $T_1 = 127\ °C + 273 = 400.\ \text{K};$ $P_1 = 2.00\ \text{atm}$

$T_2 = ?\ °C;$ $P_2 = 0.25\ \text{atm}$

$$T_2 = T_1 \times \frac{P_2}{P_1} = 400.\ \text{K} \times \frac{0.25\ \text{atm}}{2.00\ \text{atm}} = 50.\ \text{K} \qquad 50.\ \text{K} - 273 = -223\ °C$$

7.83   **Analyze the Problem:**

Property	P	V	n	R	T
Given	1.2 atm	35.0 L		$\dfrac{0.0821\ \text{L}\cdot\text{atm}}{\text{mole}\cdot\text{K}}$	5 °C $5\ °C + 273 = 278\ \text{K}$
Need			? moles		

$$n = \frac{PV}{RT} = \frac{(1.2\ \text{atm})(35.0\ \text{L})}{\left(\dfrac{0.0821\ \text{L}\cdot\text{atm}}{\text{mole}\cdot\text{K}}\right)(278\ \text{K})} = 1.8\ \text{moles of CO}_2\ \text{(2 SFs)}$$

7.85   **Analyze the Problem:**

Property	P	V	n	R	T
Given	2500. mmHg	2.00 L		$\dfrac{62.4\ \text{L}\cdot\text{mmHg}}{\text{mole}\cdot\text{K}}$	18 °C $18\ °C + 273 = 291\ \text{K}$
Need			? moles		

$$n = \frac{PV}{RT} = \frac{(2500.\ \text{mmHg})(2.00\ \text{L})}{\left(\dfrac{62.4\ \text{L} \cdot \text{mmHg}}{\text{mole} \cdot \text{K}}\right)(291\ \text{K})} = 0.275\ \text{mole of CH}_4$$

$$0.275\ \text{mole CH}_4 \times \frac{16.0\ \text{g CH}_4}{1\ \text{mole CH}_4} = 4.40\ \text{g of CH}_4\ (3\ \text{SFs})$$

7.87   Analyze the Problem: Reactant and Product

	Reactant	Product
Mass	56.0 g of $CaCO_3$	
Molar mass	1 mole of $CaCO_3$ = 100.1 g of $CaCO_3$	
Moles		? moles of CO_2 (? L of CO_2)
Molar volume		1 mole of CO_2 = 22.4 L of CO_2 (STP)
Equation	$CaCO_3(s) \xrightarrow{\Delta} CaO(s) + CO_2(g)$	

$$56.0\ \text{g CaCO}_3 \times \frac{1\ \text{mole CaCO}_3}{100.1\ \text{g CaCO}_3} \times \frac{1\ \text{mole CO}_2}{1\ \text{mole CaCO}_3} \times \frac{22.4\ \text{L CO}_2\ (\text{STP})}{1\ \text{mole CO}_2}$$

$$= 12.5\ \text{L of CO}_2\ \text{at STP}\ (3\ \text{SFs})$$

7.89   Analyze the Problem: Reactant and Product

	Reactant	Product
Volume		150 L of NH_3
Molar volume		1 mole of NH_3 = 22.4 L of NH_3 (STP)
Molar mass	1 mole of N_2 = 28.0 g of N_2	
Mass	? g of N_2	
Equation	$3H_2(g) + N_2(g) \longrightarrow 2NH_3(g)$	

$$150\ \text{L NH}_3(\text{STP}) \times \frac{1\ \text{mole NH}_3}{22.4\ \text{L NH}_3(\text{STP})} \times \frac{1\ \text{mole N}_2}{2\ \text{moles NH}_3} \times \frac{28.0\ \text{g N}_2}{1\ \text{mole N}_2} = 94\ \text{g of N}_2\ (2\ \text{SFs})$$

7.91   Analyze the Problem: Reactant and Reactant

	Reactant 1	Reactant 2
Mass	5.4 g of Al	
Molar mass	1 mole of Al = 27.0 g of Al	
Moles		? moles of O_2 (? L of O_2)
Molar volume		1 mole of O_2 = 22.4 L of O_2 (STP)
Equation	$4Al(s) + 3O_2(g) \xrightarrow{\Delta} 2Al_2O_3(s)$	

$$5.4 \text{ g Al} \times \frac{1 \text{ mole Al}}{27.0 \text{ g Al}} \times \frac{3 \text{ moles O}_2}{4 \text{ moles Al}} \times \frac{22.4 \text{ L O}_2 \text{(STP)}}{1 \text{ mole O}_2} = 3.4 \text{ L of O}_2 \text{ at STP (2 SFs)}$$

7.93 $\quad V = 941 \text{ mL} \times \dfrac{1 \text{ L}}{1000 \text{ mL}} = 0.941 \text{ L}; \quad P = 748 \text{ torr} \times \dfrac{1 \text{ mmHg}}{1 \text{ torr}} = 748 \text{ mmHg}$

Analyze the Problem:

Property	*P*	*V*	*n*	*R*	*T*
Given	748 torr (748 mmHg)	941 mL (0.941 L)		$\dfrac{62.4 \text{ L} \cdot \text{mmHg}}{\text{mole} \cdot \text{K}}$	20 °C 20 °C + 273 = 293 K
Need			? moles (? molar mass)		

$$n = \frac{PV}{RT} = \frac{(748 \text{ mmHg})(0.941 \text{ L})}{\left(\dfrac{62.4 \text{ L} \cdot \text{mmHg}}{\text{mole} \cdot \text{K}}\right)(293 \text{ K})} = 0.0385 \text{ mole}$$

$$\text{molar mass} = \frac{\text{mass}}{\text{moles}} = \frac{1.62 \text{ g}}{0.0385 \text{ mole}} = 42.1 \text{ g/mole (3 SFs)}$$

7.95 **Analyze the Problem: Reactant and Product**

	Reactant	Product
Moles	0.42 mole of NO_2	? moles of O_2 (? L of O_2)
Molar volume		1 mole of O_2 = 22.4 L of O_2 (STP)
Equation	$4NO_2(g) + 6H_2O(g) \xrightarrow{\Delta} 7O_2(g) + 4NH_3(g)$	

$$0.42 \text{ mole NO}_2 \times \frac{7 \text{ moles O}_2}{4 \text{ moles NO}_2} \times \frac{22.4 \text{ L O}_2 \text{(STP)}}{1 \text{ mole O}_2} = 16 \text{ L of O}_2 \text{ at STP (2 SFs)}$$

7.97 At STP, 1 mole of any gas occupies a volume of 22.4 L.

$$25.0 \text{ L He (STP)} \times \frac{1 \text{ mole He}}{22.4 \text{ L He (STP)}} \times \frac{4.00 \text{ g He}}{1 \text{ mole He}} = 4.46 \text{ g of He (3 SFs)}$$

7.99 Because the partial pressure of nitrogen is to be reported in torr, the atm and mmHg units (for oxygen and argon, respectively) must be converted to torr, as follows:

$$P_{\text{Oxygen}} = 0.60 \text{ atm} \times \frac{760 \text{ torr}}{1 \text{ atm}} = 460 \text{ torr} \quad \text{and} \quad P_{\text{Argon}} = 425 \text{ mmHg} \times \frac{1 \text{ torr}}{1 \text{ mmHg}} = 425 \text{ torr}$$

$$\therefore P_{\text{Nitrogen}} = P_{\text{total}} - (P_{\text{Oxygen}} + P_{\text{Argon}})$$
$$= 1250 \text{ torr} - (460 \text{ torr} + 425 \text{ torr}) = 370 \text{ torr (2 SFs)}$$

7.101 $T_1 = 15\ °C + 273 = 288\ K;$ $\qquad P_1 = 745\ mmHg;$ $\qquad V_1 = 4250\ mL$

$$T_2 = ?\ °C; \qquad P_2 = 1.20\ atm \times \frac{760\ mmHg}{1\ atm} = 912\ mmHg; \qquad V_2 = 2.50\ L \times \frac{1000\ mL}{1\ L} = 2.50 \times 10^3\ mL$$

$$T_2 = T_1 \times \frac{V_2}{V_1} \times \frac{P_2}{P_1} = 288\ K \times \frac{2.50 \times 10^3\ mL}{4250\ mL} \times \frac{912\ mmHg}{745\ mmHg} = 207\ K - 273 = -66\ °C\ (2\ SFs)$$

7.103 **Analyze the Problem: Reactant and Product**

	Reactant	Product
Mass	132 g of NaN_3	
Molar mass	1 mole of NaN_3 = 65.0 g of NaN_3	
Moles		? moles of N_2 (? L of N_2)
Molar volume		1 mole of N_2 = 22.4 L of N_2 (STP)
Equation	$2NaN_3(s) \longrightarrow 2Na(s) + 3N_2(g)$	

$$132\ g\ NaN_3 \times \frac{1\ mole\ NaN_3}{65.0\ g\ NaN_3} \times \frac{3\ moles\ N_2}{2\ moles\ NaN_3} \times \frac{22.4\ L\ N_2\ (STP)}{1\ mole\ N_2} = 68.2\ L\ of\ N_2\ at\ STP\ (3\ SFs)$$

7.105 $n = 1.00\ g\ CO_2 \times \dfrac{1\ mole\ CO_2}{44.0\ g\ CO_2} = 0.0227\ mole\ of\ CO_2$

Analyze the Problem:

Property	P	V	n	R	T
Given		4.60 L	1.00 g (0.0227 mole)	$\dfrac{62.4\ L \cdot mmHg}{mole \cdot K}$	24 °C, 24 °C + 273 = 297 K
Need	? mmHg				

$$P = \frac{nRT}{V} = \frac{(0.0227\ mole)\left(\dfrac{62.4\ L \cdot mmHg}{mole \cdot K}\right)(297\ K)}{(4.60\ L)} = 91.5\ mmHg\ (3\ SFs)$$

7.107 **Analyze the Problem: Reactant and Product**

	Reactant	Product
Mass	12.0 g of Mg	
Molar mass	1 mole of Mg = 24.3 g of Mg	
Moles		? moles of H_2
Equation	$Mg(s) + 2HCl(aq) \longrightarrow MgCl_2(aq) + H_2(g)$	

$$12.0\ g\ Mg \times \frac{1\ mole\ Mg}{24.3\ g\ Mg} \times \frac{1\ mole\ H_2}{1\ mole\ Mg} = 0.494\ mole\ of\ H_2$$

Analyze the Problem: Using the Ideal Gas Law to Calculate Volume

Property	P	V	n	R	T
Given	835 mmHg		0.494 mole H_2	$\dfrac{62.4\ L\cdot mmHg}{mole\cdot K}$	24 °C 24 °C + 273 = 297 K
Need		? L			

$$V=\frac{nRT}{P}=\frac{(0.494\ \text{mole})\left(\dfrac{62.4\ L\cdot mmHg}{mole\cdot K}\right)(297\ K)}{(835\ mmHg)}=11.0\ \text{L of }H_2\ (3\ SFs)$$

7.109 $\quad V=415\ mL\times\dfrac{1\ L}{1000\ mL}=0.415\ L$

Analyze the Problem:

Property	P	V	n	R	T
Given	734 mmHg	415 mL (0.415 L)		$\dfrac{62.4\ L\cdot mmHg}{mole\cdot K}$	23 °C 23 °C + 273 = 296 K
Need			? moles		

$$n=\frac{PV}{RT}=\frac{(734\ mmHg)(0.415\ L)}{\left(\dfrac{62.4\ L\cdot mmHg}{mole\cdot K}\right)(296\ K)}=0.0165\ \text{mole of }H_2$$

Analyze the Problem: Reactant and Product

	Reactant	Product
Mass	? grams of Al	
Molar mass	1 mole of Al = 27.0 g of Al	
Moles		0.0165 mole of H_2
Equation	$2Al(s)+3H_2SO_4(aq)\longrightarrow 3H_2(g)+Al_2(SO_4)_3(aq)$	

$$0.0165\ \text{mole }H_2\times\frac{2\ \text{moles Al}}{3\ \text{moles }H_2}\times\frac{27.0\ \text{g Al}}{1\ \text{mole Al}}=0.297\ \text{g of Al (3 SFs)}$$

Solutions

8 *(chapter number in top margin)*

8.1 The component present in the smaller amount is the solute; the component present in the larger amount is the solvent.
  a. NaCl, solute; water, solvent
  b. water, solute; ethanol, solvent
  c. oxygen, solute; nitrogen, solvent

8.3 The K^+ and I^- ions at the surface of the solid are pulled into solution by the polar water molecules, where the hydration process surrounds separate ions with water molecules.

8.5 **a.** $NaNO_3$ (an ionic solute) would be soluble in water (a polar solvent).
  b. I_2 (a nonpolar solute) would be soluble in CCl_4 (a nonpolar solvent).
  c. Sucrose (a polar solute) would be soluble in water (a polar solvent).
  d. Gasoline (a nonpolar solute) would be soluble in CCl_4 (a nonpolar solvent).

8.7 The strong electrolyte KF completely dissociates into K^+ and F^- ions when it dissolves in water. When the weak electrolyte HF dissolves in water, there are a few ions of H^+ and F^- present, but mostly dissolved HF molecules.

8.9 Strong electrolytes dissociate completely into ions.
  a. $KCl(s) \xrightarrow{H_2O} K^+(aq) + Cl^-(aq)$
  b. $CaCl_2(s) \xrightarrow{H_2O} Ca^{2+}(aq) + 2Cl^-(aq)$
  c. $K_3PO_4(s) \xrightarrow{H_2O} 3K^+(aq) + PO_4^{3-}(aq)$
  d. $Fe(NO_3)_3(s) \xrightarrow{H_2O} Fe^{3+}(aq) + 3NO_3^-(aq)$

8.11 **a.** $HC_2H_3O_2(l) \underset{H_2O}{\rightleftharpoons} H^+(aq) + C_2H_3O_2^-(aq)$ mostly molecules and a few ions
    An aqueous solution of a weak electrolyte like acetic acid will contain mostly $HC_2H_3O_2$ molecules, with a few H^+ ions and a few $C_2H_3O_2^-$ ions.
  b. $NaBr(s) \xrightarrow{H_2O} Na^+(aq) + Br^-(aq)$ ions only
    An aqueous solution of a strong electrolyte like NaBr will contain only the ions Na^+ and Br^-.
  c. $C_6H_{12}O_6(s) \xrightarrow{H_2O} C_6H_{12}O_6(aq)$ molecules only
    An aqueous solution of a nonelectrolyte like fructose will contain only $C_6H_{12}O_6$ molecules.

8.13 **a.** K_2SO_4 is a strong electrolyte because only ions are present in the K_2SO_4 solution.
  b. NH_4OH is a weak electrolyte because only a few NH_4^+ and OH^- ions are present in the solution.
  c. $C_6H_{12}O_6$ is a nonelectrolyte because only $C_6H_{12}O_6$ molecules are present in the solution.

8.15 **a.** $1 \text{ mole } K^+ \times \dfrac{1 \text{ Eq } K^+}{1 \text{ mole } K^+} = 1 \text{ Eq of } K^+$

  b. $2 \text{ moles } OH^- \times \dfrac{1 \text{ Eq } OH^-}{1 \text{ mole } OH^-} = 2 \text{ Eq of } OH^-$

c. $1 \text{ mole Ca}^{2+} \times \dfrac{2 \text{ Eq Ca}^{2+}}{1 \text{ mole Ca}^{2+}} = 2 \text{ Eq of Ca}^{2+}$

d. $3 \text{ moles CO}_3^{2-} \times \dfrac{2 \text{ Eq CO}_3^{2-}}{1 \text{ mole CO}_3^{2-}} = 6 \text{ Eq of CO}_3^{2-}$

8.17 $\quad 1.00 \text{ L} \times \dfrac{154 \text{ mEq}}{1 \text{ L}} \times \dfrac{1 \text{ Eq}}{1000 \text{ mEq}} \times \dfrac{1 \text{ mole Na}^+}{1 \text{ Eq}} = 0.154 \text{ mole of Na}^+ \text{ (3 SFs)}$

$\quad\quad 1.00 \text{ L} \times \dfrac{154 \text{ mEq}}{1 \text{ L}} \times \dfrac{1 \text{ Eq}}{1000 \text{ mEq}} \times \dfrac{1 \text{ mole Cl}^-}{1 \text{ Eq}} = 0.154 \text{ mole of Cl}^- \text{ (3 SFs)}$

8.19 In any solution, the total equivalents of anions must be equal to the equivalents of cations.
mEq of anions = 40. mEq/L Cl^- + 15 mEq/L HPO_4^{2-} = 55 mEq/L of anions
mEq of Na^+ = mEq of anions = 55 mEq/L of Na^+

8.21 a. The solution must be saturated because no additional solute dissolves.
b. The solution was unsaturated because the sugar cube dissolves completely.

8.23 a. At 20 °C, KCl has a solubility of 34 g of KCl in 100 g of H_2O. Because 25 g of KCl is less than the maximum amount that can dissolve in 100 g of H_2O at 20 °C, the KCl solution is unsaturated.

b. At 20 °C, NaNO_3 has a solubility of 88 g of NaNO_3 in 100 g of H_2O. Using the solubility as a conversion factor, we can calculate the maximum amount of NaNO_3 that can dissolve in 25 g of H_2O:

$$25 \text{ g H}_2\text{O} \times \dfrac{88 \text{ g NaNO}_3}{100 \text{ g H}_2\text{O}} = 22 \text{ g of NaNO}_3 \text{ (2 SFs)}$$

Because 11 g of NaNO_3 is less than the maximum amount that can dissolve in 25 g of H_2O at 20 °C, the NaNO_3 solution is unsaturated.

c. At 20 °C, sugar has a solubility of 204 g of $\text{C}_{12}\text{H}_{22}\text{O}_{11}$ in 100 g of H_2O. Using the solubility as a conversion factor, we can calculate the maximum amount of sugar that can dissolve in 125 g of H_2O:

$$125 \text{ g H}_2\text{O} \times \dfrac{204 \text{ g sugar}}{100 \text{ g H}_2\text{O}} = 255 \text{ g of sugar (3 SFs)}$$

Because 400. g of $\text{C}_{12}\text{H}_{22}\text{O}_{11}$ exceeds the maximum amount that can dissolve in 125 g of H_2O at 20 °C, the sugar solution is saturated, and excess undissolved sugar will be present on the bottom of the container.

8.25 a. At 20 °C, KCl has a solubility of 34 g of KCl in 100 g of H_2O.

∴ 200. g of H_2O will dissolve:

$$200. \text{ g H}_2\text{O} \times \dfrac{34 \text{ g KCl}}{100 \text{ g H}_2\text{O}} = 68 \text{ g of KCl (2 SFs)}$$

At 20 °C, 68 g of KCl will remain in solution.

b. Since 80. g of KCl dissolves at 50 °C and 68 g remains in solution at 20 °C, the mass of solid KCl that crystallizes after cooling is (80. g KCl − 68 g KCl) = 12 g of KCl. (2 SFs)

8.27 **a.** In general, the solubility of solid solutes (like sugar) increases as temperature is increased.

  b. The solubility of a gaseous solute (CO_2) is less at a higher temperature.

  c. The solubility of a gaseous solute is less at a higher temperature, and the CO_2 pressure in the can is increased. When the can of warm soda is opened, more CO_2 is released, producing more spray.

8.29 **a.** Salts containing Li^+ ions are soluble.

  b. The Cl^- salt containing Ag^+ is insoluble.

  c. Salts containing CO_3^{2-} ions are usually insoluble.

  d. Salts containing K^+ ions are soluble.

  e. Salts containing NO_3^- ions are soluble.

8.31 **a.** No solid forms; salts containing K^+ and Na^+ are soluble.

  b. Solid silver sulfide (Ag_2S) forms:

$$2AgNO_3(aq) + K_2S(aq) \longrightarrow Ag_2S(s) + 2KNO_3(aq)$$

$$2Ag^+(aq) + \cancel{2NO_3^-(aq)} + \cancel{2K^+(aq)} + S^{2-}(aq) \longrightarrow Ag_2S(s) + \cancel{2K^+(aq)} + \cancel{2NO_3^-(aq)}$$

$$2Ag^+(aq) + S^{2-}(aq) \longrightarrow Ag_2S(s) \quad \text{Net ionic equation}$$

  c. Solid calcium sulfate ($CaSO_4$) forms:

$$CaCl_2(aq) + Na_2SO_4(aq) \longrightarrow CaSO_4(s) + 2NaCl(aq)$$

$$Ca^{2+}(aq) + \cancel{2Cl^-(aq)} + \cancel{2Na^+(aq)} + SO_4^{2-}(aq) \longrightarrow CaSO_4(s) + \cancel{2Na^+(aq)} + \cancel{2Cl^-(aq)}$$

$$Ca^{2+}(aq) + SO_4^{2-}(aq) \longrightarrow CaSO_4(s) \quad \text{Net ionic equation}$$

  d. Solid copper phosphate ($Cu_3(PO_4)_2$) forms:

$$3CuCl_2(aq) + 2Li_3PO_4(aq) \longrightarrow Cu_3(PO_4)_2(s) + 6LiCl(aq)$$

$$3Cu^{2+}(aq) + \cancel{6Cl^-(aq)} + \cancel{6Li^+(aq)} + 2PO_4^{2-}(aq) \longrightarrow Cu_3(PO_4)_2(s) + \cancel{6Li^+(aq)} + \cancel{6Cl^-(aq)}$$

$$3Cu^{2+}(aq) + 2PO_4^{2-}(aq) \longrightarrow Cu_3(PO_4)_2(s) \quad \text{Net ionic equation}$$

8.33 $\text{mass percent (m/m)} = \dfrac{\text{mass of solute (g)}}{\text{mass of solution (g)}} \times 100\%$

  a. mass of solution = 25 g of KCl + 125 g of H_2O = 150. g of solution

$$\dfrac{25 \text{ g KCl}}{150. \text{ g solution}} \times 100\% = 17\% \text{ (m/m) KCl solution (2 SFs)}$$

  b. $\dfrac{12 \text{ g sugar}}{225 \text{ g solution}} \times 100\% = 5.3\% \text{ (m/m) sugar solution (2 SFs)}$

  c. $\dfrac{8.0 \text{ g CaCl}_2}{80.0 \text{ g solution}} \times 100\% = 10.\% \text{ (m/m) CaCl}_2 \text{ solution (2 SFs)}$

8.35 $\text{mass/volume percent (m/v)} = \dfrac{\text{mass of solute (g)}}{\text{volume of solution (mL)}} \times 100\%$

  a. $\dfrac{75 \text{ g Na}_2\text{SO}_4}{250 \text{ mL solution}} \times 100\% = 30.\% \text{ (m/v) Na}_2\text{SO}_4 \text{ solution (2 SFs)}$

  b. $\dfrac{39 \text{ g sucrose}}{355 \text{ mL solution}} \times 100\% = 11\% \text{ (m/v) sucrose solution (2 SFs)}$

8.37 $\text{molarity (M)} = \dfrac{\text{moles of solute}}{\text{liters of solution}}$

    a. $\dfrac{2.00 \text{ moles glucose}}{4.00 \text{ L solution}} = 0.500 \text{ M glucose solution (3 SFs)}$

    b. $\dfrac{4.00 \text{ g KOH}}{2.00 \text{ L solution}} \times \dfrac{1 \text{ mole KOH}}{56.1 \text{ g KOH}} = 0.0357 \text{ M KOH solution (3 SFs)}$

    c. $\dfrac{5.85 \text{ g NaCl}}{400. \text{ mL solution}} \times \dfrac{1 \text{ mole NaCl}}{58.5 \text{ g NaCl}} \times \dfrac{1000 \text{ mL solution}}{1 \text{ L solution}} = 0.250 \text{ M NaCl solution (3 SFs)}$

8.39   **a.** $50.0 \text{ mL solution} \times \dfrac{5.0 \text{ g KCl}}{100 \text{ mL solution}} = 2.5 \text{ g of KCl (2 SFs)}$

    b. $1250 \text{ mL solution} \times \dfrac{4.0 \text{ g NH}_4\text{Cl}}{100 \text{ mL solution}} = 50. \text{ g of NH}_4\text{Cl (2 SFs)}$

    c. $250. \text{ mL solution} \times \dfrac{10.0 \text{ mL acetic acid}}{100 \text{ mL solution}} = 25.0 \text{ mL of acetic acid (3 SFs)}$

8.41 $355 \text{ mL solution} \times \dfrac{22.5 \text{ mL alcohol}}{100 \text{ mL solution}} = 79.9 \text{ mL of alcohol (3 SFs)}$

8.43   **a.** $1 \text{ L} \times \dfrac{100. \text{ mL solution}}{1 \text{ L}} \times \dfrac{20. \text{ g mannitol}}{100. \text{ mL solution}} = 20. \text{ g of mannitol (2 SFs)}$

    b. $12 \text{ L} \times \dfrac{100. \text{ mL solution}}{1 \text{ L}} \times \dfrac{20. \text{ g mannitol}}{100. \text{ mL solution}} = 240 \text{ g of mannitol (2 SFs)}$

8.45 $100. \text{ g glucose} \times \dfrac{100 \text{ mL solution}}{5 \text{ g glucose}} \times \dfrac{1 \text{ L}}{1000 \text{ mL}} = 2 \text{ L of glucose solution (1 SF)}$

8.47   **a.** $5.0 \text{ g LiNO}_3 \times \dfrac{100 \text{ g solution}}{25 \text{ g LiNO}_3} = 20. \text{ g of LiNO}_3 \text{ solution (2 SFs)}$

    b. $40.0 \text{ g KOH} \times \dfrac{100 \text{ mL solution}}{10.0 \text{ g KOH}} = 400. \text{ mL of KOH solution (3 SFs)}$

    c. $2.0 \text{ mL formic acid} \times \dfrac{100 \text{ mL solution}}{10.0 \text{ mL formic acid}} = 20. \text{ mL of formic acid solution (2 SFs)}$

8.49   **a.** $1.00 \text{ L solution} \times \dfrac{3.00 \text{ moles NaCl}}{1 \text{ L solution}} = 3.00 \text{ moles of NaCl (3 SFs)}$

    b. $0.400 \text{ L solution} \times \dfrac{1.00 \text{ mole KBr}}{1 \text{ L solution}} = 0.400 \text{ mole of KBr (3 SFs)}$

    c. $125 \text{ mL solution} \times \dfrac{1 \text{ L solution}}{1000 \text{ mL solution}} \times \dfrac{2.00 \text{ moles MgCl}_2}{1 \text{ L solution}} = 0.250 \text{ mole of MgCl}_2 \text{ (3 SFs)}$

8.51 **a.** $2.00 \text{ L solution} \times \dfrac{1.50 \text{ moles NaOH}}{1 \text{ L solution}} \times \dfrac{40.0 \text{ g NaOH}}{1 \text{ mole NaOH}} = 120. \text{ g of NaOH (3 SFs)}$

b. $4.00 \text{ L solution} \times \dfrac{0.200 \text{ mole KCl}}{1 \text{ L solution}} \times \dfrac{74.6 \text{ g KCl}}{1 \text{ mole KCl}} = 59.7 \text{ g of KCl (3 SFs)}$

c. $25.0 \text{ mL solution} \times \dfrac{1 \text{ L solution}}{1000 \text{ mL solution}} \times \dfrac{6.00 \text{ moles HCl}}{1 \text{ L solution}} \times \dfrac{36.5 \text{ g HCl}}{1 \text{ mole HCl}}$

$= 5.48 \text{ g of HCl (3 SFs)}$

8.53 **a.** $3.00 \text{ moles KBr} \times \dfrac{1 \text{ L solution}}{2.00 \text{ moles KBr}} = 1.50 \text{ L of solution (3 SFs)}$

b. $4.78 \text{ g NaCl} \times \dfrac{1 \text{ mole NaCl}}{58.5 \text{ g NaCl}} \times \dfrac{1 \text{ L solution}}{1.50 \text{ moles NaCl}} \times \dfrac{1000 \text{ mL solution}}{1 \text{ L solution}} = 54.5 \text{ mL of solution (3 SFs)}$

c. $0.0500 \text{ mole Ca(NO}_3)_2 \times \dfrac{1 \text{ L solution}}{0.800 \text{ mole Ca(NO}_3)_2} \times \dfrac{1000 \text{ mL solution}}{1 \text{ L solution}}$

$= 62.5 \text{ mL of solution (3 SFs)}$

8.55 $C_1 V_1 = C_2 V_2$

a. $C_2 = C_1 \times \dfrac{V_1}{V_2} = 6.0 \text{ M} \times \dfrac{2.0 \text{ L}}{6.0 \text{ L}} = 2.0 \text{ M HCl solution (2 SFs)}$

b. $C_2 = C_1 \times \dfrac{V_1}{V_2} = 12 \text{ M} \times \dfrac{0.50 \text{ L}}{3.0 \text{ L}} = 2.0 \text{ M NaOH solution (2 SFs)}$

c. $C_2 = C_1 \times \dfrac{V_1}{V_2} = 25\% \times \dfrac{10.0 \text{ mL}}{100.0 \text{ mL}} = 2.5\% \text{ (m/v) KOH solution (2 SFs)}$

d. $C_2 = C_1 \times \dfrac{V_1}{V_2} = 15\% \times \dfrac{50.0 \text{ mL}}{250 \text{ mL}} = 3.0\% \text{ (m/v) H}_2\text{SO}_4 \text{ solution (2 SFs)}$

8.57 $C_1 V_1 = C_2 V_2$

a. $V_2 = V_1 \times \dfrac{C_1}{C_2} = 20.0 \text{ mL} \times \dfrac{6.00 \text{ M}}{1.50 \text{ M}} = 80.0 \text{ mL of diluted HCl solution (2 SFs)}$

b. $V_2 = V_1 \times \dfrac{C_1}{C_2} = 50.0 \text{ mL} \times \dfrac{10.0\%}{2.0\%} = 250 \text{ mL of diluted LiCl solution (2 SFs)}$

c. $V_2 = V_1 \times \dfrac{C_1}{C_2} = 50.0 \text{ mL} \times \dfrac{6.00 \text{ M}}{0.500 \text{ M}} = 600. \text{ mL of diluted H}_3\text{PO}_4 \text{ solution (3 SFs)}$

d. $V_2 = V_1 \times \dfrac{C_1}{C_2} = 75 \text{ mL} \times \dfrac{12\%}{5.0\%} = 180 \text{ mL of diluted glucose solution (2 SFs)}$

8.59 $C_1 V_1 = C_2 V_2$

a. $V_1 = V_2 \times \dfrac{C_2}{C_1} = 255 \text{ mL} \times \dfrac{0.200 \text{ M}}{4.00 \text{ M}} = 12.8 \text{ mL of the HNO}_3 \text{ solution (3 SFs)}$

b. $V_1 = V_2 \times \dfrac{C_2}{C_1} = 715 \text{ mL} \times \dfrac{0.100 \text{ M}}{6.00 \text{ M}} = 11.9 \text{ mL of the MgCl}_2 \text{ solution (3 SFs)}$

c. $V_2 = 0.100 \, \cancel{L} \times \dfrac{1000 \text{ mL}}{1 \, \cancel{L}} = 100. \text{ mL}$

$V_1 = V_2 \times \dfrac{C_2}{C_1} = 100. \text{ mL} \times \dfrac{0.150 \, \cancel{M}}{8.00 \, \cancel{M}} = 1.88 \text{ mL of the KCl solution (3 SFs)}$

8.61 **a.** $50.0 \, \cancel{\text{mL solution}} \times \dfrac{1 \, \cancel{\text{L solution}}}{1000 \, \cancel{\text{mL solution}}} \times \dfrac{1.50 \text{ moles KCl}}{1 \, \cancel{\text{L solution}}} = 0.0750 \text{ mole of KCl}$

$0.0750 \, \cancel{\text{mole KCl}} \times \dfrac{1 \, \cancel{\text{mole PbCl}_2}}{2 \, \cancel{\text{moles KCl}}} \times \dfrac{278.2 \text{ g PbCl}_2}{1 \, \cancel{\text{mole PbCl}_2}} = 10.4 \text{ g of PbCl}_2 \text{ (3 SFs)}$

b. $50.0 \, \cancel{\text{mL solution}} \times \dfrac{1 \, \cancel{\text{L solution}}}{1000 \, \cancel{\text{mL solution}}} \times \dfrac{1.50 \text{ moles KCl}}{1 \, \cancel{\text{L solution}}} = 0.0750 \text{ mole of KCl}$

$0.0750 \, \cancel{\text{mole KCl}} \times \dfrac{1 \, \cancel{\text{mole Pb(NO}_3)_2}}{2 \, \cancel{\text{moles KCl}}} \times \dfrac{1 \, \cancel{\text{L solution}}}{2.00 \, \cancel{\text{moles Pb(NO}_3)_2}} \times \dfrac{1000 \text{ mL solution}}{1 \, \cancel{\text{L solution}}}$

$= 18.8 \text{ mL of Pb(NO}_3)_2 \text{ solution (3 SFs)}$

8.63 **a.** $15.0 \, \cancel{\text{g Mg}} \times \dfrac{1 \, \cancel{\text{mole Mg}}}{24.3 \, \cancel{\text{g Mg}}} \times \dfrac{2 \, \cancel{\text{moles HCl}}}{1 \, \cancel{\text{mole Mg}}} \times \dfrac{1 \, \cancel{\text{L solution}}}{6.00 \, \cancel{\text{moles HCl}}} \times \dfrac{1000 \text{ mL solution}}{1 \, \cancel{\text{L solution}}}$

$= 206 \text{ mL of HCl solution (3 SFs)}$

b. $0.500 \, \cancel{\text{L solution}} \times \dfrac{2.00 \, \cancel{\text{moles HCl}}}{1 \, \cancel{\text{L solution}}} \times \dfrac{1 \text{ mole H}_2}{2 \, \cancel{\text{moles HCl}}} = 0.500 \text{ mole of H}_2 \text{ gas (3 SFs)}$

8.65 **a.** A solution cannot be separated by a semipermeable membrane.
　　　b. A suspension settles out upon standing.

8.67 **a.** When 1.0 mole of glycerol (a nonelectrolyte) dissolves in water, it does not dissociate into ions and so will only produce 1.0 mole of particles. Similarly, 2.0 moles of ethylene glycol (also a nonelectrolyte) dissolves as molecules to produce only 2.0 moles of particles in water. The ethylene glycol solution has more particles in 1.0 L of water and will thus have a lower freezing point.
　　　b. When 0.50 mole of the strong electrolyte KCl dissolves in water, it will produce 1.0 mole of particles because each formula unit of KCl dissociates to give two particles, K^+ and Cl^-. When 0.50 mole of the strong electrolyte $MgCl_2$ dissolves in water, it will produce 1.5 moles of particles because each formula unit of $MgCl_2$ dissociates to give three particles, Mg^{2+} and $2Cl^-$. Thus, a solution of 0.50 mole of $MgCl_2$ in 2.0 L of water will have the lower freezing point.

8.69 **a.** The 10% (m/v) starch solution has the higher solute concentration, more solute particles, and therefore the greater osmotic pressure.
　　　b. Initially, water will flow out of the 1% (m/v) starch solution into the more concentrated 10% (m/v) starch solution.
　　　c. The volume of the 10% (m/v) starch solution will increase due to inflow of water.

8.71 Water will flow from a region of higher solvent concentration (which corresponds to a lower solute concentration) to a region of lower solvent concentration (which corresponds to a higher solute concentration).
　　　a. B; the volume will rise as water flows into compartment B, which contains the 10% (m/v) starch solution.

b. A; the volume will rise as water flows into compartment A, which contains the 8% (m/v) albumin solution.

c. B; the volume will rise as water flows into compartment B, which contains the 10% (m/v) sucrose solution.

8.73 A red blood cell has the same osmotic pressure as a 5% (m/v) glucose solution or a 0.9% (m/v) NaCl solution. In a hypotonic solution (lower osmotic pressure), solvent flows from the hypotonic solution into the red blood cell. When a red blood cell is placed into a hypertonic solution (higher osmotic pressure), solvent (water) flows from the red blood cell to the hypertonic solution. Isotonic solutions have the same osmotic pressure, and a red blood cell in an isotonic solution will not change volume because the flow of solvent into and out of the cell is equal.

a. Distilled water is a hypotonic solution when compared with a red blood cell's contents.

b. A 1% (m/v) glucose solution is a hypotonic solution.

c. A 0.9% (m/v) NaCl solution is isotonic with a red blood cell's contents.

d. A 15% (m/v) glucose solution is a hypertonic solution.

8.75 Colloids cannot pass through the semipermeable dialysis membrane; water and solutions freely pass through semipermeable membranes.

a. Sodium and chloride ions will both pass through the membrane into the distilled water.

b. The amino acid alanine can pass through a dialysis membrane; the colloid starch will not.

c. Sodium and chloride ions will both be present in the water surrounding the dialysis bag; the colloid starch will not.

d. Urea will diffuse through the dialysis bag into the surrounding water.

8.77 **a.** 3; A nonelectrolyte will show no dissociation.

b. 1; A weak electrolyte will show some dissociation, producing a few ions, but mostly remaining as molecules.

c. 2; A strong electrolyte will be completely dissociated into ions.

8.79 **a.** 2; To halve the mass/volume percent (m/v), the volume would double.

b. 3; To go to one-fourth the mass/volume percent (m/v), the volume would be four times the initial volume.

8.81 A "brine" saltwater solution has a high concentration of Na^+ and Cl^- ions and is hypertonic to the cucumber. The skin of the cucumber acts like a semipermeable membrane; therefore, water flows from the more dilute solution inside the cucumber into the more concentrated brine solution that surrounds it. The loss of water causes the cucumber to become a wrinkled pickle.

8.83 **a.** Beaker 3; Solid silver chloride ($AgCl$) will precipitate when the two solutions are mixed.

b. $NaCl(aq) + AgNO_3(aq) \longrightarrow AgCl(s) + NaNO_3(aq)$

$Na^+(aq) + Cl^-(aq) + Ag^+(aq) + NO_3^-(aq) \longrightarrow AgCl(s) + Na^+(aq) + NO_3^-(aq)$

c. $Ag^+(aq) + Cl^-(aq) \longrightarrow AgCl(s)$ Net ionic equation

8.85 **a.** 2; Water will flow into the B (8% starch solution) compartment.

b. 1; Water will continue to flow equally in both directions; no change in volumes.

c. 3; Water will flow into the A (5% sucrose solution) compartment.

d. 2; Water will flow into the B (1% sucrose solution) compartment.

8.87 $80.0 \text{ g NaCl} \times \dfrac{100 \text{ g water}}{36.0 \text{ g NaCl}} = 222 \text{ g of water needed}$ (3 SFs)

8.89 At 20 °C, KNO_3 has a solubility of 32 g of KNO_3 in 100 g of H_2O.

a. 200. g of H_2O will dissolve:

$$200.\text{ g } H_2O \times \frac{32 \text{ g } KNO_3}{100 \text{ g } H_2O} = 64 \text{ g of } KNO_3 \text{ (2 SFs)}$$

Because 32 g of KNO_3 is less than the maximum amount that can dissolve in 200. g of H_2O at 20 °C, the KNO_3 solution is unsaturated.

b. 50. g of H_2O will dissolve:

$$50.\text{ g } H_2O \times \frac{32 \text{ g } KNO_3}{100 \text{ g } H_2O} = 16 \text{ g of } KNO_3 \text{ (2 SFs)}$$

Because 19 g of KNO_3 exceeds the maximum amount that can dissolve in 50. g of H_2O at 20 °C, the KNO_3 solution is saturated, and excess undissolved KNO_3 will be present on the bottom of the container.

c. 150. g of H_2O will dissolve:

$$150.\text{ g } H_2O \times \frac{32 \text{ g } KNO_3}{100 \text{ g } H_2O} = 48 \text{ g of } KNO_3 \text{ (2 SFs)}$$

Because 68 g of KNO_3 exceeds the maximum amount that can dissolve in 150. g of H_2O at 20 °C, the KNO_3 solution is saturated, and excess undissolved KNO_3 will be present on the bottom of the container.

8.91 **a.** Most CO_3^{2-} salts are insoluble.
b. Na^+ salts are soluble.
c. Most PO_4^{3-} salts are insoluble.
d. Salts containing NH_4^+ ions are soluble.
e. Most O^{2-} salts are insoluble.
f. Most OH^- salts are insoluble.

8.93 **a.** Solid silver chloride $(AgCl)$ forms:

$$AgNO_3(aq) + LiCl(aq) \longrightarrow AgCl(s) + LiNO_3(aq)$$

$$Ag^+(aq) + \cancel{NO_3^-(aq)} + \cancel{Li^+(aq)} + Cl^-(aq) \longrightarrow AgCl(s) + \cancel{Li^+(aq)} + \cancel{NO_3^-(aq)}$$

$$Ag^+(aq) + Cl^-(aq) \longrightarrow AgCl(s) \quad \text{Net ionic equation}$$

b. none; no solid forms; salts containing K^+ and Na^+ are soluble.

c. Solid barium sulfate $(BaSO_4)$ forms:

$$Na_2SO_4(aq) + BaCl_2(aq) \longrightarrow BaSO_4(s) + 2NaCl(aq)$$

$$\cancel{2Na^+(aq)} + SO_4^{2-}(aq) + Ba^{2+}(aq) + \cancel{2Cl^-(aq)} \longrightarrow BaSO_4(s) + \cancel{2Na^+(aq)} + \cancel{2Cl^-(aq)}$$

$$Ba^{2+}(aq) + SO_4^{2-}(aq) \longrightarrow BaSO_4(s) \quad \text{Net ionic equation}$$

8.95 mass of solution = 15.5 g of Na_2SO_4 + 75.5 g of H_2O = 91.0 g of solution

$$\frac{15.5 \text{ g } Na_2SO_4}{91.0 \text{ g solution}} \times 100\% = 17.0\% \text{ (m/m) } Na_2SO_4 \text{ solution (3 SFs)}$$

8.97 $\dfrac{8.0 \text{ g NaOH}}{400. \text{ mL solution}} \times \dfrac{1 \text{ mole NaOH}}{40.0 \text{ g NaOH}} \times \dfrac{1000 \text{ mL solution}}{1 \text{ L solution}} = 0.50 \text{ M NaOH solution (2 SFs)}$

8.99 **a.** $2.20 \text{ L solution} \times \dfrac{3.00 \text{ moles Al(NO}_3)_3}{1 \text{ L solution}} \times \dfrac{213.0 \text{ g Al(NO}_3)_3}{1 \text{ mole Al(NO}_3)_3}$

$= 1410 \text{ g of Al(NO}_3)_3 \text{ (3 SFs)}$

b. $75.0 \text{ mL solution} \times \dfrac{1 \text{ L solution}}{1000 \text{ mL solution}} \times \dfrac{0.500 \text{ mole C}_6\text{H}_{12}\text{O}_6}{1 \text{ L solution}} \times \dfrac{180.1 \text{ g C}_6\text{H}_{12}\text{O}_6}{1 \text{ mole C}_6\text{H}_{12}\text{O}_6}$

$= 6.75 \text{ g of C}_6\text{H}_{12}\text{O}_6 \text{ (3 SFs)}$

c. $0.150 \text{ L solution} \times \dfrac{0.320 \text{ mole NH}_4\text{Cl}}{1 \text{ L solution}} \times \dfrac{53.5 \text{ g NH}_4\text{Cl}}{1 \text{ mole NH}_4\text{Cl}}$

$= 2.57 \text{ g of NH}_4\text{Cl} \text{ (3 SFs)}$

8.101 **a.** $24 \text{ h} \times \dfrac{750 \text{ mL solution}}{12 \text{ h}} \times \dfrac{4 \text{ g amino acids}}{100 \text{ mL solution}} = 60 \text{ g of amino acids (1 SF)}$

$24 \text{ h} \times \dfrac{750 \text{ mL solution}}{12 \text{ h}} \times \dfrac{25 \text{ g glucose}}{100 \text{ mL solution}} = 380 \text{ g of glucose (2 SFs)}$

$24 \text{ h} \times \dfrac{500 \text{ mL solution}}{12 \text{ h}} \times \dfrac{10 \text{ g lipid}}{100 \text{ mL solution}} = 100 \text{ g of lipid (1 SF)}$

b. $60 \text{ g amino acids (protein)} \times \dfrac{4 \text{ kcal}}{1 \text{ g protein}} = 240 \text{ kcal}$

$380 \text{ g glucose (carbohydrate)} \times \dfrac{4 \text{ kcal}}{1 \text{ g carbohydrate}} = 1520 \text{ kcal}$

$100 \text{ g lipid (fat)} \times \dfrac{9 \text{ kcal}}{1 \text{ g fat}} = 900 \text{ kcal}$

For a total of 240 kcal + 1520 kcal + 900 kcal = 2700 kcal per day (2 SFs)

8.103 $4.5 \text{ mL propyl alcohol} \times \dfrac{100 \text{ mL solution}}{12 \text{ mL propyl alcohol}} = 38 \text{ mL of propyl alcohol solution (2 SFs)}$

8.105 $C_1V_1 = C_2V_2$

a. $C_2 = C_1 \times \dfrac{V_1}{V_2} = 0.200 \text{ M} \times \dfrac{25.0 \text{ mL}}{50.0 \text{ mL}} = 0.100 \text{ M NaBr solution (3 SFs)}$

b. $C_2 = C_1 \times \dfrac{V_1}{V_2} = 12.0\% \times \dfrac{15.0 \text{ mL}}{40.0 \text{ mL}} = 4.50\% \text{ (m/v) K}_2\text{SO}_4 \text{ solution (3 SFs)}$

c. $C_2 = C_1 \times \dfrac{V_1}{V_2} = 6.00 \text{ M} \times \dfrac{75.0 \text{ mL}}{255 \text{ mL}} = 1.76 \text{ M NaOH solution (3 SFs)}$

8.107 $C_1V_1 = C_2V_2$

a. $V_2 = V_1 \times \dfrac{C_1}{C_2} = 25.0 \text{ mL} \times \dfrac{10.0\,\%}{2.50\,\%} = 100. \text{ mL of diluted HCl solution (3 SFs)}$

b. $V_2 = V_1 \times \dfrac{C_1}{C_2} = 25.0 \text{ mL} \times \dfrac{5.00 \text{ M}}{1.00 \text{ M}} = 125 \text{ mL of diluted HCl solution (3 SFs)}$

c. $V_2 = V_1 \times \dfrac{C_1}{C_2} = 25.0 \text{ mL} \times \dfrac{6.00 \text{ M}}{0.500 \text{ M}} = 300. \text{ mL of diluted HCl solution (3 SFs)}$

8.109 mass of solution = 70.0 g of HNO_3 + 130.0 g of H_2O = 200.0 g of solution

a. $\dfrac{70.0 \text{ g HNO}_3}{200.0 \text{ g solution}} \times 100\% = 35.0\% \text{ (m/m) HNO}_3 \text{ solution (3 SFs)}$

b. $200.0 \text{ g solution} \times \dfrac{1 \text{ mL solution}}{1.21 \text{ g solution}} = 165 \text{ mL of solution (3 SFs)}$

c. $\dfrac{70.0 \text{ g HNO}_3}{165 \text{ mL solution}} \times 100\% = 42.4\% \text{ (m/v) HNO}_3 \text{ solution (3 SFs)}$

d. $\dfrac{70.0 \text{ g HNO}_3}{165 \text{ mL solution}} \times \dfrac{1 \text{ mole HNO}_3}{63.0 \text{ g HNO}_3} \times \dfrac{1000 \text{ mL solution}}{1 \text{ L solution}} = 6.73 \text{ M HNO}_3 \text{ solution (3 SFs)}$

8.111 $60.0 \text{ mL solution} \times \dfrac{1 \text{ L solution}}{1000 \text{ mL solution}} \times \dfrac{1.00 \text{ mole Al(OH)}_3}{1 \text{ L solution}} \times \dfrac{3 \text{ moles HCl}}{1 \text{ mole Al(OH)}_3}$

$\times \dfrac{1 \text{ L solution}}{6.00 \text{ moles HCl}} \times \dfrac{1000 \text{ mL HCl solution}}{1 \text{ L solution}}$

= 30.0 mL of HCl solution (3 SFs)

8.113 $80.0 \text{ mL solution} \times \dfrac{1 \text{ L solution}}{1000 \text{ mL solution}} \times \dfrac{4.00 \text{ moles HNO}_3}{1 \text{ L solution}} \times \dfrac{2 \text{ moles NO}}{8 \text{ moles HNO}_3} \times \dfrac{30.0 \text{ g NO}}{1 \text{ mole NO}}$

= 2.40 g of NO (3 SFs)

8.115 **a.** Solid silver sulfate (Ag_2SO_4) forms:

$2AgNO_3(aq) + Na_2SO_4(aq) \longrightarrow Ag_2SO_4(s) + 2NaNO_3(aq)$

$2Ag^+(aq) + 2NO_3^-(aq) + 2Na^+(aq) + SO_4^{2-}(aq) \longrightarrow$

$Ag_2SO_4(s) + 2Na^+(aq) + 2NO_3^-(aq)$

$2Ag^+(aq) + SO_4^{2-}(aq) \longrightarrow Ag_2SO_4(s)$ Net ionic equation

b. Solid lead(II) chloride ($PbCl_2$) forms:

$2KCl(aq) + Pb(NO_3)_2(aq) \longrightarrow PbCl_2(s) + 2KNO_3(aq)$

$2K^+(aq) + 2Cl^-(aq) + Pb^{2+}(aq) + 2NO_3^-(aq) \longrightarrow PbCl_2(s) + 2K^+(aq) + 2NO_3^-(aq)$

$Pb^{2+}(aq) + 2Cl^-(aq) \longrightarrow PbCl_2(s)$ Net ionic equation

c. Solid calcium phosphate ($Ca_3(PO_4)_2$) forms:

$$3CaCl_2(aq) + 2(NH_4)_3PO_4(aq) \longrightarrow Ca_3(PO_4)_2(s) + 6NH_4Cl(aq)$$

$$3Ca^{2+}(aq) + \cancel{6Cl^-(aq)} + \cancel{6NH_4^+(aq)} + 2PO_4^{3-}(aq) \longrightarrow$$

$$Ca_3(PO_4)_2(s) + \cancel{6NH_4^+(aq)} + \cancel{6Cl^-(aq)}$$

$$3Ca^{2+}(aq) + 2PO_4^{3-}(aq) \longrightarrow Ca_3(PO_4)_2(s) \quad \text{Net ionic equation}$$

d. Solid barium sulfate ($BaSO_4$) forms:

$$K_2SO_4(aq) + BaCl_2(aq) \longrightarrow BaSO_4(s) + 2KCl(aq)$$

$$\cancel{2K^+(aq)} + SO_4^{2-}(aq) + Ba^{2+}(aq) + \cancel{2Cl^-(aq)} \longrightarrow BaSO_4(s) + \cancel{2K^+(aq)} + \cancel{2Cl^-(aq)}$$

$$Ba^{2+}(aq) + SO_4^{2-}(aq) \longrightarrow BaSO_4(s) \quad \text{Net ionic equation}$$

8.117 a. mass of NaCl = 25.50 g − 24.10 g = 1.40 g of NaCl

mass of solution = 36.15 g − 24.10 g = 12.05 g of solution

$$\text{mass percent (m/m)} = \frac{1.40 \text{ g NaCl}}{12.05 \text{ g solution}} \times 100\% = 11.6\% \text{ (m/m) NaCl solution (3 SFs)}$$

b. $\text{molarity (M)} = \dfrac{1.40 \text{ g NaCl}}{10.0 \text{ mL solution}} \times \dfrac{1 \text{ mole NaCl}}{58.5 \text{ g NaCl}} \times \dfrac{1000 \text{ mL solution}}{1 \text{ L solution}}$

$$= 2.39 \text{ M NaCl solution (3 SFs)}$$

c. $C_1V_1 = C_2V_2 \quad C_2 = C_1 \times \dfrac{V_1}{V_2} = 2.39 \text{ M} \times \dfrac{10.0 \text{ mL}}{60.0 \text{ mL}} = 0.398 \text{ M NaCl solution (3 SFs)}$

9

Reaction Rates and Chemical Equilibrium

9.1 At room temperature, more of the reactants will have the energy necessary to proceed to products (the activation energy) than at the lower temperature of the refrigerator, so the rate of formation of bread mold will be faster.

9.3 Adding Br_2 molecules increases the concentration of reactants, which increases the number of collisions that take place between the reactants.

9.5 Increasing the temperature of the reaction increases the kinetic energy of the particles, which increases the number of collisions between the reactants.

9.7
  a. Adding more reactant molecules increases the number of collisions that take place between the reactants, which increases the reaction rate.
  b. Raising the temperature increases the kinetic energy of the reactant molecules, which increases the number of collisions and makes more collisions effective. The rate of reaction will be increased.
  c. Removing the catalyst raises the energy of activation, which decreases the reaction rate.
  d. Removing some reactant molecules decreases the number of collisions that take place between the reactants, which decreases the reaction rate.

9.9 A reversible reaction is one in which a forward reaction converts reactants to products, while a reverse reaction converts products to reactants.

9.11
  a. Broken glass cannot be put back together; the process is not reversible.
  b. In this physical process, heat melts a solid form of water (snow), while removing heat can change liquid water back to solid. It is reversible.
  c. A pan is warmed when heated, and cooled when heat is removed; it is reversible.

9.13
  a. When the rate of the forward reaction is faster than the rate of the reverse reaction, the process is not at equilibrium.
  b. When the concentrations of the reactants and the products do not change, the process is at equilibrium.
  c. When the rate of either the forward or reverse reaction does not change, the process is at equilibrium.

9.15 In the expression for K_c, the products are divided by the reactants, with each concentration raised to a power that is equal to its coefficient in the balanced chemical equation:

  a. $K_c = \dfrac{[CS_2][H_2]^4}{[CH_4][H_2S]^2}$ **b.** $K_c = \dfrac{[N_2][O_2]}{[NO]^2}$ **c.** $K_c = \dfrac{[CS_2][O_2]^4}{[SO_3]^2[CO_2]}$

9.17
  a. only one state (gas) is present; homogeneous equilibrium
  b. solid and gaseous states are present; heterogeneous equilibrium
  c. only one state (gas) is present; homogeneous equilibrium
  d. gaseous and solid states are present; heterogeneous equilibrium

9.19
  a. $K_c = \dfrac{[O_2]^3}{[O_3]^2}$ **b.** $K_c = [CO_2][H_2O]$

  c. $K_c = \dfrac{[H_2]^3[CO]}{[CH_4][H_2O]}$ **d.** $K_c = \dfrac{[SiCl_4][H_2]^2}{[HCl]^4}$

9.21 $K_c = \dfrac{[NO_2]^2}{[N_2O_4]} = \dfrac{[0.21]^2}{[0.030]} = 1.5 \, (2 \text{ SFs})$

9.23 $K_c = \dfrac{[CH_4][H_2O]}{[CO][H_2]^3} = \dfrac{[1.8][2.0]}{[0.50][0.30]^3} = 270 \, (2 \text{ SFs})$

9.25 $K_c = \dfrac{[CO_2]}{[CO]} = \dfrac{[0.052]}{[0.20]} = 0.26 \, (2 \text{ SFs})$

9.27   **a.**   A large K_c value indicates that the equilibrium mixture contains mostly products.
   b.   A K_c value close to 1 indicates that the equilibrium mixture contains both reactants and products.
   c.   A small K_c value indicates that the equilibrium mixture contains mostly reactants.

9.29 $K_c = \dfrac{[HI]^2}{[H_2][I_2]} = 54$

Rearrange the K_c expression to solve for $[H_2]$, and substitute in known values.

$[H_2] = \dfrac{[HI]^2}{K_c[I_2]} = \dfrac{[0.030]^2}{(54)[0.015]} = 1.1 \times 10^{-3} \text{ M} \, (2 \text{ SFs})$

9.31 $K_c = \dfrac{[NO]^2[Br_2]}{[NOBr]^2} = 2.0$

Rearrange the K_c expression to solve for $[NOBr]$, and substitute in known values.

$[NOBr]^2 = \dfrac{[NO]^2[Br_2]}{K_c} = \dfrac{[2.0]^2[1.0]}{2.0} = 2.0$

Take the square root of both sides of the equation.

$[NOBr] = \sqrt{2.0} = 1.4 \text{ M} \, (2 \text{ SFs})$

9.33   **a.**   When more reactant molecules are added to an equilibrium mixture, the system shifts in the direction of the products.
   b.   When more product molecules are added to an equilibrium mixture, the system shifts in the direction of the reactants.
   c.   When the temperature is increased for an endothermic reaction, the system shifts in the direction of the products to remove heat.
   d.   Increasing the volume of the container favors the side of the reaction with more moles of gas, so this system shifts in the direction of the reactants.
   e.   When a catalyst is added, the rates of both forward and reverse reactions increase; the equilibrium position does not change.

9.35   **a.**   When more reactant molecules are added to an equilibrium mixture, the system shifts in the direction of the products.
   b.   When the temperature is increased for an endothermic reaction, the system shifts in the direction of the products to remove heat.
   c.   When some product molecules are removed from an equilibrium mixture, the system shifts in the direction of the products.
   d.   When a catalyst is added, the rates of both forward and reverse reactions increase; the equilibrium position does not change.
   e.   When some reactant molecules are removed from an equilibrium mixture, the system shifts in the direction of the reactants.

9.37 At equilibrium, the diagram shows mostly reactants and a few products, so the equilibrium constant K_c for the reaction would have a small value.

9.39 T_2 is lower than T_1. This would cause the exothermic reaction shown to shift in the direction of products to add heat; more product is seen in the T_2 diagram.

9.41
  a. When the temperature is increased for an exothermic reaction, the system shifts in the direction of the reactants to remove heat.
  b. Decreasing the volume of the reaction container favors the side of the reaction with fewer moles of gas, so this system shifts in the direction of the products.
  c. When a catalyst is added, the rates of both forward and reverse reactions increase; the equilibrium position does not change.
  d. When more reactant molecules are added to an equilibrium mixture, the system shifts in the direction of the products.

9.43
  a. $K_c = \dfrac{[CO_2][H_2O]^2}{[CH_4][O_2]^2}$

  b. $K_c = \dfrac{[N_2]^2[H_2O]^6}{[NH_3]^4[O_2]^3}$

  c. $K_c = \dfrac{[CH_4]}{[H_2]^2}$

9.45
  a. A large K_c value indicates that the equilibrium mixture contains mostly products.
  b. A K_c value close to 1 indicates that the equilibrium mixture contains both reactants and products.
  c. A small K_c value indicates that the equilibrium mixture contains mostly reactants.
  d. A K_c value close to 1 indicates that the equilibrium mixture contains both reactants and products.

9.47
  a. $K_c = \dfrac{[HCl]^2}{[H_2][Cl_2]}$

  b. $K_c = \dfrac{[NO]^2[Br_2]}{[NOBr]^2}$

  c. $K_c = \dfrac{[Cl_2][NO]^2}{[NOCl]^2}$

  d. $K_c = \dfrac{[CO][H_2]}{[H_2O]}$

9.49 The numerator in the K_c expression gives the products in the equation, and the denominator gives the reactants.
  a. $SO_2Cl_2(g) \rightleftharpoons SO_2(g) + Cl_2(g)$
  b. $Br_2(g) + Cl_2(g) \rightleftharpoons 2BrCl(g)$
  c. $CO(g) + 3H_2(g) \rightleftharpoons CH_4(g) + H_2O(g)$
  d. $2O_2(g) + 2NH_3(g) \rightleftharpoons N_2O(g) + 3H_2O(g)$

9.51 **a.** $K_c = \dfrac{[N_2][H_2]^3}{[NH_3]^2}$

  b. $K_c = \dfrac{[3.0][0.50]^3}{[0.20]^2} = 9.4 \ (2 \ \text{SFs})$

9.53 $K_c = \dfrac{[N_2O_4]}{[NO_2]^2} = 5.0$

Rearrange the K_c expression to solve for $[N_2O_4]$, and substitute in known values.

$[N_2O_4] = K_c[NO_2]^2 = (5.0)[0.50]^2 = 1.3 \ \text{M} \ (2 \ \text{SFs})$

9.55 **a.** When more reactant O_2 molecules are added to the equilibrium mixture, the system shifts in the direction of the products.
  b. When more product O_2 molecules are added to the equilibrium mixture, the system shifts in the direction of the reactants.
  c. When more reactant O_2 molecules are added to the equilibrium mixture, the system shifts in the direction of the products.
  d. When more product O_2 molecules are added to the equilibrium mixture, the system shifts in the direction of the reactants.

9.57 Decreasing the volume of an equilibrium mixture shifts the system toward the side of the reaction that has the fewer moles of gas. No shift occurs when there are an equal number of moles of gas on both sides of the equation.
  a. With 3 moles of gas on the reactant side and 2 moles of gas on the product side, decreasing the volume will shift the system in the direction of the products.
  b. With 2 moles of gas on the reactant side and 3 moles of gas on the product side, decreasing the volume will shift the system in the direction of the reactants.
  c. With 6 moles of gas on the reactant side and 0 moles of gas on the product side, decreasing the volume will shift the system in the direction of the products.
  d. With 4 moles of gas on the reactant side and 5 moles of gas on the product side, decreasing the volume will shift the system in the direction of the reactants.

9.59 **a.** A small K_c value indicates that the equilibrium mixture contains mostly reactants.
  b. A large K_c value indicates that the equilibrium mixture contains mostly products.

9.61 Increasing the volume of an equilibrium mixture shifts the system toward the side of the reaction that has the greater number of moles of gas; decreasing the volume shifts the equilibrium toward the side of the reaction that has the fewer moles of gas.
  a. Since the product side has the greater number of moles of gas, increasing the volume of the container will increase the yield of products.
  b. Since the product side has the greater number of moles of gas, increasing the volume of the container will increase the yield of products.
  c. Since the product side has the fewer moles of gas, decreasing the volume of the container will increase the yield of products.

9.63 **a.** $\dfrac{[PCl_3][Cl_2]}{[PCl_5]} = \dfrac{[0.050][0.050]}{[0.10]} = 0.025 \ (2 \ \text{SFs})$, which is not equal to $K_c \ (4.2 \times 10^{-2})$.
  This mixture is not at equilibrium.
  b. Since 0.025 is less than K_c, the equilibrium mixture will have more of the products PCl_3 and Cl_2 and less of the reactant PCl_5; the reaction will proceed in the forward direction to establish equilibrium.

9.65   **a.** $K_c = \dfrac{[PCl_3][Cl_2]}{[PCl_5]}$

b.   Since PCl_3 and Cl_2 are formed in a 1:1 ratio, if there is 0.16 mole of PCl_3 in the flask at equilibrium, then 0.16 mole of Cl_2 is also formed, and 0.16 mole of PCl_5 must have reacted, leaving 0.60 mole − 0.16 mole = 0.44 mole of PCl_5. At equilibrium, the concentrations are $[PCl_3] = [Cl_2] = 0.16$ M, and $[PCl_5] = 0.44$ M. (2 SFs)

c. $K_c = \dfrac{[PCl_3][Cl_2]}{[PCl_5]} = \dfrac{[0.16][0.16]}{[0.44]} = 0.058$ (2 SFs)

d.   When Cl_2 (a product) is added to the equilibrium mixture, the system will shift in the direction of the reactants, and $[PCl_5]$ will increase.

9.67   **a.** $K_c = \dfrac{[CO]^2}{[CO_2]} = \dfrac{[0.030]^2}{[0.060]} = 0.015$ (2 SFs)

b.   If more CO_2 (a reactant) is added, the equilibrium will shift in the direction of the products.

c.   If the volume of the container is decreased, the equilibrium will shift toward the side of the reaction with the fewer moles of gas, which is the reactant side.

9.69   **a.**   When more product molecules are added to an equilibrium mixture, the system shifts in the direction of the reactants. This will cause a decrease in the equilibrium concentration of the product CO.

b.   When the temperature is increased for an endothermic reaction, the system shifts in the direction of the products to remove heat. This will cause an increase in the equilibrium concentration of the product CO.

c.   Increasing the volume of the reaction container favors the side of the reaction with the greater number of moles of gas, so this system shifts in the direction of the products. This will cause an increase in the equilibrium concentration of the product CO.

d.   Decreasing the volume of the reaction container favors the side of the reaction with the fewer moles of gas, so this system shifts in the direction of the reactants. This will cause a decrease in the equilibrium concentration of the product CO.

e.   When a catalyst is added, the rates of both forward and reverse reactions increase; the equilibrium position does not change. No change will be observed in the equilibrium concentration of the product CO.

f.   When the temperature is decreased for an endothermic reaction, the system shifts in the direction of the reactants to add heat. This will cause a decrease in the equilibrium concentration of the product CO.

g.   When some reactant molecules are removed from an equilibrium mixture, the system shifts in the direction of the reactants. This will cause a decrease in the equilibrium concentration of the product CO.

10.1 **a.** Acids have a sour taste.
      b. Acids neutralize bases.
      c. Acids produce H^+ ions in water.
      d. Potassium hydroxide is the name of a base.
      e. Both acids and bases are electrolytes.

10.3 Acids containing a simple nonmetal anion use the prefix *hydro*, followed by the name of the anion with its *ide* ending changed to *ic acid*. When the anion is an oxygen-containing polyatomic ion, the *ate* ending of the polyatomic anion is replaced with *ic acid*. Acids with one oxygen less than the common *ic acid* name are named as *ous acids*. Bases are named as ionic compounds containing hydroxide anions.
      a. hydrochloric acid
      b. calcium hydroxide
      c. carbonic acid
      d. nitric acid
      e. sulfurous acid
      f. iron(II) hydroxide

10.5 **a.** $Mg(OH)_2$
      b. HF
      c. H_3PO_3
      d. $LiOH$
      e. $Cu(OH)_2$

10.7 A Brønsted–Lowry acid donates a hydrogen ion (H^+), whereas a Brønsted–Lowry base accepts a hydrogen ion.
      a. HI is the acid (H^+ donor); H_2O is the base (H^+ acceptor).
      b. H_2O is the acid (H^+ donor); F^- is the base (H^+ acceptor).

10.9 To form the conjugate base, remove a hydrogen ion (H^+) from the acid.
      a. F^-, fluoride ion
      b. OH^-, hydroxide ion
      c. HCO_3^-, bicarbonate ion *or* hydrogen carbonate ion
      d. SO_4^{2-}, sulfate ion

10.11 To form the conjugate acid, add a hydrogen ion (H^+) to the base.
      a. HCO_3^-, bicarbonate ion *or* hydrogen carbonate ion
      b. H_3O^+, hydronium ion
      c. H_3PO_4, phosphoric acid
      d. HSO_3^-, bisulfite ion *or* hydrogen sulfite ion

10.13 The conjugate acid is an H^+ donor, and the conjugate base is an H^+ acceptor.
      a. In the reaction, the acid H_2CO_3 donates an H^+ to the base H_2O. The conjugate acid–base pairs are H_2CO_3/HCO_3^- and H_3O^+/H_2O.

b. In the reaction, the acid NH_4^+ donates an H^+ to the base H_2O. The conjugate acid–base pairs are NH_4^+/NH_3 and H_3O^+/H_2O.

c. In the reaction, the acid HCN donates an H^+ to the base NO_2^-. The conjugate acid–base pairs are HCN/CN^- and HNO_2/NO_2^-.

10.15 A strong acid is a good H^+ donor, whereas its conjugate base is a poor H^+ acceptor.

10.17 **a.** True

  b. False; a strong acid has a large value of K_a.

  c. False; a strong acid has a weak conjugate base.

  d. True

  e. False; a strong acid is completely ionized in aqueous solution.

10.19 Use Table 10.3 to answer (the stronger acid will be closer to the top of the table).

  a. HBr is the stronger acid.

  b. HSO_4^- is the stronger acid.

  c. H_2CO_3 is the stronger acid.

10.21 Use Table 10.3 to answer (the weaker acid will be closer to the bottom of the table).

  a. HSO_4^- is the weaker acid.

  b. HNO_2 is the weaker acid.

  c. HCO_3^- is the weaker acid.

10.23 **a.** From Table 10.3, we see that H_2O is a weaker base than HCO_3^- and that H_2CO_3 is a weaker acid than H_3O^+. Thus, the solution will contain mostly reactants at equilibrium.

  b. From Table 10.3, we see that NH_4^+ is a weaker acid than H_3O^+ and that H_2O is a weaker base than NH_3. Thus, the solution will contain mostly reactants at equilibrium.

  c. From Table 10.3, we see that NH_4^+ is a weaker acid than HNO_2 and that NO_2^- is a weaker base than NH_3. Thus, the solution will contain mostly products at equilibrium.

10.25 The larger the K_a, the stronger the acid. The stronger acid has the weaker conjugate base.

  a. H_2SO_3, which has a larger K_a than HS^-, is the stronger acid.

  b. The conjugate base, HSO_3^-, is formed by removing an H^+ from the acid H_2SO_3.

  c. The stronger acid, H_2SO_3, has the weaker conjugate base, HSO_3^-.

  d. The stronger acid, H_2SO_3, dissociates more and produces more ions.

10.27 $H_3PO_4(aq) + H_2O(l) \rightleftharpoons H_3O^+(aq) + H_2PO_4^-(aq)$

The K_a is the ratio of the [products] divided by the [reactants], with $[H_2O]$ considered constant and part of the K_a.

$$K_a = \frac{[H_3O^+][H_2PO_4^-]}{[H_3PO_4]}$$

10.29 In pure water, a small fraction of the water molecules break apart to form H^+ and OH^-. The H^+ combines with H_2O to form H_3O^+. Every time an H^+ is formed, an OH^- is also formed. Therefore, the concentration of the two must be equal in pure water.

10.31 In an acidic solution, the $[H_3O^+]$ is greater than the $[OH^-]$, which means that at 25 °C, the $[H_3O^+]$ is greater than 1×10^{-7} M and the $[OH^-]$ is less than 1×10^{-7} M.

10.33 The value of $K_w = [H_3O^+][OH^-] = 1.0 \times 10^{-14}$ at 25 °C.

If $[H_3O^+]$ needs to be calculated from $[OH^-]$, then rearranging the K_w for $[H_3O^+]$ gives

$$[H_3O^+] = \frac{1.0 \times 10^{-14}}{[OH^-]}.$$

If $[OH^-]$ needs to be calculated from $[H_3O^+]$, then rearranging the K_w for $[OH^-]$ gives

$$[OH^-] = \frac{1.0 \times 10^{-14}}{[H_3O^+]}.$$

A neutral solution has $[OH^-] = [H_3O^+] = 1 \times 10^{-7}$ M. If the $[OH^-] > [H_3O^+]$, the solution is basic; if the $[H_3O^+] > [OH^-]$, the solution is acidic.

a. $[OH^-] = \dfrac{1.0 \times 10^{-14}}{[H_3O^+]} = \dfrac{1.0 \times 10^{-14}}{[2.0 \times 10^{-5}]} = 5.0 \times 10^{-10}$ M;

since $[H_3O^+] > [OH^-]$, the solution is <u>acidic</u>.

b. $[OH^-] = \dfrac{1.0 \times 10^{-14}}{[H_3O^+]} = \dfrac{1.0 \times 10^{-14}}{[1.4 \times 10^{-9}]} = 7.1 \times 10^{-6}$ M;

since $[OH^-] > [H_3O^+]$, the solution is <u>basic</u>.

c. $[H_3O^+] = \dfrac{1.0 \times 10^{-14}}{[OH^-]} = \dfrac{1.0 \times 10^{-14}}{[8.0 \times 10^{-3}]} = 1.3 \times 10^{-12}$ M;

since $[OH^-] > [H_3O^+]$, the solution is <u>basic</u>.

d. $[H_3O^+] = \dfrac{1.0 \times 10^{-14}}{[OH^-]} = \dfrac{1.0 \times 10^{-14}}{[3.5 \times 10^{-10}]} = 2.9 \times 10^{-5}$ M;

since $[H_3O^+] > [OH^-]$, the solution is <u>acidic</u>.

10.35 The value of $K_w = [H_3O^+][OH^-] = 1.0 \times 10^{-14}$ at 25 °C.

When $[OH^-]$ is known, the $[H_3O^+]$ can be calculated by rearranging the K_w for $[H_3O^+]$:

$$[H_3O^+] = \frac{1.0 \times 10^{-14}}{[OH^-]}$$

a. $[H_3O^+] = \dfrac{1.0 \times 10^{-14}}{[OH^-]} = \dfrac{1.0 \times 10^{-14}}{[1.0 \times 10^{-9}]} = 1.0 \times 10^{-5}$ M (2 SFs)

b. $[H_3O^+] = \dfrac{1.0 \times 10^{-14}}{[OH^-]} = \dfrac{1.0 \times 10^{-14}}{[1.0 \times 10^{-6}]} = 1.0 \times 10^{-8}$ M (2 SFs)

c. $[H_3O^+] = \dfrac{1.0 \times 10^{-14}}{[OH^-]} = \dfrac{1.0 \times 10^{-14}}{[2.0 \times 10^{-5}]} = 5.0 \times 10^{-10}$ M (2 SFs)

d. $[H_3O^+] = \dfrac{1.0 \times 10^{-14}}{[OH^-]} = \dfrac{1.0 \times 10^{-14}}{[4.0 \times 10^{-13}]} = 2.5 \times 10^{-2}$ M (2 SFs)

10.37 The value of $K_w = [H_3O^+][OH^-] = 1.0 \times 10^{-14}$ at 25 °C.

When $[H_3O^+]$ is known, the $[OH^-]$ can be calculated by rearranging the K_w for $[OH^-]$:

$$[OH^-] = \frac{1.0 \times 10^{-14}}{[H_3O^+]}$$

a. $[OH^-] = \dfrac{1.0 \times 10^{-14}}{[H_3O^+]} = \dfrac{1.0 \times 10^{-14}}{[1.0 \times 10^{-3}]} = 1.0 \times 10^{-11}$ M (2 SFs)

b. $[OH^-] = \dfrac{1.0 \times 10^{-14}}{[H_3O^+]} = \dfrac{1.0 \times 10^{-14}}{[5.0 \times 10^{-6}]} = 2.0 \times 10^{-9}$ M (2 SFs)

c. $[OH^-] = \dfrac{1.0 \times 10^{-14}}{[H_3O^+]} = \dfrac{1.0 \times 10^{-14}}{[1.8 \times 10^{-12}]} = 5.6 \times 10^{-3}$ M (2 SFs)

d. $[OH^-] = \dfrac{1.0 \times 10^{-14}}{[H_3O^+]} = \dfrac{1.0 \times 10^{-14}}{[4.0 \times 10^{-13}]} = 2.5 \times 10^{-2}$ M (2 SFs)

10.39 An acidic solution has a pH less than 7.0. A basic solution has a pH greater than 7.0. A neutral solution has a pH equal to 7.0.
  a. basic (pH 7.38 > 7.0)
  b. acidic (pH 2.8 < 7.0)
  c. basic (pH 11.2 > 7.0)
  d. acidic (pH 5.54 < 7.0)
  e. acidic (pH 4.2 < 7.0)
  f. basic (pH 7.6 > 7.0)

10.41 $pH = -\log[H_3O^+]$

Since the value of $K_w = [H_3O^+][OH^-] = 1.0 \times 10^{-14}$ at 25 °C, if $[H_3O^+]$ needs to be calculated from $[OH^-]$, rearranging the K_w for $[H_3O^+]$ gives $[H_3O^+] = \dfrac{1.0 \times 10^{-14}}{[OH^-]}$.

a. $pH = -\log[H_3O^+] = -\log[1.0 \times 10^{-4}] = 4.00$ (2 SFs on the right of the decimal point)

b. $pH = -\log[H_3O^+] = -\log[3.0 \times 10^{-9}] = 8.52$ (2 SFs on the right of the decimal point)

c. $[H_3O^+] = \dfrac{1.0 \times 10^{-14}}{[1.0 \times 10^{-5}]} = 1.0 \times 10^{-9}$ M

$pH = -\log[1.0 \times 10^{-9}] = 9.00$ (2 SFs on the right of the decimal point)

d. $[H_3O^+] = \dfrac{1.0 \times 10^{-14}}{[2.5 \times 10^{-11}]} = 4.0 \times 10^{-4}$ M

$pH = -\log[4.0 \times 10^{-4}] = 3.40$ (2 SFs on the right of the decimal point)

e. $pH = -\log[H_3O^+] = -\log[6.7 \times 10^{-8}] = 7.17$ (2 SFs on the right of the decimal point)

f. $[H_3O^+] = \dfrac{1.0 \times 10^{-14}}{[8.2 \times 10^{-4}]} = 1.2 \times 10^{-11}$ M

$pH = -\log[1.2 \times 10^{-11}] = 10.92$ (2 SFs on the right of the decimal point)

10.43 $[H_3O^+] = \dfrac{1.0 \times 10^{-14}}{[OH^-]}$; $[OH^-] = \dfrac{1.0 \times 10^{-14}}{[H_3O^+]}$; $pH = -\log[H_3O^+]$

$[H_3O^+]$	$[OH^-]$	pH	Acidic, Basic, or Neutral?
1×10^{-8} M	1×10^{-6} M	8.0	Basic
1.0×10^{-3} M	1.0×10^{-11} M	3.00	Acidic
2.8×10^{-5} M	3.6×10^{-10} M	4.55	Acidic
2.4×10^{-5} M	4.2×10^{-10} M	4.62	Acidic

10.45 Acids react with active metals to form $H_2(g)$ and a salt of the metal.
    a. products: $LiCl(aq)$ and $H_2(g)$
        balanced equation: $2Li(s) + 2HCl(aq) \longrightarrow 2LiCl(aq) + H_2(g)$
    b. products: $MgCl_2(aq)$ and $H_2(g)$
        balanced equation: $Mg(s) + 2HCl(aq) \longrightarrow MgCl_2(aq) + H_2(g)$
    c. products: $SrCl_2(aq)$ and $H_2(g)$
        balanced equation: $Sr(s) + 2HCl(aq) \longrightarrow SrCl_2(aq) + H_2(g)$

10.47 The reaction of acids with carbonates or hydrogen carbonates yields $CO_2(g)$, $H_2O(l)$, and a salt.
    a. products: $LiBr(aq)$, $CO_2(g)$, and $H_2O(l)$
        balanced equation: $LiHCO_3(s) + HBr(aq) \longrightarrow LiBr(aq) + CO_2(g) + H_2O(l)$
    b. products: $MgBr_2(aq)$, $CO_2(g)$, and $H_2O(l)$
        balanced equation: $MgCO_3(s) + 2HBr(aq) \longrightarrow MgBr_2(aq) + CO_2(g) + H_2O(l)$
    c. products: $SrBr_2(aq)$, $CO_2(g)$, and $H_2O(l)$
        balanced equation: $SrCO_3(s) + 2HBr(aq) \longrightarrow SrBr_2(aq) + CO_2(g) + H_2O(l)$

10.49 In balancing a neutralization equation, the number of H^+ and OH^- must be equalized by placing coefficients in front of the formulas for the acid and base.
    a. $2HCl(aq) + Mg(OH)_2(s) \longrightarrow MgCl_2(aq) + 2H_2O(l)$
    b. $H_3PO_4(aq) + 3LiOH(aq) \longrightarrow Li_3PO_4(aq) + 3H_2O(l)$
    c. $H_2SO_4(aq) + Sr(OH)_2(s) \longrightarrow SrSO_4(aq) + 2H_2O(l)$

10.51 The products of a neutralization are water and a salt. In balancing a neutralization equation, the number of H^+ and OH^- must be equalized by placing coefficients in front of the formulas for the acid and base.
    a. $H_2SO_4(aq) + 2NaOH(aq) \longrightarrow Na_2SO_4(aq) + 2H_2O(l)$
    b. $3HCl(aq) + Fe(OH)_3(s) \longrightarrow FeCl_3(aq) + 3H_2O(l)$
    c. $H_2CO_3(aq) + Mg(OH)_2(s) \longrightarrow MgCO_3(s) + 2H_2O(l)$

10.53 In the titration equation, one mole of HCl reacts with one mole of NaOH.

$$28.6 \text{ mL NaOH solution} \times \frac{1 \text{ L NaOH solution}}{1000 \text{ mL NaOH solution}} \times \frac{0.145 \text{ mole NaOH}}{1 \text{ L NaOH solution}} \times \frac{1 \text{ mole HCl}}{1 \text{ mole NaOH}}$$

$$= 0.004\,15 \text{ mole of HCl}$$

$$5.00 \text{ mL HCl solution} \times \frac{1 \text{ L solution}}{1000 \text{ mL solution}} = 0.005\,00 \text{ L of HCl solution}$$

$$\text{molarity (M) of HCl} = \frac{\text{moles of solute}}{\text{liters of solution}} = \frac{0.004\,15 \text{ mole HCl}}{0.005\,00 \text{ L solution}}$$

$$= 0.830 \text{ M HCl solution (3 SFs)}$$

10.55 In the titration equation, one mole of H_2SO_4 reacts with two moles of KOH.

$$38.2 \text{ mL KOH solution} \times \frac{1 \text{ L KOH solution}}{1000 \text{ mL KOH solution}} \times \frac{0.162 \text{ mole KOH}}{1 \text{ L KOH solution}} \times \frac{1 \text{ mole } H_2SO_4}{2 \text{ moles KOH}}$$

$$= 0.003\ 09 \text{ mole of } H_2SO_4$$

$$25.0 \text{ mL } H_2SO_4 \text{ solution} \times \frac{1 \text{ L solution}}{1000 \text{ mL solution}} = 0.0250 \text{ L of } H_2SO_4 \text{ solution}$$

$$\text{molarity (M) of } H_2SO_4 = \frac{\text{moles of solute}}{\text{liters of solution}} = \frac{0.003\ 09 \text{ mole } H_2SO_4}{0.0250 \text{ L solution}}$$

$$= 0.124 \text{ M } H_2SO_4 \text{ solution (3 SFs)}$$

10.57 In the titration equation, one mole of H_3PO_4 reacts with three moles of NaOH.

$$16.4 \text{ mL NaOH solution} \times \frac{1 \text{ L NaOH solution}}{1000 \text{ mL NaOH solution}} \times \frac{0.204 \text{ mole NaOH}}{1 \text{ L NaOH solution}} \times \frac{1 \text{ mole } H_3PO_4}{3 \text{ moles NaOH}}$$

$$= 1.12 \times 10^{-3} \text{ mole of } H_3PO_4 \text{ (3 SFs)}$$

$$50.0 \text{ mL } H_3PO_4 \text{ solution} \times \frac{1 \text{ L solution}}{1000 \text{ mL solution}} = 0.0500 \text{ L of } H_3PO_4 \text{ solution}$$

$$\text{molarity (M) of } H_3PO_4 = \frac{\text{moles of solute}}{\text{liters of solution}} = \frac{1.12 \times 10^{-3} \text{ mole } H_3PO_4}{0.0500 \text{ L solution}}$$

$$= 0.0224 \text{ M } H_3PO_4 \text{ solution (3 SFs)}$$

10.59 (2) and (3) are buffer systems. (2) contains the weak acid H_2CO_3 and a salt containing its conjugate base HCO_3^-. (3) contains the weak acid HF and a salt containing its conjugate base F^-.

10.61 a. The purpose of the buffer system is to (3) maintain pH.
  b. The salt of the weak acid is needed to (1) provide the conjugate base and (2) neutralize added H_3O^+.
  c. The addition of OH^- is neutralized by (3) H_3O^+.
  d. When H_3O^+ is added, the equilibrium shifts in the direction of the (1) reactants.

10.63 $HNO_2(aq) + H_2O(l) \rightleftharpoons NO_2^-(aq) + H_3O^+(aq)$
Rearrange the K_a for $[H_3O^+]$ and use it to calculate the pH.

$$[H_3O^+] = K_a \times \frac{[HNO_2]}{[NO_2^-]} = (4.5 \times 10^{-4}) \times \frac{[0.10 \text{ M}]}{[0.10 \text{ M}]} = 4.5 \times 10^{-4} \text{ M}$$

$$pH = -\log[H_3O^+] = -\log[4.5 \times 10^{-4}] = 3.35 \quad \text{(2 SFs on the right of the decimal point)}$$

10.65 $HF(aq) + H_2O(l) \rightleftharpoons F^-(aq) + H_3O^+(aq)$
Rearrange the K_a for $[H_3O^+]$ and use it to calculate the pH.

$$[H_3O^+] = K_a \times \frac{[HF]}{[F^-]} = (7.2 \times 10^{-4}) \times \frac{[0.10 \text{ M}]}{[0.10 \text{ M}]} = 7.2 \times 10^{-4} \text{ M} \quad pH = -\log[7.2 \times 10^{-4}] = 3.14$$

$$[H_3O^+] = K_a \times \frac{[HF]}{[F^-]} = (7.2 \times 10^{-4}) \times \frac{[0.060 \text{ M}]}{[0.120 \text{ M}]} = 3.6 \times 10^{-4} \text{ M} \quad pH = -\log[3.6 \times 10^{-4}] = 3.44$$

The solution with 0.10 M HF/0.10 M NaF is more acidic. (pH values have 2 SFs on the right of the decimal point.)

10.67 **a.** This diagram represents a weak acid; only a few HX molecules dissociate into H_3O^+ and X^- ions.

b. This diagram represents a strong acid; all of the HX molecules dissociate into H_3O^+ and X^- ions.

c. This diagram represents a weak acid; only a few HX molecules dissociate into H_3O^+ and X^- ions.

10.69 **a.** Hyperventilation will lower the CO_2 level in the blood, which lowers the $[H_2CO_3]$, which decreases the $[H_3O^+]$ and increases the blood pH.

b. Breathing into a paper bag will increase the CO_2 level in the blood, increase the $[H_2CO_3]$, increase $[H_3O^+]$, and lower the blood pH back toward the normal range.

10.71 **a.** base; lithium hydroxide
b. salt; calcium nitrate
c. acid; hydrobromic acid
d. base; barium hydroxide
e. acid; carbonic acid
f. acid; chlorous acid

10.73 **a.** In the reaction, the acid HNO_3 donates an H^+ to the base NH_3. The conjugate acid–base pairs are HNO_3/NO_3^- and NH_4^+/NH_3. From Table 10.3, we see that NO_3^- is a weaker base than NH_3 and that NH_4^+ is a weaker acid than HNO_3. Thus, the solution will contain mostly <u>products</u> at equilibrium.

b. In the reaction, the acid HBr donates an H^+ to the base H_2O. The conjugate acid–base pairs are HBr/Br^- and H_3O^+/H_2O. From Table 10.3, we see that Br^- is a weaker base than H_2O and that H_3O^+ is a weaker acid than HBr. Thus, the solution will contain mostly <u>products</u> at equilibrium.

10.75

Acid	Conjugate Base
HI	I^-
HCl	Cl^-
NH_4^+	NH_3
H_2S	HS^-

10.77 An acidic solution has a pH less than 7.0. A neutral solution has a pH equal to 7.0. A basic solution has a pH greater than 7.0.
a. acidic (pH 5.2 < 7.0)
b. basic (pH 7.5 > 7.0)
c. acidic (pH 3.8 < 7.0)
d. acidic (pH 2.5 < 7.0)
e. basic (pH 12.0 > 7.0)

10.79 Use Table 10.3 to answer (the stronger acid will be closer to the top of the table).
a. HF is the stronger acid.
b. H_3O^+ is the stronger acid.
c. HNO_2 is the stronger acid.
d. HCO_3^- is the stronger acid.

10.81 $[H_3O^+] = \dfrac{1.0 \times 10^{-14}}{[OH^-]}$; $pH = -\log[H_3O^+]$

    a. $pH = -\log[H_3O^+] = -\log[2.0 \times 10^{-8}] = 7.70$ (2 SFs on the right of the decimal point)

    b. $pH = -\log[5.0 \times 10^{-2}] = 1.30$ (2 SFs on the right of the decimal point)

    c. $[H_3O^+] = \dfrac{1.0 \times 10^{-14}}{[3.5 \times 10^{-4}]} = 2.9 \times 10^{-11}$ M

        $pH = -\log[2.9 \times 10^{-11}] = 10.54$ (2 SFs on the right of the decimal point)

    d. $[H_3O^+] = \dfrac{1.0 \times 10^{-14}}{[0.0054]} = 1.9 \times 10^{-12}$ M

        $pH = -\log[1.9 \times 10^{-12}] = 11.72$ (2 SFs on the right of the decimal point)

10.83   **a.** basic (pH > 7.0)
       b. acidic (pH < 7.0)
       c. basic (pH > 7.0)
       d. basic (pH > 7.0)

10.85 If the pH is given, the $[H_3O^+]$ can be found by using the relationship $[H_3O^+] = 10^{-pH}$. The $[OH^-]$ can be found by rearranging $K_w = [H_3O^+][OH^-] = 1 \times 10^{-14}$.

    a. $pH = 3.00$; $[H_3O^+] = 10^{-pH} = 10^{-3.00} = 1.0 \times 10^{-3}$ M (2 SFs)

      $[OH^-] = \dfrac{1.0 \times 10^{-14}}{[H_3O^+]} = \dfrac{1.0 \times 10^{-14}}{[1.0 \times 10^{-3}]} = 1.0 \times 10^{-11}$ M (2 SFs)

    b. $pH = 6.48$; $[H_3O^+] = 10^{-pH} = 10^{-6.48} = 3.3 \times 10^{-7}$ M (2 SFs)

      $[OH^-] = \dfrac{1.0 \times 10^{-14}}{[H_3O^+]} = \dfrac{1.0 \times 10^{-14}}{[3.3 \times 10^{-7}]} = 3.0 \times 10^{-8}$ M (2 SFs)

    c. $pH = 8.85$; $[H_3O^+] = 10^{-pH} = 10^{-8.85} = 1.4 \times 10^{-9}$ M (2 SFs)

      $[OH^-] = \dfrac{1.0 \times 10^{-14}}{[H_3O^+]} = \dfrac{1.0 \times 10^{-14}}{[1.4 \times 10^{-9}]} = 7.1 \times 10^{-6}$ M (2 SFs)

    d. $pH = 11.00$; $[H_3O^+] = 10^{-pH} = 10^{-11.00} = 1.0 \times 10^{-11}$ M (2 SFs)

      $[OH^-] = \dfrac{1.0 \times 10^{-14}}{[H_3O^+]} = \dfrac{1.0 \times 10^{-14}}{[1.0 \times 10^{-11}]} = 1.0 \times 10^{-3}$ M (2 SFs)

10.87   **a.** Sour milk, with a pH of 4.5, is more acidic than maple syrup.

    b. For sour milk, the $[H_3O^+] = 10^{-pH} = 10^{-4.5} = 3 \times 10^{-5}$ M (1 SF)

      For maple syrup, the $[H_3O^+] = 10^{-pH} = 10^{-6.7} = 2 \times 10^{-7}$ M (1 SF)

    c. For sour milk, the $[OH^-] = \dfrac{1.0 \times 10^{-14}}{[H_3O^+]} = \dfrac{1.0 \times 10^{-14}}{[3 \times 10^{-5}]} = 3 \times 10^{-10}$ M (1 SF)

      For maple syrup, the $[OH^-] = \dfrac{1.0 \times 10^{-14}}{[H_3O^+]} = \dfrac{1.0 \times 10^{-14}}{[2 \times 10^{-7}]} = 5 \times 10^{-8}$ M (1 SF)

10.89 The $[OH^-]$ can be calculated from the moles of NaOH (each NaOH produces 1 OH^-) and the volume of the solution (in L).

$$0.225 \text{ g NaOH} \times \frac{1 \text{ mole NaOH}}{40.0 \text{ g NaOH}} \times \frac{1 \text{ mole OH}^-}{1 \text{ mole NaOH}} = 0.005\,63 \text{ mole of OH}^-$$

$$[OH^-] = \frac{0.005\,63 \text{ mole OH}^-}{0.250 \text{ L solution}} = 0.0225 \text{ M (3 SFs)}$$

10.91 $2.5 \text{ g HCl} \times \dfrac{1 \text{ mole HCl}}{36.5 \text{ g HCl}} = 0.069 \text{ mole of HCl}$

$$425 \text{ mL HCl solution} \times \frac{1 \text{ L solution}}{1000 \text{ mL solution}} = 0.425 \text{ L of HCl solution}$$

$$\text{molarity (M) of HCl} = \frac{\text{moles of solute}}{\text{liters of solution}} = \frac{0.069 \text{ mole HCl}}{0.425 \text{ L solution}} = 0.16 \text{ M HCl solution (2 SFs)}$$

Since HCl is a strong acid, the $[H_3O^+]$ is also 0.16 M.

$pH = -\log[H_3O^+] = -\log[0.16] = 0.80$ (2 SFs on the right of the decimal point)

10.93 **a.** $H_3PO_4(aq) + 3KOH(aq) \longrightarrow K_3PO_4(aq) + 3H_2O(l)$
   b. In the titration equation, one mole of H_3PO_4 reacts with three moles of KOH.

$$10.0 \text{ mL H}_3\text{PO}_4 \text{ solution} \times \frac{1 \text{ L H}_3\text{PO}_4 \text{ solution}}{1000 \text{ mL H}_3\text{PO}_4 \text{ solution}} \times \frac{0.560 \text{ mole H}_3\text{PO}_4}{1 \text{ L H}_3\text{PO}_4 \text{ solution}} \times \frac{3 \text{ moles KOH}}{1 \text{ mole H}_3\text{PO}_4}$$

$$\times \frac{1 \text{ L KOH solution}}{0.150 \text{ mole KOH}} \times \frac{1000 \text{ mL KOH solution}}{1 \text{ L KOH solution}} = 112 \text{ mL of KOH solution (3 SFs)}$$

10.95 **a.** To form the conjugate base, remove a hydrogen ion (H^+) from the acid.
   1. HS^- **2.** $H_2PO_4^-$

   b. **1.** $H_2S(aq) + H_2O(l) \rightleftharpoons H_3O^+(aq) + HS^-(aq)$

$$K_a = \frac{[H_3O^+][HS^-]}{[H_2S]}$$

   2. $H_3PO_4(aq) + H_2O(l) \rightleftharpoons H_3O^+(aq) + H_2PO_4^-(aq)$

$$K_a = \frac{[H_3O^+][H_2PO_4^-]}{[H_3PO_4]}$$

   c. H_2S is the weaker acid. (See Table 10.3; the weaker acid will be closer to the bottom of the table.)

10.97 In the titration equation, one mole of H_2SO_4 reacts with two moles of NaOH.

$$45.6 \text{ mL NaOH solution} \times \frac{1 \text{ L solution}}{1000 \text{ mL solution}} \times \frac{0.205 \text{ mole NaOH}}{1 \text{ L solution}} \times \frac{1 \text{ mole H}_2\text{SO}_4}{2 \text{ moles NaOH}}$$

$$= 0.004\,67 \text{ mole of H}_2\text{SO}_4$$

$$20.0 \text{ mL H}_2\text{SO}_4 \text{ solution} \times \frac{1 \text{ L solution}}{1000 \text{ mL solution}} = 0.0200 \text{ L of H}_2\text{SO}_4 \text{ solution}$$

$$\text{molarity (M) of H}_2\text{SO}_4 = \frac{\text{moles of solute}}{\text{liters of solution}} = \frac{0.004\,67 \text{ mole H}_2\text{SO}_4}{0.0200 \text{ L solution}}$$

$$= 0.234 \text{ M H}_2\text{SO}_4 \text{ solution (3 SFs)}$$

10.99 This buffer solution is made from the weak acid H_3PO_4 and a salt containing its conjugate base, $H_2PO_4^-$.

    a. Acid added: $H_2PO_4^-(aq) + H_3O^+(aq) \longrightarrow H_3PO_4(aq) + H_2O(l)$

    b. Base added: $H_3PO_4(aq) + OH^-(aq) \longrightarrow H_2PO_4^-(aq) + H_2O(l)$

    c. $H_3PO_4(aq) + H_2O(l) \rightleftharpoons H_3O^+(aq) + H_2PO_4^-(aq)$

$$K_a = \frac{[H_3O^+][H_2PO_4^-]}{[H_3PO_4]} = 7.5 \times 10^{-3}$$

Rearrange the K_a for $[H_3O^+]$ and use it to calculate the pH.

$$[H_3O^+] = K_a \times \frac{[H_3PO_4]}{[H_2PO_4^-]} = (7.5 \times 10^{-3}) \times \frac{[0.10\ \cancel{M}]}{[0.10\ \cancel{M}]} = 7.5 \times 10^{-3}\ M$$

$$pH = -\log[H_3O^+] = -\log[7.5 \times 10^{-3}] = 2.12 \text{ (2 SFs on the right of the decimal point)}$$

    d. $[H_3O^+] = K_a \times \dfrac{[H_3PO_4]}{[H_2PO_4^-]} = (7.5 \times 10^{-3}) \times \dfrac{[0.50\ \cancel{M}]}{[0.20\ \cancel{M}]} = 1.9 \times 10^{-2}\ M$

$$pH = -\log[H_3O^+] = -\log[1.9 \times 10^{-2}] = 1.72 \text{ (2 SFs on the right of the decimal point)}$$

10.101 KOH (strong base) $\longrightarrow K^+(aq) + OH^-(aq)$ (100% dissociation)

$[OH^-] = 0.050\ M = 5.0 \times 10^{-2}\ M$

    a. $[H_3O^+] = \dfrac{1.0 \times 10^{-14}}{[OH^-]} = \dfrac{1.0 \times 10^{-14}}{[5.0 \times 10^{-2}]} = 2.0 \times 10^{-13}\ M$ (2 SFs)

    b. $pH = -\log[H_3O^+] = -\log[2.0 \times 10^{-13}] = 12.70$ (2 SFs on the right of the decimal point)

    c. $H_2SO_4(aq) + 2KOH(aq) \longrightarrow K_2SO_4(aq) + 2H_2O(l)$

    d. In the titration equation, one mole of H_2SO_4 reacts with two moles of KOH.

$$40.0\ \cancel{\text{mL } H_2SO_4 \text{ solution}} \times \frac{1\ \cancel{\text{L } H_2SO_4 \text{ solution}}}{1000\ \cancel{\text{mL } H_2SO_4 \text{ solution}}} \times \frac{0.035\ \cancel{\text{mole } H_2SO_4}}{1\ \cancel{\text{L } H_2SO_4 \text{ solution}}} \times \frac{2\ \cancel{\text{moles KOH}}}{1\ \cancel{\text{mole } H_2SO_4}}$$

$$\times \frac{1\ \cancel{\text{L KOH solution}}}{0.050\ \cancel{\text{mole KOH}}} \times \frac{1000\ \text{mL KOH solution}}{1\ \cancel{\text{L KOH solution}}} = 56\ \text{mL of KOH solution (2 SFs)}$$

10.103 a. The $[H_3O^+]$ can be found by using the relationship $[H_3O^+] = 10^{-pH}$.

$$[H_3O^+] = 10^{-pH} = 10^{-4.2} = 6 \times 10^{-5}\ M \text{ (1 SF)}$$

$$[OH^-] = \frac{1.0 \times 10^{-14}}{[H_3O^+]} = \frac{1.0 \times 10^{-14}}{[6 \times 10^{-5}]} = 2 \times 10^{-10}\ M \text{ (1 SF)}$$

    b. $[H_3O^+] = 10^{-pH} = 10^{-6.5} = 3 \times 10^{-7}\ M$ (1 SF)

$$[OH^-] = \frac{1.0 \times 10^{-14}}{[H_3O^+]} = \frac{1.0 \times 10^{-14}}{[3 \times 10^{-7}]} = 3 \times 10^{-8}\ M \text{ (1 SF)}$$

    c. In the titration equation, one mole of $CaCO_3$ reacts with one mole of H_2SO_4.

$$1.0\ \cancel{\text{kL solution}} \times \frac{1000\ \cancel{\text{L solution}}}{1\ \cancel{\text{kL solution}}} \times \frac{6 \times 10^{-5}\ \cancel{\text{mole } H_3O^+}}{1\ \cancel{\text{L solution}}} \times \frac{1\ \cancel{\text{mole } H_2SO_4}}{2\ \cancel{\text{moles } H_3O^+}}$$

$$\times \frac{1\ \cancel{\text{mole } CaCO_3}}{1\ \cancel{\text{mole } H_2SO_4}} \times \frac{100.1\ \text{g } CaCO_3}{1\ \cancel{\text{mole } CaCO_3}} = 3\ \text{g of } CaCO_3 \text{ (1 SF)}$$

Answers to Combining Ideas from Chapters 7 to 10

CI.17 **a.** CH_4 $H:\overset{\displaystyle H}{\underset{\displaystyle H}{\overset{..}{\underset{..}{C}}}}:H$ or $H-\overset{\displaystyle H}{\underset{\displaystyle H}{\overset{|}{\underset{|}{C}}}}-H$

b. $7.0 \times 10^6 \text{ gal} \times \dfrac{4 \text{ qt}}{1 \text{ gal}} \times \dfrac{946 \text{ mL}}{1 \text{ qt}} \times \dfrac{0.45 \text{ g}}{1 \text{ mL}} \times \dfrac{1 \text{ kg}}{1000 \text{ g}} = 1.2 \times 10^7 \text{ kg of LNG (methane) (2 SFs)}$

c. molar mass of methane $(CH_4) = 1(12.0 \text{ g}) + 4(1.01 \text{ g}) = 16.0 \text{ g}$

$7.0 \times 10^6 \text{ gal} \times \dfrac{4 \text{ qt}}{1 \text{ gal}} \times \dfrac{946 \text{ mL}}{1 \text{ qt}} \times \dfrac{0.45 \text{ g}}{1 \text{ mL}} \times \dfrac{1 \text{ mole } CH_4}{16.0 \text{ g}} \times \dfrac{22.4 \text{ L } CH_4 \text{ (STP)}}{1 \text{ mole } CH_4}$

$= 1.7 \times 10^{10} \text{ L of LNG (methane) at STP (2 SFs)}$

d. $CH_4(g) + 2O_2(g) \xrightarrow{\Delta} CO_2(g) + 2H_2O(g) + 883 \text{ kJ}$

e. $7.0 \times 10^6 \text{ gal} \times \dfrac{4 \text{ qt}}{1 \text{ gal}} \times \dfrac{946 \text{ mL}}{1 \text{ qt}} \times \dfrac{0.45 \text{ g}}{1 \text{ mL}} \times \dfrac{1 \text{ mole } CH_4}{16.0 \text{ g}}$

$\times \dfrac{2 \text{ moles } O_2}{1 \text{ mole } CH_4} \times \dfrac{32.0 \text{ g } O_2}{1 \text{ mole } O_2} \times \dfrac{1 \text{ kg } O_2}{1000 \text{ g } O_2}$

$= 4.8 \times 10^7 \text{ kg of } O_2 \text{ (2 SFs)}$

f. $7.0 \times 10^6 \text{ gal} \times \dfrac{4 \text{ qt}}{1 \text{ gal}} \times \dfrac{946 \text{ mL}}{1 \text{ qt}} \times \dfrac{0.45 \text{ g}}{1 \text{ mL}} \times \dfrac{1 \text{ mole } CH_4}{16.0 \text{ g}} \times \dfrac{883 \text{ kJ}}{1 \text{ mole } CH_4}$

$= 6.6 \times 10^{11} \text{ kJ (2 SFs)}$

CI.19 **a.** $0.121 \text{ g } Mg \times \dfrac{1 \text{ mole } Mg}{24.3 \text{ g } Mg} \times \dfrac{1 \text{ mole } H_2}{1 \text{ mole } Mg} = 0.004\,98 \text{ mole of } H_2 \text{ (smaller number of moles)}$

$50.0 \text{ mL solution} \times \dfrac{1 \text{ L}}{1000 \text{ mL}} \times \dfrac{1.00 \text{ mole HCl}}{1 \text{ L solution}} \times \dfrac{1 \text{ mole } H_2}{2 \text{ moles HCl}} = 0.0250 \text{ mole of } H_2$

$\therefore$ Mg is the limiting reactant.

b. **Analyze the Problem**

Property	*P*	*V*	*n*	*R*	*T*
Given	750. mmHg		0.121 g (0.004 98 mole)	$\dfrac{62.4 \text{ L} \cdot \text{mmHg}}{\text{mole} \cdot \text{K}}$	33.0 °C 33.0 °C + 273 = 306 K
Need		? L			

$V = \dfrac{nRT}{P} = \dfrac{(0.004\,98 \text{ mole})\left(\dfrac{62.4 \text{ L} \cdot \text{mmHg}}{\text{mole} \cdot \text{K}}\right)(306 \text{ K})}{750. \text{ mmHg}} = 0.127 \text{ L of } H_2 \text{ (3 SFs)}$

c. $50.0 \text{ mL solution} \times \dfrac{1.00 \text{ g}}{1 \text{ mL}} = 50.0 \text{ g of solution}$

$\Delta T = T_{\text{final}} - T_{\text{initial}} = 33.0 \,°\text{C} - 22.0 \,°\text{C} = 11.0 \,°\text{C}$

$50.0 \text{ g solution} \times \dfrac{4.184 \text{ J}}{\text{g} \, °\text{C}} \times 11.0 \,°\text{C} = 2.30 \times 10^3 \text{ J} \ (3 \text{ SFs})$

d. $\dfrac{2.30 \times 10^3 \text{ J}}{0.121 \text{ g Mg}} = 1.90 \times 10^4 \text{ J/g of Mg} \ (3 \text{ SFs})$

$\dfrac{2.30 \times 10^3 \text{ J}}{0.121 \text{ g Mg}} \times \dfrac{1 \text{ kJ}}{1000 \text{ J}} \times \dfrac{24.31 \text{ g Mg}}{1 \text{ mole Mg}} = 462 \text{ kJ/mole of Mg} \ (3 \text{ SFs})$

CI.21 a. $[H_2] = \dfrac{2.02 \text{ g } H_2}{10.0 \text{ L}} \times \dfrac{1 \text{ mole } H_2}{2.02 \text{ g } H_2} = 0.100 \text{ M}$

$[S_2] = \dfrac{10.3 \text{ g } S_2}{10.0 \text{ L}} \times \dfrac{1 \text{ mole } S_2}{64.2 \text{ g } S_2} = 0.0160 \text{ M}$

$[H_2S] = \dfrac{68.2 \text{ g } H_2S}{10.0 \text{ L}} \times \dfrac{1 \text{ mole } H_2S}{34.1 \text{ g } H_2S} = 0.200 \text{ M}$

$K_c = \dfrac{[H_2S]^2}{[H_2]^2[S_2]} = \dfrac{[0.200]^2}{[0.100]^2[0.0160]} = 250. \ (3 \text{ SFs})$

b. If more H_2 (a reactant) is added, the equilibrium will shift in the direction of the products.

c. If the volume decreases from 10.0 L to 5.00 L (at constant temperature), the equilibrium will shift in the direction of the products (fewer moles of gas).

d. $[H_2] = \dfrac{0.300 \text{ mole } H_2}{5.00 \text{ L}} = 0.0600 \text{ M}$

$[H_2S] = \dfrac{2.50 \text{ moles } H_2S}{5.00 \text{ L}} = 0.500 \text{ M}$

$K_c = \dfrac{[H_2S]^2}{[H_2]^2[S_2]} = 250.$

Rearrange the expression to solve for $[S_2]$ and substitute in known values.

$[S_2] = \dfrac{[H_2S]^2}{[H_2]^2 K_c} = \dfrac{[0.500]^2}{[0.0600]^2(250.)} = 0.278 \text{ mole/L} \ (3 \text{ SFs})$

CI.23 a. $2M(s) + 6HCl(aq) \longrightarrow 2MCl_3(aq) + 3H_2(g)$

b. $34.8 \text{ mL solution} \times \dfrac{1 \text{ L solution}}{1000 \text{ mL solution}} \times \dfrac{0.520 \text{ mole HCl}}{1 \text{ L solution}} \times \dfrac{3 \text{ moles } H_2}{6 \text{ moles HCl}}$

$= 0.009 \, 05 \text{ mole of } H_2 \ (3 \text{ SFs})$

$$V = \frac{nRT}{P} = \frac{(0.009\,05 \text{ mole})\left(\dfrac{62.4 \text{ L} \cdot \text{mmHg}}{\text{mole} \cdot \text{K}}\right)(297 \text{ K})}{(720. \text{ mmHg})} \times \frac{1000 \text{ mL}}{1 \text{ L}} = 233 \text{ mL of } H_2 \text{ (3 SFs)}$$

c. $34.8 \text{ mL solution} \times \dfrac{1 \text{ L solution}}{1000 \text{ mL solution}} \times \dfrac{0.520 \text{ mole HCl}}{1 \text{ L solution}} \times \dfrac{2 \text{ moles M}}{6 \text{ moles HCl}}$

$= 6.03 \times 10^{-3} \text{ mole of M (3 SFs)}$

d. $\dfrac{0.420 \text{ g M}}{6.03 \times 10^{-3} \text{ mole M}} = 69.7 \text{ g/mole of M (3 SFs)}$

∴ the metal is gallium, Ga.

e. $2Ga(s) + 6HCl(aq) \longrightarrow 2GaCl_3(aq) + 3H_2(g)$

Introduction to Organic Chemistry: Alkanes

11

11.1 Organic compounds contain C and H and sometimes O, S, N, P, or a halogen atom. Inorganic compounds usually contain elements other than C and H.
   a. KCl is inorganic.
   b. C_4H_{10} is organic.
   c. C_2H_6O is organic.
   d. H_2SO_4 is inorganic.
   e. $CaCl_2$ is inorganic.
   f. C_3H_7Cl is organic.

11.3 **a.** Inorganic compounds are usually soluble in water.
   b. Organic compounds have lower boiling points than most inorganic compounds.
   c. Organic compounds contain carbon and hydrogen.
   d. Inorganic compounds contain ionic bonds.

11.5 **a.** Ethane boils at −89 °C.
   b. Ethane burns vigorously in air.
   c. NaBr is a solid at 250 °C.
   d. NaBr dissolves in water.

11.7 VSEPR theory predicts that the four bonds between carbon and hydrogen in methane, CH_4, will be as far apart as possible, which means that the hydrogen atoms are at the corners of a tetrahedron.

11.9 **a.** In the expanded structural formula for propane, all the C—C and C—H bonds are shown.

```
    H   H   H
    |   |   |
H — C — C — C — H
    |   |   |
    H   H   H
```

   b. In the condensed structural formula for hexane, each carbon atom and its attached hydrogen atoms are written as a group.

   $CH_3—CH_2—CH_2—CH_2—CH_2—CH_3$

   c. The skeletal formula for pentane shows the carbon skeleton as a zigzag line where the ends and corners represent C atoms.

11.11 **a.** Pentane has a carbon chain of five carbon atoms.
   b. Heptane has a carbon chain of seven carbon atoms.
   c. Hexane has a carbon chain of six carbon atoms.
   d. A ring of four carbons is cyclobutane.

11.13 **a.** CH_4
   b. $CH_3—CH_3$
   c. $CH_3—CH_2—CH_2—CH_2—CH_3$
   d. △

11.15 Two structures are isomers if they have the same molecular formula, but different arrangements of atoms.

   a. These condensed structural formulas represent the same molecule; the only difference is due to rotation of the structure. Each has a CH_3- group attached to the middle carbon in a three-carbon chain.

   b. The molecular formula of both these condensed structural formulas is C_5H_{12}. However, they represent structural isomers because the C atoms are bonded in a different order; they have different arrangements. In the first, there is a CH_3- group attached to carbon 2 of a four-carbon chain, and in the other, there is a five-carbon chain.

   c. The molecular formula of both these condensed structural formulas is C_6H_{14}. However, they represent structural isomers because the C atoms are bonded in a different order; they have different arrangements. In the first, there is a CH_3- group attached to carbon 3 of a five-carbon chain, and in the other, there is a CH_3- group on carbon 2 and carbon 3 of a four-carbon chain.

11.17   **a.**   1-fluoropropane
   b.   2,3-dimethylpentane
   c.   4-ethyl-2,2-dimethylhexane
   d.   chlorocyclopentane
   e.   2-chloropropane
   f.   methylcyclohexane

11.19 Draw the main chain with the number of carbon atoms in the ending of the name. For example, butane has a main chain of four carbon atoms, and hexane has a main chain of six carbon atoms. Attach substituents on the carbon atoms indicated. For example, in 3-methylpentane, a CH_3- group is bonded to carbon 3 of a five-carbon chain.

   a. $Br-CH_2-CH_2-CH_2-Cl$

   b.
$$CH_3-CH_2-\overset{\overset{\displaystyle CH_3}{|}}{\underset{\underset{\displaystyle CH_3}{|}}{C}}-CH_2-CH_3$$

   c.
$$CH_3-\overset{\overset{\displaystyle CH_3}{|}}{CH}-\overset{\overset{\displaystyle CH_3}{|}}{CH}-CH_2-\overset{\overset{\displaystyle CH_3}{|}}{CH}-CH_3$$

   d.
$$CH_3-\overset{\overset{\displaystyle CH_3}{|}}{CH}-\overset{\overset{\displaystyle CH_2-CH_3}{|}}{CH}-CH_2-\overset{\overset{\displaystyle CH_3}{|}}{CH}-CH_2-CH_2-CH_3$$

   e. $Br-CH_2-CH_2-Br$

11.21   **a.**

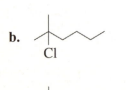

   b.

   c.

d.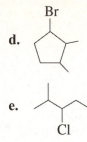

e.

11.23   **a.** $CH_3-CH_2-CH_2-CH_2-CH_2-CH_2-CH_3$

        b.   Heptane is a liquid at room temperature since it has a boiling point of 98 °C.

        c.   Heptane contains only nonpolar C—H bonds, which makes it insoluble in water.

        d.   Since the density of heptane (0.68 g/mL) is less than that of water, heptane will float on water.

        e. $C_7H_{16}(g) + 11O_2(g) \xrightarrow{\Delta} 7CO_2(g) + 8H_2O(g) + energy$

11.25   Longer carbon chains have higher boiling points. The boiling points of straight-chain alkanes are usually higher than their branched-chain isomers. Cycloalkanes have higher boiling points than their straight-chain counterparts.

        a.   Heptane has a greater molar mass and so will have a higher boiling point than pentane.

        b.   The cyclic alkane cyclopropane will have a higher boiling point than its straight-chain counterpart propane.

        c.   The straight-chain alkane hexane will have a higher boiling point than its branched isomer 2-methylpentane.

11.27   In combustion, a hydrocarbon reacts with oxygen to yield CO_2 and H_2O.

        a. $2C_2H_6(g) + 7O_2(g) \xrightarrow{\Delta} 4CO_2(g) + 6H_2O(g) + energy$

        b. $2C_8H_{18}(g) + 25O_2(g) \xrightarrow{\Delta} 16CO_2(g) + 18H_2O(g) + energy$

        c. $C_6H_{12}(g) + 9O_2(g) \xrightarrow{\Delta} 6CO_2(g) + 6H_2O(g) + energy$

11.29   **a.**   Alcohols contain a hydroxyl group (—OH) attached to a carbon chain.

        b.   Alkenes have carbon–carbon double bonds.

        c.   Aldehydes contain a carbonyl group (C=O) attached to a hydrogen atom.

        d.   Esters contain a carboxyl group (—COO—) attached to two carbon atoms.

11.31   **a.**   Ethers have an —O— group.

        b.   Alcohols have an —OH group.

        c.   Ketones have a C=O group between alkyl groups.

        d.   Carboxylic acids have a —COOH group.

        e.   Amines contain an N atom bonded to at least one carbon atom.

11.33   **a.**   Butane melts at –138 °C.

        b.   Butane burns vigorously in air.

        c.   KCl melts at 770 °C.

        d.   KCl contains ionic bonds.

        e.   Butane is a gas at room temperature.

11.35   Two structures are isomers if they have the same molecular formula, but different arrangements of atoms.

        a.   The molecular formula of both these skeletal formulas is C_6H_{12}. However, they represent structural isomers because the C atoms are bonded in a different order; they have different arrangements. In the first, there is a methyl group attached to a five-carbon ring, and in the other, there is a six-carbon ring.

        b.   The molecular formula of the first skeletal structure is C_5H_{12}; the molecular formula of the second is C_6H_{14}. They are not structural isomers.

11.37   **a.**   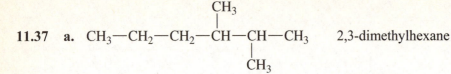   2,3-dimethylhexane

b.

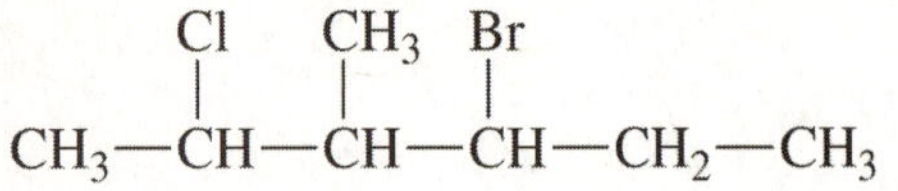

$$Cl \quad CH_3 \quad Br$$
$$CH_3—CH—CH—CH—CH_2—CH_3 \qquad \text{4-bromo-2-chloro-3-methylhexane}$$

11.39   **a.**   An alcohol is an organic compound that contains a hydroxyl group bonded to a carbon.
b.   An alkene is a hydrocarbon that contains one or more carbon–carbon double bonds.
c.   An aldehyde is an organic compound in which the carbon of a carbonyl group is bonded to a hydrogen.
d.   An alkane is a hydrocarbon that contains only carbon–carbon single bonds.
e.   A carboxylic acid is an organic compound in which the carbon of a carbonyl group is bonded to a hydroxyl group.
f.   An amine is an organic compound that contains a nitrogen atom bonded to one or more carbon atoms.

11.41   **a.**   Amines contain an N atom bonded to at least one carbon atom.
b.   Ketones have a C=O group between alkyl groups.
c.   Esters have a carboxyl group attached to two carbon chains.
d.   Alcohols have an —OH group.

11.43   **a.**   aldehyde, aromatic
b.   alkene, aldehyde, aromatic
c.   ketone

11.45   **a.**   methyl
b.   propyl
c.   chloro

11.47   **a.**   methylcyclopentane
b.   1,2-dibromo-3-chloropropane
c.   2,3-dimethylhexane
d.   3-chloro-3-ethylpentane

11.49 $Br—CH_2—CH_2—CH_2—CH_3$ 1-bromobutane

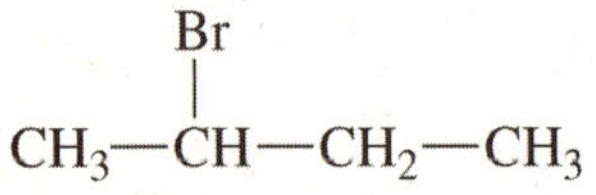

$$Br$$
$$CH_3—CH—CH_2—CH_3 \qquad \text{2-bromobutane}$$

$$CH_3$$
$$CH_3—CH—CH_2—Br \qquad \text{1-bromo-2-methylpropane}$$

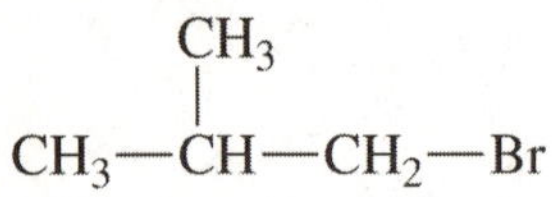

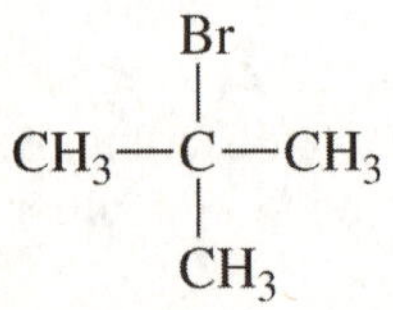

$$Br$$
$$CH_3—C—CH_3 \qquad \text{2-bromo-2-methylpropane}$$
$$CH_3$$

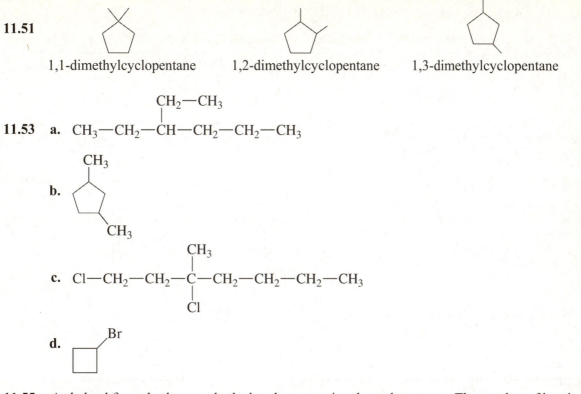

11.51

1,1-dimethylcyclopentane   1,2-dimethylcyclopentane   1,3-dimethylcyclopentane

11.53 **a.**

$$CH_3-CH_2-\overset{\overset{\displaystyle CH_2-CH_3}{|}}{CH}-CH_2-CH_2-CH_3$$

b.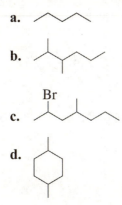

c.

$$Cl-CH_2-CH_2-\overset{\overset{\displaystyle CH_3}{|}}{\underset{\underset{\displaystyle Cl}{|}}{C}}-CH_2-CH_2-CH_2-CH_3$$

d.

11.55 A skeletal formula shows only the bonds connecting the carbon atoms. The number of bonds to hydrogen atoms is understood.

a.

b.

c.

d.

11.57 Longer carbon chains have higher boiling points. The boiling points of straight-chain alkanes are usually higher than their branched-chain isomers. Cycloalkanes have higher boiling points than their straight-chain counterparts.
  a. Pentane has a greater molar mass and so will have a higher boiling point than propane.
  b. The cyclic alkane cyclopentane will have a higher boiling point than its straight-chain counterpart pentane.
  c. The straight-chain alkane hexane will have a higher boiling point than its branched isomer 2,2-dimethylbutane.
  d. The branched-chain alkane 2-methylbutane will have a higher boiling point than its more highly branched isomer 2,2-dimethylpropane.

11.59 **a.** $2C_3H_6(g) + 9O_2(g) \xrightarrow{\Delta} 6CO_2(g) + 6H_2O(g) + \text{energy}$
  b. $C_5H_{12}(g) + 8O_2(g) \xrightarrow{\Delta} 5CO_2(g) + 6H_2O(g) + \text{energy}$
  c. $C_4H_8(g) + 6O_2(g) \xrightarrow{\Delta} 4CO_2(g) + 4H_2O(g) + \text{energy}$

11.61   **a.** $C_3H_8(g) + 5O_2(g) \xrightarrow{\Delta} 3CO_2(g) + 4H_2O(g) + energy$

      b. $2.8 \text{ kg } C_3H_8 \times \dfrac{1000 \text{ g } C_3H_8}{1 \text{ kg } C_3H_8} \times \dfrac{1 \text{ mole } C_3H_8}{44.1 \text{ g } C_3H_8} \times \dfrac{3 \text{ moles } CO_2}{1 \text{ mole } C_3H_8} \times \dfrac{44.0 \text{ g } CO_2}{1 \text{ mole } CO_2} \times \dfrac{1 \text{ kg } CO_2}{1000 \text{ g } CO_2}$

        $= 8.4 \text{ kg of } CO_2 \ \ (2 \text{ SFs})$

11.63   **a.**   ether, aromatic, alcohol, ketone
      b.   ether, aromatic, alkene, ester

11.65   ether, aromatic, amide

11.67   **a.**

$$CH_3-\underset{\underset{CH_3}{|}}{\overset{\overset{CH_3}{|}}{C}}-CH_2-\underset{\underset{CH_3}{|}}{CH}-CH_3 \qquad 2,2,4\text{-trimethylpentane } (C_8H_{18})$$

      b. $2C_8H_{18}(g) + 25O_2(g) \xrightarrow{\Delta} 16CO_2(g) + 18H_2O(g) + energy$

11.69 $CH_3-CH_2-CH_2-OH \qquad CH_3-\underset{\underset{}{}}{\overset{\overset{OH}{|}}{CH}}-CH_3 \qquad CH_3-CH_2-O-CH_3$

11.71   **a.** $CH_3-CH_2-CH_3$

      b. $C_3H_8(g) + 5O_2(g) \xrightarrow{\Delta} 3CO_2(g) + 4H_2O(g) + energy$

      c. $12.0 \text{ L } C_3H_8 \times \dfrac{1 \text{ mole } C_3H_8}{22.4 \text{ L } C_3H_8 \text{ (STP)}} \times \dfrac{5 \text{ moles } O_2}{1 \text{ mole } C_3H_8} \times \dfrac{32.0 \text{ g } O_2}{1 \text{ mole } O_2} = 85.7 \text{ g of } O_2 \ \ (3 \text{ SFs})$

      d. $12.0 \text{ L } C_3H_8 \times \dfrac{1 \text{ mole } C_3H_8}{22.4 \text{ L } C_3H_8 \text{ (STP)}} \times \dfrac{3 \text{ moles } CO_2}{1 \text{ mole } C_3H_8} \times \dfrac{44.0 \text{ g } CO_2}{1 \text{ mole } CO_2} = 70.7 \text{ g of } CO_2 \ \ (3 \text{ SFs})$

Alkenes, Alkynes, and Aromatic Compounds

12.1 **a.** A condensed structural formula with a carbon–carbon double bond is an alkene.
   b. A condensed structural formula with a carbon–carbon triple bond is an alkyne.
   c. A skeletal formula with a carbon–carbon double bond is an alkene.
   d. A skeletal formula with a carbon–carbon double bond in a ring is a cycloalkene.

12.3 **a.** This alkene has a three-carbon chain with the double bond between carbon 1 and carbon 2, and a one-carbon methyl group attached to carbon 2. The IUPAC name is 2-methylpropene.
   b. This alkyne has a five-carbon chain with the triple bond between carbon 2 and carbon 3, and a bromine atom attached to carbon 4. The IUPAC name is 4-bromo-2-pentyne.
   c. This is a five-carbon cyclic structure with a double bond (between carbon 1 and 2 of the ring), and a two-carbon ethyl group attached to carbon 4 of the ring. The IUPAC name is 4-ethylcyclopentene.
   d. This alkene has a six-carbon chain with the double bond between carbon 2 and carbon 3, and a two-carbon ethyl group attached to carbon 4. The IUPAC name is 4-ethyl-2-hexene.

12.5 **a.** 1-Pentene is the five-carbon compound with a double bond between carbon 1 and carbon 2.

   $H_2C\!=\!CH\!-\!CH_2\!-\!CH_2\!-\!CH_3$

   b. 2-Methyl-1-butene has a four-carbon chain with a double bond between carbon 1 and carbon 2, and a methyl group attached to carbon 2.

   $$\begin{array}{c} CH_3 \\ | \\ H_2C\!=\!C\!-\!CH_2\!-\!CH_3 \end{array}$$

   c. 3-Methylcyclohexene is a six-carbon cyclic compound with a double bond (between carbon 1 and carbon 2 of the ring), and a methyl group attached to carbon 3 of the ring.

   d. 4-Chloro-2-pentyne is a five-carbon compound with a triple bond between carbon 2 and carbon 3, and a chlorine atom attached to carbon 4.

   $$\begin{array}{c} Cl \\ | \\ CH_3\!-\!C\!\equiv\!C\!-\!CH\!-\!CH_3 \end{array}$$

12.7 **a.** This compound cannot have cis–trans isomers since there are two identical hydrogen atoms attached to the first carbon of the double bond.
   b. This compound can have cis–trans isomers since there are different groups attached to each carbon atom of the double bond.
   c. This compound cannot have cis–trans isomers since there are two of the same groups attached to each carbon of the double bond.

12.9 **a.** *cis*-2-Butene; this is a four-carbon compound with a double bond between carbon 2 and carbon 3. Both methyl groups are on the same side of the double bond; it is the cis isomer.
   b. *trans*-3-Octene; this compound has eight carbons with a double bond between carbon 3 and carbon 4. The alkyl groups are on opposite sides of the double bond; it is the trans isomer.
   c. *cis*-3-Heptene; this is a seven-carbon compound with a double bond between carbon 3 and carbon 4. Both alkyl groups are on the same side of the double bond; it is the cis isomer.

12.11 **a.** *trans*-1-Chloro-2-butene has a four-carbon chain with a double bond between carbon 2 and carbon 3, and a chlorine atom attached to carbon 1. The trans isomer has the alkyl groups on opposite sides of the double bond.

$$\begin{array}{ccc} H & & CH_3 \\ & C=C & \\ Cl-CH_2 & & H \end{array}$$

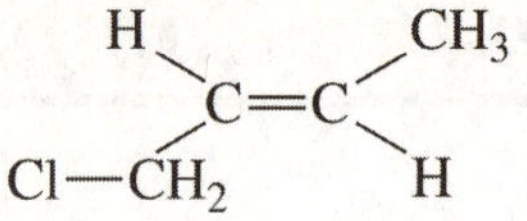

b. *cis*-2-Pentene has a five-carbon chain with a double bond between carbon 2 and carbon 3. The cis isomer has the alkyl groups on the same side of the double bond.

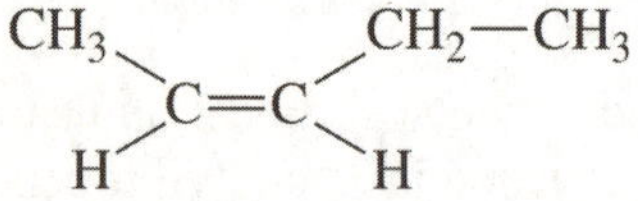

$$\begin{array}{ccc} CH_3 & & CH_2-CH_3 \\ & C=C & \\ H & & H \end{array}$$

c. *trans*-3-Heptene has a seven-carbon chain with a double bond between carbon 3 and carbon 4. The trans isomer has the alkyl groups on opposite sides of the double bond.

$$\begin{array}{ccc} CH_3-CH_2 & & H \\ & C=C & \\ H & & CH_2-CH_2-CH_3 \end{array}$$

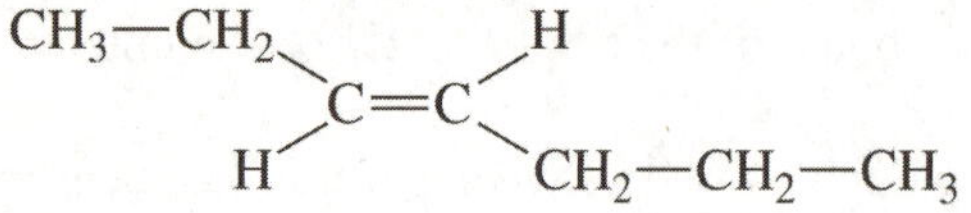

12.13 **a.** Hydrogenation of an alkene gives the saturated compound, the alkane.

$CH_3-CH_2-CH_2-CH_2-CH_3$ pentane

b. When Cl_2 is added to an alkene, the chlorine atoms add to the carbon atoms in the double bond, producing a dichloroalkane.

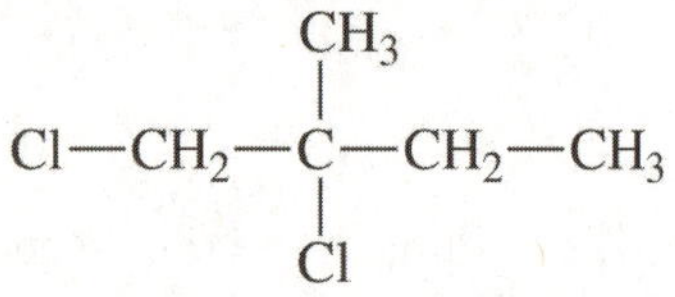

$$\begin{array}{c} CH_3 \\ | \\ Cl-CH_2-C-CH_2-CH_3 \\ | \\ Cl \end{array}$$ 1,2-dichloro-2-methylbutane

c. When Br_2 is added to a cycloalkene, the bromine atoms add to the carbon atoms in the double bond, producing a dibromocycloalkane.

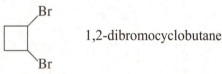   1,2-dibromocyclobutane

d. Hydrogenation of a cycloalkene gives the saturated compound, the cycloalkane.

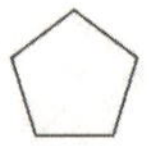

⬠   cyclopentane

e. When Cl_2 is added to an alkene, the chlorine atoms add to the carbon atoms in the double bond, producing a dichloroalkane.

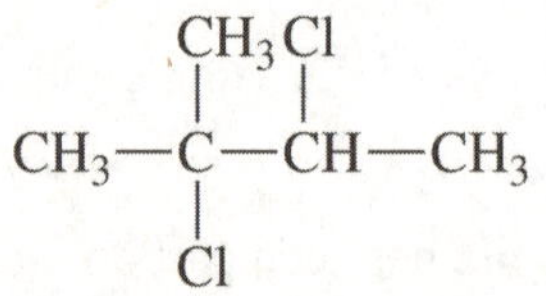

$$\begin{array}{c} CH_3\ Cl \\ |\ \ \ | \\ CH_3-C-CH-CH_3 \\ | \\ Cl \end{array}$$ 2,3-dichloro-2-methylbutane

f. Complete hydrogenation of an alkyne gives the saturated compound, the alkane.

$CH_3-CH_2-CH_2-CH_2-CH_3$ pentane

12.15 a. When HBr is added to an alkene, the product is a bromoalkane. In this case, we do not need to use Markovnikov's rule, since 2-butene is symmetrical.

$$CH_3—CH_2—\overset{\overset{\displaystyle Br}{|}}{CH}—CH_3$$

b. When HOH (water) is added to a cycloalkene, the product is a cycloalkanol. In this case, we do not need to use Markovnikov's rule, since cyclopentene is symmetrical.

c. When HCl is added to an alkene, the product is a chloroalkane. We need to use Markovnikov's rule, which says that hydrogen adds to the carbon with the greater number of hydrogens; in this case, that is carbon 1.

$$CH_3—\overset{\overset{\displaystyle Cl}{|}}{CH}—CH_2—CH_3$$

d. When HI is added to an alkene, the product is an iodoalkane. In this case, we do not need to use Markovnikov's rule, since the molecule is symmetrical.

$$CH_3—\overset{\overset{\displaystyle CH_3}{|}}{CH}—\overset{\overset{\displaystyle I}{|}}{\underset{\underset{\displaystyle CH_3}{|}}{C}}—CH_3$$

e. When HBr is added to an alkene, the product is a bromoalkane. We need to use Markovnikov's rule, which says that hydrogen adds to the carbon with the greater number of hydrogens; in this case, that is carbon 2.

$$CH_3—CH_2—\overset{\overset{\displaystyle Br}{|}}{\underset{\underset{\displaystyle CH_3}{|}}{C}}—CH_2—CH_3$$

f. When HOH (water) is added to a cycloalkene, the product is a cycloalkanol. We need to use Markovnikov's rule, which says that hydrogen adds to the carbon with the greater number of hydrogens; in this case, that is carbon 2 of the ring.

12.17 a. Hydrogenation of an alkene gives the saturated compound, the alkane.

$$H_2C{=}\overset{\overset{\displaystyle CH_3}{|}}{C}—CH_3 + H_2 \xrightarrow{Pt} CH_3—\overset{\overset{\displaystyle CH_3}{|}}{CH}—CH_3$$

b. When HCl is added to a cycloalkene, the product is a chlorocycloalkane. In this case, we do not need to use Markovnikov's rule, since the structure is symmetrical.

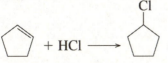

c. When Br_2 is added to an alkene, the bromine atoms add to the carbon atoms in the double bond, producing a dibromoalkane.

$$CH_3—CH{=}CH—CH_2—CH_3 + Br_2 \longrightarrow CH_3—\overset{\overset{\displaystyle Br}{|}}{CH}—\overset{\overset{\displaystyle Br}{|}}{CH}—CH_2—CH_3$$

d. When HOH (water) is added to an alkene, the product is an alcohol. We need to use Markovnikov's rule, which says that hydrogen adds to the carbon with the greater number of hydrogens; in this case, that is carbon 1.

$$H_2C{=}CH{-}CH_3 + HOH \xrightarrow{H^+} CH_3{-}\underset{\underset{OH}{|}}{CH}{-}CH_3$$

e. When Cl_2 is added to an alkyne, the chlorine atoms add to the carbon atoms in the triple bond, producing a tetrachloroalkane.

$$CH_3{-}C{\equiv}C{-}CH_3 + 2Cl_2 \longrightarrow CH_3{-}\underset{\underset{Cl}{|}}{\overset{\overset{Cl}{|}}{C}}{-}\underset{\underset{Cl}{|}}{\overset{\overset{Cl}{|}}{C}}{-}CH_3$$

12.19 A polymer is a very large molecule composed of small units (monomers) that are repeated many times.

12.21 $3\ H_2C{=}CH$ (with CH_3) $\longrightarrow$ polymer chain with repeating $-C-C-$ units bearing H, CH_3, H substituents

12.23 polymer chain: $-C-C-C-C-C-C-$ with F, H, F, H, F, H substituents (top and bottom)

12.25
a. Cyclohexane has the formula C_6H_{12}.
b. Benzene has one hydrogen atom bonded to each carbon.
c. Cyclohexane contains only single bonds.

12.27 Aromatic compounds that contain a benzene ring with a single substituent are usually named as benzene derivatives. A benzene ring with a methyl substituent is named toluene. The methyl group is attached to carbon 1, and the ring is numbered to give the lower numbers to other substituents. If two groups are in the 1,2-position, this is *ortho-* (*o-*); 1,3- is *meta-* (*m-*); and 1,4- is *para-* (*p-*).
a. 1-chloro-2-methylbenzene, *o*-chloromethylbenzene, 2-chlorotoluene, *o*-chlorotoluene
b. ethylbenzene
c. 1,3,5-trichlorobenzene
d. 1,3-dimethylbenzene, *m*-dimethylbenzene, 3-methyltoluene, *m*-methyltoluene, *m*-xylene
e. 3-bromo-5-chloro-1-methylbenzene, 3-bromo-5-chlorotoluene
f. isopropylbenzene

12.29
a. benzene ring with CH_3
b. benzene ring with Br and Cl

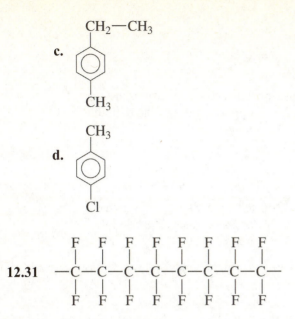

c.

CH$_2$—CH$_3$

CH$_3$

d.

CH$_3$

Cl

12.31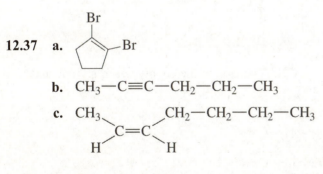

12.33
a. Propane has three carbon atoms and two carbon–carbon single bonds.
b. Cyclopropane has three carbon atoms and three carbon–carbon single bonds in a ring.
c. Propene has three carbon atoms, one carbon–carbon single bond, and one carbon–carbon double bond.
d. Propyne has three carbon atoms, one carbon–carbon single bond, and one carbon–carbon triple bond.

12.35
a. This alkene has a five-carbon chain with a double bond between carbon 1 and carbon 2, and a methyl group attached to carbon 2. The IUPAC name is 2-methyl-1-pentene.
b. This alkene has a six-carbon chain with the double bond between carbon 1 and carbon 2. The substituents are a bromine atom attached to carbon 4 and a methyl group on carbon 5. The IUPAC name is 4-bromo-5-methyl-1-hexene.
c. This is a five-carbon cyclic structure with a double bond. The IUPAC name is cyclopentene.
d. This alkyne has a five-carbon chain with the triple bond between carbon 2 and carbon 3. The IUPAC name is 2-pentyne.

12.37

a.

Br

Br

b. CH$_3$—C≡C—CH$_2$—CH$_2$—CH$_3$

c.

CH$_3$ CH$_2$—CH$_2$—CH$_2$—CH$_3$

C═C

H   H

12.39
a. These structures represent a pair of structural isomers. Both have the molecular formula C_5H_7Cl. In one isomer, the chlorine is attached to one of the carbons in the double bond; in the other isomer, the carbon bonded to the chlorine is not part of the double bond.
b. These structures are cis–trans isomers. In the cis isomer, the two methyl groups are on the same side of the double bond. In the trans isomer, the methyl groups are on opposite sides of the double bond.

12.41
a. *cis*-3-heptene
b. *trans*-2-methyl-3-hexene
c. *trans*-2-heptene

12.43 a.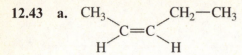

cis-2-pentene; both alkyl groups are on the same side of the double bond.

trans-2-pentene; the alkyl groups are on opposite sides of the double bond.

b.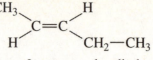

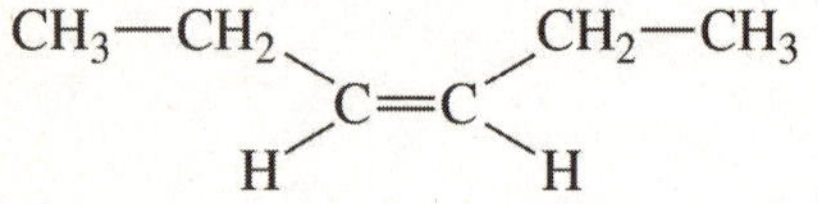

cis-3-hexene; both alkyl groups are on the same side of the double bond.

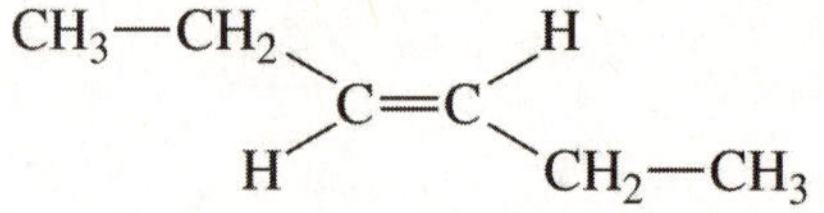

trans-3-hexene; the alkyl groups are on opposite sides of the double bond.

12.45 During hydrogenation, the multiple bonds are converted to single bonds and two H atoms are added for each bond converted.
   a. 3-methylpentane
   b. cyclohexane
   c. pentane

12.47 a. 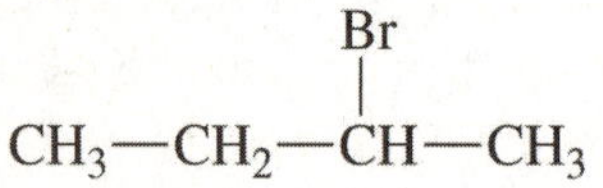
$$CH_3-CH_2-\overset{\overset{\displaystyle Br}{|}}{CH}-CH_3$$

   b.

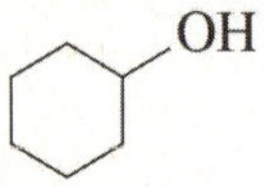

   c. 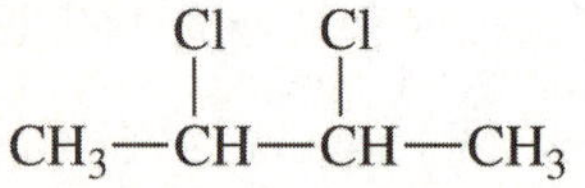
$$CH_3-\overset{\overset{\displaystyle Cl}{|}}{CH}-\overset{\overset{\displaystyle Cl}{|}}{CH}-CH_3$$

12.49 a. The reaction of H_2 in the presence of a nickel catalyst changes alkenes into alkanes. The reactant must be cyclohexene.

   b. Br_2 adds to alkenes to give a dibromoalkane. Since there are bromine atoms on carbon 2 and carbon 3 of the five-carbon chain, the double bond in the reactant must have been between carbon 2 and carbon 3. The reactant is named 2-pentene.

12.51 Styrene is $H_2C=CH$ and acrylonitrile is $H_2C=\overset{\overset{\displaystyle CN}{|}}{CH}$. A section of the copolymer of styrene and acrylonitrile would be

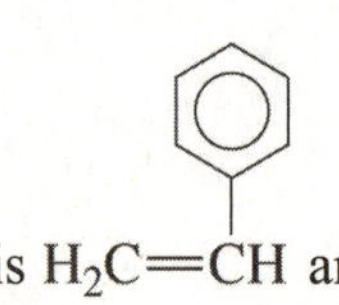

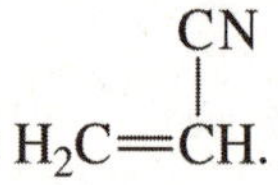

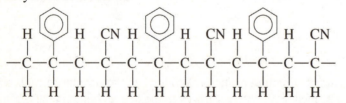

12.53 Aromatic compounds that contain a benzene ring with a single substituent are usually named as benzene derivatives. A benzene ring with a methyl or amino substituent is named toluene or aniline, respectively. The methyl or amino group is attached to carbon 1, and the ring is numbered to give the lower numbers to other substituents.
   a. 3-methylaniline, *p*-methylaniline
   b. 1-chloro-2-methylbenzene, 2-chlorotoluene, *o*-chlorotoluene
   c. 1-ethyl-4-methylbenzene, *p*-ethylmethylbenzene, 4-ethyltoluene, *p*-ethyltoluene

12.55 **a.** The prefix *p-* means that the two groups are in the 1 and 4 positions on the ring.

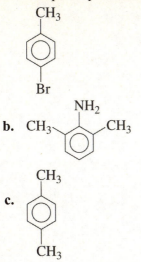

b.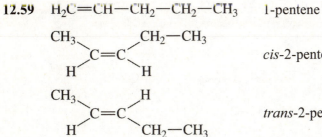

c.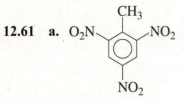

12.57 Molar mass of bombykol $(C_{16}H_{30}O) = 16(12.0\,g) + 30(1.01\,g) + 1(16.0\,g) = 238.3\,g/mole$

$$50\;\text{ng} \times \frac{1\;\text{g}}{10^9\;\text{ng}} \times \frac{1\;\text{mole}}{238.3\;\text{g}} \times \frac{6.02 \times 10^{23}\;\text{molecules}}{1\;\text{mole}} = 1 \times 10^{14}\;\text{molecules of bombykol}\;(1\;\text{SF})$$

12.59 $H_2C=CH-CH_2-CH_2-CH_3$ 1-pentene

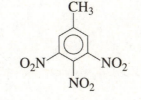 *cis*-2-pentene

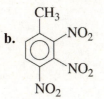 *trans*-2-pentene

12.61 **a.**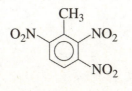

b.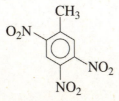

Alcohols, Phenols, Thiols, and Ethers

13.1 **a.** This compound has a two-carbon chain. The final *e* from ethane is dropped, and *ol* is added to indicate an alcohol. The IUPAC name is ethanol.

b. This compound has a four-carbon chain with a hydroxyl group attached to carbon 2. The IUPAC name is 2-butanol.

c. This is the skeletal formula of a five-carbon chain with a hydroxyl group attached to carbon 2. The IUPAC name is 2-pentanol.

d. This compound has a six-carbon ring with a hydroxyl group attached to carbon 1, and a methyl group attached to carbon 4 of the ring. The IUPAC name is 4-methylcyclohexanol.

e. This compound is a phenol because the —OH group is attached to a benzene ring. For a phenol, the carbon atom attached to the —OH group is understood to be carbon 1; no number is needed to give the location of the —OH group. This compound also has a bromine atom attached to carbon 3 of the ring; the IUPAC name is 3-bromophenol.

13.3 **a.** 1-Propanol has a three-carbon chain with a hydroxyl group attached to carbon 1.

$$CH_3—CH_2—CH_2—OH$$

b. 3-Pentanol has a five-carbon chain with a hydroxyl group attached to carbon 3.

$$\overset{\displaystyle OH}{\underset{\displaystyle |}{CH_3—CH_2—CH—CH_2—CH_3}}$$

c. 2-Methyl-2-butanol has a four-carbon chain with a methyl group and a hydroxyl group attached to carbon 2.

$$\begin{array}{c} OH \\ | \\ CH_3—C—CH_2—CH_3 \\ | \\ CH_3 \end{array}$$

d. *p*-Chlorophenol has an —OH group attached to carbon 1 of a benzene ring, and a chlorine attached to carbon 4 of the ring (*para*- position).

e. 2-Bromo-4-chlorophenol has an —OH group attached to carbon 1 of a benzene ring, a bromine atom attached to carbon 2, and a chlorine attached to carbon 4 of the ring.

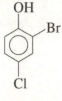

13.5 **a.** The IUPAC name of the ether with a one-carbon alkyl group and a two-carbon alkyl group attached to an oxygen atom is methoxyethane. The common name is ethyl methyl ether.

b. The IUPAC name of the ether with a one-carbon alkyl group and a six-carbon cycloalkyl group attached to an oxygen atom is methoxycyclohexane. The common name is cyclohexyl methyl ether.

[]

    c. The IUPAC name of the ether with a two-carbon alkyl group and a four-carbon cycloalkyl group attached to an oxygen atom is ethoxycyclobutane. The common name is cyclobutyl ethyl ether.

    d. The IUPAC name of the ether with a one-carbon alkyl group and a three-carbon alkyl group attached to an oxygen atom is 1-methoxypropane. The common name is methyl propyl ether.

13.7   **a.** Ethyl propyl ether has a two-carbon group and a three-carbon group attached to oxygen by single bonds.

$$CH_3-CH_2-O-CH_2-CH_2-CH_3$$

    b. Cyclopropyl ethyl ether has a two-carbon group and a three-carbon cycloalkyl group attached to oxygen by single bonds.

$$CH_3-CH_2-O-\triangleleft$$

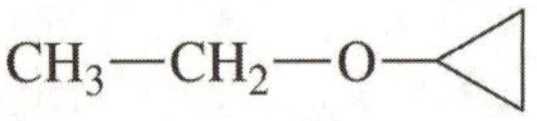

    c. Methoxycyclopentane has a one-carbon group and a five-carbon cycloalkyl group attached to oxygen by single bonds.

$$O-CH_3$$

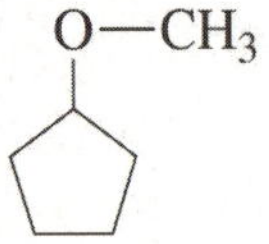

    d. 1-Ethoxy-2-methylbutane has a four-carbon chain with a methyl group attached to carbon 2, and an ethoxy group attached to carbon 1.

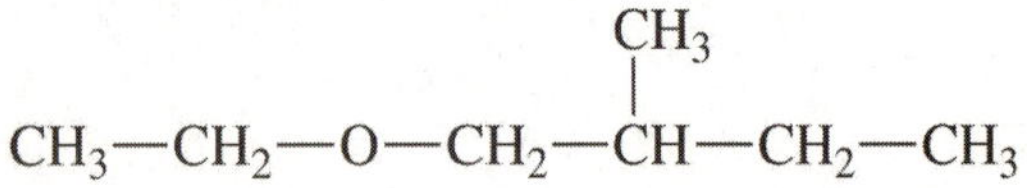

$$CH_3-CH_2-O-CH_2-\overset{\overset{\displaystyle CH_3}{|}}{CH}-CH_2-CH_3$$

    e. 2,3-Dimethoxypentane has a five-carbon chain with two methoxy groups attached, one to carbon 2 and the other to carbon 3.

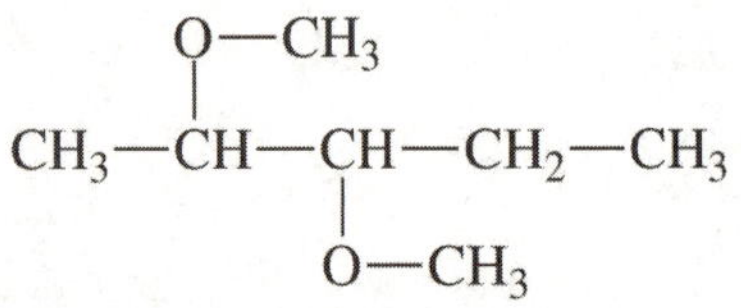

$$CH_3-\overset{\overset{\displaystyle O-CH_3}{|}}{CH}-\underset{\underset{\displaystyle O-CH_3}{|}}{CH}-CH_2-CH_3$$

13.9   **a.** 2-Pentanol and 2-methoxybutane both have a molecular formula of $C_5H_{12}O$, but one is an alcohol and the other is an ether; they are structural isomers.

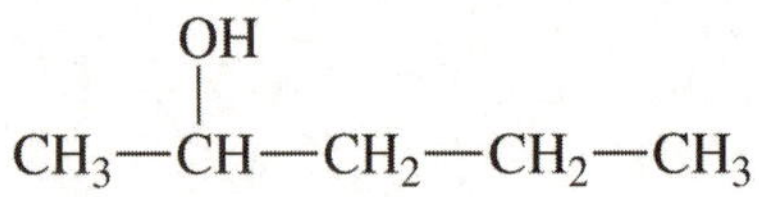

$$CH_3-\overset{\overset{\displaystyle OH}{|}}{CH}-CH_2-CH_2-CH_3 \quad \text{2-pentanol}$$

$$CH_3-\overset{\overset{\displaystyle O-CH_3}{|}}{CH}-CH_2-CH_3 \quad \text{2-methoxybutane}$$

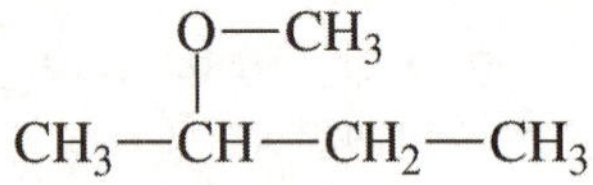

    b. 2-Butanol has a molecular formula of $C_4H_{10}O$, while cyclobutanol is C_4H_8O; they are not structural isomers.

$$CH_3-\overset{\overset{\displaystyle OH}{|}}{CH}-CH_2-CH_3 \quad \text{2-butanol}$$

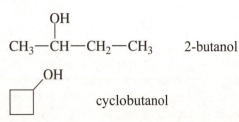 cyclobutanol

c. Ethyl propyl ether and 2-methyl-1-butanol both have a molecular formula of $C_5H_{12}O$, but one is an ether and the other is an alcohol; they are structural isomers.

$$CH_3—CH_2—O—CH_2—CH_2—CH_3 \quad \text{ethyl propyl ether}$$

$$\begin{array}{c} CH_3 \\ | \\ HO—CH_2—CH—CH_2—CH_3 \end{array} \quad \text{2-methyl-1-butanol}$$

13.11 Cyclic ethers with five atoms have common names derived from *furan*; those with six atoms in the ring have names derived from *pyran*. A six-atom cyclic ether with two oxygen atoms is named *dioxane*.
   a. tetrahydrofuran
   b. 3-methylfuran
   c. 5-methyl-1,3-dioxane

13.13 The carbon bonded to the hydroxyl group (—OH) is attached to one alkyl group in a primary (1°) alcohol, except for methanol; to two alkyl groups in a secondary (2°) alcohol; and to three alkyl groups in a tertiary (3°) alcohol.
   a. primary (1°) alcohol
   b. primary (1°) alcohol
   c. tertiary (3°) alcohol
   d. secondary (2°) alcohol

13.15 **a.** Methanol molecules can form hydrogen bonds and will have a higher boiling point than the alkane ethane.
   b. 1-Butanol molecules can form hydrogen bonds and will have a higher boiling point than diethyl ether, which cannot form hydrogen bonds with other ether molecules.
   c. 1-Butanol molecules can form hydrogen bonds and will have a higher boiling point than the alkane pentane.

13.17 **a.** Soluble; ethanol with a short carbon chain is soluble because the hydroxyl group forms hydrogen bonds with water.
   b. Slightly soluble; ethers with up to four carbon atoms are slightly soluble in water because they can form a few hydrogen bonds with water.
   c. Insoluble; an alcohol with a carbon chain of five or more carbon atoms is not soluble in water.

13.19 **a.** Methanol has a polar —OH group that can form hydrogen bonds with water, but the alkane ethane does not.
   b. 2-Propanol is more soluble in water than 1-butanol because 2-propanol has a shorter carbon chain.
   c. 1-Propanol is more soluble because it can form more hydrogen bonds with water than the ether can.

13.21 Dehydration is the removal of an H— and an —OH from adjacent carbon atoms of an alcohol to form a water molecule and the corresponding alkene.
   a. $CH_3—CH_2—CH{=}CH_2$
   b.
   c.
   d. $CH_3—CH_2—CH{=}CH—CH_3$

13.23 An ether is formed when the components of H_2O are eliminated from two alcohols; the alkyl portion of one alcohol combines with the alkoxy portion of the other alcohol.
   a. $CH_3—O—CH_3$
   b. $CH_3—CH_2—CH_2—O—CH_2—CH_2—CH_3$

13.25 Alcohols can produce alkenes and ethers by the loss of water (dehydration).

    a. CH₃—CH₂—OH

    b. Since this ether has two different alkyl groups, it must be formed from two different alcohols.
    CH₃—OH   and   CH₃—CH₂—OH

    c.

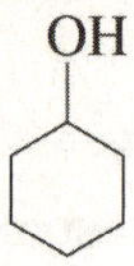

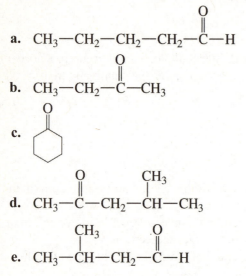

13.27 A primary alcohol oxidizes to an aldehyde, and a secondary alcohol oxidizes to a ketone.

    a. CH₃—CH₂—CH₂—CH₂—C(=O)—H

    b. CH₃—CH₂—C(=O)—CH₃

    c.

    d. CH₃—C(=O)—CH₂—CH(CH₃)—CH₃

    e. CH₃—CH(CH₃)—CH₂—C(=O)—H

13.29   **a.** An aldehyde is the product of the oxidation of a primary alcohol.
    CH₃—OH

    b. A ketone is the product of the oxidation of a secondary alcohol.

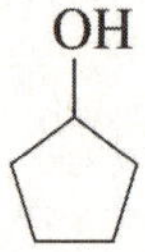

    c. A ketone is the product of the oxidation of a secondary alcohol.
    CH₃—CH(OH)—CH₂—CH₃

    d. An aldehyde is the product of the oxidation of a primary alcohol.

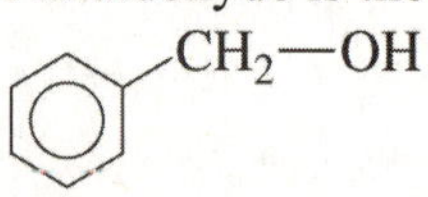

    e. A ketone is the product of the oxidation of a secondary alcohol.

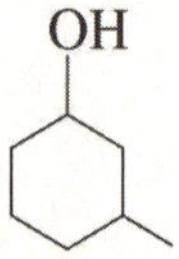

13.31 phenol (aromatic + hydroxyl group)

13.33   **a.** alcohol   **b.** ether   **c.** thiol
        d. alcohol   **e.** ether   **f.** cyclic ether
        g. alcohol   **h.** phenol

13.35 **a.** 2-chloro-4-methylcyclohexanol
    b. methoxybenzene, methyl phenyl ether
    c. 2-propanethiol
    d. 2,4-dimethyl-2-pentanol
    e. 1-methoxypropane, methyl propyl ether
    f. 2-methylfuran
    g. 4-bromo-2-pentanol
    h. *meta*-cresol, 3-methylphenol, *m*-methylphenol

13.37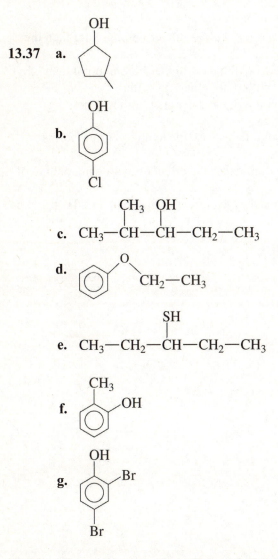

13.39 Write the carbon chain first, and place the —OH group on the carbon atoms in the chain to give different structural formulas. Shorten the chain by one carbon, and attach a methyl group and —OH group to give different compounds.

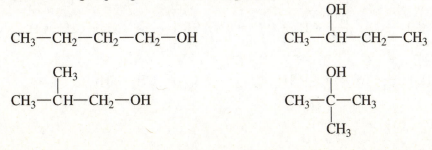

13.41   The carbon bonded to the hydroxyl group (—OH) is attached to one alkyl group in a primary (1°) alcohol, except for methanol; to two alkyl groups in a secondary (2°) alcohol; and to three alkyl groups in a tertiary (3°) alcohol.

    a.   secondary (2°) alcohol

    b.   primary (1°) alcohol

    c.   primary (1°) alcohol

    d.   secondary (2°) alcohol

    e.   primary (1°) alcohol

    f.   tertiary (3°) alcohol

13.43   **a.**   1-Propanol molecules can form hydrogen bonds and will have a higher boiling point than the alkane butane.

    b.   1-Propanol molecules can form hydrogen bonds and will have a higher boiling point than ethyl methyl ether, which cannot form hydrogen bonds with other ether molecules.

    c.   1-Butanol has a greater molar mass than ethanol and will have a higher boiling point.

13.45   **a.**   Soluble; 2-propanol with a short carbon chain is soluble because the hydroxyl group forms hydrogen bonds with water.

    b.   Insoluble; the long carbon chain in dipropyl ether diminishes the effect of hydrogen bonding of water to the —O— group.

    c.   Insoluble; the long carbon chain in 1-hexanol diminishes the effect of the polar —OH group on hydrogen bonding with water.

13.47   **a.**   Dehydration of an alcohol produces an alkene.

$$CH_3-CH=CH_2$$

    b.   Oxidation of a primary alcohol produces an aldehyde.

$$CH_3-CH_2-\overset{\overset{\textstyle O}{\|}}{C}-H$$

    c.   Dehydration of an alcohol produces an alkene.

$$CH_3-CH=CH-CH_3$$

    d.   Dehydration of an alcohol produces an alkene.

    e.   Oxidation of a secondary alcohol produces a ketone.

13.49   **a.** $CH_3-CH_2-CH_2-OH \xrightarrow[\text{Heat}]{H^+} CH_3-CH=CH_2 + HCl \longrightarrow CH_3-\overset{\overset{\textstyle Cl}{|}}{CH}-CH_3$

    b. $CH_3-\overset{\overset{\textstyle OH}{|}}{\underset{\underset{\textstyle CH_3}{|}}{C}}-CH_3 \xrightarrow[\text{Heat}]{H^+} CH_3-\overset{\overset{\textstyle}{}}{\underset{\underset{\textstyle CH_3}{|}}{C}}=CH_2 + H_2 \xrightarrow{Pt} CH_3-\overset{\overset{\textstyle}{}}{\underset{\underset{\textstyle CH_3}{|}}{CH}}-CH_3$

c. $CH_3-CH_2-CH_2-OH \xrightarrow[\text{Heat}]{H^+} CH_3-CH{=}CH_2 + H_2O \xrightarrow[\text{Heat}]{H^+} CH_3-\overset{\overset{\displaystyle OH}{|}}{CH}-CH_3$

$\xrightarrow{[O]} CH_3-\overset{\overset{\displaystyle O}{\|}}{C}-CH_3$

13.51 Testosterone contains cycloalkane, cycloalkene, ketone, and alcohol functional groups.

13.53 The name 4-hexyl-1,3-benzenediol tells us that there is a six-carbon alkyl group attached to carbon 4 of a benzene ring, and hydroxyl groups attached to carbon 1 and carbon 3 of the ring.

$CH_2-CH_2-CH_2-CH_2-CH_2-CH_3$

13.55 **a.** 2,5-Dichlorophenol is a benzene ring with a hydroxyl group on carbon 1, and chlorine atoms on carbon 2 and carbon 5.

b. 3-Methyl-1-butanethiol is a four-carbon chain with a methyl group on carbon 3, and a thiol group on carbon 1.

$CH_3-\overset{\overset{\displaystyle CH_3}{|}}{CH}-CH_2-CH_2-SH$

trans-2-Butene-1-thiol is similar in structure to 3-methyl-1-butanethiol except that there is a double bond between carbon 2 and carbon 3, and the carbon chains on the double bond are on opposite sides of the double bond.

$\underset{H}{\overset{CH_3}{\diagdown}}C{=}C\underset{CH_2-SH}{\overset{H}{\diagup}}$

c. Pentachlorophenol is a benzene ring with one hydroxyl group and five chlorine atoms attached to the ring.

13.57 Since the compound is synthesized from a primary alcohol and oxidizes to give a carboxylic acid, it must be an aldehyde.

$CH_3-\overset{\overset{\displaystyle CH_3}{|}}{CH}-\overset{\overset{\displaystyle O}{\|}}{C}-H$

14

Aldehydes, Ketones, and Chiral Molecules

14.1   **a.** A carbonyl group (C=O) attached to two carbon atoms within the carbon chain makes this compound a ketone.
   b. A carbonyl group (C=O) attached to a hydrogen atom at the end of the carbon chain makes this compound an aldehyde.
   c. A carbonyl group (C=O) attached to two carbon atoms within the carbon chain makes this compound a ketone.
   d. A carbonyl group (C=O) attached to a hydrogen atom at the end of the carbon chain makes this compound an aldehyde.

14.3   **a.** These compounds are structural isomers of C_3H_6O: The first is a ketone, and the second is an aldehyde.
   b. These compounds are structural isomers of $C_5H_{10}O$: The first is a ketone with the carbonyl group on carbon 3, and the second is a ketone with the carbonyl group on carbon 2.
   c. These compounds are not structural isomers: The first has a molecular formula of C_4H_8O, and the second has a molecular formula of $C_5H_{10}O$.

14.5   **a.** 3-bromobutanal
   b. 2-pentanone
   c. 2-methylcyclopentanone
   d. 3-bromobenzaldehyde

14.7   **a.** acetaldehyde
   b. methyl propyl ketone
   c. formaldehyde

14.9   **a.**
$$CH_3-\overset{\overset{\displaystyle O}{\|}}{C}-H$$

   b.
$$CH_3-\overset{\overset{\displaystyle CH_3}{|}}{CH}-\overset{\overset{\displaystyle O}{\|}}{C}-CH_2-CH_3$$

   c.
$$CH_3-\overset{\overset{\displaystyle O}{\|}}{C}-CH_2-CH_2-CH_2-CH_3$$

   d.
$$CH_3-CH_2-CH_2-\overset{\overset{\displaystyle CH_3}{|}}{CH}-CH_2-\overset{\overset{\displaystyle O}{\|}}{C}-H$$

14.11   The name 4-methoxybenzaldehyde tells us that there is a methyl ether at carbon 4 of the ring in benzaldehyde.

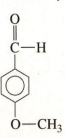

14.13 **a.** CH₃—C—H will have the higher boiling point since aldehydes have a polar carbonyl group and form dipole–dipole attractions that alkanes like propane do not.

$$CH_3-\overset{\displaystyle O}{\overset{\displaystyle \|}{C}}-H$$

b. Pentanal has a longer carbon chain, more electrons, and more dispersion forces than propanal, which give pentanal a higher boiling point.

c. 1-Butanol has a polar hydroxyl group and can form hydrogen bonds, which are stronger than the dipole–dipole attractions in butanal; 1-butanol will have the higher boiling point.

14.15 **a.** $CH_3-\overset{\displaystyle O}{\overset{\displaystyle \|}{C}}-\overset{\displaystyle O}{\overset{\displaystyle \|}{C}}-CH_2-CH_3$ is more soluble in water because it has two polar carbonyl groups and can form more hydrogen bonds with water.

b. Propanal is more soluble in water because it has a shorter carbon chain than pentanal, in which the longer hydrocarbon chain diminishes the effect on solubility of the polar carbonyl group.

c. Acetone is more soluble in water because it has a shorter carbon chain than 2-pentanone, in which the longer hydrocarbon chain diminishes the effect on solubility of the polar carbonyl group.

14.17 No. A hydrocarbon chain of eight carbon atoms reduces the effect on solubility of the polar carbonyl group.

14.19 **a.** An aldehyde can be oxidized to a carboxylic acid.

$$H-\overset{\displaystyle O}{\overset{\displaystyle \|}{C}}-OH$$

b. None; a ketone cannot be further oxidized.

c. An aldehyde can be oxidized to a carboxylic acid.

d. None; a ketone cannot be further oxidized.

14.21 **a.** An aldehyde will react with Tollens' reagent.
b. A ketone will react with neither Tollens' reagent nor Benedict's reagent.
c. An aldehyde with an adjacent hydroxyl group will react with both Tollens' reagent and Benedict's reagent.

14.23 In reduction, an aldehyde will give a primary alcohol, and a ketone will give a secondary alcohol.
a. Butyraldehyde is the four-carbon aldehyde; it will be reduced to a four-carbon primary alcohol.
$$CH_3-CH_2-CH_2-CH_2-OH$$

b. Acetone is a three-carbon ketone; it will be reduced to a three-carbon secondary alcohol.
$$CH_3-\overset{\displaystyle OH}{\overset{\displaystyle |}{CH}}-CH_3$$

c. 3-Bromohexanal is a six-carbon aldehyde with a bromine atom on carbon 3; it reduces to the corresponding six-carbon primary alcohol with a bromine atom on carbon 3.
$$CH_3-CH_2-CH_2-\overset{\displaystyle Br}{\overset{\displaystyle |}{CH}}-CH_2-CH_2-OH$$

d. 2-Methyl-3-pentanone is a five-carbon ketone with a methyl group attached to carbon 2. It will be reduced to a five-carbon secondary alcohol with a methyl group attached to carbon 2.
$$CH_3-\overset{\displaystyle CH_3}{\overset{\displaystyle |}{CH}}-\overset{\displaystyle OH}{\overset{\displaystyle |}{CH}}-CH_2-CH_3$$

14.25   **a.**   hemiacetal
       b.   hemiacetal
       c.   acetal
       d.   hemiacetal
       e.   acetal

14.27   A hemiacetal forms when an alcohol is added to the carbonyl of an aldehyde or ketone.

     a.
$$CH_3-\underset{\underset{OH}{|}}{\overset{\overset{O-CH_3}{|}}{C}}-H$$

     b.
$$CH_3-\underset{\underset{OH}{|}}{\overset{\overset{O-CH_3}{|}}{C}}-CH_3$$

     c.
$$CH_3-CH_2-CH_2-\underset{\underset{OH}{|}}{\overset{\overset{O-CH_3}{|}}{C}}-H$$

14.29   An acetal forms when a second molecule of alcohol reacts with a hemiacetal.

     a.
$$CH_3-\underset{\underset{O-CH_3}{|}}{\overset{\overset{O-CH_3}{|}}{C}}-H$$

     b.
$$CH_3-\underset{\underset{O-CH_3}{|}}{\overset{\overset{O-CH_3}{|}}{C}}-CH_3$$

     c.
$$CH_3-CH_2-CH_2-\underset{\underset{O-CH_3}{|}}{\overset{\overset{O-CH_3}{|}}{C}}-H$$

14.31   **a.**   Achiral; there are no carbon atoms attached to four different groups.

     b.   Chiral;
$$CH_3-\overset{\overset{Br}{|}}{CH}-CH_2-CH_3 \quad \textit{chiral carbon}$$

     c.   Chiral;
$$\textit{chiral carbon}\quad CH_3-\overset{\overset{Br}{|}}{CH}-\overset{\overset{O}{\|}}{C}-H$$

     d.   Achiral;   there are no carbon atoms attached to four different groups.

14.33   **a.**
$$CH_3-\overset{\overset{CH_3}{|}}{C}=CH-CH_2-CH_2-\overset{\overset{CH_3}{|}}{CH}-CH_2-CH_2-OH \quad \textit{chiral carbon}$$

     b.
$$H_2N-\overset{\overset{CH_3}{|}}{CH}-\overset{\overset{O}{\|}}{C}-OH$$
               chiral carbon

14.35 a.

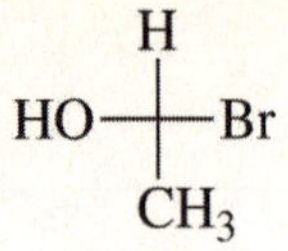

$$\begin{array}{c} H \\ HO{-}\!\!\!\!{-}\!\!\!\!{-}Br \\ CH_3 \end{array}$$

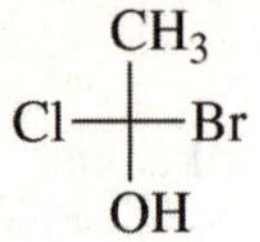

b.

$$\begin{array}{c} CH_3 \\ Cl{-}\!\!\!\!{-}\!\!\!\!{-}Br \\ OH \end{array}$$

c.

$$\begin{array}{c} CHO \\ HO{-}\!\!\!\!{-}\!\!\!\!{-}H \\ CH_2CH_3 \end{array}$$

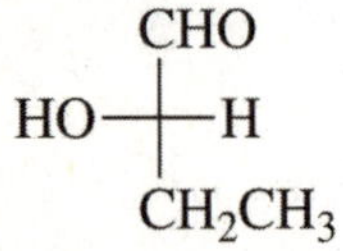

14.37 Enantiomers are nonsuperimposable mirror images.
   a. identical structures (no chiral carbons)
   b. enantiomers
   c. enantiomers
   d. enantiomers

14.39 The C$=$O double bond has a dipole because the oxygen atom is highly electronegative compared to the carbon atom. In the C$=$C double bond, both atoms have the same electronegativity, and there is no dipole.

14.41 a. An aldehyde will react with Tollens' reagent and produce a silver mirror.
   b. An aldehyde will react with Tollens' reagent and produce a silver mirror.
   c. An ether will not react with Tollens' reagent.

14.43 a.

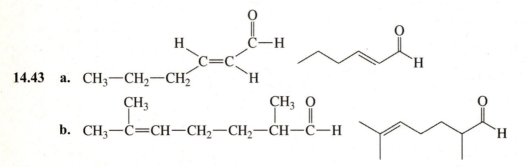

b. $CH_3{-}\overset{\displaystyle CH_3}{\underset{}{C}}{=}CH{-}CH_2{-}CH_2{-}\overset{\displaystyle CH_3}{\underset{}{CH}}{-}\overset{\displaystyle O}{\overset{\|}{C}}{-}H$

14.45 a. 2-bromo-4-chlorocyclopentanone
   b. 2,4-dibromobenzaldehyde
   c. 3-chloropropanal
   d. 5-chloro-3-hexanone
   e. 2-chloro-3-pentanone

14.47 a.

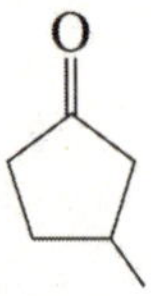

b. 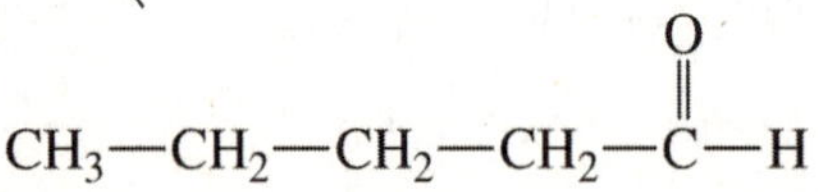 $CH_3{-}CH_2{-}CH_2{-}CH_2{-}\overset{\displaystyle O}{\overset{\|}{C}}{-}H$

c. $CH_3{-}\overset{\displaystyle O}{\overset{\|}{C}}{-}CH_2{-}CH_3$

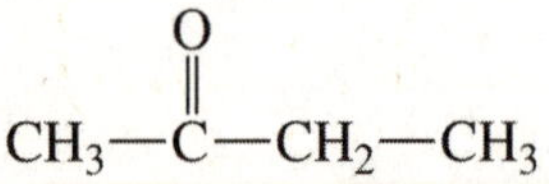

d. 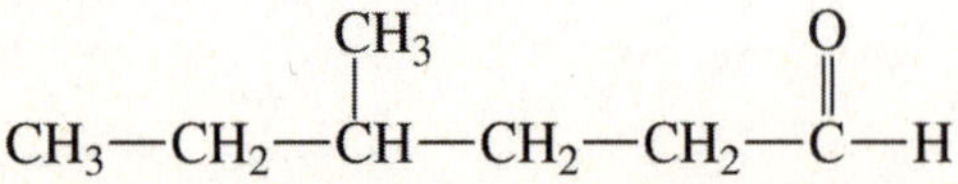 $CH_3{-}CH_2{-}\overset{\displaystyle CH_3}{\underset{}{CH}}{-}CH_2{-}CH_2{-}\overset{\displaystyle O}{\overset{\|}{C}}{-}H$

14.49   Compounds **a** and **b** are soluble in water because they have a polar group with an oxygen atom that hydrogen bonds with water and fewer than five carbon atoms.

14.51   **a.** $CH_3—CH_2—CH_2—OH$

$$\begin{array}{c}O\\\|\end{array}$$
b. 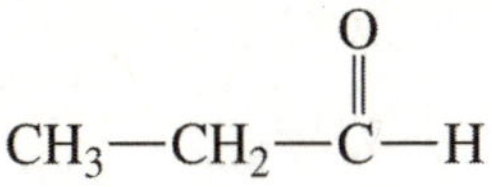 $CH_3—CH_2—C—H$

c. $CH_3—CH_2—OH$

14.53   A chiral carbon is bonded to four different groups.

$$\begin{array}{ccc}Cl & Cl\\ | & |\end{array}$$
a. 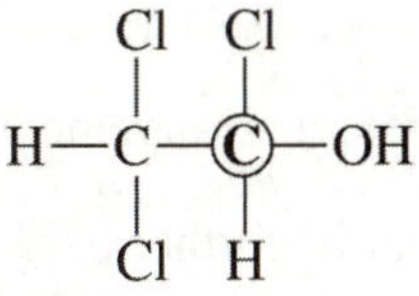 $H—C—\textcircled{C}—OH$
$$\begin{array}{cc}Cl & H\end{array}$$

b.   none

c.   none

$$\begin{array}{cc}NH_2 & O\\ | & \|\end{array}$$
d. 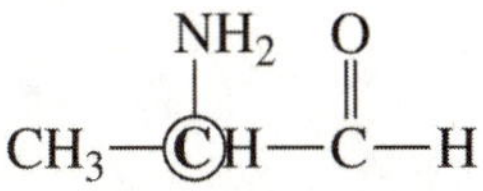 $CH_3—\textcircled{C}H—C—H$

$$\begin{array}{c}Br\\ |\end{array}$$
e. 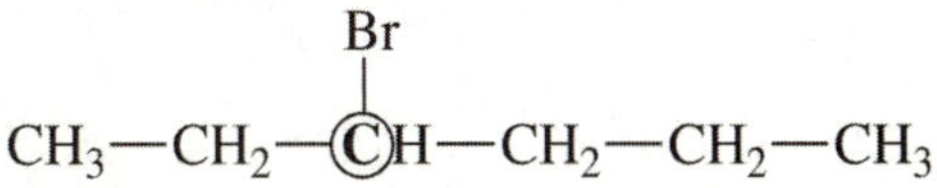 $CH_3—CH_2—\textcircled{C}H—CH_2—CH_2—CH_3$

f.   none

14.55   Enantiomers are nonsuperimposable mirror images.
   a.   enantiomers
   b.   identical compounds (no chiral carbons)
   c.   identical compounds
   d.   identical compounds (no chiral carbons)

14.57   Primary alcohols oxidize to aldehydes and then to carboxylic acids. Secondary alcohols oxidize to ketones.

$$\begin{array}{ccc}O & & O\\ \| & \text{Further} & \|\end{array}$$
a. 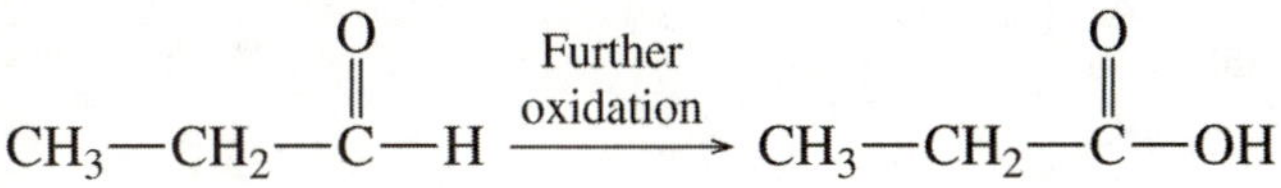 $CH_3—CH_2—C—H \xrightarrow{\text{oxidation}} CH_3—CH_2—C—OH$

$$\begin{array}{c}O\\ \|\end{array}$$
b. $CH_3—C—CH_2—CH_2—CH_3$

$$\begin{array}{c}O\\ \|\end{array}$$
c. $CH_3—CH_2—CH_2—C—OH$

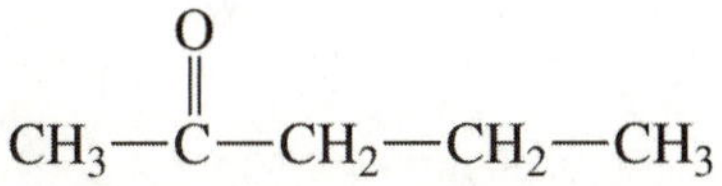

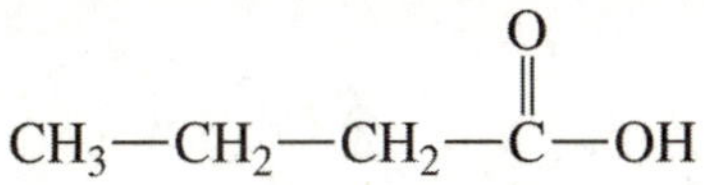

d.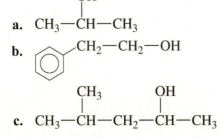

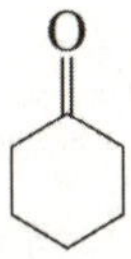

14.59   In reduction, an aldehyde will give a primary alcohol, and a ketone will give a secondary alcohol.

$$\begin{array}{c}OH\\ |\end{array}$$
a. $CH_3—CH—CH_3$

b. $CH_2—CH_2—OH$

$$\begin{array}{cccc}CH_3 & & OH\\ | & & |\end{array}$$
c. $CH_3—CH—CH_2—CH—CH_3$

14.61   a.   propanal
      b.   2-pentanone
      c.   2-butanol
      d.   cyclohexanone

14.63   a.   acetal; propanal and methanol
      b.   hemiacetal; butanone and ethanol
      c.   acetal; cyclohexanone and ethanol

14.65   a.   True; both **A** and **B** have the molecular formula $C_5H_{10}O$, but a different arrangement of atoms.
      b.   False; **A** is 3-pentanone, and **C** is 2-pentanone.
      c.   True; both **B** and **C** are 2-pentanone.
      d.   True; both **C** and **D** have the molecular formula $C_5H_{10}O$, but a different arrangement of atoms.

14.67   Since the compound is synthesized from a secondary alcohol and cannot be further oxidized, it must be a ketone.

$$CH_3-\overset{\overset{\displaystyle O}{\|}}{C}-CH_2-CH_3 \qquad \text{butanone}$$

14.69 $CH_3-CH_2-CH_2-\overset{\overset{\displaystyle O}{\|}}{C}-H \qquad \text{butanal}$

$$CH_3-\overset{\overset{\displaystyle CH_3}{|}}{CH}-\overset{\overset{\displaystyle O}{\|}}{C}-H \qquad \text{2-methylpropanal}$$

$$CH_3-\overset{\overset{\displaystyle O}{\|}}{C}-CH_2-CH_3 \qquad \text{butanone}$$

14.71   **A** $CH_3-CH_2-CH_2-OH \qquad \text{1-propanol}$

      B $CH_3-CH{=}CH_2 \qquad \text{propene}$

      C $CH_3-CH_2-\overset{\overset{\displaystyle O}{\|}}{C}-H \qquad \text{propanal}$

15

Carbohydrates

15.1 Photosynthesis requires CO_2, H_2O, and the energy from the Sun. Respiration requires O_2 from the air and glucose from our foods.

15.3 Monosaccharides are composed of a chain of three to eight carbon atoms—one in a carbonyl group as an aldehyde or ketone, and the rest attached to hydroxyl groups. A monosaccharide cannot be split or hydrolyzed into smaller carbohydrates. A disaccharide consists of two monosaccharide units joined together. A disaccharide can be hydrolyzed into two monosaccharide units.

15.5 Hydroxyl groups are found in all monosaccharides, along with a carbonyl on the first or second carbon that gives an aldehyde or ketone functional group.

15.7 A ketopentose contains hydroxyl and ketone functional groups and has five carbon atoms.

15.9   **a.** This six-carbon monosaccharide has a carbonyl group on carbon 2; it is a ketohexose.
       b. This five-carbon monosaccharide has a carbonyl group on carbon 1; it is an aldopentose.

15.11 A Fischer projection is a two-dimensional representation of the three-dimensional structure of a molecule. In the D stereoisomer, the —OH group on the chiral carbon atom at the bottom of the chain is on the right side, whereas in the L stereoisomer, the —OH group appears on the left side.

15.13   **a.** This structure is the D stereoisomer since the hydroxyl group on the chiral carbon farthest from the carbonyl group is on the right.
       b. This structure is the D stereoisomer since the hydroxyl group on the chiral carbon farthest from the carbonyl group is on the right.
       c. This structure is the L stereoisomer since the hydroxyl group on the chiral carbon farthest from the carbonyl group is on the left.
       d. This structure is the D stereoisomer since the hydroxyl group on the chiral carbon farthest from the carbonyl group is on the right.

15.15

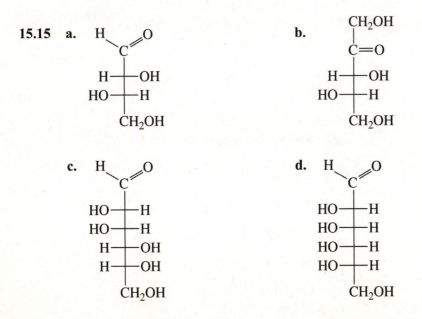

15.17   L-Glucose is the mirror image of D-glucose.

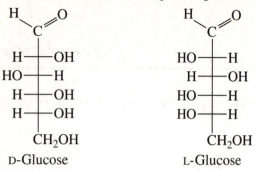

D-Glucose   L-Glucose

15.19   In D-galactose, the —OH group on carbon 4 extends to the left; in D-glucose, this —OH group goes to the right.

15.21   **a.**   Glucose is also called blood sugar.
        b.   Galactose is not metabolized in the condition called galactosemia.
        c.   Fructose is also called fruit sugar.

15.23   In the cyclic structure of glucose, there are five carbon atoms and an oxygen atom.

15.25   In the α anomer, the —OH group on carbon 1 is drawn down; in the β anomer, the —OH group on carbon 1 is drawn up.

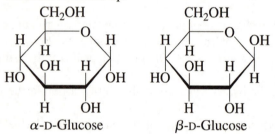

α-D-Glucose   β-D-Glucose

15.27   **a.**   This is the α anomer because the —OH group on carbon 2 is down.
        b.   This is the α anomer because the —OH group on carbon 1 is down.

15.29

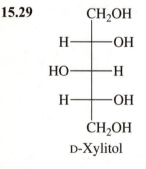

D-Xylitol

15.31   **a.**   Oxidation product: Reduction product (sugar alcohol):

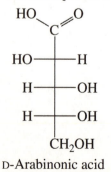 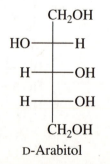

D-Arabinonic acid   D-Arabitol

15.33 **a.** When this disaccharide is hydrolyzed, galactose and glucose are produced. The glycosidic bond is a *β*-1,4 bond since the ether bond is drawn up from carbon 1 of the galactose unit, which is on the left in the drawing, to carbon 4 of the glucose on the right. *β*-Lactose is the name of this disaccharide since the —OH group on carbon 1 of the glucose unit is drawn up.

b. When this disaccharide is hydrolyzed, two molecules of glucose are produced. The glycosidic bond is an *α*-1,4 bond since the ether bond is drawn down from carbon 1 of the glucose unit on the left to carbon 4 of the glucose on the right. *α*-Maltose is the name of this disaccharide since the —OH group on the rightmost glucose unit is drawn down.

15.35 **a.** *β*-Lactose is a reducing sugar because the free —OH group in the hemiacetal undergoes mutarotation, which gives an aldehyde group that can reduce other substances.

b. *α*-Maltose is a reducing sugar because the free —OH group in the hemiacetal undergoes mutarotation, which gives an aldehyde group that can reduce other substances.

15.37 **a.** Another name for table sugar is sucrose.
b. Lactose is the disaccharide found in milk and milk products.
c. Maltose is also called malt sugar.
d. When lactose is hydrolyzed, the products are the monosaccharides galactose and glucose.

15.39 **a.** Amylose is an unbranched polymer of glucose units joined by *α*-1,4-glycosidic bonds. Amylopectin is a branched polymer of glucose units joined by *α*-1,4- and *α*-1,6-glycosidic bonds.

b. Amylopectin, which is produced in plants, is a branched polymer of glucose units joined by *α*-1,4- and *α*-1,6-glycosidic bonds. The branches in amylopectin occur about every 25 glucose units. Glycogen, which is produced in animals, is a highly branched polymer of glucose units joined by *α*-1,4- and *α*-1,6-glycosidic bonds. The branches in glycogen occur about every 10 to 15 glucose units.

15.41 **a.** Cellulose is not digestible by humans.
b. Amylose and amylopectin are the storage forms of carbohydrates in plants.
c. Amylose is the polysaccharide that contains only *α*-1,4-glycosidic bonds.
d. Glycogen is the most highly branched polysaccharide.

15.43 **a.** Isomaltose is a disaccharide.
b. Isomaltose consists of two *α*-D-glucose units.
c. The glycosidic link in isomaltose is an *α*-1,6-glycosidic bond.
d. The structure shown is *α*-isomaltose.
e. *α*-Isomaltose is a reducing sugar; the free —OH group in the hemiacetal undergoes mutarotation, which gives an aldehyde group that can reduce other substances.

15.45 **a.** Melezitose is a trisaccharide.
b. Melezitose contains two units of the aldohexose *α*-D-glucose and one unit of the ketohexose *β*-D-fructose.
c. Melezitose, like sucrose, is not a reducing sugar; melezitose does not have a hemiacetal, and therefore it cannot undergo mutarotation to form the aldehyde group needed for reduction.

15.47 D-Fructose is a ketohexose with the carbonyl group on carbon 2; D-galactose is an aldohexose where the carbonyl group is on carbon 1. In the Fischer projection of D-galactose, the —OH group on carbon 4 is drawn on the left; in fructose, the —OH group on carbon 4 is on the right.

15.49 D-Galactose is the mirror image of L-galactose. In the Fischer projection of D-galactose, the —OH groups on carbon 2 and carbon 5 are drawn on the right side, but are on the left for carbon 3 and carbon 4. In L-galactose, the —OH groups are reversed: carbon 2 and carbon 5 have —OH groups on the left, and carbon 3 and carbon 4 have —OH groups on the right.

15.51 a.

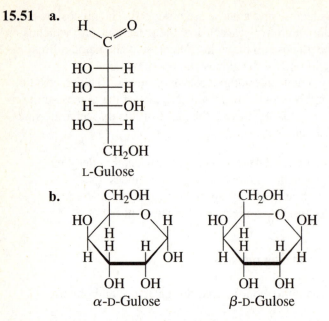

L-Gulose

b.

α-D-Gulose   β-D-Gulose

15.53 Since D-sorbitol can be oxidized to D-glucose, it must contain the same number of carbons with the same groups attached as glucose. The difference is that sorbitol has only hydroxyl groups, while glucose has an aldehyde group. In sorbitol, the aldehyde group is changed to a hydroxyl group.

CH₂OH ⟵ This hydroxyl group is an aldehyde in glucose.

```
      CH2OH
   H ——— OH
  HO ——— H
   H ——— OH
   H ——— OH
      CH2OH
```

15.55 When the α-galactose forms an open-chain structure in water, it can close to form either α- or β-galactose.

15.57

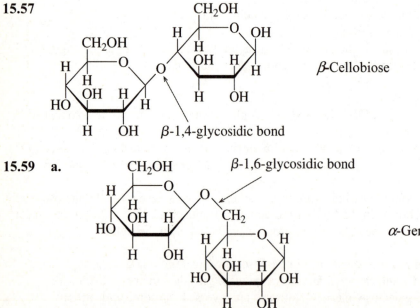

β-Cellobiose

β-1,4-glycosidic bond

15.59 a.

β-1,6-glycosidic bond

α-Gentiobiose

b. Yes. Gentiobiose is a reducing sugar. The ring on the right has a free —OH group in the hemi-acetal which can undergo mutarotation, giving an aldehyde group that can reduce other substances.

22 22222222

Answers to Combining Ideas from Chapters 11 to 15

CI.25 **a.**

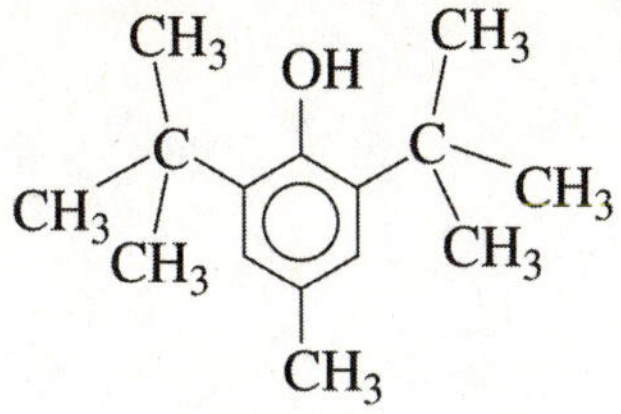

b.

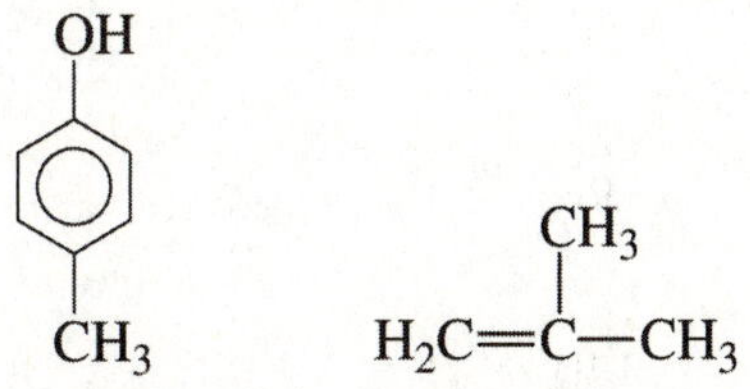

4-Methylphenol   2-Methylpropene

c. molecular formula $C_{15}H_{24}O$

molar mass of BHT $(C_{15}H_{24}O) = 15(12.0\text{ g}) + 24(1.01\text{ g}) + 1(16.0\text{ g}) = 220.\text{ g/mole (3 SFs)}$

d. 50. ppm BHT = 50. mg BHT/kg cereal

$$15\text{ oz} \times \frac{1\text{ lb}}{16\text{ oz}} \times \frac{1\text{ kg cereal}}{2.20\text{ lb}} \times \frac{50.\text{ mg BHT}}{1\text{ kg cereal}} = 21\text{ mg of BHT (2 SFs)}$$

CI.27 **a.**

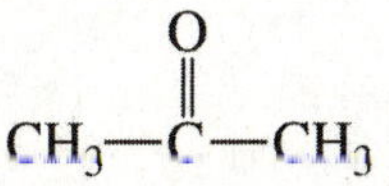

b. molecular formula C_3H_6O

molar mass of propanone $(C_3H_6O) = 3(12.0\text{ g}) + 6(1.01\text{ g}) + 1(16.0\text{ g}) = 58.1\text{ g/mole (3 SFs)}$

c.

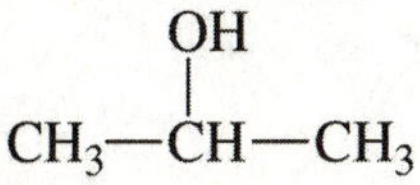

CI.29 **a.** **A**, **B**, and **C** are all glucose units.
b. An α-1,6-glycosidic bond connects monosaccharides **A** and **B**.
c. An α-1,4-glycosidic bond connects monosaccharides **B** and **C**.
d. The anomer shown is β-panose.
e. Panose is a reducing sugar because the anomeric carbon 1 of **C** is a hemiacetal that opens and closes during mutarotation to form the open-chain aldehyde that can reduce other substances.

CI.31 **a.**

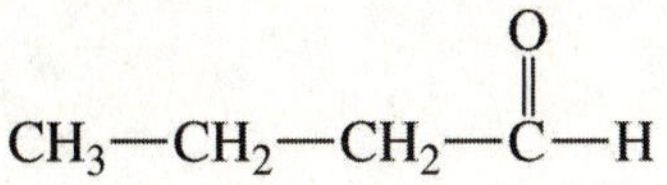

b.

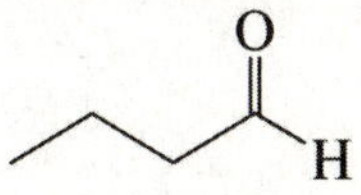

c. The IUPAC name of butyraldehyde is butanal.
d. $CH_3-CH_2-CH_2-CH_2-OH$

16.1 Methanoic acid (formic acid) is the carboxylic acid that is responsible for the pain associated with ant stings.

16.3 **a.** CH$_3$—CH$_2$—CH$_2$—$\overset{\overset{\displaystyle O}{\|}}{C}$—OH   butanoic acid

b. CH$_3$—$\overset{\overset{\displaystyle CH_3}{|}}{CH}$—$\overset{\overset{\displaystyle O}{\|}}{C}$—OH   2-methylpropanoic acid

16.5 **a.** Ethanoic acid (acetic acid) is the carboxylic acid with two carbons.
b. Butanoic acid (butyric acid) is the carboxylic acid with four carbons.
c. 3-Methylhexanoic acid is a six-carbon carboxylic acid with a methyl group on carbon 3 of the chain.
d. 3,4-Dibromobenzoic acid is an aromatic carboxylic acid with bromine atoms on carbon 3 and carbon 4 of the ring.

16.7 **a.** 2-Chloroethanoic acid is a carboxylic acid that has a two-carbon chain with a chlorine atom on carbon 2.

Cl—CH$_2$—$\overset{\overset{\displaystyle O}{\|}}{C}$—OH

b. 3-Hydroxypropanoic acid is a carboxylic acid that has a three-carbon chain with a hydroxyl group on carbon 3.

HO—CH$_2$—CH$_2$—$\overset{\overset{\displaystyle O}{\|}}{C}$—OH

c. α-Methylbutyric acid is a carboxylic acid that has a four-carbon chain with a methyl group on the carbon adjacent to the carboxyl group.

CH$_3$—CH$_2$—$\overset{\overset{\displaystyle CH_3}{|}}{CH}$—$\overset{\overset{\displaystyle O}{\|}}{C}$—OH

d. 3,5-Dibromoheptanoic acid is a carboxylic acid that has a seven-carbon chain with bromine atoms attached to carbon 3 and carbon 5.

CH$_3$—CH$_2$—$\overset{\overset{\displaystyle Br}{|}}{CH}$—CH$_2$—$\overset{\overset{\displaystyle Br}{|}}{CH}$—CH$_2$—$\overset{\overset{\displaystyle O}{\|}}{C}$—OH

16.9 Aldehydes and primary alcohols oxidize to produce the corresponding carboxylic acid.

a. H—$\overset{\overset{\displaystyle O}{\|}}{C}$—OH

b. CH$_3$—$\overset{\overset{\displaystyle O}{\|}}{C}$—OH

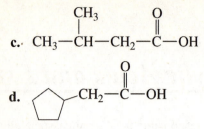

c. $CH_3-\overset{\overset{\displaystyle CH_3}{|}}{CH}-CH_2-\overset{\overset{\displaystyle O}{\|}}{C}-OH$

d. cyclopentane$-CH_2-\overset{\overset{\displaystyle O}{\|}}{C}-OH$

16.11 **a.** Butanoic acid has a greater molar mass and would have a higher boiling point than ethanoic acid.

b. Propanoic acid can form dimers, effectively doubling the molar mass, which gives propanoic acid a higher boiling point than 1-propanol.

c. Butanoic acid can form dimers, effectively doubling the molar mass, which gives butanoic acid a higher boiling point than butanone.

16.13 **a.** Propanoic acid is the most soluble of the group because it has the fewest number of carbon atoms in its hydrocarbon chain. Solubility of carboxylic acids decreases as the number of carbon atoms in the hydrocarbon chain increases.

b. Propanoic acid is more soluble than 1-hexanol because it has fewer carbon atoms in its hydrocarbon chain. Propanoic acid is also more soluble because the carboxyl group forms more hydrogen bonds with water than does the hydroxyl group of an alcohol. An alkane is not soluble in water.

16.15 **a.** $CH_3-CH_2-CH_2-\overset{\overset{\displaystyle O}{\|}}{C}-OH + H_2O \rightleftharpoons CH_3-CH_2-CH_2-\overset{\overset{\displaystyle O}{\|}}{C}-O^- + H_3O^+$

b.

$CH_3-CH_2-CH_2-CH_2-\overset{\overset{\displaystyle O}{\|}}{C}-OH + H_2O \rightleftharpoons CH_3-CH_2-CH_2-CH_2-\overset{\overset{\displaystyle O}{\|}}{C}-O^- + H_3O^+$

16.17 **a.**

$CH_3-CH_2-CH_2-CH_2-\overset{\overset{\displaystyle O}{\|}}{C}-OH + NaOH \longrightarrow CH_3-CH_2-CH_2-CH_2-\overset{\overset{\displaystyle O}{\|}}{C}-O^-Na^+ + H_2O$

b. $CH_3-\overset{\overset{\displaystyle Cl}{|}}{CH}-\overset{\overset{\displaystyle O}{\|}}{C}-OH + NaOH \longrightarrow CH_3-\overset{\overset{\displaystyle Cl}{|}}{CH}-\overset{\overset{\displaystyle O}{\|}}{C}-O^-Na^+ + H_2O$

c. benzene$-\overset{\overset{\displaystyle O}{\|}}{C}-OH$ + NaOH $\longrightarrow$ benzene$-\overset{\overset{\displaystyle O}{\|}}{C}-O^-Na^+$ + H_2O

16.19 A carboxylic acid salt is named by replacing the *ic* ending of the acid name with *ate*.
a. sodium pentanoate
b. sodium 2-chloropropanoate (sodium α-chloropropioniate)
c. sodium benzoate

16.21 **a.** This is an aldehyde since it has a carbonyl group bonded to a hydrogen atom.
b. This is an ester since it has a carboxyl group bonded to two carbon groups.
c. This is a ketone since it has a carbonyl group bonded to two carbon groups.
d. This is a carboxylic acid since it has a carboxyl group bonded to a hydrogen atom.

16.23 A carboxylic acid reacts with an alcohol to form an ester and water. In an ester, the —H of the carboxylic acid is replaced by an alkyl group.

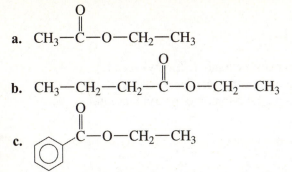

a. $CH_3-\overset{\overset{\displaystyle O}{\|}}{C}-O-CH_2-CH_3$

b. $CH_3-CH_2-CH_2-\overset{\overset{\displaystyle O}{\|}}{C}-O-CH_2-CH_3$

c. (phenyl ring)$-\overset{\overset{\displaystyle O}{\|}}{C}-O-CH_2-CH_3$

16.25 A carboxylic acid and an alcohol react to give an ester with the elimination of water.

a. $CH_3-CH_2-\overset{\overset{\displaystyle O}{\|}}{C}-O-CH_2-CH_2-CH_3$

b. $CH_3-CH_2-CH_2-CH_2-\overset{\overset{\displaystyle O}{\|}}{C}-O-\overset{\overset{\displaystyle CH_3}{|}}{CH}-CH_3$

16.27 a. The carboxylic acid part of the ester is from methanoic acid (formic acid), and the alcohol part is from methanol (methyl alcohol).

b. The carboxylic acid part of the ester is from ethanoic acid (acetic acid), and the alcohol part is from methanol (methyl alcohol).

c. The carboxylic acid part of the ester is from butanoic acid (butyric acid), and the alcohol part is from methanol (methyl alcohol).

d. The carboxylic acid part of the ester is from 3-methylbutanoic acid (β-methylbutyric acid), and the alcohol part is from cthanol (ethyl alcohol).

16.29 a. The alcohol part of the ester is from methanol (methyl alcohol), and the carboxylic acid part is from methanoic acid (formic acid). The ester is named methyl methanoate (methyl formate).

b. The alcohol part of the ester is from ethanol (ethyl alcohol), and the carboxylic acid part is from propanoic acid (propionic acid). The ester is named ethyl propanoate (ethyl propionate).

c. The alcohol part of the ester is from methanol (methyl alcohol), and the carboxylic acid part is from butanoic acid (butyric acid). The ester is named methyl butanoate (methyl butyrate).

d. The alcohol part of the ester is from 2-methyl-1-propanol, and the carboxylic acid part is from pentanoic acid. The ester is named 2-methylpropyl pentanoate.

16.31 a. The alkyl part of the ester comes from the one-carbon methanol, and the carboxylate part comes from the two-carbon acetic acid.

$CH_3-\overset{\overset{\displaystyle O}{\|}}{C}-O-CH_3$

b. The alkyl part of the ester comes from the four-carbon 1-butanol, and the carboxylate part comes from the one-carbon formic acid.

$H-\overset{\overset{\displaystyle O}{\|}}{C}-O-CH_2-CH_2-CH_2-CH_3$

c. The alkyl part of the ester comes from the two-carbon ethanol, and the carboxylate part comes from the five-carbon pentanoic acid.

$CH_3-CH_2-CH_2-CH_2-\overset{\overset{\displaystyle O}{\|}}{C}-O-CH_2-CH_3$

d. The alkyl part of the ester comes from the three-carbon 1-propanol that has a bromine atom attached to carbon 2, and the carboxylate part comes from the three-carbon propanoic acid.

$$CH_3-CH_2-\overset{\displaystyle O}{\overset{\|}{C}}-O-CH_2-\overset{\displaystyle Br}{\overset{|}{C}H}-CH_3$$

16.33 **a.** The flavor and odor of bananas is due to pentyl ethanoate (pentyl acetate).
   b. The flavor and odor of oranges is due to octyl ethanoate (octyl acetate).
   c. The flavor and odor of apricots is due to pentyl butanoate (pentyl butyrate).

16.35 **a.** $CH_3-CH_2-\overset{\displaystyle O}{\overset{\|}{C}}-OH$

   b. $CH_3-CH_2-CH_2-CH_2-OH$

   c. $CH_3-\overset{\displaystyle O}{\overset{\|}{C}}-O-CH_3$

16.37 Acid hydrolysis of an ester adds water in the presence of acid and gives an alcohol and a carboxylic acid.

16.39 Acid hydrolysis of an ester gives the carboxylic acid and the alcohol that were combined to form the ester; base hydrolysis of an ester gives the salt of the carboxylic acid and the alcohol that combined to form the ester.

   a. $CH_3-CH_2-\overset{\displaystyle O}{\overset{\|}{C}}-O^-Na^+$ and CH_3-OH

   b. $CH_3-\overset{\displaystyle O}{\overset{\|}{C}}-OH$ and $CH_3-CH_2-CH_2-OH$

   c. $CH_3-CH_2-CH_2-\overset{\displaystyle O}{\overset{\|}{C}}-OH$ and CH_3-CH_2-OH

   d. ⬡$-\overset{\displaystyle O}{\overset{\|}{C}}-OH$ and CH_3-CH_2-OH

   e. ⬡$-\overset{\displaystyle O}{\overset{\|}{C}}\diagdown_{O^-Na^+}$ and CH_3-CH_2-OH

16.41 $CH_3-CH_2-CH_2-CH_2-\overset{\displaystyle O}{\overset{\|}{C}}-OH$ butanoic acid

$CH_3-\overset{\displaystyle CH_3}{\overset{|}{C}H}-\overset{\displaystyle O}{\overset{\|}{C}}-OH$ 2-methylpropanoic acid

16.43 $CH_3-\overset{\displaystyle O}{\overset{\|}{C}}-O-CH_3$ methyl ethanoate

$H-\overset{\displaystyle O}{\overset{\|}{C}}-O-CH_2-CH_3$ ethyl methanoate

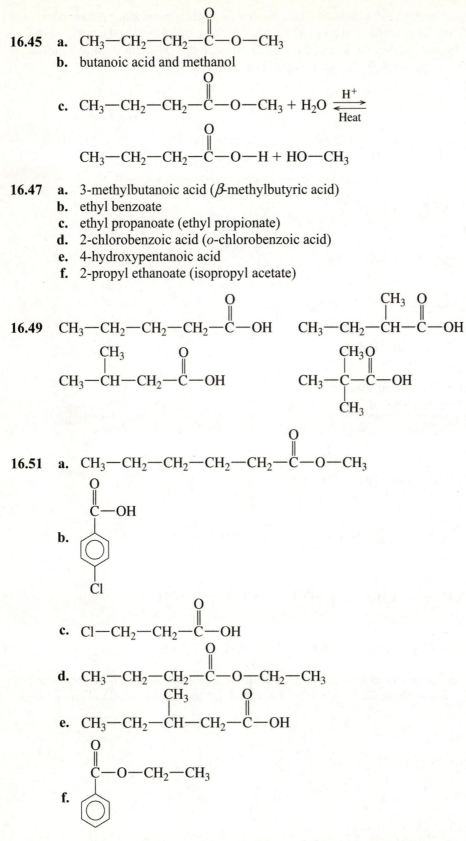

16.45 **a.** $CH_3-CH_2-CH_2-\overset{\displaystyle O}{\overset{\displaystyle \|}{C}}-O-CH_3$

     b. butanoic acid and methanol

     c. $CH_3-CH_2-CH_2-\overset{\displaystyle O}{\overset{\displaystyle \|}{C}}-O-CH_3 + H_2O \underset{Heat}{\overset{H^+}{\rightleftharpoons}}$

               $CH_3-CH_2-CH_2-\overset{\displaystyle O}{\overset{\displaystyle \|}{C}}-O-H + HO-CH_3$

16.47 **a.** 3-methylbutanoic acid (*β*-methylbutyric acid)
     b. ethyl benzoate
     c. ethyl propanoate (ethyl propionate)
     d. 2-chlorobenzoic acid (*o*-chlorobenzoic acid)
     e. 4-hydroxypentanoic acid
     f. 2-propyl ethanoate (isopropyl acetate)

16.49 $CH_3-CH_2-CH_2-CH_2-\overset{\displaystyle O}{\overset{\displaystyle \|}{C}}-OH$ $CH_3-CH_2-\overset{\displaystyle CH_3}{\overset{\displaystyle |}{CH}}-\overset{\displaystyle O}{\overset{\displaystyle \|}{C}}-OH$

      $CH_3-\overset{\displaystyle CH_3}{\overset{\displaystyle |}{CH}}-CH_2-\overset{\displaystyle O}{\overset{\displaystyle \|}{C}}-OH$ $CH_3-\overset{\displaystyle CH_3}{\underset{\displaystyle CH_3}{\overset{\displaystyle |}{\underset{\displaystyle |}{C}}}}-\overset{\displaystyle O}{\overset{\displaystyle \|}{C}}-OH$

16.51 **a.** $CH_3-CH_2-CH_2-CH_2-CH_2-\overset{\displaystyle O}{\overset{\displaystyle \|}{C}}-O-CH_3$

     b. *(benzene ring with)* $\overset{\displaystyle O}{\overset{\displaystyle \|}{C}}-OH$ *and* Cl *substituent*

     c. $Cl-CH_2-CH_2-\overset{\displaystyle O}{\overset{\displaystyle \|}{C}}-OH$

     d. $CH_3-CH_2-CH_2-\overset{\displaystyle O}{\overset{\displaystyle \|}{C}}-O-CH_2-CH_3$

     e. $CH_3-CH_2-\overset{\displaystyle CH_3}{\overset{\displaystyle |}{CH}}-CH_2-\overset{\displaystyle O}{\overset{\displaystyle \|}{C}}-OH$

     f. *(benzene ring with)* $\overset{\displaystyle O}{\overset{\displaystyle \|}{C}}-O-CH_2-CH_3$

16.53 **a.** Ethanoic acid has a higher boiling point than 1-propanol because two molecules of ethanoic acid hydrogen bond to form a dimer, which effectively doubles the molar mass and requires a higher temperature to reach the boiling point.
     b. Ethanoic acid has the higher boiling point because it forms hydrogen bonds, whereas butane does not.

16.55 Of the three compounds, methyl formate would have the lowest boiling point since it has only dipole–dipole attractions. Both acetic acid and 1-propanol can form hydrogen bonds, but because acetic acid can form dimers and double the effective molar mass, it has the highest boiling point. Methyl formate, 32 °C; 1-propanol, 97 °C; acetic acid, 118 °C.

16.57 **a**, **c**, and **d** are soluble in water.

16.59

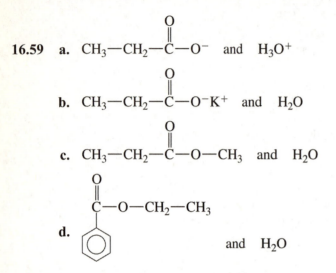

a. $CH_3-CH_2-\overset{\overset{\displaystyle O}{\|}}{C}-O^-$ and H_3O^+

b. $CH_3-CH_2-\overset{\overset{\displaystyle O}{\|}}{C}-O^-K^+$ and H_2O

c. $CH_3-CH_2-\overset{\overset{\displaystyle O}{\|}}{C}-O-CH_3$ and H_2O

d. phenyl-$\overset{\overset{\displaystyle O}{\|}}{C}-O-CH_2-CH_3$ and H_2O

16.61 **a.** 3-methylbutanoic acid and methanol
b. 3-chlorobenzoic acid and ethanol
c. hexanoic acid and ethanol

16.63 **a.** $CH_3-CH_2-\overset{\overset{\displaystyle O}{\|}}{C}-OH$ and $HO-\overset{\overset{\displaystyle CH_3}{|}}{CH}-CH_3$

b. $CH_3-\overset{\overset{\displaystyle CH_3}{|}}{CH}-\overset{\overset{\displaystyle O}{\|}}{C}-O^-Na^+$ and $HO-CH_2-CH_2-CH_3$

16.65 **a.** $H_2C{=}CH_2 + HOH \xrightarrow{H^+} CH_3-CH_2-OH \xrightarrow{[O]} CH_3-\overset{\overset{\displaystyle O}{\|}}{C}-OH$

b. $CH_3-CH_2-CH_2-CH_2-OH \xrightarrow{[O]} CH_3-CH_2-CH_2-\overset{\overset{\displaystyle O}{\|}}{C}-OH$

16.67 In basic solution, the ester undergoes saponification to form the carboxylate salt potassium benzoate and methanol, which are soluble in water. When HCl is added, the salt is converted to benzoic acid, which is insoluble.

phenyl-$\overset{\overset{\displaystyle O}{\|}}{C}-O-CH_3 + KOH \xrightarrow{Heat}$ phenyl-$\overset{\overset{\displaystyle O}{\|}}{C}-O^-K^+ + CH_3-OH$

16.69 **a.** $CH_3-\overset{\overset{\displaystyle O}{\|}}{C}-O-CH_2-CH_2-CH_3$

b. $CH_3-\overset{\overset{\displaystyle O}{\|}}{C}-OH + HO-CH_2-CH_2-CH_3 \underset{Heat}{\overset{H^+}{\rightleftharpoons}} CH_3-\overset{\overset{\displaystyle O}{\|}}{C}-O-CH_2-CH_2-CH_3 + H_2O$

c. $CH_3-\overset{\displaystyle O}{\overset{\|}{C}}-O-CH_2-CH_2-CH_3 + H_2O \underset{Heat}{\overset{H^+}{\rightleftharpoons}} CH_3-\overset{\displaystyle O}{\overset{\|}{C}}-OH + HO-CH_2-CH_2-CH_3$

d.

$CH_3-\overset{\displaystyle O}{\overset{\|}{C}}-O-CH_2-CH_2-CH_3 + NaOH \xrightarrow{Heat} CH_3-\overset{\displaystyle O}{\overset{\|}{C}}-O^-Na^+ + HO-CH_2-CH_2-CH_3$

e. molar mass of propyl acetate ($C_5H_{10}O_2$) = 5(12.0 g) + 10(1.01 g) + 2(16.0 g) = 102.1 g/mole

$$1.58 \; g \; C_5H_{10}O_2 \times \frac{1 \; mole \; C_5H_{10}O_2}{102.1 \; g \; C_5H_{10}O_2} \times \frac{1 \; mole \; NaOH}{1 \; mole \; C_5H_{10}O_2} \times \frac{1000 \; mL \; solution}{0.208 \; mole \; NaOH}$$

= 74.4 mL of a 0.208 M NaOH solution (3 SFs)

17.1   Lipids provide energy along with protection, and insulation for the organs in the body. Lipids are also an important component of cell membranes.

17.3   Because lipids are not soluble in water, a polar solvent, they are nonpolar molecules.

17.5   All fatty acids contain a long chain of carbon atoms with a carboxylic acid group. Saturated fatty acids contain only carbon–carbon single bonds; unsaturated fatty acids contain one or more double bonds.

17.7   **a.** Palmitic acid

b. Oleic acid

17.9   **a.** Lauric acid has only carbon–carbon single bonds; it is saturated.
b. Linolenic acid has three carbon–carbon double bonds; it is polyunsaturated.
c. Palmitoleic acid has one carbon–carbon double bond; it is monounsaturated.
d. Stearic acid has only carbon–carbon single bonds; it is saturated.

17.11   In a cis fatty acid, the hydrogen atoms are on the same side of the double bond, which produces a kink in the carbon chain. In a trans fatty acid, the hydrogen atoms are on opposite sides of the double bond, which gives a carbon chain without any kink.

17.13   In an omega-3 fatty acid, there is a double bond beginning at carbon 3 counting from the methyl group. In an omega-6 fatty acid, there is a double bond beginning at carbon 6 counting from the methyl group.

17.15   Arachidonic acid and PGE_1 are both carboxylic acids with 20 carbon atoms. The differences are that arachidonic acid contains four cis double bonds and no other functional groups, whereas PGE_1 has one trans double bond, one ketone functional group, and two hydroxyl functional groups. In addition, a part of the PGE_1 chain forms a cyclopentane ring.

17.17   Prostaglandins raise or lower blood pressure, stimulate contraction and relaxation of smooth muscle, and may cause inflammation and pain.

17.19   Palmitic acid is the 16-carbon saturated fatty acid (16:0), and myricyl alcohol is a 30-carbon long-chain alcohol.

$$CH_3-(CH_2)_{14}-\overset{\displaystyle O}{\overset{\displaystyle \|}{C}}-O-(CH_2)_{29}-CH_3$$

17.21   Triacylglycerols are composed of fatty acids and glycerol. In this case, the fatty acid is stearic acid, an 18-carbon saturated fatty acid (18:0).

$$CH_2-O-\overset{\overset{\displaystyle O}{\|}}{C}-(CH_2)_{16}-CH_3$$
$$CH-O-\overset{\overset{\displaystyle O}{\|}}{C}-(CH_2)_{16}-CH_3$$
$$CH_2-O-\overset{\overset{\displaystyle O}{\|}}{C}-(CH_2)_{16}-CH_3$$

17.23 Glyceryl tripalmitate (tripalmitin) has three palmitic acids (a 16-carbon saturated fatty acid, 16:0) forming ester bonds with glycerol.

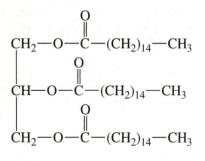

17.25 Glyceryl tricaprylate (tricaprylin) has three caprylic acids (an 8-carbon saturated fatty acid, 8:0) forming ester bonds with glycerol.

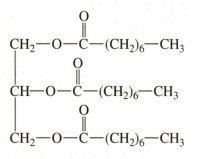

17.27 Safflower oil has a lower melting point because it contains mostly polyunsaturated fatty acids, whereas olive oil contains a large amount of monounsaturated oleic acid. A polyunsaturated fatty acid has two or more kinks in its carbon chain, which means it does not have as many dispersion forces compared to the hydrocarbon chains in olive oil.

17.29 Although coconut oil comes from a plant source, it contains large amounts of saturated fatty acids and small amounts of unsaturated fatty acids. Since coconut oil contains the same kinds of fatty acids as animal fat, coconut oil has a melting point similar to the melting point of animal fats.

17.31 Hydrogenation of an unsaturated triacylglycerol adds H_2 to each of the double bonds, producing a saturated triacylglycerol containing only carbon–carbon single bonds.

$$CH_2-O-\overset{\overset{\displaystyle O}{\|}}{C}-(CH_2)_7-CH{=}CH-(CH_2)_7-CH_3$$
$$CH-O-\overset{\overset{\displaystyle O}{\|}}{C}-(CH_2)_7-CH{=}CH-(CH_2)_7-CH_3 + 3H_2 \xrightarrow{\text{Ni}}$$
$$CH_2-O-\overset{\overset{\displaystyle O}{\|}}{C}-(CH_2)_7-CH{=}CH-(CH_2)_7-CH_3$$

$$CH_2-O-\overset{\overset{\displaystyle O}{\|}}{C}-(CH_2)_{16}-CH_3$$
$$CH-O-\overset{\overset{\displaystyle O}{\|}}{C}-(CH_2)_{16}-CH_3$$
$$CH_2-O-\overset{\overset{\displaystyle O}{\|}}{C}-(CH_2)_{16}-CH_3$$

17.33 Acid hydrolysis of a fat gives glycerol and the fatty acids.

$$
\begin{array}{l}
\text{CH}_2\text{—O—C—(CH}_2)_{12}\text{—CH}_3 \\
\quad\quad\quad\overset{\text{O}}{\overset{\|}{}} \\
\text{CH—O—C—(CH}_2)_{12}\text{—CH}_3 + 3\text{H}_2\text{O} \xrightarrow{\ \text{H}^+\ } \text{CH—OH} + 3\text{HO—C—(CH}_2)_{12}\text{—CH}_3 \\
\quad\quad\quad\overset{\text{O}}{\overset{\|}{}} \\
\text{CH}_2\text{—O—C—(CH}_2)_{12}\text{—CH}_3 \quad\quad\quad \text{CH}_2\text{—OH}
\end{array}
$$

17.35 Basic hydrolysis (saponification) of fat gives glycerol and the salts of the fatty acids.

$$
\begin{array}{l}
\text{CH}_2\text{—O—C—(CH}_2)_{12}\text{—CH}_3 \\
\text{CH—O—C—(CH}_2)_{12}\text{—CH}_3 + 3\text{NaOH} \longrightarrow \text{CH—OH} + 3\text{Na}^{+}\ ^{-}\text{O—C—(CH}_2)_{12}\text{—CH}_3 \\
\text{CH}_2\text{—O—C—(CH}_2)_{12}\text{—CH}_3 \quad\quad\quad \text{CH}_2\text{—OH}
\end{array}
$$

17.37 A triacylglycerol is composed of glycerol with three hydroxyl groups that form ester links with three long-chain fatty acids. In olestra, six to eight long-chain fatty acids form ester links with the hydroxyl groups on sucrose, a sugar. The olestra cannot be digested because our pancreatic lipase enzyme cannot break down the large olestra molecule.

17.39
$$
\begin{array}{l}
\text{CH}_2\text{—O—C—(CH}_2)_{16}\text{—CH}_3 \\
\text{CH—O—C—(CH}_2)_{16}\text{—CH}_3 \\
\text{CH}_2\text{—O—C—(CH}_2)_{16}\text{—CH}_3
\end{array}
$$

17.41 A triacylglycerol consists of glycerol and three fatty acids. A glycerophospholipid also consists of glycerol, but has two fatty acids with the hydroxyl group on the third carbon attached by a phosphate bond to phosphoric acid, which is attached by a phosphate ester bond to an ionized amino alcohol.

17.43
$$
\begin{array}{l}
\text{CH}_2\text{—O—C—(CH}_2)_{14}\text{—CH}_3 \\
\text{CH—O—C—(CH}_2)_{14}\text{—CH}_3 \\
\text{CH}_2\text{—O—P—O—CH}_2\text{—CH}_2\text{—}\overset{+}{\text{N}}\text{H}_3 \\
\quad\quad\quad\ \text{O}^-
\end{array}
$$

17.45 This glycerophospholipid is a cephalin. It contains glycerol, oleic acid, stearic acid, a phosphate group, and ethanolamine.

17.47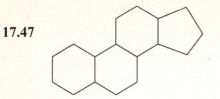

17.49   Bile salts act to emulsify fat globules, allowing the fat to be more easily digested by lipases.

17.51   Lipoproteins are large, spherically shaped structures that transport lipids in the bloodstream. They consist of an outside layer of glycerophospholipids and proteins surrounding an inner core of hundreds of nonpolar lipids and cholesteryl esters.

17.53   Chylomicrons have a lower density than VLDLs. They pick up triacylglycerols from the intestine, whereas VLDLs transport triacylglycerols synthesized in the liver.

17.55   "Bad" cholesterol is the cholesterol carried by LDLs that can form deposits in the arteries called plaque, which narrows the arteries.

17.57   Both progesterone and testosterone contain the steroid nucleus, a ketone group, a double bond in ring A, and two methyl groups. Testosterone has a hydroxyl group on ring D, whereas progesterone has an acetyl group on ring D.

17.59   Cortisol (**b**), estrogen (**c**), and testosterone (**d**) are steroid hormones.

17.61   The lipids in a cell membrane are glycerophospholipids with smaller amounts of sphingolipids and cholesterol.

17.63   The function of the lipid bilayer in the cell membrane is to keep the cell contents separated from the outside environment and to allow the cell to regulate the movement of substances into and out of the cell.

17.65   The integral proteins extend through the lipid bilayer and appear on both the inner and outer surfaces of cellular membranes. Peripheral proteins appear on only one of the surfaces, outer or inner.

17.67   The carbohydrates (glycoproteins and glycosphingolipids) on the surface of cells act as receptors for cell recognition and chemical messengers, such as neurotransmitters.

17.69   Substances move through cell membranes by passive transport, facilitated transport, and active transport.

17.71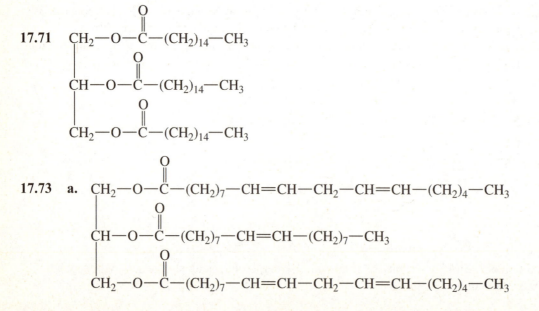

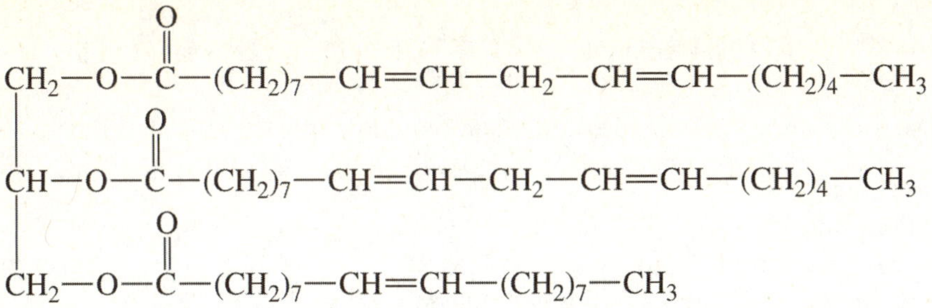

$$
\begin{array}{l}
CH_2-O-\overset{\displaystyle O}{\overset{\|}{C}}-(CH_2)_7-CH=CH-CH_2-CH=CH-(CH_2)_4-CH_3 \\
CH-O-\overset{\displaystyle O}{\overset{\|}{C}}-(CH_2)_7-CH=CH-CH_2-CH=CH-(CH_2)_4-CH_3 \\
CH_2-O-\overset{\displaystyle O}{\overset{\|}{C}}-(CH_2)_7-CH=CH-(CH_2)_7-CH_3
\end{array}
$$

b. 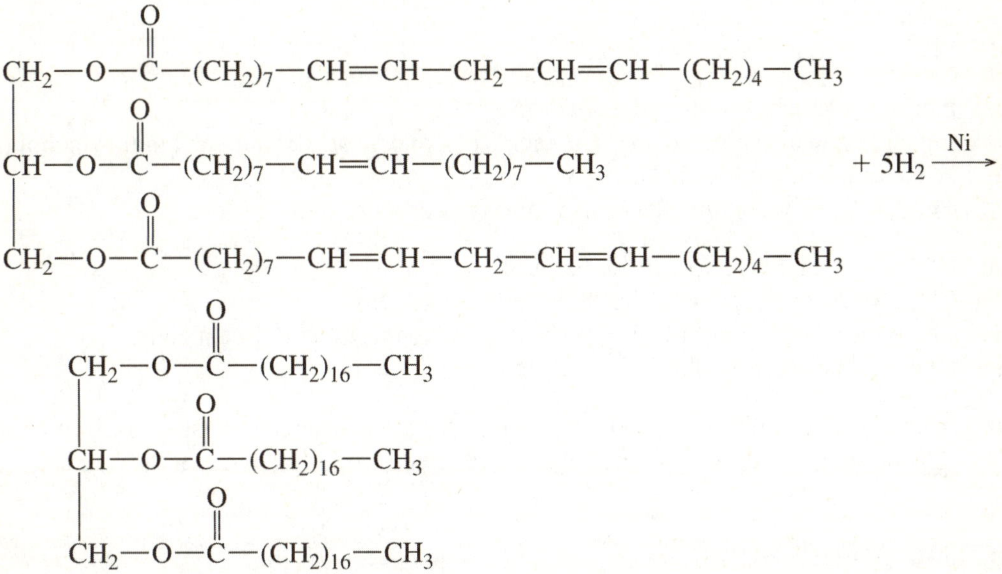
$$
\begin{array}{l}
CH_2-O-\overset{\displaystyle O}{\overset{\|}{C}}-(CH_2)_7-CH=CH-CH_2-CH=CH-(CH_2)_4-CH_3 \\
CH-O-\overset{\displaystyle O}{\overset{\|}{C}}-(CH_2)_7-CH=CH-(CH_2)_7-CH_3 \qquad\qquad +\ 5H_2 \xrightarrow{\text{Ni}} \\
CH_2-O-\overset{\displaystyle O}{\overset{\|}{C}}-(CH_2)_7-CH=CH-CH_2-CH=CH-(CH_2)_4-CH_3
\end{array}
$$

$$
\begin{array}{l}
CH_2-O-\overset{\displaystyle O}{\overset{\|}{C}}-(CH_2)_{16}-CH_3 \\
CH-O-\overset{\displaystyle O}{\overset{\|}{C}}-(CH_2)_{16}-CH_3 \\
CH_2-O-\overset{\displaystyle O}{\overset{\|}{C}}-(CH_2)_{16}-CH_3
\end{array}
$$

17.75 a. Carnauba is a wax. Vegetable oil and glyceryl tricaprate (tricaprin) are triacylglycerols.

b. 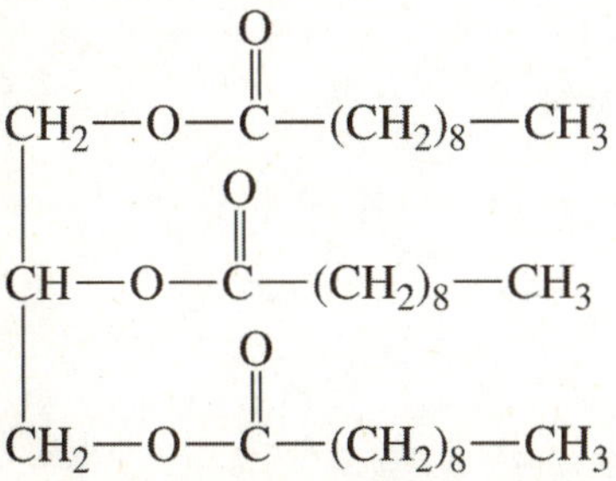
$$
\begin{array}{l}
CH_2-O-\overset{\displaystyle O}{\overset{\|}{C}}-(CH_2)_8-CH_3 \\
CH-O-\overset{\displaystyle O}{\overset{\|}{C}}-(CH_2)_8-CH_3 \qquad \text{Glyceryl tricaprate (tricaprin)} \\
CH_2-O-\overset{\displaystyle O}{\overset{\|}{C}}-(CH_2)_8-CH_3
\end{array}
$$

17.77 a. A typical unsaturated fatty acid has a cis double bond.
   b. A cis unsaturated fatty acid contains hydrogen atoms on the same side of each double bond. A trans unsaturated fatty acid has hydrogen atoms on opposite sides of each double bond.

c. 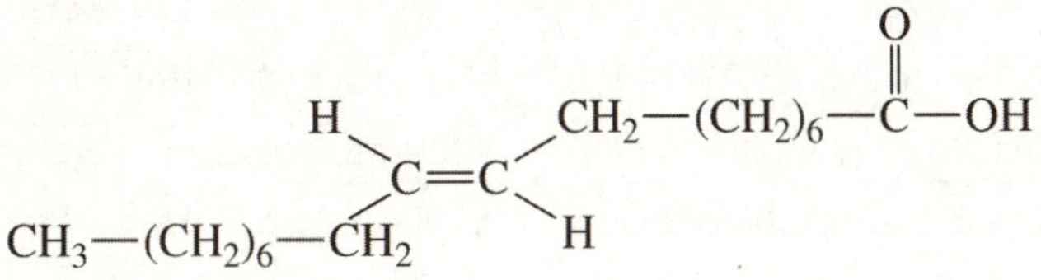
$$CH_3-(CH_2)_6-CH_2 \quad \overset{H}{\underset{}{}}C=C\overset{CH_2-(CH_2)_6-\overset{\displaystyle O}{\overset{\|}{C}}-OH}{\underset{H}{}}$$

17.79 a. $46\ \text{g fat} \times \dfrac{9\ \text{kcal}}{1\ \text{g fat}} = 410\ \text{kcal from fat} \qquad \dfrac{410\ \text{kcal}}{830\ \text{kcal}} \times 100\% = 49\%\ \text{fat (2 SFs)}$

   b. $29\ \text{g fat} \times \dfrac{9\ \text{kcal}}{1\ \text{g fat}} = 260\ \text{kcal from fat} \qquad \dfrac{260\ \text{kcal}}{520\ \text{kcal}} \times 100\% = 50\%\ \text{fat (2 SFs)}$

c. $18 \text{ g fat} \times \dfrac{9 \text{ kcal}}{1 \text{ g fat}} = 160 \text{ kcal from fat} \qquad \dfrac{160 \text{ kcal}}{560 \text{ kcal}} \times 100\% = 29\% \text{ fat (2 SFs)}$

The fats in these foods are from animal sources and would be mostly saturated fats.

17.81 **a.** Beeswax is a wax.
b. Cholesterol is a steroid.
c. Lecithin is a glycerophospholipid.
d. Glyceryl tripalmitate (tripalmitin) is a triacylglycerol.
e. Sodium stearate is a soap.
f. Safflower oil is a triacylglycerol.

17.83 **a.** Estrogen contains the steroid nucleus (**5**).
b. Cephalin contains glycerol (**1**), fatty acids (**2**), phosphate (**3**), and an amino alcohol (**4**).
c. Waxes contain fatty acid (**2**).
d. Triacylglycerols contain glycerol (**1**) and fatty acids (**2**).

17.85 **a.** HDL (**4**) is known as "good" cholesterol.
b. LDL (**3**) transports most of the cholesterol to the cells.
c. Chylomicrons (**1**) carry triacylglycerols from the intestine to the fat cells.
d. HDL (**4**) transports cholesterol to the liver.

17.87 **a.** Adding NaOH will hydrolyze lipids such as glyceryl tristearate (tristearin), forming glycerol and salts of the fatty acids that are soluble in water and would wash down the drain.

b.

c. Tristearin = $C_{57}H_{110}O_6$

molar mass of tripalmitolein $(C_{57}H_{110}O_6) = 57(12.0 \text{ g}) + 110(1.01 \text{ g}) + 6(16.0 \text{ g}) = 891 \text{ g/mole}$

$10.0 \text{ g tristearin} \times \dfrac{1 \text{ mole tristearin}}{891 \text{ g tristearin}} \times \dfrac{3 \text{ moles NaOH}}{1 \text{ mole tristearin}} \times \dfrac{1000 \text{ mL solution}}{0.500 \text{ mole NaOH}}$

$= 67.3 \text{ mL of NaOH solution (3 SFs)}$

18.1   In a primary (1°) amine, there is one carbon group (and two hydrogens) attached to a nitrogen atom.

18.3   **a.** This is a primary (1°) amine; there is only one alkyl group (and two hydrogens) attached to the nitrogen atom.
   b. This is a secondary (2°) amine; there are two alkyl groups (and one hydrogen) attached to the nitrogen atom.
   c. This is the skeletal formula of a primary (1°) amine; there is only one alkyl group (and two hydrogens) attached to the nitrogen atom.
   d. This is a tertiary (3°) amine; there are two alkyl groups and one aromatic group (and no hydrogens) attached to the nitrogen atom.
   e. This is a tertiary (3°) amine; there are three alkyl groups (and no hydrogens) attached to the nitrogen atom.

18.5   The common name of an amine consists of naming the alkyl groups bonding to the nitrogen atom in alphabetical order. In the IUPAC name, the *e* in the name of the corresponding alkane is replaced with *amine*.
   a. A two-carbon alkyl group attached to —NH_2 is ethylamine. In the IUPAC name, the *e* in ethane is replaced with *amine* to give ethanamine.
   b. A one-carbon and a three-carbon alkyl group attached to nitrogen form methylpropylamine. The IUPAC name is *N*-methyl-1-propanamine.
   c. A one-carbon and two two-carbon alkyl groups attached to nitrogen form diethylmethylamine. The IUPAC name is *N*-ethyl-*N*-methylethanamine.
   d. A three-carbon isopropyl group attached to nitrogen forms isopropylamine. The IUPAC name is 2-propanamine.

18.7   **a.** The carboxylic acid has priority over the amine in naming. The IUPAC name is 4-aminopentanoic acid.
   b. The amine has priority over the halogen atom in naming. The IUPAC name is 2-chloroaniline or *ortho*-chloroaniline.
   c. The aldehyde has priority over the amine in naming. The IUPAC name is 3-aminopropanal.
   d. The alcohol has priority over the amine in naming. The IUPAC name is 5-amino-3-hexanol.

18.9   **a.** $Cl-CH_2-CH_2-NH_2$

   b.

   c. $CH_3-CH_2-CH_2-CH_2-\overset{\overset{H}{|}}{N}-CH_2-CH_2-CH_3$

   d. $CH_3-CH_2-\overset{\overset{NH_2}{|}}{CH}-\overset{\overset{O}{||}}{C}-H$

18.11 Amines have higher boiling points than hydrocarbons but lower boiling points than alcohols of similar mass. Boiling point increases with molecular mass.

 a. $CH_3—CH_2—OH$ has the higher boiling point because the $—OH$ group forms stronger hydrogen bonds than the $—NH_2$ group.

 b. $CH_3—CH_2—CH_2—NH_2$ has the higher boiling point because it has a greater molar mass.

 c. $CH_3—CH_2—CH_2—NH_2$ has the higher boiling point because it is a primary amine that forms hydrogen bonds. A tertiary amine cannot form hydrogen bonds with other tertiary amines.

18.13 As a primary amine, propylamine can form two hydrogen bonds, which gives it the highest boiling point. Ethylmethylamine, a secondary amine, can form one hydrogen bond, and butane cannot form hydrogen bonds. Thus, butane has the lowest boiling point of the three compounds.

18.15 Amines with six or fewer carbon atoms are soluble in water. In larger amines, the nonpolar hydrocarbon groups diminish the effect of hydrogen bonding.

 a. Yes; amines with six or fewer carbon atoms hydrogen bond with water molecules and are soluble in water.

 b. Yes; amines with six or fewer carbon atoms hydrogen bond with water molecules and are soluble in water.

 c. No; an amine with nine carbon atoms has large hydrocarbon sections that make it insoluble in water.

 d. Yes; amines with six or fewer carbon atoms hydrogen bond with water molecules and are soluble in water.

18.17 Amines, which are weak bases, accept a proton from water to give a hydroxide ion and the related ammonium ion.

 a. $CH_3—NH_2 + H_2O \rightleftharpoons CH_3—\overset{+}{N}H_3 + OH^-$

 b. $CH_3—NH—CH_3 + H_2O \rightleftharpoons CH_3—\overset{+}{N}H_2—CH_3 + OH^-$

 c.

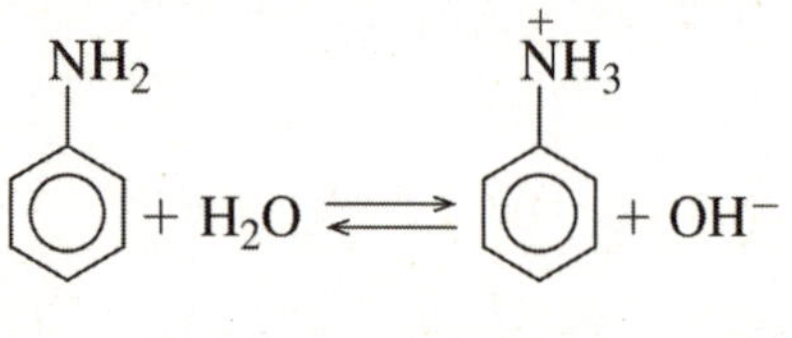

18.19 Amines, which are weak bases, combine with the proton from HCl to yield the ammonium chloride salt.

 a. $CH_3—\overset{+}{N}H_3\,Cl^-$

 b. $CH_3—\overset{+}{N}H_2—CH_3\,Cl^-$

 c.

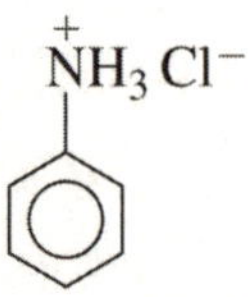

18.21 a.

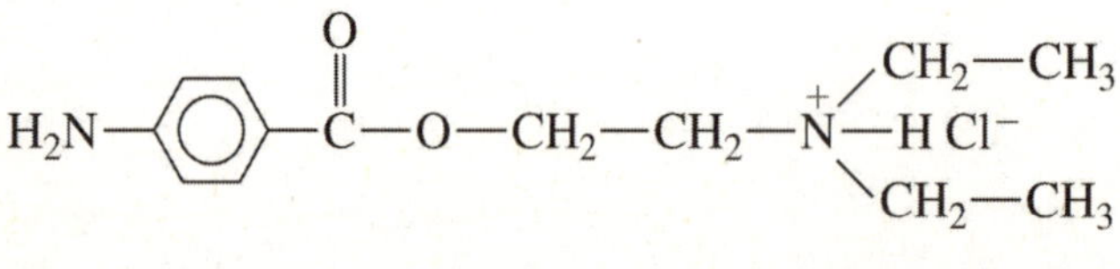

 b. The ammonium salt Novocain is more soluble in water and body fluids than the amine procaine.

18.23 Heterocyclic amines contain one or more nitrogen atoms in a ring.
   a. Piperidine is a six-atom ring with one nitrogen atom and no double bonds.
   b. Pyrimidine is a six-atom ring with two nitrogen atoms and three double bonds.
   c. Pyrrole is a five-atom ring with one nitrogen atom and two double bonds.

18.25 The six-atom ring with one nitrogen atom and no double bonds in Ritalin is piperidine.

18.27 The five-atom ring with one nitrogen atom and two double bonds in serotonin is pyrrole.

18.29 Carboxylic acids react with amines to form amides with the elimination of water.

   a. $CH_3-\overset{\displaystyle O}{\overset{\|}{C}}-NH_2$

   b. $CH_3-\overset{\displaystyle O}{\overset{\|}{C}}-\overset{\displaystyle H}{\overset{|}{N}}-CH_2-CH_3$

   c. Ph $-\overset{\displaystyle O}{\overset{\|}{C}}-\overset{\displaystyle H}{\overset{|}{N}}-CH_2-CH_2-CH_3$

18.31 **a.** *N*-methylethanamide (*N*-methylacetamide); the "*N*-methyl" means that there is a one-carbon alkyl group attached to the nitrogen. The "ethanamide" component tells us that the carbonyl portion has two carbon atoms.
   b. Butanamide (butyramide) has a four-carbon carbonyl portion bonded to an amino group.
   c. Methanamide (formamide) has only the carbonyl carbon bonded to the amino group.
   d. *N*-methylbenzamide; the "*N*-methyl" means that there is a one-carbon alkyl group attached to the nitrogen. The "benzamide" component tells us that this is the amide of benzoic acid.

18.33 **a.** This is an amide of propionic acid, which has three carbon atoms.

   $CH_3-CH_2-\overset{\displaystyle O}{\overset{\|}{C}}-NH_2$

   b. This is an amide of pentanoic acid, which has five carbon atoms.

   $CH_3-CH_2-CH_2-CH_2-\overset{\displaystyle O}{\overset{\|}{C}}-NH_2$

   c. The nitrogen atom in *N*-ethylbenzamide is bonded to a two-carbon ethyl group. The "benzamide" component tells us that this is the amide of benzoic acid.

   Ph $-\overset{\displaystyle O}{\overset{\|}{C}}-\overset{\displaystyle H}{\overset{|}{N}}-CH_2-CH_3$

   d. This is an amide of butyric acid, which has four carbon atoms. The "*N*-ethyl" means that there is a two-carbon alkyl group attached to the nitrogen.

   $CH_3-CH_2-CH_2-\overset{\displaystyle O}{\overset{\|}{C}}-\overset{\displaystyle H}{\overset{|}{N}}-CH_2-CH_3$

18.35 **a.** Ethanamide has the higher melting point because it can form more hydrogen bonds as a primary amide than can *N*-methylethanamide, which is a secondary amide.
   b. Propionamide has the higher melting point because it forms hydrogen bonds, but butane does not.
   c. *N*-methylpropanamide, a secondary amide, has the higher melting point because it can form more hydrogen bonds than the tertiary amide *N,N*-dimethylpropanamide can.

18.37   Acid hydrolysis of an amide gives the carboxylic acid and the ammonium salt.

a. $CH_3-\overset{\overset{O}{\|}}{C}-OH$ and $\overset{+}{N}H_4\,Cl^-$

b. $CH_3-CH_2-\overset{\overset{O}{\|}}{C}-OH$ and $\overset{+}{N}H_4\,Cl^-$

c. $CH_3-CH_2-CH_2-\overset{\overset{O}{\|}}{C}-OH$ and $CH_3-\overset{+}{N}H_3\,Cl^-$

d. ⬡$-\overset{\overset{O}{\|}}{C}-OH$ and $\overset{+}{N}H_4\,Cl^-$

18.39   A neurotransmitter is a chemical compound that transmits an impulse from a nerve cell to a target cell.

18.41   When a nerve impulse reaches the axon terminal, it stimulates the release of neurotransmitters into the synapse.

18.43   A neurotransmitter must be removed from its receptor so that new signals can come from the nerve cells.

18.45   Acetylcholine is a neurotransmitter that communicates between the nervous system and muscle cells.

18.47   Dopamine is a neurotransmitter that controls muscle movement, regulates the sleep–wake cycle, and helps to improve cognition, attention, memory, and learning.

18.49   Serotonin is a neurotransmitter that helps to decrease anxiety and improve mood, learning, and memory; it also reduces appetite and induces sleep.

18.51   Histamine is a neurotransmitter that causes allergic reactions, which may include inflammation, watery eyes, itchy skin, and hay fever.

18.53   Excess glutamate in the synapse can lead to destruction of brain cells.

18.55   GABA is a neurotransmitter that regulates muscle tone, sleep, and anxiety.

18.57   amine, carboxylic acid, amide, aromatic, ester

18.59   phenol, aromatic, alcohol, amine

18.61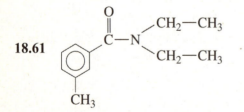

18.63   Excitatory neurotransmitters, like glutamate, open ion channels and stimulate the receptors to send more signals.

18.65   Dopamine, norepinephrine, and epinephrine all have catechol (3,4-dihydroxyphenyl) and amine components.

18.67 **a.** tetraethylammonium bromide; quaternary (4°) ammonium salt

  b. 1-pentanamine (pentylamine); primary (1°) amine

  c. *N*-ethyl-1-propanamine (ethylpropylamine); secondary (2°) amine

18.69 **a.** An amino group is bonded to carbon 3 of a five-carbon alkane chain.

$$\underset{\displaystyle CH_3-CH_2-\underset{|}{\overset{\displaystyle \overset{NH_2}{|}}{CH}}-CH_2-CH_3}{}$$

  b. A six-carbon cycloalkyl group (and two hydrogens) are bonded to a nitrogen atom.

  c. This is an ammonium salt with two methyl groups bonded to the nitrogen atom.

$$CH_3-\overset{\displaystyle \overset{CH_3}{|}}{\underset{}{N}}H_2\ Cl^-$$

  d. Three two-carbon ethyl groups are bonded to a nitrogen atom.

$$CH_3-CH_2-\overset{\displaystyle \overset{CH_2-CH_3}{|}}{N}-CH_2-CH_3$$

18.71 **a.** An alcohol with an —OH group such as 1-butanol forms stronger hydrogen bonds than an amine and has a higher boiling point than an amine.

  b. Ethylamine, a primary amine, forms more hydrogen bonds and has a higher boiling point than dimethylamine, which forms fewer hydrogen bonds as a secondary amine.

18.73 **a.** Ethylamine is a small amine that is soluble because it forms hydrogen bonds with water. Dibutylamine has two large nonpolar alkyl groups that decrease its solubility in water.

  b. Trimethylamine is a small tertiary amine that is soluble because it hydrogen bonds with water. *N*-ethylcyclohexylamine has a large nonpolar cycloalkyl group that decreases its solubility in water.

18.75 **a.** *N*-ethylethanamide; the "*N*-ethyl" means that there is a two-carbon alkyl group attached to the nitrogen. The "ethanamide" component tells us that the carbonyl portion has two carbon atoms.

  b. Propanamide has a three-carbon carbonyl portion bonded to an amino group.

  c. 3-Methylbutanamide has a four-carbon chain with a methyl substituent on carbon 3 as its carbonyl portion bonded to an amino group.

18.77 **a.** The alkaloid from the bark of the cinchona tree used in treating malaria is quinine.

  b. The alkaloid found in tobacco is nicotine.

  c. The alkaloid found in coffee and tea is caffeine.

  d. The alkaloids that are painkillers found in the opium poppy plant are morphine and codeine.

18.79 **a.** An ammonium salt and a strong base produce the amine, a salt, and water.

$$CH_3-CH_2-\overset{\displaystyle \overset{CH_3}{|}}{N}H + NaCl + H_2O$$

  b. An amine in water accepts a proton from water, which produces an ammonium ion and OH⁻.

$$CH_3-CH_2-\overset{+}{N}H_2-CH_3 +\ OH^-$$

18.81 carboxylate salt, aromatic, amine, halogen

18.83 Tryptophan contains a carboxylic acid group that is not present in serotonin. Serotonin has a hydroxyl group (—OH) on the aromatic ring that is not present in tryptophan.

18.85 SSRI stands for selective serotonin reuptake inhibitor.

18.87 $CH_3—CH_2—CH_2—NH_2$ $CH_3—CH_2—\overset{\overset{\displaystyle H}{|}}{N}—CH_3$ $CH_3—\overset{\overset{\displaystyle CH_3}{|}}{N}—CH_3$

        Propylamine (1°)   Ethylmethylamine (2°)   Trimethylamine (3°)

$CH_3—\overset{\overset{\displaystyle CH_3}{|}}{CH}—NH_2$ Isopropylamine (1°)

18.89
    a.   aromatic, amine, amide, carboxylic acid, cycloalkene
    b.   aromatic, ether, alcohol, amine
    c.   aromatic, carboxylic acid
    d.   phenol, amine, carboxylic acid
    e.   aromatic, ether, heterocyclic amine, ketone
    f.   aromatic, amine, heterocyclic amine

18.91 Dopamine is needed in the brain, where it is important in controlling muscle movement. Since dopamine cannot cross the blood–brain barrier, persons with low levels of dopamine are given L-dopa, which can cross the blood–brain barrier, where it is converted to dopamine.

Amino Acids and Proteins

19.1   **a.**   Hemoglobin, which carries oxygen in the blood, is a transport protein.
       b.   Collagen, which is a major component of tendons and cartilage, is a structural protein.
       c.   Keratin, which is found in hair, is a structural protein.
       d.   Amylases, which catalyze the breakdown of starch, are enzymes.

19.3   All α-amino acids contain a carboxylate group and an ammonium group on the alpha-carbon.

19.5   **a.**

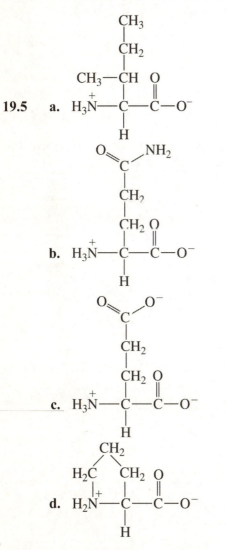

       b.

       c.

       d.

19.7   **a.**   Isoleucine has an alkyl (hydrocarbon) R group making it a nonpolar amino acid, which would be hydrophobic.
       b.   Glutamine has an R group that contains the polar amide group making glutamine a polar neutral amino acid, which would be hydrophilic.
       c.   Glutamic acid has an R group containing a polar carboxylic acid group. Glutamic acid is a polar acidic amino acid, which would be hydrophilic.
       d.   Proline has an alkyl (hydrocarbon) R group making it a nonpolar amino acid, which would be hydrophobic.

19.9 Amino acids have both three-letter and one-letter abbreviations.
   a. Ala is the three-letter abbreviation for the amino acid alanine.
   b. V is the one-letter abbreviation for the amino acid valine.
   c. Lys is the three-letter abbreviation for the amino acid lysine.
   d. Cys is the three-letter abbreviation for the amino acid cysteine.

19.11 In the L enantiomer, the —NH_3^+ group is on the left side of the horizontal line of the Fischer projection; in the D enantiomer, the —NH_3^+ group is on the right.

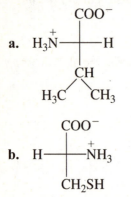

19.13 A zwitterion is a molecule with both positive and negative charges. In the case of an amino acid, the zwitterion form has a positively charged ammonium group and a negatively charged carboxylate group on the α-carbon.

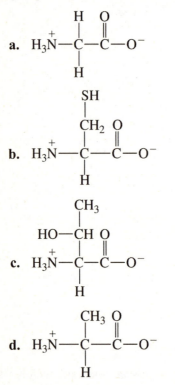

19.15 At low pH (highly acidic), the —COO^- group of the zwitterion accepts H^+ to become —COOH and the amino acid has a positive charge overall.

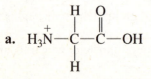

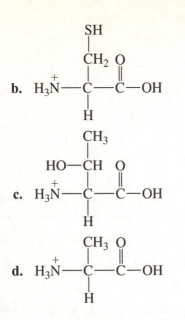

b. (structure)

c. (structure)

d. (structure)

19.17 **a.** When valine is in a solution with a <u>pH above its pI</u>, the $-NH_3^+$ group loses H^+ to form an uncharged amino group ($-NH_2$). The negative charge on the ionized carboxylate group ($-COO^-$) gives valine an overall negative charge (1−).

b. When valine is in a solution with a <u>pH below its pI</u>, the $-COO^-$ group gains H^+ to form an uncharged carboxylic acid group ($-COOH$). The positive charge on the ionized ammonium group ($-NH_3^+$) gives valine an overall positive charge (1+).

c. In a solution with a <u>pH equal to its pI</u> (6.0), valine is in its zwitterion form, containing both a carboxylate anion ($-COO^-$) and an ammonium cation ($-NH_3^+$), which give an overall charge of zero (0).

19.19 In a peptide, the amino acids are joined by peptide bonds (amide bonds). The first amino acid has a free $-NH_3^+$ group, and the last one has a free $-COO^-$ group.

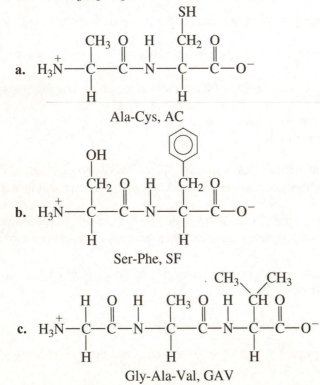

a. Ala-Cys, AC

b. Ser-Phe, SF

c. Gly-Ala-Val, GAV

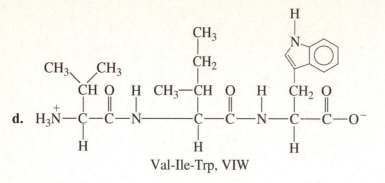

Val-Ile-Trp, VIW

19.21 The primary structure of a protein is the order of amino acids; the bonds that hold the amino acids together in a protein are amide or peptide bonds.

19.23 The possible primary structures of a tripeptide of one valine and two methionines are Val-Met-Met (VMM), Met-Val-Met (MVM), and Met-Met-Val (MMV).

19.25 The primary structure remains unchanged and intact as hydrogen bonds form between carbonyl oxygen atoms and amino hydrogen atoms of peptide bonds in the polypeptide chain.

19.27 In the α helix, hydrogen bonds form between the carbonyl oxygen atom and the amino hydrogen atom of a peptide bond in the next turn of the helical chain. In the β-pleated sheet, hydrogen bonds occur between parallel peptides or across sections of a long polypeptide chain.

19.29 **a.** The two cysteines have —SH groups, which react to form a disulfide bond.
   b. Glutamic acid is acidic and lysine is basic; an ionic bond, or salt bridge, is formed between the —COO⁻ in the R group of Glu and the —NH₃⁺ in the R group of Lys.
   c. Serine has a polar —OH group that can form a hydrogen bond with the carboxyl group of aspartic acid.
   d. Two leucines have R groups that are hydrocarbons and nonpolar. They would have a hydrophobic interaction.

19.31 **a.** The R group of cysteine contains a —SH group that can form a disulfide bond with another cysteine.
   b. Leucine and valine will be found on the inside of the protein structure since they have nonpolar R groups that are hydrophobic.
   c. Cysteine and aspartic acid would be on the outside of the protein since they have R groups that are polar.
   d. The order of the amino acids (the primary structure) provides the R groups whose interactions determine the tertiary structure of the protein.

19.33 **a.** Disulfide bonds and ionic bonds join different sections of the protein chain to give a three-dimensional shape. Disulfide bonds and ionic bonds are important in the tertiary and quaternary structures.
   b. Peptide bonds join the amino acid building blocks in the primary structure of a polypeptide.
   c. Hydrogen bonds that hold adjacent polypeptide chains together are found in the secondary structures of β-pleated sheets.
   d. In the secondary structure of α helices, hydrogen bonding occurs between amino acids in the same polypeptide to give a coiled shape to the protein.

19.35 The products of complete hydrolysis would be the amino acids glycine, alanine, and serine.

19.37 The dipeptides that could be produced by partial hydrolysis of this tetrapeptide are His-Met (HM), Met-Gly (MG), and Gly-Val (GV).

19.39 Hydrolysis splits the amide linkages in the primary structure.

19.41 **a.** Placing an egg in boiling water coagulates the proteins of the egg by disrupting hydrogen bonds and hydrophobic interactions.

  b. The alcohol on the swab coagulates the proteins of any bacteria present on the surface of the skin by forming hydrogen bonds and disrupting hydrophobic interactions.

  c. The heat from an autoclave will coagulate the proteins of any bacteria on the surgical instruments by disrupting hydrogen bonds and hydrophobic interactions.

  d. Heat will coagulate the surrounding proteins to close the wound by disrupting hydrogen bonds and hydrophobic interactions.

19.43 **a.** Yes, a combination of rice and garbanzo beans provides all the essential amino acids; garbanzo beans contain the lysine missing in rice.

  b. No, a combination of lima beans and cornmeal does not provide all the essential amino acids; both are deficient in the amino acid tryptophan.

  c. No, a combination of garbanzo beans and lima beans does not provide all the essential amino acids; both are deficient in the amino acid tryptophan.

19.45 **a.** Because a pH of 10.5 is more basic and above the pI of cysteine, the $-NH_3^+$ group loses H^+ to form an uncharged amino group ($-NH_2$). The negative charge on the ionized carboxylate group ($-COO^-$) gives cysteine an overall negative charge (1–), as in diagram 1.

  b. Since the pI of cysteine is 5.1, at that pH cysteine exists as a zwitterion with an overall charge of zero (0) as in diagram 3.

  c. Because a pH of 1.8 is more acidic and below the pI of cysteine, the $-COO^-$ group gains H^+ to form an uncharged carboxylic acid group ($-COOH$). The positive charge on the ionized ammonium group ($-NH_3^+$) gives cysteine an overall positive charge (1+), as in diagram 2.

19.47 The possible primary structures of a tripeptide of one valine and two serines are Val-Ser-Ser (VSS), Ser-Val-Ser (SVS), and Ser-Ser-Val (SSV).

19.49 **a.** Asparagine and serine are both polar neutral amino acids; their R groups can interact by hydrogen bonding.

  b. The polar neutral amino acid cysteine contains the $-SH$ group; two cysteines can form a disulfide bond.

  c. Leucine and alanine are both nonpolar amino acids; their R groups have a hydrophobic interaction.

19.51 At low pH (highly acidic), the $-COO^-$ group of the zwitterion accepts H^+ and the polar neutral amino acids will have an overall charge of 1+. Polar basic amino acids will have a charge of 2+.

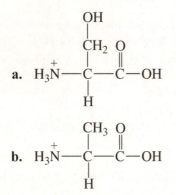

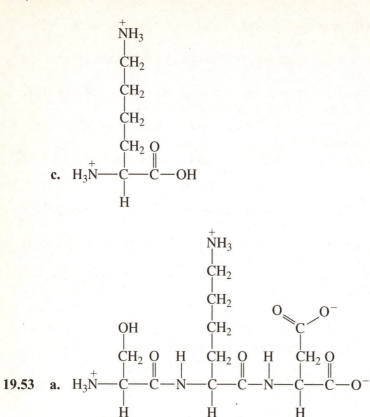

c.

19.53 a.

b. This segment contains polar R groups, which would be found on the surface of a globular protein where they can hydrogen bond with water.

19.55 a. Collagen is found in connective tissue, blood vessels, skin, tendons, ligaments, the cornea of the eye, and cartilage.
b. Collagen consists of three polypeptides woven together like a braid, called a triple helix.

19.57 A polypeptide with a high content of amino acids with large R groups, like His, Met, and Leu, would be expected to have more α-helical than β-pleated sheet sections. In an α helix, these large R groups could extend toward the outside of the helix, away from the central corkscrew shape.

19.59 Serine is a polar amino acid, whereas valine is nonpolar. Serine would move to the outside surface of the protein where it can form hydrogen bonds with water. However, valine, which is nonpolar, would be pushed to the center of the tertiary structure where it is stabilized by forming hydrophobic interactions.

19.61 a. Because it has a nonpolar R group, proline will be found in hydrophobic regions.
b. Because they have polar R groups, lysine and glutamic acid will be found in hydrophilic regions.
c. The basic R group of lysine and the acidic R group of glutamic acid can form a salt bridge.

19.63 a. The amino acids in aspartame are aspartic acid and phenylalanine.
b. The dipeptide in aspartame would be named aspartylphenylalanine.
c. The abbreviated form of the name for the dipeptide in aspartame would be named Asp-Phe or DF.

19.65 The acid from the lemon juice and the mechanical whipping (agitation) of the egg white denature the proteins, which turn into solids as meringue.

19.67 **a.** Since the pI of serine is 5.7, at that pH serine exists as a zwitterion with an overall charge of zero (0).

  b. Because a pH of 2.0 is more acidic and below the pI of threonine (5.6), the —COO^- group gains H^+ to form an uncharged carboxylic acid group (—COOH). The positive charge on the ionized ammonium group (—NH_3^+) gives threonine an overall positive charge (1+).

  c. Because a pH of 3.0 is more acidic and below the pI of isoleucine (6.0), the —COO^- group gains H^+ to form an uncharged carboxylic acid group (—COOH). The positive charge on the ionized ammonium group (—NH_3^+) gives isoleucine an overall positive charge (1+).

  d. Because a pH of 9.0 is more basic and above the pI of leucine (6.0), the —NH_3^+ group loses H^+ to form an uncharged amino group (—NH_2). The negative charge on the ionized carboxylate group (—COO^-) gives leucine an overall negative charge (1−).

19.69 **a.** Glutamic acid will have a negative charge at pH 6.0 and will migrate toward the positive electrode.

  b. Arginine will have a positive charge at pH 6.0 and will migrate toward the negative electrode.

  c. Since 6.0 is the pI for leucine, leucine will have no net charge at pH 6.0 and will remain where it was placed.

  d. There are six possible primary structures of a tripeptide with one unit each of glutamic acid, arginine, and leucine: Glu-Arg-Leu (ERL), Glu-Leu-Arg (ELR), Arg-Glu-Leu (REL), Arg-Leu-Glu (RLE), Leu-Glu-Arg (LER), and Leu-Arg-Glu (LRE).

19.71 **a.** The secondary structure of a protein depends on hydrogen bonds to form a helix or a pleated sheet; the tertiary structure is determined by the interactions of R groups such as disulfide bonds and salt bridges, and determines the three-dimensional shape of the protein.

  b. Nonessential amino acids can be synthesized by the body, but essential amino acids must be supplied by the diet.

  c. Polar amino acids have hydrophilic R groups, whereas nonpolar amino acids have hydrophobic R groups.

  d. Dipeptides contain two amino acids, whereas tripeptides contain three amino acids.

20.1 Chemical reactions in the body can occur without enzymes, but the rates are too slow at the relatively mild conditions of normal body temperature and pH. Catalyzed reactions, which are many times faster, provide the amounts of products needed by the cell at a particular time.

20.3 **a.** An enzyme (**2**) has a tertiary structure that recognizes the substrate.
    b. The combination of an enzyme with the substrate is the enzyme–substrate complex (**1**).
    c. The substrate (**3**) has a structure that fits the active site of the enzyme.

20.5 **a.** The equation for an enzyme-catalyzed reaction is:

$$E + S \rightleftharpoons ES \longrightarrow EP \longrightarrow E + P$$

E = enzyme, S = substrate, ES = enzyme–substrate complex,
EP = enzyme–product complex, P = products

    b. The active site is a region or pocket within the tertiary structure of an enzyme that accepts the substrate, aligns the substrate for reaction, and catalyzes the reaction.

20.7 **a.** Oxidoreductases catalyze oxidation–reduction reactions.
    b. Transferases move (or transfer) groups, such as amino or phosphate groups, from one substance to another.
    c. Hydrolases use water to split bonds in molecules (hydrolysis) such as carbohydrates, peptides, and lipids.

20.9 **a.** A hydrolase would catalyze the hydrolysis of sucrose.
    b. An isomerase would catalyze the conversion of glucose to fructose.
    c. A transferase would catalyze the transfer of an amino group from one molecule to another.

20.11 **a.** A lyase such as a decarboxylase removes CO_2 from a molecule.
    b. The transfer of an amino group to another molecule would be catalyzed by a transferase.

20.13 **a.** Succinate oxidase catalyzes the oxidation of succinate.
    b. Glutamine synthetase catalyzes the combination of glutamate and ammonia to form glutamine.
    c. Alcohol dehydrogenase removes 2H from an alcohol.

20.15 Isoenzymes are slightly different forms of an enzyme that catalyze the same reaction in different organs and tissues of the body.

20.17 A doctor might run tests for the enzymes CK and LDH to determine if the patient had a heart attack.

20.19 **a.** Decreasing the substrate concentration decreases the rate of reaction.
    b. The reaction will slow or stop because the enzyme will be denatured at low pH.
    c. The reaction will slow or stop because the high temperature will denature the enzyme.
    d. The reaction will go faster as long as there are polypeptides to react.

20.21 From the graph, the optimum pH values for the enzymes are approximately: pepsin, pH 2; sucrase, pH 6; trypsin, pH 8.

20.23 **a.** If the inhibitor has a structure similar to the structure of the substrate, the inhibitor is competitive.
    b. If adding more substrate cannot reverse the effect of the inhibitor, the inhibitor is noncompetitive.
    c. If the inhibitor competes with the substrate for the active site, it is a competitive inhibitor.

    d. If the structure of the inhibitor is not similar to the structure of the substrate, the inhibitor is noncompetitive.

    e. If adding more substrate reverses the inhibition, the inhibitor is competitive.

20.25 **a.** Methanol has the condensed structural formula CH_3—OH, whereas ethanol is CH_3—CH_2—OH.

    b. Ethanol has a structure similar to methanol and could compete for the active site.

    c. Ethanol is a competitive inhibitor of methanol oxidation.

20.27 Enzymes that act on proteins are proteases, and would digest the proteins of the organ where they are produced if they were active immediately upon synthesis. Therefore, digestive enzymes are produced in one organ and transported to the site of digestion where they are activated.

20.29 In feedback control, the product binds to the first enzyme in a series, changing the shape of the active site. If the active site can no longer bind the substrate effectively, the reaction will stop.

20.31 When a regulator molecule binds to an allosteric site, the shape of the enzyme is altered, which makes the active site more reactive or less reactive, and thereby increases or decreases the rate of the reaction.

20.33 **a.** (3) A negative regulator slows down a reaction, but its shape is different from that of the substrate.

    b. (4) An enzyme that binds a regulator molecule that differs from the substrate is an allosteric enzyme.

    c. (1) A zymogen is produced as an inactive enzyme.

20.35 **a.** Thiamine or vitamin B_1 is a cofactor (coenzyme), which is required by this enzyme for activity.

    b. The Zn^{2+} is a cofactor, which is required by this enzyme for activity.

    c. If the active form of an enzyme consists of only polypeptide chains, a cofactor is not required.

20.37 **a.** Pantothenic acid (vitamin B_5) is part of coenzyme A.

    b. Tetrahydrofolate (THF) is a reduced form of folic acid.

    c. Niacin (vitamin B_3) is a component of NAD^+.

20.39 **a.** A deficiency of vitamin D or cholecalciferol can lead to rickets.

    b. A deficiency of ascorbic acid or vitamin C can lead to scurvy.

    c. A deficiency of niacin or vitamin B_3 can lead to pellagra.

20.41 Vitamin B_6 is a water-soluble vitamin, which means that any excess of vitamin B_6 is eliminated from the body each day.

20.43 **a.** The oxidation of a glycol to an aldehyde and carboxylic acid is catalyzed by an oxidoreductase.

    b. At high concentration, ethanol, which acts as a competitive inhibitor of ethylene glycol, would saturate the alcohol dehydrogenase enzyme to allow the ethylene glycol to be removed from the body without producing oxalic acid.

20.45 **a.** Fresh pineapple contains an enzyme that breaks down protein, which means that a gelatin dessert containing fresh pineapple would not turn solid upon cooling. The high temperatures used to prepare canned pineapple denature the enzyme so it can no longer break down protein.

    b. The enzyme in fresh pineapple juice can be used to tenderize tough meat because the enzyme breaks down proteins.

20.47 The many different reactions that take place in cells require different enzymes because enzymes react with only a certain type of substrate.

20.49 In chemistry laboratories, reactions are often run at high temperatures using catalysts that are strong acids or bases. Enzymes, which function at physiological temperatures and pH, are proteins that are denatured rapidly if high temperatures or acids or bases are used.

20.51   Enzymes lower the activation energy by binding the substrate in the active site of the enzyme in a position that is more favorable for the reaction to proceed, thereby requiring less energy to convert reactants to products.

20.53   **a.**   The disaccharide lactose is a substrate (S).
      b.   The suffix *ase* in lactase indicates that it is an enzyme (E).
      c.   The suffix *ase* in lipase indicates that it is an enzyme (E).
      d.   Trypsin is an enzyme that hydrolyzes polypeptides (E).
      e.   Pyruvate is a substrate (S).
      f.   The suffix *ase* in transaminase indicates that it is an enzyme (E).

20.55   **a.**   Urea is the substrate for urease.
      b.   Succinate is the substrate for succinate dehydrogenase.
      c.   Aspartate is the substrate for aspartate transaminase.
      d.   Phenylalanine is the substrate for phenylalanine hydroxylase.

20.57   **a.**   The transfer of an acyl group is catalyzed by a transferase.
      b.   Oxidases are classified as oxidoreductases.
      c.   A lipase, which uses water to split ester bonds in lipids, is classified as a hydrolase.
      d.   A decarboxylase is classified as a lyase.

20.59   In the lock-and-key model, the substrate sucrose fits the exact shape of the active site in the enzyme sucrase.

20.61   A heart attack may be the cause. Normally the enzymes LDH and CK are present only in low levels in the blood.

20.63   The optimum temperature for an enzyme is the temperature at which the enzyme is fully active and most effective.

20.65   **a.**   The rate of catalysis will slow and stop as a high temperature denatures the enzyme.
      b.   The rate of the catalyzed reaction will slow or stop when the reaction mixture is placed in ice.
      c.   The reaction will slow or stop because pH 2 is much lower than the optimum pH of the enzyme.

20.67   **a.**   An enzyme is saturated if adding more substrate does not increase the rate of reaction.
      b.   When increasing the substrate concentration increases the rate of reaction, the enzyme is not saturated.

20.69   In reversible inhibition, the inhibitor can dissociate from the enzyme, whereas in irreversible inhibition, the inhibitor forms a strong covalent bond with the enzyme and does not dissociate. Irreversible inhibitors act as poisons to enzymes.

20.71   **a.**   (3) An irreversible inhibitor forms a covalent bond with an R group in the active site.
      b.   (1) A competitive inhibitor has a structure similar to the substrate.
      c.   (1) The addition of more substrate reverses the inhibition of a competitive inhibitor.
      d.   (2) A noncompetitive inhibitor bonds to the surface of the enzyme, causing a change in the shape of the enzyme and active site.

20.73   **a.**   Antibiotics such as amoxicillin are irreversible inhibitors.
      b.   Antibiotics such as amoxicillin inhibit enzymes needed to form cell walls in bacteria, not humans.

20.75   **a.**   When pepsinogen enters the stomach, the low pH cleaves a peptide from its protein chain to form pepsin.
      b.   An active protease would digest the proteins of the stomach rather than the proteins in the foods.

20.77   An allosteric enzyme contains sites for regulators that alter the enzyme and speed up or slow down the rate of the catalyzed reaction.

20.79 In feedback control, the end product of the reaction pathway binds to the enzyme to slow down or stop the first reaction in the reaction pathway. It acts as a negative regulator.

20.81   **a.**   The Mg^{2+} is a cofactor, which is required by this enzyme for activity.
       b.   A protein that is catalytically active as a tertiary protein structure does not require a cofactor.
       c.   Folic acid is a cofactor (coenzyme), which is required by this enzyme for activity.

20.83   **a.**   Coenzyme A (**3**) requires pantothenic acid (B_5).
       b. NAD^+ (**1**) requires niacin (B_3).
       c.   TPP (**2**) requires thiamine (B_1).

20.85 A vitamin combines with an enzyme only when the enzyme and coenzyme are needed to catalyze a reaction. When the enzyme is not needed, the vitamin dissociates for use by other enzymes in the cell.

20.87   **a.**   A deficiency of niacin can lead to pellagra (**3**).
       b.   A deficiency of vitamin A can lead to night blindness (**1**).
       c.   A deficiency of vitamin D can lead to weak bone structure (**2**).

20.89   **a.**   The reactants are lactose and water, and the products are glucose and galactose.
       b.

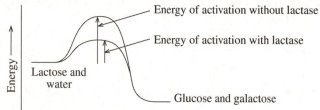

       c.   By lowering the energy of activation, the enzyme furnishes a lower energy pathway by which the reaction can take place.

20.91   **a.**   In this reaction, oxygen is added to an aldehyde. The enzyme that catalyzes this reaction would be an oxidoreductase.
       b.   In this reaction, a dipeptide is hydrolyzed. The enzyme that catalyzes this reaction would be a hydrolase.
       c.   In this reaction, water is added to a double bond. The enzyme that catalyzes the additon of a group without hydrolysis would be a lyase.

Answers to Combining Ideas from Chapters 16 to 20

CI.31 **a.**

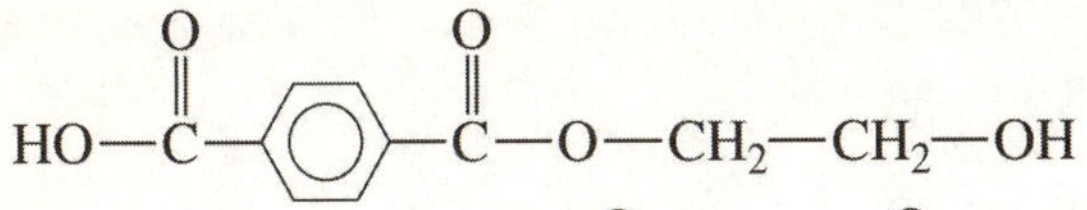

b.

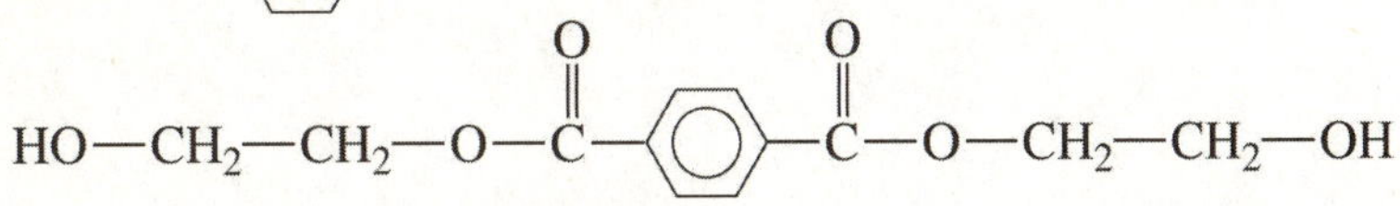

c. 2.4×10^9 lb PETE $\times \dfrac{1 \text{ kg PETE}}{2.20 \text{ lb PETE}} = 1.1 \times 10^9$ kg of PETE (2 SFs)

d. 1.1×10^9 kg PETE $\times \dfrac{1000 \text{ g PETE}}{1 \text{ kg PETE}} \times \dfrac{1 \text{ mL PETE}}{1.38 \text{ g PETE}} \times \dfrac{1 \text{ L PETE}}{1000 \text{ mL PETE}}$

$= 8.0 \times 10^8$ L of PETE (2 SFs)

e. 8.0×10^8 L PETE $\times \dfrac{1 \text{ landfill}}{2.7 \times 10^7 \text{ L PETE}} = 30$ landfills (2 SFs)

CI.33 **a.** Epibatidine contains the heterocyclic amines pyridine and pyrrolidine.
b. The molecular formula of epibatidine is $C_{11}H_{13}N_2Cl$.
c. molar mass of epibatidine ($C_{11}H_{13}N_2Cl$)

$= 11(12.0 \text{ g}) + 13(1.01 \text{ g}) + 2(14.0 \text{ g}) + 1(35.5 \text{ g}) = 209$ g/mole (3 SFs)

d. 60. kg body mass $\times \dfrac{2.5 \ \mu\text{g epibatidine}}{1 \text{ kg body mass}} \times \dfrac{1 \text{ g epibatidine}}{10^6 \ \mu\text{g epibatidine}}$

$= 1.5 \times 10^{-4}$ g of epibatidine (2 SFs)

e. 60. kg body mass $\times \dfrac{2.5 \ \mu\text{g epibatidine}}{1 \text{ kg body mass}} \times \dfrac{1 \text{ g epibatidine}}{10^6 \ \mu\text{g epibatidine}} \times \dfrac{1 \text{ mole epibatidine}}{209 \text{ g epibatidine}}$

$\times \dfrac{6.02 \times 10^{23} \text{ molecules epibatidine}}{1 \text{ mole epibatidine}}$

$= 4.3 \times 10^{17}$ molecules of epibatidine (2 SFs)

CI.35 **a.**

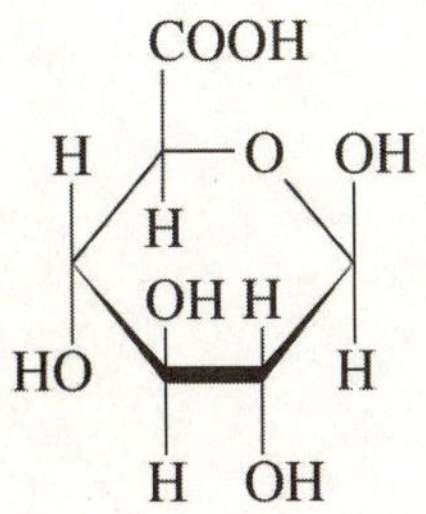

β-D-Gluconic acid

b.

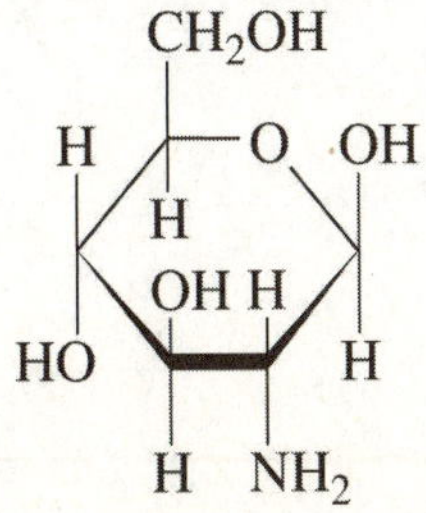

β-D-Glucosamine

c.

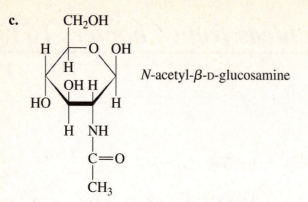

N-acetyl-β-D-glucosamine

d. They are β-1,4- and β-1,3-glycosidic bonds.

e.

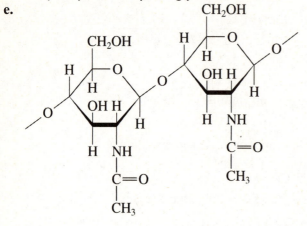

Nucleic Acids and Protein Synthesis

21.1   Purine bases (e.g., adenine, guanine) have a double-ring structure; pyrimidines (e.g., cytosine, thymine, uracil) have a single ring.
    a.   Thymine is a pyrimidine base.
    b.   This single-ring base is the pyrimidine cytosine.

21.3   DNA contains two purines, adenine (A) and guanine (G), and two pyrimidines, cytosine (C) and thymine (T). RNA contains the same bases, except thymine (T) is replaced by the pyrimidine uracil (U).
    a.   Thymine is a base present in DNA.
    b.   Cytosine is a base present in both DNA and RNA.

21.5   Nucleotides contain a base, a sugar, and a phosphate group. The nucleotides found in DNA would all contain the sugar deoxyribose. The four nucleotides are deoxyadenosine-5′-monophosphate (dAMP), deoxyguanosine-5′-monophosphate (dGMP), deoxycytidine-5′-monophosphate (dCMP), and deoxythymidine-5′-monophosphate (dTMP).

21.7   **a.**   Adenosine is a nucleoside found in RNA.
    b.   Deoxycytidine is a nucleoside found in DNA.
    c.   Uridine is a nucleoside found in RNA.
    d.   Cytidine-5′-monophosphate is a nucleotide found in RNA.

21.9

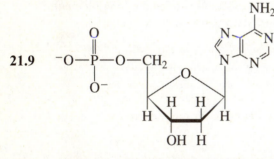

21.11   The nucleotides in nucleic acid polymers are held together by phosphodiester bonds between the 3′—OH of a sugar (ribose or deoxyribose) and the phosphate group on the 5′-carbon of another sugar.

21.13

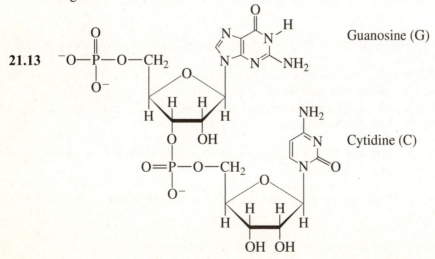

21.15 The two DNA strands are held together by hydrogen bonds between the complementary bases in each strand.

21.17 **a.** Since T pairs with A, if one strand of DNA has the sequence 5′—A A A A A A—3′, the second strand would be 3′—T T T T T T—5′.

b. Since C pairs with G, if one strand of DNA has the sequence 5′—G G G G G G—3′, the second strand would be 3′—C C C C C C—5′.

c. Since T pairs with A, and C pairs with G, if one strand of DNA has the sequence 5′—A G T C C A G G T—3′, the second strand would be 3′—T C A G G T C C A—5′.

d. Since T pairs with A, and C pairs with G, if one strand of DNA has the sequence 5′—C T G T A T A C G T T A—3′, the second strand would be 3′—G A C A T A T G C A A T—5′.

21.19 The enzyme helicase unwinds the DNA helix to prepare the parent DNA strand for the synthesis of daughter DNA strands.

21.21 First, the two DNA strands separate in a way that is similar to the unzipping of a zipper. Then the enzyme DNA polymerase begins to copy each strand by pairing each of the bases in the strands with its complementary base: A pairs with T and C with G. Finally, a phosphodiester bond joins the base to the new, growing strand. This process produces two exact copies of the original DNA.

21.23 The three types of RNA are messenger RNA (mRNA), ribosomal RNA (rRNA), and transfer RNA (tRNA).

21.25 A ribosome consists of a small subunit and a large subunit that contain rRNA combined with proteins.

21.27 In transcription, the sequence of nucleotides on a DNA template strand is used to produce the base sequences of a messenger RNA. The DNA unwinds, and one strand is copied as complementary bases are placed in the mRNA molecule. In RNA, U (uracil) is paired with A in DNA.

21.29 To form mRNA, the bases in the DNA template strand are paired with their complementary bases: G with C, C with G, T with A, and A with U. The strand of mRNA would have the following sequence: 5′—G G C U U C C A A G U G—3′.

21.31 In eukaryotic cells, genes contain sections called exons that code for proteins and sections called introns that do not code for proteins.

21.33 An operon is a section of DNA that regulates the synthesis of one or more proteins.

21.35 When the lactose level is low in *E. coli*, a repressor produced by the mRNA from a regulatory gene binds to the control site, which blocks the synthesis of mRNA from the genes and thereby prevents the synthesis of protein.

21.37 A codon is a three-base sequence (triplet) in mRNA that codes for a specific amino acid in a protein.

21.39 **a.** The codon CUU in mRNA codes for the amino acid leucine (Leu).
b. The codon UCA in mRNA codes for the amino acid serine (Ser).
c. The codon GGU in mRNA codes for the amino acid glycine (Gly).
d. The codon AGG in mRNA codes for the amino acid arginine (Arg).

21.41 At the beginning of an mRNA, the codon AUG signals the start of protein synthesis; thereafter, the AUG codon specifies the amino acid methionine.

21.43 A codon is a base triplet in the mRNA template. An anticodon is the complementary triplet on a tRNA for a specific amino acid.

21.45 The three steps in translation are initiation, chain elongation, and termination.

21.47   **a.**   The codons ACC, ACA, and ACU in mRNA all code for threonine: — Thr — Thr — Thr — .

         b.   The codons UUU and UUC code for phenylalanine, and CCG and CCA both code for proline: — Phe — Pro — Phe — Pro — .

         c.   The codon UAC codes for tyrosine, GGG for glycine, AGA for arginine, and UGU for cysteine: — Tyr — Gly — Arg — Cys — .

21.49   The new amino acid is joined by a peptide bond to the growing peptide chain. The ribosome moves to the next codon, which attaches to a tRNA carrying the next amino acid.

21.51   **a.**   The mRNA sequence would be: 5′ — CGA AAA GUU UUU — 3′.

         b.   The tRNA triplet anticodons would be: GCU, UUU, CAA, and AAA.

         c.   From the table of mRNA codons, the amino acids would be: — Arg — Lys — Val — Phe — .

21.53   In a substitution mutation, a base in DNA is replaced by a different base.

21.55   In a frameshift mutation caused by a deletion or an addition, all the codons from the mutation onward are changed, which changes the order of amino acids in the rest of the polypeptide chain.

21.57   The normal triplet TTT in DNA forms the codon AAA in mRNA. AAA codes for lysine. The mutation TTC in DNA forms the codon AAG in mRNA, which also codes for lysine. Thus, there is no effect on the amino acid sequence.

21.59   **a.**   — Thr — Ser — Arg — Val — is the amino acid sequence produced by normal DNA.

         b.   — Thr — Thr — Arg — Val — is the amino acid sequence produced by a mutation.

         c.   — Thr — Ser — Gly — Val — is the amino acid sequence produced by a mutation.

         d.   — Thr — STOP; protein synthesis would terminate early. If this mutation occurs early in the formation of the polypeptide, the resulting protein will probably be nonfunctional.

         e.   The new protein will contain the sequence — Asp — Ile — Thr — Gly — .

         f.   The new protein will contain the sequence — His — His — Gly — .

21.61   **a.**   Both codons GCC and GCA code for alanine.

         b.   A vital ionic cross-link in the tertiary structure of hemoglobin cannot be formed when the polar glutamic acid is replaced by valine, which is nonpolar. The resulting hemoglobin is malformed and less capable of carrying oxygen.

21.63   *E. coli* bacterial cells contain several small circular plasmids of DNA that can be isolated easily. After the recombinant DNA is formed, *E. coli* multiply rapidly, producing many copies of the recombinant DNA in a relatively short time.

21.65   The cells of the *E. coli* are soaked in a detergent solution that disrupts the plasma membrane and releases the cell contents including the plasmids, which are then collected.

21.67   When a gene has been obtained using restriction enzymes, it is mixed with the plasmids that have been opened by the same enzymes. When mixed together in a fresh *E. coli* culture, the sticky ends of the DNA fragments bond with the sticky ends of the plasmid DNA to form a recombinant DNA.

21.69   In DNA fingerprinting, restriction enzymes cut a sample of DNA into fragments, which are sorted by size by gel electrophoresis. A radioactive probe that adheres to specific DNA sequences exposes an X-ray film placed over the gel and creates a pattern of dark and light bands known as a DNA fingerprint.

21.71   A virus contains either DNA or RNA, but not both, inside a protein coat.

21.73   **a.**   An RNA-containing virus must make viral DNA from the RNA to produce proteins for the protein coat, which allows the virus to replicate and leave the cell to infect new cells.

         b.   A virus that uses reverse transcription is called a retrovirus.

21.75 Nucleoside analogs such as AZT and ddI are similar to the nucleosides required to make viral DNA in reverse transcription. When they are incorporated into viral DNA, the lack of a hydroxyl group on the 3′-carbon in the sugar prevents the formation of the sugar–phosphate bonds and stops the replication of the virus.

21.77 a.

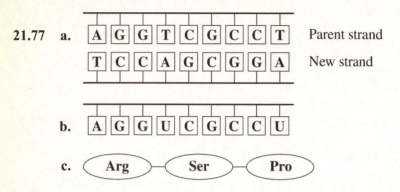

Parent strand

New strand

b.

c. Arg — Ser — Pro

21.79 DNA contains two purines, adenine (A) and guanine (G), and two pyrimidines, cytosine (C) and thymine (T). RNA contains the same bases, except thymine (T) is replaced by the pyrimidine uracil (U).
  a. Cytosine is a pyrimidine base.
  b. Adenine is a purine base.
  c. Uracil is a pyrimidine base.

21.81 a. Deoxythymidine is a nucleoside containing the base thymine and the sugar deoxyribose.
  b. Adenosine contains the base adenine and the sugar ribose.
  c. Cytidine contains the base cytosine and the sugar ribose.
  d. Deoxyguanosine contains the base guanine and the sugar deoxyribose.

21.83 Thymine and uracil are both pyrimidines, but thymine has a methyl group on carbon 5.

21.85

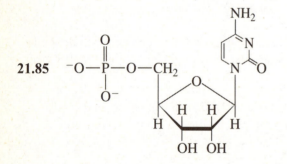

21.87 Both RNA and DNA are polymers of nucleotides connected through phosphodiester bonds between alternating sugar and phosphate groups with bases extending out from each sugar.

21.89 Because A bonds with T, DNA containing 28% A will also have 28% T. Thus the sum of A + T is 56%, which leaves 44% divided equally between G and C: 22% G and 22% C.

21.91 There are two hydrogen bonds between A and T in DNA.

21.93 a. 3′—C T G A A T C C G—5′
  b. 5′—A C G T T T G A T C G A—3′
  c. 3′—T A G C T A G C T A G C—5′

21.95 DNA polymerase synthesizes the leading strand continuously in the 5′ to 3′ direction. The lagging strand is synthesized in small segments called Okazaki fragments because it must grow in the 3′ to 5′ direction and DNA polymerase can only work in the 5′ to 3′ direction.

21.97 One strand of the parent DNA is found in each of the two copies of the daughter DNA molecule.

21.99 **a.** Transfer RNA (tRNA) is the smallest type of RNA.
b. Ribosomal RNA (rRNA) makes up the highest percentage of RNA in the cell.
c. Messenger RNA (mRNA) carries genetic information from the nucleus to the ribosomes.

21.101 **a.** ACU, ACC, ACA, and ACG are all codons for the amino acid threonine.
b. UCU, UCC, UCA, UCG, AGU, and AGC are all codons for the amino acid serine.
c. UGU and UGC are codons for the amino acid cysteine.

21.103 **a.** AAG codes for lysine.
b. AUU codes for isoleucine.
c. CGA codes for arginine.

21.105 Using the genetic code, the codons indicate the following amino acid sequence:
START — Tyr — Gly — Gly — Phe — Leu — STOP

21.107 The anticodon on tRNA consists of the three complementary bases to the codon in mRNA.
a. UCG
b. AUA
c. GGU

21.109 There are nine amino acids in the peptide oxytocin. The codon for each amino acid contains three nucleotides, plus the start and stop codon triplets, which makes a minimum total of $(9 \times 3) + 3 + 3 = 33$ nucleotides.

21.111 A DNA virus attaches to a cell and injects viral DNA that uses the host cell to produce copies of DNA to make viral RNA. A retrovirus injects viral RNA from which complementary DNA is produced by reverse transcription.

22.1 The digestion of polysaccharides takes place in stage 1.

22.3 In metabolism, a catabolic reaction breaks apart large molecules, releasing energy.

22.5   **a.** (3) The smooth endoplasmic reticulum is the site for the synthesis of fats and steroids.
  b. (1) Lysosomes contain hydrolytic enzymes.
  c. (2) The Golgi complex modifies products from the rough endoplasmic reticulum.

22.7 When a phosphate group is cleaved from ATP, sufficient energy is released for energy-requiring processes in the cell.

22.9   **a.** $PEP \longrightarrow pyruvate + P_i + 14.8$ kcal/mole
  b. $ADP + P_i + 7.3$ kcal/mole $\longrightarrow ATP$
  c. Combined: $PEP + ADP \longrightarrow ATP + pyruvate + 7.5$ kcal/mole

22.11   **a.** Pantothenic acid is a component of coenzyme A.
  b. Niacin is the vitamin component of NAD^+.
  c. Ribitol is the sugar alcohol that is a component of riboflavin in FAD.

22.13 In biochemical systems, oxidation is usually accompanied by the gain of oxygen or loss of hydrogen. Loss of oxygen or gain of hydrogen usually accompanies reduction.
  a. The reduced form of NAD^+ is abbreviated NADH.
  b. The oxidized form of $FADH_2$ is abbreviated FAD.

22.15 When a carbon–carbon double bond is formed, the coenzyme that picks up hydrogen is FAD.

22.17 Hydrolysis is the main reaction involved in the digestion of carbohydrates.

22.19   **a.** Lactose $+ H_2O \longrightarrow$ galactose + glucose
  b. Sucrose $+ H_2O \longrightarrow$ glucose + fructose
  c. Maltose $+ H_2O \longrightarrow$ glucose + glucose

22.21 Glucose is the starting compound of glycolysis.

22.23 In the initial steps of glycolysis, ATP molecules are required to add phosphate groups to glucose (phosphorylation reactions).

22.25 When fructose-1,6-bisphosphate splits, the three-carbon intermediates glyceraldehyde-3-phosphate and dihydroxyacetone phosphate are formed.

22.27 ATP is produced directly in glycolysis in two places. In reaction 7, a phosphate group from 1,3-bisphosphoglycerate is transferred to ADP and yields ATP. In reaction 10, a phosphate group from phosphoenolpyruvate is transferred directly to ADP to yield another ATP molecule.

22.29   **a.** In glycolysis, phosphorylation is catalyzed by the enzyme hexokinase in reaction 1 and by phosphofructokinase in reaction 3.
  b. In glycolysis, direct transfer of a phosphate group is catalyzed by the enzyme phosphoglycerate kinase in reaction 7 and by pyruvate kinase in reaction 10.

22.31 **a.** One ATP is required in the phosphorylation of glucose to glucose-6-phosphate.

  b. One NADH is produced in the conversion of glyceraldehyde-3-phosphate to 1,3-bisphosphoglycerate.

  c. Two ATPs and two NADHs are produced when glucose is converted to pyruvate.

22.33 **a.** In reaction 1 of glycolysis, a hexokinase uses ATP to phosphorylate glucose.

  b. In reactions 7 and 10 of glycolysis, phosphate groups are transferred from 1,3-bisphosphoglycerate and phosphoenolpyruvate directly to ADP to produce ATP.

  c. In reaction 4 of glycolysis, the six-carbon molecule fructose-1,6-bisphosphate is split into two three-carbon molecules, glyceraldehyde-3-phosphate and dihydroxyacetone phosphate.

22.35 Galactose reacts with ATP to yield galactose-1-phosphate, which is converted to glucose-6-phosphate, an intermediate in glycolysis. Fructose reacts with ATP to yield fructose-1-phosphate, which is cleaved to give dihydroxyacetone phosphate and glyceraldehyde. Dihydroxyacetone phosphate isomerizes to glyceraldehyde-3-phosphate, and glyceraldehyde is phosphorylated to glyceraldehyde-3-phosphate, which is an intermediate in glycolysis.

22.37 **a.** Low levels of ATP will activate phosphofructokinase and increase the rate of glycolysis.

  b. High levels of ATP will inhibit phosphofructokinase and slow or stop glycolysis.

22.39 A cell converts pyruvate to acetyl-CoA only under aerobic conditions; there must be sufficient oxygen available.

22.41 The oxidation of pyruvate converts NAD^+ to NADH and produces acetyl-CoA and CO_2.

$$\underset{\text{Pyruvate}}{CH_3-\overset{\overset{\displaystyle O}{\|}}{C}-COO^-} + NAD^+ + HS-CoA \longrightarrow \underset{\text{Acetyl CoA}}{CH_3-\overset{\overset{\displaystyle O}{\|}}{C}-S-CoA} + CO_2 + NADH$$

22.43 When pyruvate is reduced to lactate, the NAD^+ is used to oxidize glyceraldehyde-3-phosphate, regenerating NADH, which allows glycolysis to continue, producing a small but needed amount of ATP.

22.45 During fermentation, the three-carbon compound pyruvate is reduced to ethanol while decarboxylation removes one carbon as carbon dioxide, CO_2.

22.47 Glycogenesis is the synthesis of glycogen from glucose molecules.

22.49 Muscle cells break down glycogen to glucose-6-phosphate, which enters glycolysis.

22.51 Glycogen phosphorylase cleaves the glycosidic bonds at the ends of glycogen chains to remove glucose monomers as glucose-1-phosphate.

22.53 When there are no glycogen stores remaining in the liver, gluconeogenesis synthesizes glucose from noncarbohydrate compounds such as pyruvate and lactate.

22.55 The enzymes in glycolysis that are also used in their reverse directions for gluconeogenesis are phosphoglucose isomerase, aldolase, triose phosphate isomerase, glyceraldehyde-3-phosphate dehydrogenase, phosphoglycerate kinase, phosphoglycerate mutase, and enolase.

22.57 **a.** Low glucose levels activate glucose synthesis (gluconeogenesis).

  b. Glucagon, produced when glucose levels are low, activates gluconeogenesis.

  c. Insulin, produced when glucose levels are high, inhibits gluconeogenesis.

22.59 $2.5 \; \cancel{h} \times \dfrac{350 \; \cancel{kcal}}{1 \; \cancel{h}} \times \dfrac{1 \; \text{mole ATP}}{7.3 \; \cancel{kcal}} = 120 \; \text{moles of ATP (2 SFs)}$

22.61   Metabolism includes all the reactions in cells that provide energy and material for cell growth.

22.63   Stage 1 involves the digestion of large food polymers, such as polysaccharides and proteins.

22.65   A eukaryotic cell has a nucleus, whereas a prokaryotic cell does not.

22.67   ATP is the abbreviation for adenosine triphosphate.

22.69   ATP $\longrightarrow$ ADP + P_i + 7.3 kcal/mole (or 31 kJ/mole)

22.71   FAD is the abbreviation for flavin adenine dinucleotide.

22.73 NAD^+ is the abbreviation for nicotinamide adenine dinucleotide.

22.75   The reduced forms of these coenzymes include hydrogen obtained from an oxidation reaction.
    a. The reduced form of FAD is abbreviated $FADH_2$.
    b. The reduced form of NAD^+ is abbreviated NADH.

22.77   Lactose undergoes digestion in the mucosal cells of the small intestine to yield galactose and glucose.

22.79   Glucose is the reactant and pyruvate is the product of glycolysis.

22.81   **a.** Reactions 1 and 3 of glycolysis involve phosphorylation of hexoses with ATP.
    b. Reactions 7 and 10 of glycolysis involve direct substrate phosphorylation that generates ATP.

22.83   Reaction 4, catalyzed by aldolase, converts fructose-1,6-bisphosphate into two three-carbon intermediates.

22.85   Phosphoglucose isomerase converts glucose-6-phosphate to the isomer fructose-6-phosphate.

22.87   Pyruvate is converted to lactate when oxygen is not present in the cell (anaerobic conditions) to regenerate NAD^+ for glycolysis.

22.89   Phosphofructokinase is an allosteric enzyme that is activated by high levels of AMP and ADP because the cell needs to produce more ATP. When ATP levels are high due to a decrease in energy needs, ATP inhibits phosphofructokinase, which reduces its catalysis of fructose-6-phosphate.

22.91   The rate of glycogenolysis increases when blood glucose levels are low and glucagon has been secreted, which accelerates the breakdown of glycogen.

22.93   The breakdown of glycogen (glycogenolysis) in the liver produces glucose.

22.95   **a.** A low blood glucose level increases the rate of glycogenolysis in the liver.
    b. Insulin, secreted when glucose levels are high, decreases the rate of glycogenolysis in the liver.
    c. Glucagon, secreted when glucose levels are low, increases the rate of glycogenolysis in the liver.
    d. High levels of ATP decrease the rate of glycogenolysis in the liver.

22.97   **a.** High blood glucose levels decrease the rate of gluconeogenesis.
    b. Insulin, produced when glucose levels are high, decreases the rate of gluconeogenesis.
    c. Glucagon, secreted when glucose levels are low, increases the rate of gluconeogenesis.
    d. High levels of ATP decrease the rate of gluconeogenesis.

22.99   The cells in the liver, but not skeletal muscle, contain a phosphatase enzyme needed to convert glucose-6-phosphate to free glucose that can diffuse through cell membranes into the bloodstream. Glucose-6-phosphate, which is the end product of glycogenolysis in muscle cells, cannot diffuse easily across cell membranes.

22.101 Insulin increases the rate of glycogenesis and glycolysis and decreases the rate of glycogenolysis. Glucagon decreases the rate of glycogenesis and glycolysis and increases the rate of glycogenolysis.

22.103 The Cori cycle is a cyclic process that involves the flow of lactate and glucose between muscle and the liver. Lactate produced during anaerobic exercise is transported to the liver where it is oxidized to pyruvate, which is used to synthesize glucose. Glucose enters the bloodstream and returns to the muscle to rebuild glycogen stores.

22.105 **a.** $24 \, h \times \dfrac{60 \, min}{1 \, h} \times \dfrac{60 \, s}{1 \, min} \times \dfrac{2 \times 10^6 \, ATP}{1 \, s \, cell} \times 10^{13} \, cells \times \dfrac{1 \, mole \, ATP}{6.02 \times 10^{23} \, ATP} \times \dfrac{7.3 \, kcal}{1 \, mole \, ATP}$

$= 21 \, kcal \; (2 \, SFs)$

b. $24 \, h \times \dfrac{60 \, min}{1 \, h} \times \dfrac{60 \, s}{1 \, min} \times \dfrac{2 \times 10^6 \, ATP}{1 \, s \, cell} \times 10^{13} \, cells \times \dfrac{1 \, mole \, ATP}{6.02 \times 10^{23} \, ATP} \times \dfrac{507 \, g \, ATP}{1 \, mole \, ATP}$

$= 1500 \, g \; of \; ATP \; (2 \, SFs)$

Metabolism and Energy Production

23.1 The citric acid cycle is also known as the Krebs cycle and the tricarboxylic acid cycle.

23.3 One turn of the citric acid cycle converts 1 acetyl-CoA to $2CO_2$, $3NADH + 3H^+$, $FADH_2$, GTP (ATP), and HS—CoA.

23.5 Two reactions, reactions 3 and 4, involve oxidation and decarboxylation which reduces the length of the carbon chain by one carbon in each reaction.

23.7 NAD^+ is reduced by the oxidation reactions 3, 4, and 8 of the citric acid cycle.

23.9 In reaction 5, GDP undergoes a direct phosphate transfer to yield GTP, which is used to convert ADP to ATP and regenerates GDP for the citric acid cycle.

23.11 a. The six-carbon compounds in the citric acid cycle are citrate and isocitrate.
      b. Decarboxylation reactions remove carbon atoms as CO_2, which reduces the number of carbon atoms in the chain (reactions 3 and 4).
      c. The five-carbon compound in the citric acid cycle is α-ketoglutarate.
      d. Several reactions are oxidation reactions:

          isocitrate $\longrightarrow$ α-ketoglutarate (reaction 3); α-ketoglutarate $\longrightarrow$ succinyl-CoA (reaction 4);

          succinate $\longrightarrow$ fumarate (reaction 6); malate $\longrightarrow$ oxaloacetate (reaction 8)
      e. Secondary alcohols are oxidized in reactions 3 and 8.

23.13 a. Citrate synthase joins acetyl-CoA to oxaloacetate.
      b. Succinate dehydrogenase and aconitase form a carbon–carbon double bond.
      c. Fumarase adds water to the double bond in fumarate.

23.15 a. NAD^+ accepts a hydrogen from the oxidation and decarboxylation of isocitrate.
      b. GDP accepts a phosphate group in the formation of succinate.

23.17 Isocitrate dehydrogenase and α-ketoglutarate dehydrogenase are allosteric enzymes, which increase or decrease the flow of materials through the citric acid cycle.

23.19 High levels of ADP means there are low levels of ATP. To provide more ATP for the cell, the reaction rate of the citric acid cycle increases.

23.21 Cyt c (Fe^{3+}) is the abbreviation for the oxidized form of cytochrome c.

23.23 a. The loss of H^+ and 2 e^- is oxidation.
      b. The gain of $2H^+$ and 2 e^- is reduction.

23.25 NADH molecules provide the hydrogen ions and electrons for electron transport at complex I.

23.27 Their order in electron transport is: $FADH_2$, CoQ, cytochrome c (Fe^{3+}).

23.29 The mobile carrier coenzyme Q transfers electrons from complex I to complex III.

23.31   When NADH transfers electrons to complex I, NAD^+ is produced (oxidation).

23.33   **a.** $NADH + H^+ + \underline{CoQ} \longrightarrow \underline{NAD^+} + CoQH_2$

        b. $CoQH_2 + 2cyt\ c\ (Fe^{3+}) \longrightarrow CoQ + \underline{2cyt\ c\ (Fe^{2+}) + 2H^+}$

23.35   In oxidative phosphorylation, the energy from the oxidation reactions in electron transport is used to drive ATP synthesis.

23.37   Protons return to a lower-energy environment in the mitochondrial matrix by passing through the F_O channel of ATP synthase. During the process, energy is released to drive the synthesis of ATP in the F_1 section of ATP synthase.

23.39   Glycolysis and the citric acid cycle produce reduced coenzymes NADH and $FADH_2$, which enter electron transport where the release of hydrogen ions and electrons is used to generate energy for the synthesis of ATP.

23.41   ATP synthase consists of two protein complexes, F_O and F_1.

23.43   The loose (L) site in ATP synthase begins the synthesis of ATP by binding ADP and P_i.

23.45   Glycolysis takes place in the cytoplasm, not in the mitochondria. Because NADH cannot cross the mitochondrial membrane, the hydrogen ions and electrons from NADH are used to form glycerol-3-phosphate, which crosses the mitochondrial membrane. Then the hydrogen ions and electrons are transferred to FAD to form $FADH_2$. The resulting $FADH_2$ produces only two ATPs for each NADH produced in glycolysis.

23.47   **a.**   Three ATPs are produced from the oxidation of NADH in electron transport.
        b.   Six ATPs are produced in glycolysis when glucose degrades to two pyruvate molecules.
        c.   Six ATPs are produced when two pyruvate molecules are oxidized to 2 acetyl-CoA and $2CO_2$.

23.49   **a.**   Succinate is part of the citric acid cycle.
        b. $CoQH_2$ is part of electron transport.
        c.   FAD is part of both the citric acid cycle and electron transport.
        d.   Cyt c (Fe^{2+}) is part of electron transport.
        e.   Citrate is part of the citric acid cycle.

23.51   citrate $\longrightarrow$ isocitrate

        succinyl-CoA $\longrightarrow$ succinate

        malate $\longrightarrow$ oxaloacetate

23.53   **a.**   reactant: citrate   product: isocitrate
        b.   reactant: succinate   product: fumarate
        c.   reactant: fumarate   product: malate

23.55   **a.**   Aconitase uses H_2O.
        b.   Succinate dehydrogenase uses FAD.
        c.   Isocitrate dehydrogenase uses NAD^+.

23.57   **a.**   Aconitase catalyzes a hydration (4) reaction.
        b.   Succinate dehydrogenase catalyzes an oxidation (1) reaction.
        c.   Isocitrate dehydrogenase catalyzes an oxidation (1) and decarboxylation (2) reaction.

23.59 The oxidation reactions of the citric acid cycle produce a source of reduced coenzymes for electron transport and ATP synthesis.

23.61 The oxidized coenzymes NAD^+ and FAD needed for the citric acid cycle are regenerated by electron transport, which requires oxygen.

23.63   **a.** Citrate and isocitrate are six-carbon compounds in the citric acid cycle.
  b. α-Ketoglutarate is a five-carbon compound.
  c. The compounds α-ketoglutarate, succinyl-CoA, and oxaloacetate have keto groups.

23.65   **a.** In reaction 4, α-ketoglutarate, a five-carbon keto acid, is decarboxylated.
  b. In reactions 2 and 7, double bonds in aconitate and fumarate are hydrated.
  c. NAD^+ is reduced in reactions 3, 4, and 8.
  d. In reactions 3 and 8, a secondary hydroxyl group in isocitrate and malate is oxidized.

23.67   **a.** NAD^+ is the coenzyme for the oxidation of a secondary hydroxyl group in isocitrate to a keto group in α-ketoglutarate.
  b. The coenzymes NAD^+ and CoA are needed in the oxidation and decarboxylation of α-ketoglutarate to succinyl-CoA.

23.69   **a.** High levels of NADH inhibit isocitrate dehydrogenase and α-ketoglutarate dehydrogenase to slow the rate of the citric acid cycle.
  b. High levels of ATP inhibit isocitrate dehydrogenase to slow the rate of the citric acid cycle.

23.71 The transfer of electrons by complexes I, III, and IV generates energy to pump protons out of the matrix into the intermembrane space.

23.73   **a.** Amytal and rotenone block electron flow from complex I to coenzyme Q.
  b. Antimycin A blocks the flow of electrons from complex III to cytochrome *c*.
  c. Cyanide and carbon monoxide block electron flow from cytochrome *c* to complex IV.

23.75 In the chemiosmotic model, energy is released as protons flow through ATP synthase back to the mitochondrial matrix and is utilized for the synthesis of ATP.

23.77 In the intermembrane space, there is a higher concentration of protons, which reduces the pH and forms an electrochemical gradient. As a result, protons flow into the matrix, where the proton concentration is lower and the pH is higher.

23.79 Two ATP molecules are produced from the energy generated by the electrons from $FADH_2$ moving through electron transport to oxygen.

23.81 The oxidation of glucose to pyruvate by glycolysis produces 6 ATPs. Two ATPs are formed by direct phosphorylation along with 2 NADHs. Because the 2 NADHs are produced in the cytosol, the electrons are transferred to form 2 $FADH_2$ molecules which produces an additional 4 ATPs. The oxidation of glucose to CO_2 and H_2O produces 36 ATPs.

23.83 The ATP synthase extends through the inner mitochondrial membrane with the F_O part in contact with the proton gradient in the intermembrane space, whereas the F_1 complex is in the matrix.

23.85 As protons from the proton gradient move through the ATP synthase to return to the matrix, energy is released and used to drive ATP synthesis at the F_1 ATP synthase.

23.87 A hibernating bear has more brown fat which can be used during the winter to generate heat rather than ATP energy.

23.89 **a.** $6 \text{ moles ATP} \times \dfrac{7.3 \text{ kcal}}{1 \text{ mole ATP}} = 44 \text{ kcal (2 SFs) (from glycolysis)}$

b. $6 \text{ moles ATP} \times \dfrac{7.3 \text{ kcal}}{1 \text{ mole ATP}} = 44 \text{ kcal (2 SFs) (2 pyruvate molecules to 2 acetyl-CoA)}$

c. $24 \text{ moles ATP} \times \dfrac{7.3 \text{ kcal}}{1 \text{ mole ATP}} = 180 \text{ kcal (2 SFs) (2 acetyl-CoA in the citric acid cycle)}$

d. $36 \text{ moles ATP} \times \dfrac{7.3 \text{ kcal}}{1 \text{ mole ATP}} = 260 \text{ kcal (2 SFs) (complete oxidation of glucose to } CO_2 \text{ and } H_2O)$

23.91 If the combustion of glucose produces 680 kcal in a calorimeter, but only 260 kcal (from 36 ATPs) in cells, the efficiency of glucose use in the cells is 260 kcal/680 kcal or 38%.

23.93 $1.0 \text{ }\mu\text{g acetyl-CoA} \times \dfrac{1 \text{ g acetyl-CoA}}{10^6 \text{ }\mu\text{g acetyl-CoA}} \times \dfrac{1 \text{ mole acetyl-CoA}}{809 \text{ g acetyl-CoA}} \times \dfrac{12 \text{ moles ATP}}{1 \text{ mole acetyl-CoA}}$

$= 1.5 \times 10^{-8} \text{ mole of ATP (2 SFs)}$

24

Metabolic Pathways for Lipids and Amino Acids

24.1 The bile salts emulsify fat to give small fat globules for lipase hydrolysis.

24.3 Fats are released from fat stores when blood glucose and glycogen stores are depleted.

24.5 Glycerol is converted to glycerol-3-phosphate, and then to dihydroxyacetone phosphate, which is an intermediate of glycolysis.

24.7 Fatty acids are activated in the cytosol at the outer mitochondrial membrane.

24.9 The coenzymes FAD, NAD^+, and HS—CoA are required for β-oxidation.

24.11 The designation β-carbon is based on the common names of carboxylic acids in which the α-carbon is the carbon adjacent to the carboxyl group.

  a. $CH_3-CH_2-CH_2-CH_2-CH_2-\underset{\beta}{CH_2}-CH_2-\overset{\displaystyle O}{\overset{\|}{C}}-S-CoA$

  b. $CH_3-(CH_2)_{14}-\underset{\beta}{CH_2}-CH_2-\overset{\displaystyle O}{\overset{\|}{C}}-S-CoA$

  c. $CH_3-CH_2-CH=\underset{\beta}{CH}-CH_2-\overset{\displaystyle O}{\overset{\|}{C}}-S-CoA$

24.13 **a.** and **b.** $CH_3-(CH_2)_4-\underset{\beta}{CH_2}-\underset{\alpha}{CH_2}-\overset{\displaystyle O}{\overset{\|}{C}}-S-CoA$

  c. Three β-oxidation cycles are needed.
  d. Four acetyl-CoAs are produced from a C_8 fatty acid.

24.15 The hydrolysis of ATP to AMP hydrolyzes ATP to ADP, and ADP to AMP, which provides the same amount of energy as the hydrolysis of two ATPs to two ADPs.

24.17 **Analyze the Problem**

Number of Carbon Atoms	Number of β-Oxidation Cycles	Number of $FADH_2$	Number of NADH	Number of Acetyl-CoAs
22	10	10	10	11

  a. A C_{22} fatty acid will go through 10 β-oxidation cycles.
  b. The β-oxidation of a chain of 22 carbon atoms produces 11 acetyl-CoA molecules.
  c. ATP yield for each molecule of behenic acid (C_{22}):

ATP Production from Behenic Acid (C_{22})	
Activation of behenic acid to behenoyl-CoA	−2 ATP
$10 \ \text{FADH}_2 \times \dfrac{2 \text{ ATP}}{\text{FADH}_2}$ (electron transport)	20 ATP
$10 \ \text{NADH} \times \dfrac{3 \text{ ATP}}{\text{NADH}}$ (electron transport)	30 ATP
$11 \ \text{acetyl-CoA} \times \dfrac{12 \text{ ATP}}{\text{acetyl-CoA}}$ (citric acid cycle)	132 ATP
Total	180 ATP

24.19 Ketogenesis is the synthesis of ketone bodies from excess acetyl-CoA from fatty acid oxidation, which occurs when glucose is not available for energy, particularly in starvation, fasting, low-carbohydrate diets, fasting, alcoholism, and diabetes.

24.21 Acetoacetate undergoes reduction using $NADH + H^+$ to yield β-hydroxybutyrate.

24.23 High levels of ketone bodies lead to ketosis, a condition characterized by acidosis (a drop in blood pH values), excessive urination, and strong thirst.

24.25 Fatty acid synthesis takes place in the cytosol of cells in the liver and adipose tissue.

24.27 Fatty acid synthesis starts when acetyl-CoA, HCO_3^-, and ATP produce malonyl-CoA.

24.29 **a.** (3) Malonyl-CoA transacylase converts malonyl-CoA to malonyl-ACP.
    b. (1) Acetyl-CoA carboxylase combines acetyl-CoA with bicarbonate to yield malonyl-CoA.
    c. (2) Acetyl-CoA transacylase converts acetyl-CoA to acetyl-ACP.

24.31 **a.** A C_{10} fatty acid requires the formation of 4 malonyl-ACP, which uses $4 \ HCO_3^-$.
    b. Four ATPs are required to produce 4 malonyl-CoA.
    c. Five acetyl-CoAs are needed to make 1 acetyl-ACP and 4 malonyl-ACP.
    d. A C_{10} fatty acid requires 4 malonyl-ACP and 1 acetyl-ACP.
    e. A C_{10} fatty acid chain requires 4 cycles with 2 NADPH/cycle or a total of 8 NADPH.
    f. The four cycles remove a total of $4 \ CO_2$.

24.33 The digestion of proteins begins in the stomach and is completed in the small intestine.

24.35 Hormones, heme, purines and pyrimidines for nucleotides, proteins, nonessential amino acids, amino alcohols, and neurotransmitters require nitrogen obtained from amino acids.

24.37 The reactants are an amino acid and an α-keto acid, and the products are a new amino acid and a new α-keto acid.

24.39 In transamination, an amino group is transferred from an amino acid to an α-keto acid, creating a new amino acid and a new α-keto acid.

a.
$$\text{H}-\overset{\displaystyle \overset{\text{O}}{\|}}{\text{C}}-\text{COO}^-$$

b.
$$\text{HS}-\text{CH}_2-\overset{\displaystyle \overset{\text{O}}{\|}}{\text{C}}-\text{COO}^-$$

c.
$$\text{CH}_3-\overset{\displaystyle \overset{\text{CH}_3}{|}}{\text{CH}}-\overset{\displaystyle \overset{\text{O}}{\|}}{\text{C}}-\text{COO}^-$$

24.41 In oxidative deamination, the amino group in an amino acid such as glutamate is removed as an ammonium ion. The reaction requires NAD^+.

$$\overset{\overset{\displaystyle \overset{+}{N}H_3}{|}}{^-OOC-CH-CH_2-CH_2-COO^-} + H_2O + NAD^+ \xrightarrow{\text{Glutamate dehydrogenase}}$$

Glutamate

$$\overset{\overset{\displaystyle O}{\|}}{^-OOC-C-CH_2-CH_2-COO^-} + NH_4^+ + NADH + H^+$$

α-Ketoglutarate

24.43 The body converts NH_4^+ to urea because NH_4^+ is toxic if allowed to accumulate.

24.45 $\overset{\overset{\displaystyle O}{\|}}{H_2N-C-NH_2}$

24.47 The carbon atom in urea is obtained from the CO_2 produced by the citric acid cycle.

24.49 Glucogenic amino acids can be used to produce intermediates for gluconeogenesis (glucose synthesis).

24.51
a. Carbon atoms from alanine form the citric acid cycle intermediate oxaloacetate.
b. Carbon atoms from asparagine form the citric acid cycle intermediate oxaloacetate.
c. Carbon atoms from valine form the citric acid cycle intermediate succinyl-CoA.
d. Carbon atoms from glutamine form the citric acid cycle intermediate α-ketoglutarate.

24.53 The amino acids that humans can synthesize are called nonessential amino acids.

24.55 Glutamine synthetase catalyzes the addition of an amino group to glutamate to form glutamine using energy from the hydrolysis of ATP.

24.57 PKU is the abbreviation for **p**henyl**k**eton**u**ria.

24.59 **a.** and **b.** $CH_3-(CH_2)_8-\underset{\beta}{CH_2}-\underset{\alpha}{CH_2}-\overset{\overset{\displaystyle O}{\|}}{C}-CoA$

Analyze the Problem

Number of Carbon Atoms	Number of β-Oxidation Cycles	Number of $FADH_2$	Number of NADH	Number of Acetyl-CoAs
12	5	5	5	6

c. Five cycles of β-oxidation are needed.
d. Six acetyl-CoA units are produced.
e. ATP yield for each molecule of lauric acid (C_{12}):

ATP Production from Lauric Acid (C_{12})	
Activation of lauric acid to lauroyl-CoA	−2 ATP
$5\ FADH_2 \times \dfrac{2\ ATP}{FADH_2}$ (electron transport)	10 ATP
$5\ NADH \times \dfrac{3\ ATP}{NADH}$ (electron transport)	15 ATP
$6\ acetyl\text{-}CoA \times \dfrac{12\ ATP}{acetyl\text{-}CoA}$ (citric acid cycle)	72 ATP
Total	95 ATP

24.61 Triacylglycerols are hydrolyzed to monoacylglycerols and fatty acids in the small intestine, which are reformed into triacylglycerols in the intestinal lining for transport as lipoproteins to the tissues.

24.63 Fats can be stored in unlimited amounts in adipose tissue compared with the limited storage of carbohydrates as glycogen.

24.65 The fatty acids cannot diffuse across the blood–brain barrier.

24.67 **a.** Glycerol is converted to glycerol-3-phosphate and to dihydroxyacetone phosphate, which can enter glycolysis or gluconeogenesis.
   b. Activation of fatty acids occurs in the cytosol at the outer mitochondrial membrane.
   c. The energy cost is equal to two ATPs.
   d. Only fatty acyl-CoA can move into the intermembrane space for transport by carnitine into the matrix.

24.69 **a.** NAD^+ is involved in β-oxidation.
   b. β-Oxidation occurs in the mitochondrial matrix.
   c. Malonyl-ACP is involved in fatty acid synthesis.
   d. Cleavage of a two-carbon acetyl group occurs in β-oxidation.
   e. Acyl carrier protein is involved in fatty acid synthesis.
   f. Acetyl-CoA carboxylase is involved in fatty acid synthesis.

24.71 **a.** High blood glucose stimulates fatty acid synthesis.
   b. Secretion of glucagon stimulates fatty acid oxidation.

24.73 Ammonium ions are toxic if allowed to accumulate in the liver.

24.75 **a.** Citrulline reacts with aspartate in the urea cycle.
   b. Carbamoyl phosphate reacts with ornithine in the urea cycle.

24.77 **a.** Carbon atoms from serine form the citric acid cycle intermediate oxaloacetate.
   b. Carbon atoms from lysine form the citric acid cycle intermediate acetyl-CoA.
   c. Carbon atoms from methionine form the citric acid cycle intermediate succinyl-CoA.
   d. Carbon atoms from glutamate form the citric acid cycle intermediate α-ketoglutarate.

24.79 Serine is degraded to pyruvate, which is oxidized to acetyl-CoA. The oxidation produces $NADH + H^+$, which provides three ATPs. In one turn of the citric acid cycle, the acetyl-CoA provides 12 ATPs. Thus, serine can provide a total of 15 ATPs.

24.81 **a.** $14 \text{ kg fat} \times \dfrac{1000 \text{ g fat}}{1 \text{ kg fat}} \times \dfrac{0.491 \text{ mole ATP}}{1 \text{ g fat}} = 6900 \text{ moles of ATP (2 SFs)}$

   b. $6900 \text{ moles ATP} \times \dfrac{7.3 \text{ kcal}}{1 \text{ mole ATP}} = 5.0 \times 10^4 \text{ kcal (2 SFs)}$

24.83 **a.**

$$\underset{\text{Valine}}{CH_3-\overset{\displaystyle CH_3}{\overset{|}{CH}}-\overset{\displaystyle \overset{+}{N}H_3}{\overset{|}{CH}}-\overset{\displaystyle O}{\overset{\|}{C}}-O^-}$$

   b.

$$\underset{\text{Isoleucine}}{CH_3-CH_2-\overset{\displaystyle CH_3}{\overset{|}{CH}}-\overset{\displaystyle \overset{+}{N}H_3}{\overset{|}{CH}}-\overset{\displaystyle O}{\overset{\|}{C}}-O^-}$$

   c.

$$\underset{\text{Aspartic acid}}{{}^-O-\overset{\displaystyle O}{\overset{\|}{C}}-CH_2-\overset{\displaystyle \overset{+}{N}H_3}{\overset{|}{CH}}-\overset{\displaystyle O}{\overset{\|}{C}}-O^-}$$

Answers to Combining Ideas from Chapters 21 to 24

CI.37 **a.** GTP is part of the citric acid cycle.

  b. $CoQH_2$ is part of electron transport.

  c. $FADH_2$ is part of both the citric acid cycle and electron transport.

  d. Cyt *c* is part of electron transport.

  e. Succinate dehydrogenase is part of the citric acid cycle.

  f. Complex I is part of electron transport.

  g. Isocitrate is part of the citric acid cycle.

  h. NAD^+ is part of both the citric acid cycle and electron transport.

CI.39 **a.** The components of acetyl-CoA are aminoethanethiol, pantothenic acid (vitamin B_5), and phosphorylated ADP.

  b. Coenzyme A carries an acetyl group to the citric acid cycle for oxidation.

  c. The acetyl group links to the sulfur atom (—S—) in the aminoethanethiol part of CoA.

  d. molar mass of acetyl-CoA ($C_{23}H_{38}N_7O_{17}P_3S$)

  $= 23(12.0 \text{ g}) + 38(1.01 \text{ g}) + 7(14.0 \text{ g}) + 17(16.0 \text{ g}) + 3(31.0 \text{ g}) + 1(32.1 \text{ g}) = 809 \text{ g/mole}$

  e. $1.0 \text{ mg acetyl-CoA} \times \dfrac{1 \text{ g acetyl-CoA}}{1000 \text{ mg acetyl-CoA}} \times \dfrac{1 \text{ mole acetyl-CoA}}{809 \text{ g acetyl-CoA}} \times \dfrac{12 \text{ moles ATP}}{1 \text{ mole acetyl-CoA}}$

  $= 1.5 \times 10^{-5} \text{ mole of ATP (2 SFs)}$

CI.41 **a.**

  b. molar mass of glyceryl tripalmitate ($C_{51}H_{98}O_6$)

  $= 51(12.0 \text{ g}) + 98(1.01 \text{ g}) + 6(16.0 \text{ g}) = 807 \text{ g/mole (3 SFs)}$

  c. **Analyze the Problem**

Number of Carbon Atoms	Number of β-Oxidation Cycles	Number of $FADH_2$	Number of NADH	Number of Acetyl-CoAs
16	7	7	7	8

ATP Production from Palmitic Acid (C_{16})	
Activation of palmitic acid to palmitoyl-CoA	−2 ATP
$7 \text{ FADH}_2 \times \dfrac{2 \text{ ATP}}{\text{FADH}_2}$ (electron transport)	14 ATP
$7 \text{ NADH} \times \dfrac{3 \text{ ATP}}{\text{NADH}}$ (electron transport)	21 ATP
$8 \text{ acetyl-CoA} \times \dfrac{12 \text{ ATP}}{\text{acetyl-CoA}}$ (citric acid cycle)	96 ATP
Total	129 ATP

$\therefore$ 1 mole of palmitic acid will yield 129 moles of ATP.

d. $1 \text{ pat butter} \times \dfrac{0.50 \text{ oz butter}}{1 \text{ pat butter}} \times \dfrac{1 \text{ lb}}{16 \text{ oz}} \times \dfrac{454 \text{ g}}{1 \text{ lb}} \times \dfrac{80. \text{ g glyceryl tripalmitate}}{100. \text{ g butter}}$

$\times \dfrac{1 \text{ mole glyceryl tripalmitate}}{807 \text{ g glyceryl tripalmitate}} \times \dfrac{3 \text{ moles palmitic acid}}{1 \text{ mole glyceryl tripalmitate}} \times \dfrac{129 \text{ moles ATP}}{1 \text{ mole palmitic acid}} \times \dfrac{7.3 \text{ kcal}}{1 \text{ mole ATP}}$

= 40. kcal (2 SFs)

e. $45 \text{ min} \times \dfrac{1 \text{ h}}{60 \text{ min}} \times \dfrac{750 \text{ kcal}}{1 \text{ h}} \times \dfrac{1 \text{ pat butter}}{40. \text{ kcal}}$ = 14 pats of butter (2 SFs)

CI.43 **a.** The disaccharide maltose will produce more ATP per mole than the monosaccharide glucose.

b. The C_{18} fatty acid stearic acid will produce more ATP per mole than the C_{14} fatty acid myristic acid.

c. The six-carbon molecule glucose will produce more ATP per mole than two two-carbon molecules of acetyl-CoA.

d. The C_8 fatty acid caprylic acid will produce more ATP per mole than the six-carbon molecule glucose.

e. The six-carbon compound citrate occurs earlier in the citric acid cycle than the four-carbon compound succinate and will produce more ATP per mole in one turn of the cycle.